1982
SEASON

THE COMPLETE HANDBOOK OF
PRO FOOTBALL

T3-BFD-872

Other Sports Books from SIGNET

1982
SEASON
THE COMPLETE HANDBOOK OF
PRO FOOTBALL

EDITED BY ZANDER HOLLANDER

A SIGNET BOOK
NEW AMERICAN LIBRARY
TIMES MIRROR

ACKNOWLEDGMENTS

Can a record-setting, world-famous athlete best known for running over hurdles in his underwear find happiness in a helmet in San Francisco? Al Davis and player strikes aside, this may be the most intriguing question of the NFL's 63rd season. Renaldo Nehemiah, the hurdler-turned-footballer, has bested pro football players in the past—as a two-time overall winner of "The Superstars" (see page 24). But this, of course, is a different ball game.

For this ninth annual edition of the handbook, we acknowledge our own set of superstars—the writers on the facing page, contributing editors Eric Compton and Howard Blatt, and Frank Kelly, Bob Decker, Rich Rossiter, Beri Greenwald, Dot Gordineer, Pat Murphy, JoAnn Alfano, Phyllis Hollander, Jim Heffernan, Joe Browne, Fran Connors, Dick Maxwell and the NFL team publicists.

Zander Hollander

SIGNET, SIGNET CLASSICS, MENTOR, PLUME, MERIDIAN AND NAL BOOKS are published by The New American Library Inc. 1633 Broadway New York, New York 10019

First Printing, August 1982

1 2 3 4 5 6 7 8 9

PRINTED IN THE UNITED STATES OF AMERICA

CONTENTS

Editor's Note: The material herein includes trades and rosters up to final printing deadline.

Professor Walsh and The Making of Montana

By DAVE NEWHOUSE

The white hair is the first clue. The eyeglasses, though larger and more California jet-set than those found in Ivy lecture halls, add to the scholarly appearance. Finally, there's the hand against the chin in the reflective manner of Rodin's famous statue.

The professor.

This is the image Bill Walsh has and one he abhors. In fact, the very mention of it is enough to make him throw erasers in rage and scribble furiously on the blackboard.

"I don't see myself as a professor. But, for some reason as my hair turned white, I became more professorial," he said. "I'm not laid-back. I'm as expressive as any football coach on the field. It's not always the King's English. It's not classroom, either. I'm not some guru."

The blue eyes are so clear and deep, one gets the impression by looking into them of being in space and drifting forever. Those eyes want to see and learn, and they have seen first-hand the wild game and tribesmen of Nairobi, and would love someday to gaze upon the Sphinx.

The student.

"He [Walsh] had me throw the football with different velocities, at different heights," Joe Montana said, remembering his first meeting with the professor. "I had never done that before.

"He watched me with one hand on the elbow and the other hand on his chin. He seemed to be very intense . . . studying me very hard."

Dave Newhouse, coauthor of "The Jim Plunkett Story," is sports columnist for the Oakland Tribune.

His MVP trophy at Super Bowl XVI says it for Joe Montana.

Bill Walsh gets a Super lift after the 49ers nip the Bengals.

It was a perfect match from the beginning, the student quarterback and the teacher of quarterbacks. Walsh had been searching for the right quarterback to grasp his concept of offense and carry it to its most logical conclusion: the Super Bowl. Montana was looking for a mentor who would take his raw football talents and competitive, inquisitive mind and blend them, shape them, into something special.

And that's precisely what happened. No quarterback has ever moved to the front of Walsh's class with the speed and success of Montana. Montana completed Quarterback 1A with honors and the San Francisco 49ers completed an unbelievable three-year turnaround under Walsh by defeating Cincinnati, 26–21, in Super Bowl XVI.

Walsh and Montana have much in common despite their roles and a quarter-century of age difference. Both wanted to be triumphant in NFL leadership roles. But Walsh was passed over as a head coach for years and Montana was not thought to be blue-chip material (Walsh drafted him in the third round in 1979).

The two men share another common bond, this one more ironic: as youngsters, each of them wasn't interested in football as a career. Walsh didn't think about coaching until after graduating from college. He first considered teaching or a place in the business world. Montana was ready to quit football as an 11-year-old Midget League player. If his father hadn't interceded, Montana might well be playing major-league baseball.

"He could play all nine positions," his father, Joe Sr., recalled.

"Joe hung out with his nephews back then. They quit football and he wanted to as well. I told him he could quit at the end of the season if he wanted, but not in the middle. Somewhere in life, if things got rough, he might quit because he had done it once before. I never heard another word from him about quitting."

Quite the contrary. Young Joe Montana's refusal to quit would in later years become his stamp of greatness.

Bill Walsh's junior college coach in the San Francisco Bay Area detected no hidden coaching genius in Walsh bursting to break free.

"I could tell you stories and say, 'Oh, yes, I knew he was going to be a great coach back then,'" said Herb Hudson, who turned Walsh from an end into a lefthanded quarterback at College of San Mateo.

"How do you know? Bill asked questions, but he didn't show that much interest in coaching. It's so hard to tell."

It sure is. Hudson also coached a "big, ol' slow-moving guy who was injured his second year with us. I didn't even see the humor in him that he shows now." Hudson referred to John Madden, like Walsh, a late-bloomer as coaching material.

"Bill probably knew everyone's assignment when he played for me," said Bob Bronzan, Walsh's coach at San Jose State. "He was a walk-on, a tough kid, who started a goodly number of games for us at end."

Bronzan also coached a small, jut-jawed quarterback by the name of Dick Vermeil. The coach must have been prescient in the letters of recommendation he wrote in each of Walsh's and Vermeil's academic files upon graduation.

"I said that they would have 'rare and unusual reputations in coaching football.' It was like I was looking into a crystal ball."

Walsh entered the military, planning on attending graduate school when he got out. Washington High School in Fremont, Cal., was looking for a football coach. By this time Walsh was married and having to buy groceries, so he applied for the job and was accepted.

Washington High was 1–27 in football the previous three years. However, a new freeway by the school led to the quadrupling of enrollment to 2,900 students. In Walsh's second year, the team went 9–1 and won the conference championship. Walsh credits the highway system, more than his own, for the about-face.

He moved on to the University of California as an assistant under Marv Levy, now the Kansas City Chiefs' coach.

"I hired Bill because he was alert, smart, ambitious and personal," Levy said. "More than most coaches at the time, he was interested in ideas. Other coaches were interested in fundamentals. Bill had an abundance of ideas, though his ideas were ahead of his fundamentals. Now he is a master of fundamentals."

Walsh moved across the bay to Stanford as an assistant, then spent one year, 1966, as receivers coach of the Oakland Raiders. Billy Cannon was Oakland's tight end at the time.

"Bill didn't do a lot of talking, but he did a lot of listening," said Dr. Billy Cannon, now a dentist in Baton Rouge, La. "I didn't understand it then, but in retrospect he was a thinker who was feeling his way, trying to learn all he can. He wasn't trying to impress people, but to observe people."

It was at this stage of his life that Bill Walsh, 36, planned a career change. He went to graduate school, financing it through his position of general manager-coach of the semipro San Jose Apaches. Walsh had been turned down twice for the San Jose State job and, feeling rebuffed, he wanted eventually to get out of football. However, when the Cincinnati Bengals asked Walsh to be their offensive coordinator, he couldn't refuse.

"He gave me my only good year in the NFL," said Sam Wyche, then a Bengal quarterback of average ability and now the 49ers' quarterback coach.

Walsh had a parade of quarterbacks during his eight years in Cincinnati—Wyche, Virgil Carter, Greg Cook and Ken Anderson. Cook led the AFL in passing proficiency once and Anderson led the NFL twice in the same category.

Then Paul Brown stepped down as the Bengals' head coach. Walsh wanted the job badly, but Brown promoted another assistant, Bill (Tiger) Johnson. Rejected in Cincinnati, he moved on to San Diego in 1976 and transformed Dan Fouts, a quarterback going nowhere, into one of the NFL's best passers in the amazingly short span of one season.

Stanford needed a head coach in 1977. Realizing that he wasn't having any luck becoming an NFL head coach through the assistant's ranks—he had also failed at one time in his pursuit of the top job in Houston—Walsh decided to try a new approach, as a college coach.

In two years at Stanford, Walsh produced two NCAA passing champions, Guy Benjamin and Steve Dils, and two bowl victories. But he didn't land the head coach post with the Rams.

Meanwhile in San Francisco, the 49ers were self-destructing under Joe Thomas. Owner Edward J. DeBartolo Jr. fired Thomas and brought in Walsh as general manager-head coach.

At last, Walsh had what he wanted—and more—an NFL coaching job and total control. Over the next three years, the 49ers improved dramatically from 2–14 to 6–10 to 13–3 and a Super Bowl championship over Paul Brown's Bengals.

Ah, sweet vindication! However, Walsh is quick to praise Brown for helping shape his coaching expertise.

"From Paul Brown, I learned the administrative, organizational aspect of football, and teaching theory," he said.

"Bob Bronzan was a great football technician . . . great football mind. He taught me the work ethic as well.

"From Marv Levy, I learned the Wing-T. I learned more about football in my one year with the Oakland Raiders than anywhere else. It is very detailed, fully-dimensional football. I wasn't there long, but I learned a system."

Somewhere along the line, Walsh developed a sense of humor. He dressed up as a hotel bellman to greet the 49ers upon their arrival at the Super Bowl (Walsh preceded the team to Michigan after accepting a Coach-of-the-Year award in Washington, D.C., the previous evening).

"I'm not trying to be the commander-in-chief," he said. "You don't run around saluting all the time. Often I'm the butt of humor, but it's self-imposed."

Walsh has the ability to put on and take off pressure. It's the same thing in tennis. "He is a fierce competitor who fights over every point," said Frankie Albert, former 49er quarterback and head coach who plays tennis with Walsh.

Walsh was a boxer in college and he still shadowboxes. Though 50, he acts and dresses as an athlete. The night the 49ers on the Super Bowl, Walsh showed up at the victory party in a jogging suit.

Who's not laid-back?

Joseph Clifford Montana Jr. is an only child who began zeroing in on targets at a young age.

"He'd sit by his bedroom window, set a target in the yard and shoot at it with his beebee gun," said his mother.

Theresa and Joe Montana Sr. raised a polite son who cares deeply about humans and animals. He hates to see either hurt.

"I told Joey that he would get further with people if he were polite, not nasty," Theresa said. "One time when Joey was four, he sat quietly in a chair while we were visiting a man. The man couldn't believe that Joey could just sit there the whole time."

Joe Sr. manages a finance company in Monongahela, Pa., 30 miles south of Pittsburgh. Theresa works as his secretary.

"Joey doesn't like to hurt people's feelings," Theresa said. "He always puts everyone else before himself. If the 49ers had never gotten rid of [quarterback Steve] DeBerg, Joey wouldn't have tried to push for first because he was so close to DeBerg. Joey is a very easy-going person, but don't walk up his back too often."

As a boy, Joe Jr. would be picked on and not retaliate. Joe Sr. instructed his son that he didn't want him to start fights, but that there comes a point when a person must defend himself.

Such a moment came when Joe Jr. was a quarterback at Ringgold High School in Monongahela. Another Ringgold quarterback much bigger than Joe often picked on him. Finally, Joe's back having been walked up, he tore into the other boy and whipped him soundly. End of problem.

At Ringgold, Montana began his propensity for pulling out last-minute victories. That is, after he learned not to line up behind the guard, his most embarrassing moment in football.

He received a scholarship to Notre Dame, and while in college married his high school sweetheart. The marriage didn't work out.

"It was bad timing," he says now.

As a Notre Dame sophomore, Montana became the Goose Gossage of college football, saving one game after another. A shoulder separation forced him to miss the next season. When he came back in 1977, he was third-string. Notre Dame beat Pittsburgh, lost to Mississippi and was losing, 24–14, to Purdue with a minute left in the third quarter when Montana got his first chance of the season. Notre Dame won, 31–24.

The Irish, with Montana as a starter, won their next eight games, including a Cotton Bowl annihilation of previously undefeated Texas, and claimed the national championship.

Montana lacked the same magic as a senior as Notre Dame lost to Missouri and Michigan to plummet in the polls. However, Montana saved his best for the last against Houston in the Cotton Bowl.

He came down with the shakes at halftime as his temperature dropped *below* normal to 94. He lay on the locker-room floor, covered with blankets and was fed hot soup. Somehow, somewhere, he found the strength to return to the game. When he got back in, Houston was leading, 34–12, in the fourth quarter.

What followed was one of the greatest comebacks in college football history. Montana threw a touchdown pass to Kris Haines with no time left to bring Notre Dame to within a point, 34–33. Then Montana passed to Haines for the two-point conversion that

Montana had NFL's best completion percentage (63.7) in '81.

gave the Irish a 35–34 victory.

Montana's game-saving heroics became part of legend at Notre Dame, but they didn't interest the NFL.

"The question about Joe at the time was his hot-and-cold streaks," Walsh said. "The scouts universally said that he wasn't a consistent player. My final impression was that it could have been the Notre Dame system, which certainly wasn't the same [pro-type] system we had at Stanford. I felt we could overcome that."

Walsh's system is based on the pass setting up the run instead of vice-versa. He believes in high-percentage passes that reduce the possibility of turnovers. Walsh's system, which worked perfectly in the Super Bowl, sometimes calls for lots of passing early in the game, when teams are expecting the run. If the plan works and the 49ers get an early lead, which happened against Cincinnati, then Walsh will reverse his plan and take minutes off the clock in the second half with ball control.

Walsh's intial impression of Montana after watching him throw passes to UCLA's James Owens before the 1979 draft (the 49ers drafted Owens in the second round that year) was that here was a diamond in the rough.

"My philosophy in a quarterback is looking for things we can utilize," Walsh said. "With Carter it was his competitiveness and grit. With Anderson, it was his arm initially. With Fouts, it was his nerve, expecially under pressure.

"With Joe, it was his resourcefulness. And like Joe Namath, he has beautiful, gazelle-like movement with his feet. Joe Montana is a nimble, quick athlete with great instincts for football and competition."

Montana played in spots as an NFL rookie, after which Walsh had the opportunity to draft Brigham Young quarterback Marc Wilson. Walsh passed up Wilson, now with the Oakland Raiders, because "we felt our future was with Joe."

Walsh looked like a prophet when Montana pulled off a 1980 comeback to match the one in the Cotton Bowl. The 49ers trailed New Orleans, 35–7, at halftime. Montana brought them back to a 38–35 overtime victory, officially documented as the greatest come-from-behind win in NFL annals.

"A lot of people are afraid to be in that situation," Montana said. "It doesn't bother me. Maybe it's my competitiveness, but I'm just as relaxed in that situation as when I'm not. I've always been competitive, whether it was throwing rocks as a kid or playing in the NFL."

He led the NFL in passing percentage (63.7) in 1981—another Walsh accomplishment. Montana rescued the 49ers from defeat against Pittsburgh and Los Angeles, but topped himself in the playoffs.

Dallas led San Francisco, 27–21, in the NFC championship game when the 49ers got the ball back with less than five minutes to play and the Cowboy end zone 89 yards away. Montana marched his team to a touchdown—a spectacular pass play to Dwight Clark that will forever be known in San Francisco as The Catch—to pull out a 28–27 triumph.

"Joe has the ability to become the superb quarterback of the 1980s," Walsh said. "He's about 85 percent of the football player that he will be in five, six years. The only thing that could hold him back is the injury factor. At 193 pounds, he's not big as quarterbacks go."

"Anyone would like to be [the quarterback of the '80s]," Montana said of that possibility. "You have to think you're going to be, whether you are or not. If you don't, you never will be."

Montana took his time with that comment and the following one:

"Jealousy could come through because something I might have said two years ago when we weren't winning will be taken differently now that we've won the Super Bowl. So I have to be careful not to say anything that might hurt someone else or be taken the wrong way."

Doesn't like to hurt the feelings of others, his mother said.

The student quarterback couldn't believe the beauty of the animals he saw in Kenya or the poverty he witnessed in the Massai tribe during the photographers' safari he went on with his second wife, Cass, after the Super Bowl.

"*I love animals and wanted to see them in their natural habitat,*" *Joe Montana said.*

"*The Massai are sheepherders, though they have goats and cattle, too. At night, they bring the animals in beside their huts. That brings the flies.*

"*There was this little Massai boy, about two. He stood in the doorway of the hut with a full goatee . . . of flies. He never used his hand to brush them away. He just stared at us as we drove away.*"

The professor coach will not teach quarterbacks forever.

"*I don't see myself coaching at 60 or even 55,*" *Bill Walsh said. "At 55, I can see myself in a general manager's role or possibly in television. At 60, I can see myself lecturing college students.*"

What? The non-professor . . . as a professor?

The Funniest Men In the Game

By LARRY FELSER

Phyllis George, the set decoration on "The NFL Today," was fluffing her hair and otherwise preparing for an interview with one of the Los Angeles Rams "on location"—that is, on one of the Pacific beaches south of LA.

While George primped, the cameras focused upon her. In mid-primp, the cameraman noticed something strange in the background. From out of the surf emerged a figure which resembled the world's largest sea urchin. As it clomped its way toward the unsuspecting George, it became clear that the figure was a man, a huge man, in a wet suit.

Larry Felser gets his kicks as columnist for the Buffalo Evening News.

Just as Phyllis smiled sweetly into the lens, she was enveloped by the grunting, snorting apparition in the wet suit. The cameras kept running as George shrieked in distress, the intruder carrying her off toward the sea.

That was Fred Dryer's way of arriving for the interview.

His career placed in limbo by the Rams' chaotic front office last year, Dryer may no longer have the exposure that made him one of the funniest men in football, but he and his antics will live long after him.

When he was with the New York Giants, Dryer's roommate in 1970 was Matt Hazeltine, the linebacker who was winding down his career.

"They lived in an East Side pad," recalled Ed Croke, the Giants' publicity director, "and Hazeltine said that Dryer put 10 years on his life. Dryer liked to drop water bags off the roof of hotels and he also would ring doorbells of the single women in their apartment house, asking to borrow sugar. Nothing wrong with that, but Dryer would be stark naked."

Of course, Dryer's audience for those solos can't be compared with that of Jack (Hacksaw) Reynolds during Super Bowl XVI. The 49er linebacker got his nickname because he once sawed a car in two, but Super Sunday was something else. Remember the dramatic goal-line stand by the San Francisco defense which virtually assured the 49er victory over Cincinnati?

Reynolds was so excited that as he left the field, he realized that the capacity of his kidneys was no match for the time left on the game clock. He also had the feeling that the 49er offense, playing conservatively to protect its lead, would likely be on the field for just three plays, then punt back to the Bengals.

No time to duck off the field into a men's room. So, time for a defensive huddle.

As his teammates gathered around him on the sidelines, Reynolds relieved himself on the artificial turf of the Pontiac Silverdome. Almost in front of 80,000 spectators. Not too far away from the gaze of 100 million television watchers.

Not only that, but Reynolds had so much tape around his hands that he required assistance in accomplishing his Super Bowl first.

In a sport that takes itself seriously, there is little humor during the game, but there are the light moments in the clubhouse. Joe Gordon, the Steelers' publicity chief, notes that three of the leading Pittsburgh pranksters are Lynn Swann, John Stallworth and Terry Bradshaw. They like to put cups of water in an unsuspecting player's shoulder pads, hide shoes and fill helmets with shaving cream.

Shaving cream always has been a staple for locker room laughs. One time the *Buffalo News* Sunday Magazine was doing a piece on Bills' linebacker Jim Haslett and nose tackle Fred Smerlas. A photographer came to Rich Stadium to take pictures of the pair. While awaiting the cameraman, Smerlas fell asleep next to his locker. Haslett filled Smerlas' helmet with shaving cream, and a picture of the sleeping Smerlas and Haslett booby-trapping the helmet ran on the magazine cover.

Training camp is pro football's most tedious period, a time when grown men, some of them with grown children at home, are confined to quarters. The Washington Redskins, for instance, train in rural Carlisle, Pa., where, as Sonny Jurgensen used to say, "the late-late show starts at 7:30." The result? To break the monotony, the players sometimes conduct themselves like adolescents.

When boredom reaches the screaming point each summer in the Kansas City Chiefs' camp in Liberty, Mo., the victim is usually some new assistant coach.

A pay phone will ring incessantly in the hall, near the coach's room. The phone is right alongside the door leading to the room of center Jack Rudnay, the Chiefs' most relentless practical joker.

"Hello," answers the coach.

"Is it raining in Liberty?" asks the caller.

"Of course not," answers the coach. "The sun is shining outside. There's no chance of rain."

"There is now," the caller responds, and the coach is doused with a garden hose.

In the Philadelphia Eagles' camp one summer, placekicker Tony Franklin's teammates got the distinct idea that he had become too full of himself and was showboating for the fans each day.

One morning at practice, the goalposts where Franklin did his kicking were decorated with blown-up balloons in the form of hot dogs. There were even bigger balloons tied to Franklin's locker, and the equipment manager had put a new tape on the locker-room stereo: "I Wish I Was An Oscar Meyer Weiner."

Equipment managers are often the curse of hot-shot rookies in training camp. Bobby Yarborough, who has been with the Chiefs as equipment man or associate trainer since the team's beginning, finds it risky to be a resident good-humor man with Jack Rudnay still on the roster.

One time, Yarborough finished his day's work in camp and eagerly retired to his room—only to find it full of live chickens.

Morrie Kono, equipment man with the Cleveland Browns, broke in offensive tackle Doug Deiken with an oldie. Deiken told Kono he had broken a shoelace and needed a replacement.

"Left or right?" asked Kono.

"Left," answered Deiken, in rookie innocence, as the veteran Browns guffawed.

Dan Dowe of the Miami Dolphins has been known to cement rookies' shoes to the locker-room floor, and he once changed around all the Dolphins' football pants. Bob Kuechenberg, who found himself with pants whose beltline finished several inches below his navel, led a vigilante party which dunked Dowe into his whirlpool bath.

The Minnesota Vikings always are a veteran-dominated team. They aren't impressed with hot-shot rookies. When Ed Marinaro, now an actor on the TV series, "Hill Street Blues," was a rookie in 1972, he came in with a glittering reputation as a ball-carrier. To make it worse, he was an Ivy Leaguer, having set his record at Cornell.

Grady Alderman, then the most senior of the Vikings, invited Marinaro to join the veterans in a card game in their dormitory room. Marinaro thought the invitation was a badge of honor until he found out that he was there only to run for coffee and anything else the older guys wanted.

Marinaro drove to camp in a Porsche that first season. Not only was it a Porsche, but a purple Porsche. One day, Ed came out of the locker room to discover that his car had been stolen. He went down to the police station to file a report. In the midst of his filing, the news came that the car was in the middle of the Vikings' practice field.

The doors were locked. The keys were missing. Marinaro, assuming that the culprits would eventually produce his keys, left the car on the field overnight.

The next morning, as he was dressing for practice, he was informed that coach Bud Grant wanted to see him. Grant was pacing impatiently and there were about 1,000 fans waiting to watch practice when Marinaro came out.

"What is your car doing in the middle of the practice field?" demanded the coach. "What in hell were you doing last night?"

After a lame explanation, which didn't seem to go over with the coach, Marinaro returned to the locker room. His keys were in his stall. Sheepishly, he dashed out on the field and, in full uniform, drove the car off the playing surface.

Those who only see Grant as The Great Stone Face on the sidelines know nothing of the Viking coach as a practical joker. The Viking office staff, though, has learned to expect all sorts of pranks from him. As a naturalist and fisherman at home with wildlife, he has been known for placing salamanders in desk drawers of the secretaries, and once he smuggled a rooster into the ladies' room.

The girls turned the tables on him one day when they borrowed a 10-foot python from the Minneapolis zoo and placed it on Grant's desk. As cool as a coach with a 50-point lead in the Super Bowl, Grant wrapped the python around his neck and went about his business.

Equipment manager Sid Brooks of the San Diego Chargers is known as a maestro of mischief. Among his victims has been offensive lineman Ed White, who joined the team in 1978 after a decade with the Vikings. He is regarded as one of the messiest Chargers. White came into the clubhouse one day and discovered a portable toilet in front of his locker, with all his gear inside.

White himself is an instigator. When he was with the Vikings he knew that line coach Jerry Burns had an aversion to insects and creepy crawlers. He'd buy rubber spiders and snakes, put them in the film can and watch Burns go nuts.

"One day I rigged this line along the ceiling so this rubber

Minnesota's Bud Grant did not recoil at the sight of a python.

spider slowly dropped down in front of Burns as he was showing the films," White recalled. "He was so terrified he kicked over the projector. Bud Grant loved it."

New York Giant punter Dave Jennings has been with the team since his rookie year in 1974 and he has witnessed his share of clubhouse capers.

"When John McVay was head coach, he had this hit-of-the-week award," Jennings said. "We'd always holler for the guy who won it to make a speech. They never did until Andy (Boom Boom) Selfridge, a linebacker and special-teams man, won it and suddenly turned off the lights, got into the spotlight of the projector and proceeded to do George C. Scott's opening speech from the movie *Patton*. Selfridge had us rolling on the floor."

Even the straight-laced Dallas Cowboys have had their share of laughs. In training camp Roger Staubach, the straightest of straight arrows, was relaxing on his bed, reading a book, when he heard his door open and then close quickly.

He looked up to find a naked woman smiling down at him. Outside, Craig Morton and several other Cowboy teammates roared at Roger's embarrassment.

The old-timers claim the funny men are tame compared to the old days, and they may have a point.

When Larry Eisenhauer played defensive end for the old Boston Patriots in the '60s, he used to psyche himself up for a game by banging his head against his metal locker. He also kept a large chicken bone in his locker and he'd tell visitors, "That's from Jack Kemp's neck." Kemp, now a congressman, used to play against the Pats when he was Buffalo's quarterback.

Those were the days of traveling by propeller-driven aircraft, so teams used to spend weeks on the road and play two or three western games at a clip. When the Pats stayed in San Diego it was at the Stardust Country Club, which had a cocktail lounge where the afternoon entertainment was a mermaid swimming in a pool that was visible through windows behind the back bar.

Eisenhauer's father, called "the Chief," was a Long Island construction company owner who used to make some of those trips. He was bigger than Larry. One afternoon, "The Chief" strolled out of his room in his bathing suit and asked Larry the whereabouts of the hotel swimming pool.

"Just walk around that corner, Dad, and you'll see some steps. Climb up and you'll see that pool right there. Jump in."

As soon as his father disappeared around the corner, Larry and his pals dashed into the cocktail lounge. The pool to which "The Chief" had been directed was, of course, not the one reserved for guests.

Larry collapsed in laughter as the lounge patrons, anticipating the appearance of a voluptuous mermaid, were startled instead by the sudden appearance of a mini-whale.

In the '50s, the Chicago Bears' resident humorist was their all-pro guard, Stan Jones. Jones, now defensive line coach for the Denver Broncos, still comes up with the good lines. When George Halas, 87-year-old patriarch of the Bears, suddenly began pulling all the strings for the team late last year, Jones quipped that "Halas coming out of retirement to run the Bears is like Orville Wright returning to become president of United Airlines."

There weren't many yuks when Paul Brown was winning championships with the Cleveland Browns, but what few there were usually were provided by the backup quarterback, George Ratterman.

Brown invented the messenger guards, who shuttled in the plays from the coach at the sidelines, thereby removing the quarterback from the responsibility. Ratterman wasn't thrilled about it, but then again, he didn't get to play much in relief of Hall of Famer Otto Graham.

There was one game in which he did appear which his teammates never forgot. When the messenger guard came racing into the huddle with Brown's decision, Ratterman told him, "I don't like that play. Go back and tell Brown to give you another one."

Ratterman was only kidding, but the guard was just 15 yards

from Brown when he finally heard the quarterback beseeching him, "Come back! Come back!"

In a game between Philadelphia and Buffalo last year, Eagle nose tackle Charley Johnson complained bitterly to the officials that Will Grant, the Bills' center, was holding him on almost every play. Finally, Grant became fed up with Johnson's complaints.

"Yeah, Charley, you're right. I am holding you," Grant confessed. "And I'm doing a damn good job of it, too."

The "Thanksgiving Turkey Caper" is an old number, but no one pulls it off with more aplomb than Sam Wyche, the San Francisco 49ers' quarterback coach. It goes like this:

About a week before Thanksgiving, a letter from the "Ajax Meat Packing Co." is received by each of the team's rookies. The letter will congratulate the player on a fine season, then invite him out to the meat-packing plant to accept, with Ajax's best wishes, a fat turkey—for free.

The letter also includes detailed, complex road maps on how to reach the place where the turkeys will be given out. The directions, of course, lead to nowhere.

The beauty part is that there always is an "Ajax" meat company listed in the phone book. It receives many phone calls from bewildered rookies, asking for a clarification on the directions. The response is almost always, "What turkey? What football team?"

Wyche was so good at writing the letter that he would catch unsuspecting veterans as well as rookies.

Even the college draft has its lighter side. One year, the Browns were especially secretive about whom they were seeking. Nate Wallack, the team's public relations director, was in the press room, jotting down some notes, when he was called to the phone in another office.

An inquisitive reporter, noticing that Wallack left his notepad on a desk, glanced over to see what Nate had written. Wallack's pad contained these notations: 3 cb, 4 rb, 3 lb.

Naturally, the reporter thought he had a scoop. The Browns were going to draft three cornerbacks, four running backs and three linebackers. The writer confronted Wallack with his find.

"Are you kidding?" said Wallack. "That's our lunch order: three corned beef, four roast beef and three lox-and-bagels."

Even the officials find a few laughs.

Jim Tunney, one of the top referees in the NFL, is a noted speaker at motivational seminars during the offseason. He always gets a chuckle with his definition of a fan:

"That's the guy who sits in the 50th row of the grandstand and can see even the most minute mistake we might make, but when he gets back to the parking lot can't find his own automobile."

The Myth and Magic of Monday Night Football

By PETE ALFANO

The casual air that marked their preparation earlier in the evening slowly begins to fade. There is a feeling of tension now and anticipation even though they have done this a hundred times before. From his vantage point in the truck, director Chet Forte oversees a bank of monitors and whispers the countdown into their earphones, sounding like the mission controller at Cape Canaveral. "Two minutes to air time.... One minute, thirty seconds..." And while 50 million Americans turn their TV dials to ABC and rush into the kitchen for some last-minute refreshments, the three men in the yellow-gold blazers take a deep breath and wait for their cue, like entertainers poised in the wings of a Las Vegas nightclub.

Then, precisely on the hour, the familiar staccato voice of Howard Cosell fills the airwaves, welcoming nearly one-third of the nation to another edition of Monday Night Football, one of television's longest-running and most successful series. With his customary flair for dramatics, Cosell sets the scene and introduces the principals. For example:

"Hel-lo every-one, this is How-ard Co-sell and this is Chicago, the Win-dy City, where George Pa-pa Bear Halas has waited seemingly an eternity for a winnah."

Viewers are probably convinced by now they are going to witness an event of historic proportions. It is only when Cosell's sidekicks, country boy Don Meredith and the urbane Frank Gifford, deliver their own more low-key appraisals, that fans remember this is a football game, not World War III.

Pete Alfano is a sports feature writer for Long Island's Newsday.

Introducing... "The Dandy Don, Howard and Frank Show."

And yet, not just any football game. One day after all the other National Football League teams have shared the spotlight and fans have been treated to nearly seven hours of second helpings of games and postgame shows and slow-motion, stop-action, reverse-angle replays, their appetities still are whetted by the prospect of Monday Night Football. And it doesn't really matter whether the featured teams are in last place, wallowing in mediocrity, or play-off bound, Monday night games stand above the others.

Victory on Monday night is the next best thing to winning the Super Bowl. Losing reads like a Shakespearian tragedy.

"We have been known to make or break a player's career," said Chet Forte, the director of Monday Night Football who has been with the program since its inception in 1970. "All the players' peers are watching and if a guy is playing a poor game, we say it."

ABC cameras follow the action in a Steeler-49er game.

Sometimes, nothing needs to be said. Dave Smith was a receiver for the Pittsburgh Steelers from 1970–72 and he is best known for the Monday Night Blunder. He caught a pass and was headed for the end zone for an apparent touchdown. So far, so good. Then, as he crossed the goal line, Smith spiked the ball in celebration. The problem was that it wasn't really the goal line but the five-yard line. The play was ruled a fumble and the opposing team recovered. Smith's career, however, never recovered.

What makes Monday Night Football unique is ABC's show-business treatment. Although Cosell, Meredith and Gifford will dabble in x's and o's and weakside blitzes, they are conscious of being performers who also are expected to be entertaining, although, theoretically, never at the expense of the game. The ratings prove that fans like this approach, although critics abound. In recent seasons, CBS radio has taken to broadcasting Monday Night Football, inviting the audience to turn down the TV sound and listen to football announcers who take the sport seriously.

But Chet Forte says this is just so much propaganda. Fans enjoy the byplay in the booth, he says, especially when Meredith and Cosell are disagreeing. They like the tomfoolery and the light approach as much as they thrill to a long touchdown pass or kickoff return.

"I think the key thing in the beginning was that we treated this as a happening," said Don Ohlmeyer, an associate producer when Monday Night Football began and later the president of NBC Sports. "It was far more entertainment oriented. We tried to reach out for the non-football fan. We tried to create an excitement like the old Tonight Show where something outrageous would happen and you would be afraid to turn it off."

Cosell has been the focal point, the one credited for the success of Monday Night Football. He is called "Humble Howard," the way a skinny person is called "Fats." Cosell is anything but modest. He is what the rest of the nation perceives as a typical "New Yawker," abrasive, obnoxious, condescending, overbearing, shrill . . . and those are some of the nicer things said about him. Some of the unkind thoughts have included death threats from those who do not share his opinions.

He is, however, also the preeminent television sports journalist, a man who went beyond merely giving the scores and boosting the egos of the pampered athlete. Oh, Cosell can be as doting as any sportscaster when he is plugging something of interest or praising a favorite player, but Cosell was an outspoken pioneer in addressing serious issues in sports and he still is the industry's conscience.

"Howard is Howard," Chet Forte said.

"Howard is Howard," Don Ohlmeyer added.

"Howard is Howard," Gifford agreed.

Get the picture?

It was these unique qualities that Roone Arledge, then president of ABC Sports and now president of ABC News and Sports, was looking for when he assembled an announcing team for the first year of Monday Night Football.

"The rationalization for using Howard was that we wanted someone who would tell it like it is," Chet Forte said. "Announcers at the time never criticized anyone. But Howard made Monday Night Football different from the beginning."

"Howard has great visability," Gifford said. "He was judged

the most unpopular and most popular sportscaster in the same poll."

In 1970, Cosell's partners were Meredith and Keith Jackson. Arledge had chosen Jackson because he was a professional announcer, not a former athlete, although Arledge had first sought out Gifford, who still had one year remaining on his contract at CBS.

"Roone talked to me before it all started," Gifford said, "and we talked about a lot of things. I knew he was set on Howard and I suggested Don. I really had a good idea what they were trying to do."

Meredith had been a pretty good quarterback for the Dallas Cowboys but what made him appealing was his good looks and irreverence. Several network officials feared that football fans might object to the fun these announcers would have at the expense of the sport, but they also understood the need for personalities in the booth to compete against programs like M*A*S*H.

Meredith, with his folksy down-home humor and "aw, shucks, Howard" manner of dealing with Cosell, was ideal. As a former quarterback, it was obvious Meredith understood football as well as anyone but he never thought of it as life and death.

Despite a successful first season, Arledge made a change in the broadcast team in 1971 when Gifford became available. Critics speculated that Jackson was moved to college football because Cosell did not like him, but the prevailing opinion was that Arledge was looking for another pretty face to win favor with the ladies.

Gifford was handsome and mild-mannered, not one to bring the kettle to a boil. His voice was the neutral tone taught in announcing school. He was a traditionalist who called the plays while Cosell and Meredith jousted. It was difficult to imagine him offending anyone.

So, not only were the voices distinctive, but the roles were, too. And Cosell, Meredith and Gifford seemed to like one another, although at first Gifford did not seem comfortable with the show-biz style. "TV is so structured that people believe we read from a script," Gifford said. "But no one ever told us what to do or say. And I never construed our function as poking fun at the game. I wouldn't have been part of that."

"We were more of an improvisational group," Meredith has said. "People look at us announcers in our kind of elevated position of authority and they think we're supposed to know what goes on down on the field all the time. Heck, there were times when I was down there playing when I didn't know what was going on."

They had perceived weaknessess, too. Gifford was considered bland and Meredith was too closely identified with the Cowboys.

The director calls the shots in the production truck.

It became all too evident on one Monday night when Dallas was routed by the St. Louis Cardinals, 35–0. Meredith was so shaken he rambled almost incoherently on the air. His loyalty was tempered, however, as the years passed and many of his former teammates retired.

Gifford played for the New York Giants and did his best not to show it. It wasn't hard; the Giants had become perennial losers after he retired. Cosell never played football but fans were convinced he played favorites. The mail he received would lead you to believe he hated every team. Which usually is the mark of a good journalist.

Fans weren't the only critics either. A number of sportswriters and columnists objected to the side-show atmosphere created by Monday Night Football. Perhaps many of them had covered Monday night games and observed first-hand the celebrities Cosell, Meredith and Gifford had become. They were much in demand when they came to town, the honored guests at luncheons and cocktail parties. They often gave as many interviews as the players. Perhaps the reporters were jealous.

"There usually is a mayor's luncheon, parties—in some cases, too much partying—it's really a festival on Monday night," Gifford said. It's an unbelievable, exciting evening and none of us has been jaded by it. I'm amazed all this craziness still goes on."

In San Francisco during 1970, Forte observed that fans had raised as many as 50 banners praising Monday Night Football and "Humble Howard," "Dandy Don" and "Faultless Frank." When the cameras zeroed in on these banners during the game, reporters charged that ABC had printed the signs.

"That's nonsense," Forte said. "Why those fans did it that night I'll never know. But they began to do it everywhere we went. Some were funny, others crude; some knocked Howard."

ABC would not apologize to the purists who thought football was all serious business. Newspapers did not have to worry about ratings. Thus in the early years, Hollywood stars and starlets as well as politicians and authors would visit the TV booth at halftime, to plug a movie or a series or a book, knowing they were reaching a big audience.

Singer John Denver's agent called to ask whether Denver might appear at halftime. Other guests included Burt Reynolds, John Wayne, Farrah Fawcett and Bo Derrick. It was worth it just to see Cosell, tall and slightly hunched, flattering a beautiful actress like a gawking schoolboy.

"It was like a supermarket with all these people waiting in line," Gifford said. "It made me cringe. I didn't like it from the start. But I remember the time in the mid-seventies when Ronald Reagan and former Beatle John Lennon were in the booth waiting to be interviewed at halftime. I turned around and there was Reagan with his arm around Lennon trying to explain what was going on in a football game. It was vastly amusing."

But there was another reason for staying tuned at halftime. And that was the highlights, another of Roone Arledge's innovations. He knew that fans might switch to another show at halftime, especially if the game was dull or one-sided. So he had Cosell narrate the highlights of Sunday's games. Because the other networks did not make widespread use of tapes at the time, the Monday Night highlights were the only glimpse many fans had of other games. Now, it has become a matter of prestige to appear on the highlights.

And the highlights also became another forum for controversy "Most of the negative mail we get is about the highlights," Chet Forte said. "When Miami had those good teams, people there thought they should be on every week. When Howard and I appeared on a local TV show there once, the station told people what hotel we were staying at. Both of us received death threats. It wasn't funny.

"And in Pittsburgh one year, they wanted to take us to court because we weren't showing the Steelers enough on the highlights."

Even those behind the scenes came under scrutiny. Forte remembers a game when a player was injured and a stretcher was summoned. As the player lay motionless, Forte directed a cameraman with a hand-held camera to move in for a closeup. Instead of breaking for the commercial, Forte continued focusing on the injured player as teammates carried him off the field.

"Well, two minutes later, Roone Arledge calls me and says he had just gotten a call from Rozelle," Forte said. "Roone said, 'Pete wants to know if you're going to follow the player to the hospital and into surgery?' I think Rozelle was only half-kidding."

ABC improvised because it had no assurances every game would be exciting. Schedules were prepared in advance and could not take into account whether preseason contenders would become midseason busts.

Despite being consistent losers, the Giants and Jets appeared at least once a year because of ABC's desire to maximize interest in the New York market. In 1981, however, when both teams made the playoffs, they were not on the schedule.

Anyway, games involving the Cowboys and Steelers are not necessarily going to be exciting. This is when the Monday Night crew is expected to sustain interest while being honest. Critics, however, have charged that Cosell, in particular, will not admit a game is terrible until the second half when prime-time is ending in the East and people are going to sleep.

Forte remembers a game in 1973 when Oakland was trouncing the Oilers, 35–0, in Houston. An Oiler fan was sleeping in the stands and Forte directed a cameraman to take a shot of this. The fan awoke unexpectedly and made an obscene gesture seen by millions of viewers. "He's just saying, 'we're No. 1,'" Meredith said coyly, saving an embarrassing moment.

It was as if Monday Night Football lived a charmed existence. Everything worked so smoothly. "But Don and I have said over and over that we're constantly amazed that we get on the air and amazed we get off," Gifford said. "It is three hours of live TV and incredible things can happen, things that are emotional, electric, that wouldn't have any humor for anyone. And at the time they happen it is tense although hilarious, too."

Interestingly enough, none of the networks were interested in the rights to prime-time football in 1970. Sports programming on a weekday night was considered unthinkable. Even baseball still was playing its World Series and playoff games during the day. It was NFL commissioner Pete Rozelle who suggested nighttime football. He wanted to capitalize on professional football's soaring popularity. He was interested in making new fans, especially among women. But he was taking a chance. Would football be overexposed? How many Sunday football widows would give up their husbands and Monday night, too?

Besides, CBS had a successful lineup on Monday night and was the leader in the Nielsen ratings. NBC was a comfortable second and reluctant to overdo its football coverage. These two networks wanted to restrict football to its traditional Sunday time slot.

ABC was last in the ratings. Arledge argued that a bold stroke was needed to improve the network's ratings, that there was everything to gain and little to lose. Besides, this would enable ABC to get its foot in the door with the NFL and a piece of the action.

"If this were happening now when we are competitive," Chet Forte said, "we might turn it down. But back then, Roone wanted to take a chance. Besides, the Hughes Network was negotiating with the NFL for nighttime football and we could have lost some of our affiliates to them."

The gamble paid off like a longshot at the track. "The early years were a wonderful, exciting time," Don Ohlmeyer said. "We were fighting to change people's habits. We were trying not to alienate the hard-core fan. We were all presentation and hype. The announcers were mobbed like rock stars in every city we went. I nicknamed the show, 'The Brother Love Traveling Freak Show.'"

The first game was played on Sept. 21, 1970, in Cleveland between the Browns and the New York Jets. The Jets had won Super Bowl III the previous year and were led by quarterback Joe Namath—Joe Willie Namath, as Cosell always said—football's biggest and most controversial star. The winners that night were the Browns and ABC. Monday Night Football had scored a huge ratings success that would change the habits of millions of people.

Variety Magazine, for instance, reported that business at movie theatres dropped considerably and many theatres were contemplating remaining closed on Mondays. Bowling leagues suffered a decline in participation as many bowlers switched to another night.

Restaurants and bars also lost patrons until enlightened entrepreneurs decided to exploit Monday Night Football instead of fight it. They installed television and large screens and made the games

The cameraman endures the elements except under the domes.

available to their patrons. In 1979, when Monday Night Football was completing its first decade, Miami-Dade Community College in Florida offered a course entitled, "Understanding and Enjoying Monday Night Football." A course made for student-athletes.

And in free-wheeling Southern California, a so-called "Church of Monday Night Football" was born and its disciples were urged never to miss a game. "Monday Night Football," according to Bud Grant, coach of the Minnesota Vikings, "was a week-long pep rally. A circus."

There were no studies made, however, to determine how many marriages were broken up by Monday Night Football.

"In the beginning, we didn't think it would be a great success," Chet Forte said. "We were flabbergasted by it. It was a tremendous endeavor."

Meredith even won an Emmy Award for his work on the show

during its first year. Thus, it came as a surprise when he left Monday Night Football in 1974 and signed a contract with NBC. He would be an analyst on NBC's Sunday games and, more importantly, he would be given an opportunity to act in a TV series and TV movies.

ABC auditioned Fred Williamson, the good-looking former defensive back from the Kansas City Chiefs and himself an actor, for three games, then hired Alex Karras, another irreverent type, who had been an outstanding defensive lineman for the Detroit Lions. Karras was a bear of a man, who delighted in poking fun at foreign born, soccer-style field-goal kickers. "I keeek a touchdown, I keeek a touchdown," Karras would say.

Because Monday Night Football was entrenched, the loss of Meredith did not hurt the ratings. Karras proved to be a capable replacement. He will be remembered for an observation he made during a game when the camera zoomed in on Marvin Upshaw, a player who had shaved his head. With the lights bouncing off Upshaw's gleaming bald head, Karras observed: "There's Marvin Upshaw from the University of Mars."

Karras, though, also became interested in acting and left after the 1976 season. Meredith returned, having satisfied his own need to appear in the movies. "He was a different guy," Chet Forte said. "At NBC, he was one of only two guys in the booth and so he had to study. I saw him one day after he came back and he had this big pad with all the plays written on it. I said, 'Hey, what happened to you?'"

ABC did not want Meredith to come across as an expert. It wanted his wit and charm and his detachment. It wanted him to continue to use Cosell as a foil, to argue with him in the booth. Meredith picked up as if he never had been away. And in recent seasons, even Gifford has become more animated, showing he can be witty and critical as well as capable of balancing his play-by-play duties with his role of refereeing the Cosell-Meredith matches. "Boys, boys, come on now," he will say, admonishing his partners.

Cosell pretends to enjoy jokes at his expense, although insiders say that privately he does not respect Gifford and Meredith as journalists or consider them equals. Then again, Cosell does not think too many people are his equal. Meredith and Gifford are friends and have become polished TV performers.

"People have tried to stir us up over the years," Gifford said, "but we get along. We can be argumentative and there is good-natured ribbing. If I have changed, I'm not aware of it. People look at it and say that I'm nuts and bolts, Howard is philosophical and Don is country. It's true I try to choreograph things; I'm in charge of making sure the commercials go on and the station breaks."

ABC did give in to one request Meredith made when the NFL increased its regular-season schedule to 16 games. He did not want to be obligated to do every broadcast plus the preseason games. So in 1979 Fran Tarkenton, the former quarterback of the Minnesota Vikings, became the fourth member of Monday Night Football cast. The "Scrambler" was a lower-case version of Meredith although Tarkenton was not as folksy or irreverent. He also was more of an analyst while Meredith might wonder aloud, "I don't know what they're doing out there, Howard."

The ratings have not suffered when Tarkenton has substituted for Meredith or for Cosell, or when Howard was broadcasting the baseball playoffs and World Series.

Monday Night Football also has been expanded to an occasional Sunday and Thursday night edition. Chet Forte worries about overexposure but thus far his fears have not been borne out. What other television program can tamper with the days of the week?

As it enters its 13th season, Monday Night Football has become part of American lifestye. In 1981, the game enjoyed its highest ratings ever. Forte, however, says he is concerned that the picture could change when Cosell decides to leave. "We will only know how it does when Howard isn't here anymore," Forte said. "He built this thing. I threw a lot onto his shoulders from the start."

Forte also worries what would happen should one of the two other networks eventually outbid ABC for Monday Night Football or if all three networks have to share it as part of a television package with the NFL. "I know they can do it well, but I don't think you can do it as basic football," Forte says.

Don Ohlmeyer disagrees. "It's been a while since the show was a happening," he points out. "You don't see many celebrities in the booth anymore. Sure, the show will change when Howard leaves. That reality though, will have to be faced and sometime soon.

"But if everyone is candid, you could agree that now the show would be successful on any network. On Tuesday morning, people don't say. 'Did you see the game last night?' They say, 'Did you see Monday Night Football?'"

There will be a time, too, when Meredith will leave again, this time for good, and Gifford also. Perhaps their successors will inherit a faithful audience unable to break the Monday night habit. Or, perhaps, viewers will miss Cosell, Meredith and Gifford. If that's the case, then the little song Meredith sings when a game no longer is in doubt may well apply: "Turn out the lights, the party's over."

TONY DORSETT'S TOUGHEST BATTLE

By FRANK LUKSA

The scene is worth a replay because it foretold all that was to come. Flash back to the second game of the 1981 regular season when Tony Dorsett of the Dallas Cowboys rushed for 129 yards against St. Louis. As usual, a swarm of media locusts cornered him and sought answers to why he was off to such a blistering pace.

"I feel more confident." Dorsett said. "More knowledgeable about what's going on. That awareness helps a running back. I'm just ready. I have a point to prove this year in the NFL."

What's the point?

"The point is . . . you're seeing it."

What a sight to behold. Dorsett rushed for a club-record 1,646 yards. In only five seasons, he became the Cowboys' career leading runner with 6,270 yards, surpassing Don Perkins who had 6,217. He set another club record for most 100-yard games (9) in a season, earned Pro Bowl and first-time all-pro honors, plus designation as the National Conference Offensive Player of the Year.

"This is the first year I can really say I reached my goals," Dorsett said when it was over. "I came in as a loud-mouthed rookie saying I could gain 1,500 yards. But I didn't know what it took to do it."

Now he knows. He also knows something else. He will be expected to do it again. Do it better, in fact. To do less will be to fail before the ever-demanding public eye. To do as well will

Frank Luksa follows Tony Dorsett's and the Cowboys' fortunes for the Dallas Times-Herald.

Tony Dorsett was 1981 NFL runnerup in yards rushing (1,646).

mean lack of progress. To do better...that is Dorsett's toughest battle.

Such is the world of the exceptional athlete. He competes as much against himself as his opponents. Dorsett understands the match-up. He has accepted the challenge.

"I'll just have to keep on keeping on. In any business you always want to improve," he says. "Hopefully, 1,600 yards won't be the highlight of my career. I can't stop there. I know it won't be easy. It's going to take a lot of work by a lot of people because what an individual accomplishes in this game depends on the group. All I know is I want to do better."

Already, he has done something no runner in football history can match. That is, rush for more than 1,000 yards 11 seasons in a row, beginning with his junior year at Hopewell High School in Pennsylvania. He did it again as a senior, then each of four seasons at the University of Pittsburgh (for a then NCAA-record total of 6,082 yards) and five more for the Cowboys.

Yet at the pro level, Dorsett never believed those years of 1,007, 1,325, 1,107 and 1,185 yards reflected the full flower of his talent. Neither, for that matter, did coach Tom Landry.

No question that Dorsett was the running-game catalyst as a 1977 rookie when Dallas won Super Bowl XII. Or that he helped rush them back to Super Bowl XIII. Or that in games where he gained more than 100 yards, including playoffs, the Cowboys' record was 28–1.

In terms of return on the money, an estimated $1.1-million original contract spread over five years, Dorsett more than paid back the investment. His Heisman Trophy credentials were legitimate. His selection as a No. 1 draft choice via a trade with Seattle—he was the second player chosen behind Ricky Bell, who went to Tampa Bay—was a masterpiece deal.

Yet Landry long held reservations about Dorsett. He once expressed them this way: "If Tony's willing to work hard enough year-round to prepare himself physically for the season ahead, then there's no limit to what he might do. He's capable of going into the 1,500-yard area every year if he's in top condition."

This was an oblique nudge from the coach. But for at least three years Dorsett ignored it and showed only token interest in the club's offseason conditioning program. To Landry, this was like failing to stand for the national anthem.

Since Dorsett is smallish by NFL yardsticks (5–11, 190 pounds), Landry feared for his physical well-being anyway. Further, if he wasn't in hardrock shape—at least by Landry's strict definition—the coach became injury-wary of his tailback and eased up at times on his workload.

Dallas fans greet Dorsett after loss in 1980 NFC title game.

The result was a muted but distinct disagreement between the pair. Dorsett never foot-stamped about it to cause a public rumpus. He stated his case in the manner of someone reciting the Dow-Jones average. His was a mild assertion that he could handle an average of 20–25 carries per game.

"I'm one who doesn't believe you prolong a guy's career by using him 50 percent of his potential," he said. "Maybe he (Landry) has his reasons. I bet he does. He's seen a lot of backs beat up in the business."

Exactly. Dorsett knew all along why Landry wasn't giving him free rein. He was raising a question and answering it at the same time. The answer being that Landry restrained Dorsett because he didn't believe the runner had prepared himself to handle it.

The change began at midseason, 1980.

"I've reached the point where I'm using him more effectively than I did earlier," Landry said then. "I was a little concerned about his size in years past. I tried to protect him to some extent to where he could make it through the season. Recently, I've been using him more and he's responded to it."

Dorsett was turned loose against the New York Giants to rush for 183 yards. It was the second-best game of his career, topped only by a 206-yard burst against Philadelphia as a rookie. Ironically, this was the only time Dorsett ran for more than 100 yards in a losing cause as Dallas fell, 38–35.

Still, that outing was a turning point. Beginning there, his finishing eight-game total was 879 yards and a 5.2-per-carry average. Such was the springboard for the 1,646-yard breakthrough in '81. Strung together, it means Dorsett has averaged 105 yards over the last 24 regular-season outings.

That burst put him in heady company. Only three backs in NFL history have gained more yardage after five seasons than Dorsett with 6,270. They are Walter Payton of Chicago (6,926) and Jim Brown of Cleveland (6,463 playing a shorter schedule). He's well ahead of the five-year pace of O. J. Simpson of Buffalo (5,181) and Franco Harris of Pittsburgh (5,133). Further, Dorsett already ranks 14th among all-time leading NFL rushers and will enter his sixth season at a peak-producing age of 26.

There's more. Dorsett owns the top seven rushing games in Dallas history, ranging from 206 to 154 yards, and eight of the top 10. His longest touchdown runs have been 84, 77 and 75. Besides that, the guy has caught 177 passes to rank No. 9 among all Cowboy receivers.

As Dorsett mentioned early last season, the NFL was seeing a different model. It was no accidental transformation, either. He planned on it. He worked for it like never before. As to why he chose to do so, there are a number of reasons.

Dorsett's personal life stabilized. He married for the first time in the spring of '81. Following the ceremony in Hawaii, he and wife Julie settled into Tony's 5,000-square-foot, 12-room home. Surprisingly to many, it has a rural location—on a one-acre plot in Wylie, a small northern suburb of Dallas.

Then there was the matter of wounded ego. During roll calls of the NFL's premier running backs, Earl Campbell and Payton led all lists. Billy Sims was making noise in Detroit. There was league-wide respect for the Kamikaze style of Philadelphia's Wilbert Montgomery. Others endorsed William Andrews of Atlanta.

Sometimes Dorsett was mentioned in their company. Sometime he wasn't. Regardless, he felt he belonged. He also realized the only way in was to prove it. He began by hitting the practice field to log 50 offseason workouts. Landry watched, and smiled.

"If I'm going to accomplish what I want to in the pros, it's time to get my act together," said the halfback.

Thereafter, the fruits of his labor fell into Dorsett's lap. Landry named him a team captain, an unthinkable role for a player once tagged with a bad-guy image. Then he ran him through a banner season with 342 carries, not only a Dallas record but 52 more than Tony's previous high. The reason was simple. Landry judged him fit to handle it and regretted only the fact he didn't run him more, since Tony lost the NFL rushing title to New Orleans rookie George Rogers by only 27 yards.

The other major downer of a 12–4 season came in the NFC championship against San Francisco. The 49ers won in the final minute, 28–27, to qualify for Super Bowl XVI, which they captured quite easily over Cincinnati, 26–21.

But at least another facet of Dorsett's reputation had been altered along the way. Opponents who felt they could intimidate him physically came up empty this time around. Dorsett could always, as teammate Jay Saldi put it, "make 10 yards by the time you blink." But his toughness was suspect to alien eyes.

"Tony has improved, I think, 15–20 percent this year over any year he's played," noted New York Giant safety Beasley Reece. "In the past we could get real physical with Tony. Either he'd go out of the game or get nicked up.

"He's much improved now. A much tougher player. Looking at film, the way he bounces off tacklers and runs through people, he has to be the best back in football now."

Still, there are longtime Dorsett watchers who blink at his reply to the question of what it'll take to return Dallas to the Super Bowl. He endorses the very thing he used to avoid.

"It all boils down to the offseason program," he says. "The last two years we came up a game short of the Super Bowl (20–7 to the Eagles in '80) and this year by one point. That should be enough to make everyone participate in the offseason program. That's where you get started.

"I think it might even be tougher because our schedule looks tougher. But they say the third time's a charm, so hopefully we'll be able to make it. I miss the Super Bowl. I think I got spoiled going my first two years. I really want to get back there."

To understand the magnitude of such a statement, one must recall Dorsett's early carefree, and careless, days as a Cowboy. Those were the times when he made Monday morning headlines running for 100-something yards and Tuesday morning headlines for running into trouble.

There was a punch-out with a local bartender. Followed by a station-house booking for arguing with police who had stopped a car in which Dorsett was riding in the back seat. Curfew violations in training camp. Then what became known locally as The Big Sleep, Dorsett snoring through a Saturday morning workout and losing his starting job the next day. What made it worse was his family had traveled from Pennsylvania to watch him play. There also was a noisy contract renegotiation which, before the Cowboys arranged to pay him $320,000 last year, found him threatening to bolt the team.

Odd how the fastest player on the team never could dodge even a minor transgression. He was thrown for no gain or a loss every time. Sad, too, because Dorsett wound up badly misrepresenting himself. He has yet to display a malicious, ornery or even bad-tempered side. He's soft-spoken, polite, especially enjoys the company of children and has never sparked a word of jealousy from a teammate. In short, he's a downright agreeable fellow.

Despite an early notion that the media had abused him by reporting his misdeeds, Dorsett never has ducked questions or anyone who asked them. From opening day as a Cowboy, he's been an easy-talking, cooperative and, most of all, patient interview.

A stammering, overwhelmed teenager from a 12-watt radio station receives the same attention as the metropolitan columnist. To the most tedious repetitious inquiries his replies are detailed and expansive. Dorsett's postgame locker-room habit is to talk on and on until one of two things occur: the team bus leaves or the interviewers, finally satisfied, wander away.

This was the way Myrtle Dorsett taught her youngest son, born Anthony Drew Dorsett in Rochester, Pa. All seven of the Dorsett children received the same training in manners and values worth maintaining.

"It was important to me that the kids went to church and school. Those were the most important things in their life," she says. "I never did like for them to fight a lot or swear. I always liked for them to have respect for grown folks. I never liked for them to talk back to grown folks."

From Westley Dorsett, his father, Tony learned ambition.

"My dad didn't want me to work in the steel mill like he did. He always told me there was no future there, to go out and accomplish as much as I could so I wouldn't end up in the steel mill. My dad didn't go to school but he's not a dumb man. He knows a lot."

Few know as much about running, or are as instinctively gifted in the art, as Dorsett. In a way, he's handicapped with the Cowboys because they are multitalented on offense. Their weapons are many and varied . . . Danny White, Drew Pearson, Tony Hill, Billy Joe DuPree. No one player carries the whole load and that suits Dorsett.

"I don't want those pressures," he says. "I think I respond under pressure situations but I honestly don't want to be the dominant force in our offense. Like if you stop Tony Dorsett, you've stopped the Cowboy offense. I don't want that type situation for myself.

"I like the situation where if we're going to have a running game, then I'm going to be basically responsible for it. That's great. I love it. But I don't want the whole team riding on my shoulders. That's a lot of pressure.

"I've had people say to me, 'Earl [Campbell] is a great back but he's only a 16-game back.' I find that hard to believe, but if you look at it over the years and playoffs, maybe there's something to it. If Houston's running game is stopped, that was the story. They were out of the playoffs. Whereas with us, we have more things that work. This is a happier atmosphere to work in."

The Landry-Dorsett relationship has firmed into one of mutual respect. If Dorsett's toughest battle lies ahead in terms of improving upon a sensational season, Landry will furnish the opportunity to do it.

That much was certain during a postgame exchange between Landry and some guy with a tape recorder. He shoved the microphone under the coach's nose and in his best radio voice inquired: "Did you plan to use Dorsett a lot today?"

Landry's reply well-serves his plans for Dorsett this season. "I plan to use Dorsett *all* the time," he said.

How Cris Collinsworth Won TV's Football "Superstars"

By HOWARD BLATT

Collinsworth (far right) won the 100-yard dash over such rivals as (l. to r.) Charle Young, Mark Gastineau and Kellen Winslow.

Cris Collinsworth doesn't have to be reminded that, by comparison to his muscular NFL brethren, he looks like the "before" portion of an ad for a body-building salon.

"My skinny old body won't win any prizes," says the 6–4, 192-pound wide receiver for the Cincinnati Bengals, "When I took the NFL physical, I couldn't believe some of those linemen. The receivers were afraid to take off their shirts."

Of course, Collinsworth's "skinny old body" won its share of

Howard Blatt is a sports copy editor at the New York Daily News.

Collinsworth showed Wimbledon touch in winning the tennis.

Richard Todd (left) and Billy Sims vie on obstacle course.

prizes during an all-pro rookie season that saw him lead the Bengals to the Super Bowl with 67 regular-season catches for a team-record 1,009 yards and eight TDs. He added five more receptions for 107 yards as Cincinnati fell to San Francisco in Supe XVI.

Then, when the season was over, Collinsworth provided the ultimate proof that, when it comes to athletic versatility, bulging biceps are not the last word. The Cincinnati scarecrow won the football competition in the preliminary round of TV's "The Superstars," besting such titans as the Jets' Mark Gastineau, the 49ers' Jack (Hacksaw) Reynolds, the Chargers' Kellen Winslow and the Lions' Billy Sims.

Collinsworth edged Green Bay receiver James Lofton by a single point and topped San Francisco pass-catcher Dwight Clark by four to win $13,800 in the football event held Feb. 12–14 at Key Biscayne, Fla. Following those top three were, in order of finish: the Rams' Nolan Cromwell, Gastineau, Sims, Reynolds, Winslow, the Dolphins' Don Strock, the 49ers' Charle Young, the Jets' Richard Todd and the Giants' Rob Carpenter.

Collinsworth, a four-sport star (football, basketball, baseball and track) at Astronaut High School in Titusville, Fla., has always been the adaptable type. The 23-year-old bachelor began his foot-

Green Bay wide receiver James Lofton wheeled home second to another wide receiver, San Francisco's Dwight Clark.

Dwight Clark rowed home fifth to winner Nolan Cromwell.

Mark Gastineau (above) and Billy Sims (facing page) pressed . .

Dwight Clark proved master of the links.

and pressed... and wound up in a first-place tie.

ball career at the University of Florida as a quarterback, but was later switched to wide receiver, where he flourished.

The keys to Collinsworth's triumph in the football competition were winning performances on the tennis court (he beat Clark, 6–1 in the finals), and in the 100-yard dash (he nipped Lofton by .28 seconds with a time of 10.10). In addition, he was second in swimming (to Gastineau), third in the half-mile (behind Lofton and Cromwell), third in bowling (behind Winslow and Sims), fourth on the obstacle course and fifth in golf.

Since Superstars rules require competitors to participate in only seven of 10 events, Collinsworth wisely decided to forego the competition in weightlifting (won by Gastineau and Sims), rowing (won by Cromwell) and bicycle racing (won by Clark).

Collinsworth's preliminary-round conquest earned him a spot in the men's finals, where he won the tennis event and finished fourth overall to add another $9,300 to his winnings. World-class hurdler Renaldo Nehemiah won the overall men's title for a second year in a row.

Collinsworth went on to the World Superstars competition, where he tied Gastineau for third place and earned $15,600. He was also a member of the Cincinnati Bengals team that lost to the Oakland Athletics in the Super Teams finals in Honolulu, and his loser's share netted him an overall Superstars' total of $48,791.

Not a bad pay day for a skinny guy in the land of the behemoths.

Betting on Pro Football: Why You Can't Win

By DAVE SCHULZ

Never before has the pro football betting public been given as much information and as much pregame analysis as it gets now.

This information explosion is not entirely new to sport. Horse racing has long had its past performances in the *Daily Racing Form* and similar publications. Horse race selectors are standard figures in the sports departments of most big-city newspapers.

Even baseball bettors have long had available a plethora of statistics as well as the probable pitchers listed every day among the major-league results and standings on the sports pages of just about every daily paper in the country.

And such a data deluge is common to professional football. Point spreads are published for next week's games immediately after the previous weekend's schedule is over. The spreads are updated daily to reflect such things as injuries, intrasquad dissension, a new-found kicking star and—most importantly—the amount of money being bet.

Representatives of three major Las Vegas sports books arrive at a consensus and put out a line—an "outlaw line"—on Monday morning for big bettors and selected handicappers, and they are allowed to wager limited amounts. These bets are monitored closely. If the odds-makers detect any significant betting tendency on one game, or a group of games, they will adjust the line according before the point spread is available to the general public. This gives the average bettor a full five days to study the line before deciding on which teams to bet.

Why then, can't the average fan win betting football?

"Vigorish."

"He bets with his heart, not his head."

"He just likes the action, he doesn't really want to win."

"Sucker bets."

Book author, editor and once an owner of thoroughbred race horses, Dave Schulz has won and lost—more often—on everything from jai alai to pro football.

"No cash management. He doesn't know when to push hard and when to pull back."

These are just some of the answers from the real pros—those who make money from pro football betting. But they don't necessarily make it betting on games; some are selectors for daily or specialized football newspapers, others take bets, some have written books on the subject and then, of course, there are the touts who offer their selections for a fee.

In gambling, as with most business transactions, there is a handling fee. This "vigorish"—or juice—is the 10 percent surcharge that the loser pays, in addition to his losing wager. Thus a bettor will have to put up $110 to win $100.

If our Sunday gambler breaks even on his selections, winning two games and losing two against the point spreads, he must still come up with $20 vigorish for the bookmaker, the bookie. The origin of the word vigorish is said to have come from middle or Eastern Europe, where Yiddish was spoken, and where it meant winnings or profit.

Even if a gambler can guess right half the time during an entire season, he would still be behind. Because of the vigorish, a bettor must win 52.9 percent of the time just to break even.

Assuming the cost of business—paying the juice—is no particular problem, the next obstacle is deciding which teams to bet.

"I love a man with an opinion," says Sparky, an investment broker with a medium-sized business.* Medium-sized in this case means a $10,000 or $12,000 profit on Sunday is considered a bad day.

"People love the home team. They really don't care what the point spread is, so we can adjust accordingly," enthuses Sparky. "It's great to do business in New York where half the people love the Giants and the other half love the Jets, but they have strong opinions either way. They could get a better line out of town, but how many people know a bookie in Pittsburgh or Minneapolis?"

In addition to being blinded by loyalty to the home team, another fan problem is that he sometimes knows too much without being able to be objective.

"The basic fan is aware of rivalries between players, say in the defensive backfield," offers Mac, a southern Californian who has been both a big bettor and a smallish bookmaker. "It could be the rookie-veteran thing or whatever, but the fan feels maybe this

*Bookmakers are not without humor. Sparky, like most bookies, requires a code name for use when his clients call in on the telephone. Sparky's clients all have names like tuna, snapper, and minnow. They're all fish to Sparky, which may be a commentary on what he thinks their chances for survival are.

could hurt his team's performance. In comes a team with a big quarterback and a couple of great receivers and the fan figures his quarreling secondary is going to get picked apart. What he forgets is that the players are professional enough to leave the fighting in the locker room or, if not, the coach senses the situation and makes some adjustment in the pass rush or the linebacker assignments to neutralize the other team's passing game. And the fan is patting himself on the back before the game for having the good sense to go against his favorites. But a little knowledge is a dangerous thing."

This too much/too little knowledge also affects the home team's opposition. The average fan gets very little information about the other team, except in the week before the game. Unless, of course, it is one of the stronger teams in the league and it tends to get more press and television coverage. Even then, the local sportswriters often play up what appear to be weaknesses in the strong teams in an effort to give the local fans hope. The end result is that the average fan will let his emotions rule the decision on who to bet and how much to put on the game.

Brad Thomas, a handicapper and selector for the daily sports newspaper *Sports Eye,* feels this lack of well-rounded information is a common reason the average guy loses.

"They have a favorite team and they want to bet it no matter what," Thomas says. "They don't realize, or at least forget, that the point spread is the equalizing factor. Many people look at these lines or point spreads and can't believe a strong team like Dallas or San Diego is only a six-point favorite over a weaker team. What they are not taking into account are factors like momentum.

Most professional pro football handicappers feel that fans aren't willing to put effort into their betting. A guy wouldn't go out and plunk down several hundred dollars for a video recorder or a sound system, without learning a few things about the equipment, yet that same guy will risk that much money and more on a Sunday afternoon after reading one local paper and maybe getting some TV guy's predictions.

Some bettors rely on tout services that offer anything from a regular weekly service spotlighting three to five games, a best bet of the week to a "lock of the year." Whatever these guys charge has to be included in the losses or deducted from the winnings, which makes the odds against John Q. Bettor just that much longer.

Some tout services charge you only on winning selections. The big touts pull in as much as $2 million a season. Others are fly-by-nighters who scrape up enough money for a telephone listing and a few newspaper ads.

Like the old man of the mountain asks, "If these guys know so much, why are they selling the information instead of backing it with their own money?" Obviously, the answer is that they know better, and they know their bettors.

All of this information gathering, scrutinizing official injury reports, analyzing personnel changes, assessing attitudes and momentum and weighing dozens of other factors make up the fine art of handicapping. There is a breed of pro football gambler who has no trouble picking winners, even against the point spreads, in a majority of the games. But they are still losers because they don't know how to bet.

"This is generally true because every guy is looking for a big pot of gold," says Benjamin Lee Eckstein, a freelance sportswriter and handicapper for several major Eastern daily newspapers. "The average guy lacks discipline and control needed to win. He gets carried away, betting with his heart instead of his head."

And you thought picking winners was everything! According to Sonny Reizner, who runs the Castaways Sports Book in Las Vegas and who is one of the three men responsible for the Las Vegas line published in many newspapers, "Just about every losing player fails to take advantage of his winning streaks and falls into big trouble when he is losing."

What the wise old Reizner is saying is a paraphrase of the gambling axiom, "press your winnings, back off from losses"— meaning increase the amount of your wagers when on a winning streak, decrease when you're on a losing streak.

Knowing how to bet means selectively choosing among games and going after the right ones. It is almost impossible to make money pecking away with small bets and hoping for a high winning percentage. The routine bets are just to keep you interested. It's the occasional big score that turns a punter into a winner. And a big score does not mean playing parlays, round robins, teasers and other sucker bets.

As *Sports Eye's* Thomas puts it, "The average guy is really greedy and wants to win it all, every time. He is unwilling to look for spots, wait for the right games. He wants the action, the home team, everything that is on television."

Control, discipline, knowing when to hold back or push your luck—in business this is called cash management. It's what Sonny Reizner and other Las Vegas pros like Lem Banker and Ernie Kauffman advocate.

As articulated by Eckstein, good cash management in betting is almost the opposite of good investment strategy elsewhere. You don't want to hedge your bets too much or diversify a lot or else you can get eaten alive by the vigorish. It is better, wagering wise,

Super Bowl Betting Scoreboard

Up until last season one man was responsible for the national line on pro football games. He was Bob Martin, now retired, who worked for the Stardust Casino and Sports Book on the Las Vegas Strip. One of his crowning achievements was his line for Los Angeles-Pittsburgh in Super Bowl XIV.

The Rams were surprise winners of the NFC title and looked like no match for the Steelers. In trying to determine the line, Martin said at the time that a one-touchdown difference wasn't enough and two touchdowns was too much, so he settled on 11 points. Pittsburgh won by 12, 31–19.

In the listing of Super Bowl results that follow, the point spreads given are as they were on the closing national line. The spreads may have varied from city to city and in the days prior to Super Sunday.

Year	Winner (Point Spread)	Loser
1967	Green Bay (−14) 35	Kansas City 10
1968	Green Bay (−13½) 33	Oakland 14
1969	New York Jets (+18) 16	Baltimore 7
1970	Kansas City (+13) 23	Minnesota 7
1971	Baltimore (+2½) 16	Dallas 13
1972	Dallas (−5½) 24	Miami 3
1973	Miami (+2) 14	Washington 7
1974	Miami (−7) 24	Minnesota 7
1975	Pittsburgh (−3½) 16	Minnesota 6
1976	Pittsburgh (−7) 21	Dallas 17
1977	Oakland (−4½) 32	Minnesota 14
1978	Dallas (−5½) 27	Denver 10
1979	Pittsburgh (−4) 35	Dallas 31
1980	Pittsburgh (−11) 31	Los Angeles 19
1981	Oakland (+3) 27	Philadelphia 10
1982	San Francisco (−1½) 26	Cincinnati 21

to put all your eggs in one, maybe two games, on a Sunday.

All the people interviewed for this article said that Joe Average bets on too many games.

Every bettor uses a system of some sort, where certain key categories are emphasized and others are minimized, discarded or otherwise overlooked. Even flipping a coin can be a system— random chance, if you will. But trying to reduce pro football to an arithmetic formula is virtually impossible.

One of those who holds this position is Larry Merchant, newspaper columnist and selector who detailed a season's worth of betting in his book, "The National Football Lottery."

"I don't believe in systems," he states bluntly. "Systems substitute mathematical equations for human equations, a fatal flaw because humans must operate them."

Then, striking at the heart of the reason why people bet, Merchant says a system "would turn an essentially romantic pastime into a grind."

Yet what Merchant and virtually every other pro football handicapper does is use a system of sorts. They may not realize it, or even admit to it, but they all have their prejudices, their likes and dislikes about what is important to winning football games and what isn't. If you track their choices you will find each has tendencies, whether it is favoring a strong pass rush over a strong passing attack as the deciding factor, or picking a team with good running and so-so passing over a strong passing team with so-so ground attack or whatever. What makes it more complicated— and why many handicappers don't realize they have a system— is that they don't always follow it. They make exceptions to the rules, or they let intangibles like momentum, will-to-win and hot or cold streaks override the system.

The fact remains, though, that many systems have some validity and can work well for a short while or in certain, limited circumstances. That's when the successful gambler should start to press his winnings.

Washington Post horse and football handicapper Gerry Strine, co-author of "Covering the Spread: How to Bet Pro Football," advises, "When you're winning regularly, you are clearly doing something right and you should take advantage of it while it lasts." But he quickly adds, "If you hit a cold spell, don't try to break out of it by doubling up, figuring it can't go on. It can, and you probably can't."

Yet every season that's just what tens of thousands of betting fans do: fight a winning streak, feed a losing one.

What is there to consider? First of all, let's realize there are no bargains on Sunday morning. The first scan early in the week determined any "hole in the line" or mistake in the point spreads. Mistakes may happen in college football, where there are 30 to 35 Division I games on a Saturday or, more likely, in college basketball, where there can be 25 or 30 games a night. But there are few mistakes in pro football, and these are ironed out early in the week.

It may be a lesson in humility, but the truth is what you bet, or whatever everybody else bets, really doesn't have anything to do with the outcome of the game. The coaches get paid on the win-loss percentage and not how often they cover the spread.

Linesmakers don't make mistakes. Big underdogs might win a game outright, or slight favorites might blow the other team out of the stadium. But that doesn't make the line wrong; all it means is that half the people who bet the game were willing to risk their money that the results would have been reversed.

Lines are made or changed to attract wagering on both teams. For example, Denver opens up a 3-point favorite over Kansas City and all the early money comes in on the Broncos. Sparky (the New York bookie) moves the line to 3½ to try to attract KC money, but the Denver money keeps coming. He then makes the decision to raise the line to 4½ or 5 points, Denver favored. What he is saying is, "If you can get a better line on Denver somewhere else, go get it, I'm only interested in Kansas City money to balance my book."

The average guy, of course, doesn't have access to a lot of bookmakers, so he is forced to lay a lot of points on Denver or skip the game altogether. Neither is to his advantage, especially if Denver winds up a 4-point winner on the day.

With all these factors going against them, it is amazing that as many fans bet as much money on pro football games as often as they do. And as though these aren't enough reasons to shun wagering on football, there are still others.

They are called sucker bets and go by names like parlay, teaser and round robins, which is really just a series of parlays.

"Teasers and parlays," advises handicapper Eckstein, "are crazy bets. The returns are bigger, but the shifts in odds are in the bookie's favor. Even though the dollar payoff is higher than in straight bets, the percentages are worse."

So there you have it. From the mouths of experts. You can make a riddle out of it: "Who is emotional, unknowledgeable, gets the worst of odds situations engaging in an illegal activity while proving there is a sucker born every minute (at least on Sundays and Monday nights) and is willing to lose money to make his point?

If you don't know the answer, I'll book your bets.

INSIDE THE NFC

By PAUL ATTNER

PREDICTED ORDER OF FINISH

EAST	CENTRAL	WEST
Dallas	Detroit	San Francisco
New York Giants	Tampa Bay	Atlanta
Philadelphia	Chicago	Los Angeles
Washington	Green Bay	New Orleans
St. Louis	Minnesota	

NFC Champion: San Francisco

San Francisco's meteoric climb to the Super Bowl championship last season should serve as an inspiration to the rest of the conference. There are some bad teams in the NFC that suddenly might think they can duplicate the 49ers' miracle year and that could produce some improved football in the conference this season. The only problem is those darn 49ers should get better themselves, especially now that they have a legitimate tight end in Russ Francis and a potential game-breaker in Renaldo (Skeets) Nehemiah.

If Bill Walsh's boys stay in relatively good health, it seems unlikely that anyone else is good enough to catch them, except possibly Dallas. The Cowboys failed twice to beat San Francisco in 1981 and they are starting to become a bit old, unlike those young colts in San Francisco.

Of course, Dallas has to win its own division first over improving New York and revenge-motivated Philadelphia. Don't overlook Washington, either, after the Redskins' 8–3 finish in their last 11 last season. Even St. Louis, which keeps adding young talent, could pull off a few surprises. The Cardinals just happen to be in the wrong division to be really dangerous.

Paul Attner covers the Washington Redskins for the Washington Post.

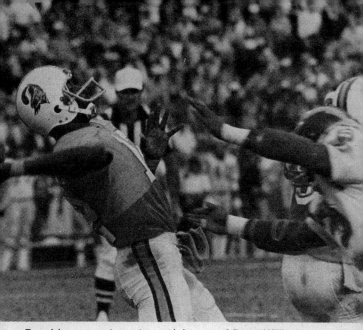

Bucs' hopes rest on strong right arm of Doug Williams.

Los Angeles and Atlanta both are capable of pushing San Francisco, but they also have enough roller-coaster players to wind up with the same kind of disappointing seasons they endured last year. With Bert Jones at quarterback, the Rams should be over their signal-caller shuffle. And stability at that position can go a long way toward turning any talented team into a contender. Atlanta is just fragile enough to be destroyed by injuries to a few key players. Look what happened last season when linebacker Joel Williams went down. That's not a healthy situation for a run to the Super Bowl.

Talking about unhealthy situations, how about the Central Division? These teams are either all pretty good or all pretty bad, but at least they are even. And such even play produces a lot of .500 records. Maybe this is the year Detroit gets all of its talent coordinated and stamps its superiority on the division. If not, Tampa Bay has the defense to be a champion. Minnesota, however, is going backwards and Green Bay always seems to be treading in the same space.

Still, the season may be academic anyway, as long as Walsh continues to think clearly. His creativeness last year was something to behold and it became the 49ers' secret weapon. So far, no device has been found to counteract Walsh's power.

ATLANTA FALCONS

TEAM DIRECTORY: Chairman: Rankin Smith, Sr.; Pres.: Rankin Smith, Jr.; Exec. VP: Eddie LeBaron; GM: Tom Braatz; Dir. Pub. Rel.: Charlie Dayton; Head Coach: Leeman Bennett. Home field: Atlanta Stadium (60,748). Colors: Red, black, silver and white.

SCOUTING REPORT

OFFENSE: What's a coach to do? Leeman Bennett figured if his offense caught fire last season, the Falcons had to wind up in the Super Bowl. So the club broke just about every offensive record in its books, leading the NFC with 426 points, only to have Bennett's pride and joy, his defense, all but collapse.

Now the task is for the offense to maintain its high level while Bennett revives the defense. It may not take that much, since the team lost seven games by a total of only 18 points and six by three or less.

Maybe even better play from quarterback Steve Bartkowski, a true superstar, might do the job even if the defense stays the same. All he did last year was throw for 30 touchdowns and break most of his seasonal records. In Alfred Jenkins and the rest of the receiving corps, he has speedy, reliable targets. In William Andrews, he has only the fifth back in NFL history to notch a combined 2,000 yards rushing and receiving. That's a tough group to defense.

The offensive linemen likewise are no slouches and the line could get better if tackle Warren Bryant comes back at full strength from an arm injury.

DEFENSE: Where do you begin telling a sad story? Perhaps with injuries. There were just enough to this unit—especially damaging was the loss of linebacker Joel Williams—to throw off the chemistry and create a season-long struggle. Without Williams, the Falcons lacked a good pass rush and gave opponents too long to pass. The result was that the Falcons gave up more yards passing than any season in their history.

So Bennett better keep Williams healthy somehow this season. That way, linebacker Al Richardson can go back to concentrating more on pass defense, which should strengthen that area. Surely, safeties Tom Pridemore and Bob Glazebrook can improve their coverage and take some of the burden off talented corners Kenny Johnson and Bobby Butler.

Even without Williams' blitzing, the pass rush needs to be

Alfred Jenkins came out to snare 70 passes.

more consistent. Only nose man Don Smith stood out last season despite constant double-teaming. And there is a need for more depth everywhere.

KICKING GAME: Sometimes spotty play by the Falcons' special teams helped contribute to a couple of losses last season. John James was among the weakest of the conference's punters, but Mick Luckhurst, the new field-goal kicker, scored 114 points, third best in the NFC.

THE ROOKIES: The Falcons hope Gerald Riggs, a speedster from Arizona State, will push Lynn Cain for a starting job and complement Andrews with some added quickness. Second-round choice Doug Rogers of Stanford could be a long-shot starter at defensive end, but needs to improve.

OUTLOOK: There is talent enough here to get the Falcons back in the playoffs. But the biggest need is more consistency, so the

FALCONS VETERAN ROSTER

HEAD COACH—Leeman Bennett. Assistant Coaches—Jerry Glanville, Mike McDonnell, Wayne McDuffie, John North, Jimmy Raye, Doug Shively, Jim Stanley, Bill Walsh, Dick Wood.

No.	Name	Pos.	Ht.	Wt.	NFL Exp.	College
31	Andrews, William	RB	6-0	200	4	Auburn
10	Bartkowski, Steve	QB	6-4	213	8	California
	Blount, Tony	S	6-1	195	2	Virginia
66	Bryant, Warren	T	6-6	270	6	Kentucky
23	Butler, Bobby	CB	5-11	170	2	Florida State
21	Cain, Lynn	RB	6-1	205	4	Southern California
50	Curry, Buddy	LB	6-3	221	3	North Carolina
59	Davis, Paul	LB	6-1	215	2	North Carolina
55	Daykin, Tony	LB	6-1	215	6	Georgia Tech
74	Faumuina, Wilson	DE	6-5	275	6	San Jose State
89	Francis, Wallace	WR	5-11	190	10	Arkansas-Pine Bluff
34	Gaison, Blane	S	6-0	185	2	Hawaii
36	Glazebrook, Bob	S	6-1	200	5	Fresno State
64	Howell, Pat	G	6-5	253	4	Southern California
85	Jackson, Alfred	WR	5-11	176	5	Texas
6	James, John	P	6-3	200	11	Florida
84	Jenkins, Alfred	WR	5-10	170	8	Morris Brown
37	Johnson, Kenny	CB	5-10	176	3	Mississippi State
20	Jones, Earl	CB	6-0	178	3	Norfolk State
14	Jones, June	QB	6-4	200	5	Portland State
78	Kenn, Mike	T	6-6	257	5	Michigan
54	Kuykendall, Fulton	LB	6-5	225	8	UCLA
51	Laughlin, Jim	LB	6-0	212	3	Ohio State
22	Lawrence, Rolland	CB	5-10	179	9	Tabor
18	Luckhurst, Mick	K	6-0	180	2	California
39	Mayberry, James	RB	5-11	210	4	Colorado
75	Merrow, Jeff	DE	6-4	255	8	West Virginia
87	Mikeska, Russ	TE	6-3	225	4	Texas A&M
80	Miller, Junior	TE	6-4	235	3	Nebraska
45	Moriarty, Tom	S	6-0	180	6	Bowling Green
15	Moroski, Mike	QB	6-4	200	4	California-Davis
96	Musser, Neal	LB	6-2	218	2	North Carolina State
27	Pridemore, Tom	S	5-10	180	5	West Virginia
56	Richardson, Al	LB	6-2	206	3	Georgia Tech
33	Robinson, Bo	RB	6-2	225	4	West Texas State
67	Sanders, Eric	T	6-6	255	2	Nevada-Reno
70	Scott, Dave	G	6-4	265	7	Kansas
61	Scully, John	C	6-5	255	2	Notre Dame
65	Smith, Don	DT	6-5	248	4	Miami
16	Smith, Reggie	WR	6-4	168	5	North Carolina Central
25	Strong, Ray	RB	5-9	184	5	Nevada-Las Vegas
72	Teague, Matthew	DE	6-5	240	2	Prairie View
68	Thielemann, R.C.	G	6-4	247	6	Arkansas
57	Van Note, Jeff	C	6-2	247	14	Kentucky
52	White, Lyman	LB	6-0	217	2	Louisiana State
58	Williams, Joel	LB	6-0	215	4	Wisconsin-LaCrosse
30	Woerner, Scott	S	6-0	195	2	Georgia
79	Yeates, Jeff	DE	6-3	248	11	Boston College
63	Zele, Mike	DT	6-3	236	4	Kent State

TOP FIVE DRAFT CHOICES

Rd.	Name	Sel. No.	Pos.	Ht.	Wt.	College
1	Riggs, Gerald	9	RB	6-1	230	Arizona State
2	Rogers, Doug	36	DE	6-5	255	Stanford
3	Bailey, Stacey	63	WR	6-1	161	San Jose State
4	Brown, Reggie	95	RB	5-11	209	Oregon
5	Mansfield, Von	122	DB	5-11	177	Wisconsin

club can get off its roller-coaster ride of alternating winning and losing seasons. The keys will be improved defense and better depth.

FALCON PROFILES

STEVE BARTKOWSKI 29 6–4 213   Quarterback

The Golden Boy is now everyone's golden quarterback...What franchise wouldn't give up a lot to obtain this talented man?...Only weakness in his armor is a problem with short passes...Sometimes his touch is not quite right, but who cares? He can throw pinpoint bombs that go 50 yards or more...No one in football can throw the ball long as well as he does...His 1981 statistics: 297 completions, 3,829 yards, 30 touchdowns...A bit high on the interceptions with 23...Born Nov. 12, 1952, in Des Moines, Iowa...Attended California.

WILLIAM ANDREWS 26 6–0 200   Running Back

"Tackling him is like tackling a bowling ball," says Steve Bartkowski...Has become one of the league's elite runners in just three seasons after being third-round draft choice out of Auburn...Rugged, durable, consistent...What else could you want in a running back?...Even has wonderful hands as receiver...Ran for 1,301 yards and caught 81 passes for another 735 yards to go over the 2,000 mark combined, a rare feat...Played in shadow of both Joe Cribbs and James Brooks in college...Born Dec. 25, 1955, in Thomasville, Ga....Thrives from abundance of work, a rare trait in this league.

LYNN CAIN 26 6–1 205   Running Back

One of those fine years that was overshadowed by play of running mate William Andrews...Rushing total of 542 way down from 1980, but caught 55 passes to become receiving threat out of the backfield...Has gained over 1,400 yards in his two years as regular in Falcon attack...Blocked for Heisman winner Charles White at USC and was drafted in fourth round in 1979 draft . . . That was the year Falcons landed Andrews. Not a bad draft . . . Born Oct. 16, 1955, in Los Angeles . . . "I ran up the middle in college. At least in the pros I can go outside," he says.

ALFRED JENKINS 30 5–10 170   Wide Receiver

It says 5–10 but if you believe that, there's a bridge in Brooklyn I'd like you to buy . . . Maybe 5–8 at the most, so how does he survive and play so well? . . . Quickness, my friend, and some wonderful determination . . . Scooted around for 70 receptions last year, by far the best of his career. His 1,356 receiving yards were among the league's best . . . That's an average of almost 20 yards a catch . . . And he pulled in 13 passes for touchdowns . . . Born Nov. 7, 1951, in Franklin, La. . . . Has done some television and public relations work . . . Attended Morris Brown, then played in WFL . . . Was named the league MVP after leading Birmingham to the only WFL title, in 1974.

JEFF VAN NOTE 36 6–2 247   Center

Ranks as one of the league's best centers despite advanced age . . . "Age isn't a factor because he takes care of himself," says coach Leeman Bennett . . . Relies heavily on film study to find weaknesses of opponents . . . Multi-year Pro Bowl selection . . . Had only one holding penalty in 1980 . . . Couldn't make it as linebacker, so he went to the Continental Football League and learned to be a center . . . That was nothing for him, since he arrived at Kentucky as a running back and left as a linebacker . . . Born Feb. 7, 1946, in South Orange, N.J.

TOM PRIDEMORE 26 5–10 180   Safety

In the offseason, he changes from pads to business suits and becomes member of the West Virginia House of Delegates . . . Youngest member when he won election in 1980 . . . Not a bad football player, either . . . Ranks among the best at his position, intercepting seven passes last year to give him 12 for his career . . . Always the secondary leader in tackles . . . He's the best goal-line free safety in football, according to his coaches...Born April 29, 1956, in Ansted, W. Va., where he still lives...Attended West Virginia, where he ranks in top five in interceptions...Came into league needing to work on his pass coverage.

BUDDY CURRY 24 6–3 221   Linebacker

Helped fill Falcon need for quickness at linebacker...Settled into position and is fast becoming one of the best around...His forte is aggressiveness...He loves to hit and run and that seems to fire up the rest of the Falcon defense...Can drop back on pass defense and still come up fast against the run...Falcons thought so much of him that he was allowed to call defensive signals as a rookie...Good balance makes it difficult for blockers to knock him off his feet...Already reminding fans of Tommy Nobis...Born June 4, 1958, in Danville, Va....Works in the car leasing business.

JOEL WILLIAMS 25 6–0 215   Linebacker

Proved his value to the team by being injured for most of the season...Without him, the Falcons' defense was ordinary at best...One player probably shouldn't make that much difference, but he did...When he's healthy, is among the linebackers who rush the passer most effectively...Atlanta needs his blitzing ability to take pressure off its secondary...Had 16 sacks his rookie season...Wasn't even drafted out of Wisconsin-LaCrosse...Asked for free-agent tryout with Miami, then was signed by Atlanta...Born Dec. 13, 1956, in Miami, Fla...Grew up a couple of blocks from Dolphins' training camp in Biscayne.

WALLACE FRANCIS 30 5–11 190   Wide Receiver

With the Falcons relying more on their backs as receivers, Francis' catch total fell off for second straight year, slipping to 30 from high of 74 in 1979...Play of Alfred Jenkins has been part of the reason, too...Remains a quality receiver with big-play potential...Unheralded player at Arkansas A&M...Enjoys life, with outgoing personality...Born Nov. 7, 1951, in Franklin, La....President of own public relations firm . . . Also attends divinity school . . . Took him five seasons as a pro to finally earn starting position.

JUNIOR MILLER 24 6–4 235   **Tight End**

Has solidified Falcon tight end situation . . . Caught 78 passes in first two seasons in the league . . . Has all-pro ability . . . Don't overlook his blocking ability when evaluating his talents . . . He was so good that the Falcons ignored other needs to draft him No. 1 two years ago . . . Consensus All-America his senior season at Nebraska . . . Born Nov. 26, 1957, in Midland, Tex. . . . Runs the 40 in 4.6 . . . That's one reason he averaged 18 yards a catch during his college career . . . Falcons say his future will be determined by how hard he works in off-season.

COACH LEEMAN BENNETT . . . Somehow, he must figure

out a way to keep the Falcons on an even keel, so they can get off this roller coaster they've been on the last few seasons . . . Team went from 6–10 also-rans to 12–4 playoff qualifiers to 7–9 also-rans, despite having one of the most dangerous offenses in the league . . . Defense got worse instead of better . . . Was coach of the year in some corners two seasons ago . . . Went with youngsters on defense and that backfired on him a bit . . . Injuries didn't help much, either . . . Served 14 years as an assistant in both college and pro ranks before finally getting a head coaching spot . . . Born June 20, 1938, in Paducah, Ky. . . . Played and coached at Kentucky, where he really wasn't much of an athlete . . . A receiver coach at Los Angeles before getting job with Atlanta.

GREATEST LINEBACKER

By the time he retired in 1976, his knees were so banged up it was amazing he could even walk, much less play football of the caliber fans had come to expect of Tommy Nobis. This tough,

tough man had the ability and the desire to go down as one of the all-time greats, despite those knees that took so much punishment and endured the surgeon's knife.

With it all he performed nobly for 11 NFL seasons. No other Falcon linebacker has come close to his production. Even as late as his next-to-last season, he was able to lead the team in tackles, a position he held nine times as a Falcon. But it was his younger days, when he was an all-pro after having been the first player ever drafted by the team, that stand out in the memory of fans. One afternoon against New Orleans in 1974, he had 15 individual tackles, eight of which saved touchdowns.

That kind of effort was commonplace for Nobis in his college days at Texas, when he was a two-time All-American, an Outland Trophy winner and a man with so much promise.

INDIVIDUAL FALCON RECORDS

Rushing

Most Yards Game:	167	William Andrews, vs New Orleans, 1979
Season:	1,308	William Andrews, 1980
Career:	3,632	William Andrews, 1979–81

Passing

Most TD Passes Game:	4	Randy Johnson, vs Chicago, 1969
	4	Steve Bartkowski, vs New Orleans, 1980
	4	Steve Bartkowski, vs St. Louis, 1981
Season:	31	Steve Bartkowski, 1980
Career:	108	Steve Bartkowski, 1975–81

Receiving

Most TD Passes Game:	3	Alfred Jenkins, vs New Orleans, 1981
Season:	13	Alfred Jenkins, 1981
Career:	38	Alfred Jenkins, 1975–81

Scoring

Most Points Game:	18	Alfred Jenkins, vs New Orleans, 1981
Season:	114	Mick Luckhurst, 1981
Career:	270	Nick Mike-Mayer, 1973–77
Most TDs Game:	3	Lynn Cain, vs Oakland, 1979
	3	Alfred Jenkins, vs New Orleans, 1981
Season:	13	Alfred Jenkins, 1981
Career:	38	Alfred Jenkins, 1975–81

CHICAGO BEARS

TEAM DIRECTORY: Chairman/Pres: George Halas; VP: Edward McCaskey; Exec. VP/GM: Jim Finks; Treasurer: Jerome Vainisi; Dir. Pro Scouting: Bill Tobin; Dir. Pub. Rel.: Patrick McCaskey; Head Coach: Mike Ditka. Home field: Soldier Field (64,410). Colors: Orange, Navy blue and white.

Walter Payton is fourth among all-time NFL rushers.

SCOUTING REPORT

OFFENSE: Simply put, there was hardly any offense in Chicago last year. The booing fans generated more energy than the Bears' offense in most games. Even 58 points in their last two wins couldn't salvage another dismal year in the Windy City. Now new coach Mike Ditka, an offensive-minded coach, will try to bring his old team a new look.

Until he makes a change at quarterback, that may be difficult. Under Vince Evans' direction, the Bears were 26th in the league in overall offense last year and he was last, by a lot, in the NFC passing stats. Rookie Jim McMahon, picked fifth overall, may have to hasten his adjustment from BYU to the pros.

Ditka says Walter Payton has at least five years left, will be used as much as in the past, but will be more productive. Payton probably will believe it when he sees it. Matt Suhey seems set at fullback and the return of James Scott will help the receiving corps, which has a possible star in Ken Margerum. Ditka couldn't be more unhappy about the tight end spot.

Improvement from Noah Jackson and Keith Van Horne and the return of tackle Dennis Lick, who was injured last season, could solidify the line.

DEFENSE: Thanks to the maneuvering of crack defensive co-ordinator Buddy Ryan, the Bears were able to straighten out their defense and make it effective by midway through last season. Ryan was rewarded by being retained by owner George Halas, even before Ditka was hired.

Ryan again will be throwing all types of formations and personnel shifts at opponents, in part to cover up for some glaring personnel problems. One plus was the development of rookie Mike Singletary, whose leap into a starting role at linebacker heralded the start of the Bears' turnaround. Otis Wilson needs to be more disciplined at his outside linebacking spot. Room also has to be made for the return from injury of Jerry Muckensturm, the man Singletary replaced, and ex-Patriot Rod Shoate.

Now that Alan Page has retired, Ryan needs to fill a hole in his defensive front, possibly with Brad Shearer. Dan Hampton is solid, but Al Harris has dislodged Mike Hartenstine at end. A better pass rush would aid a secondary that got good play last year from rookie cornerback Reuben Henderson and another solid season from strong safety Gary Fencik.

KICKING GAME: Bob Thomas was hurt for much of last season, which enabled John Roveto to take over the field-goal duties.

BEARS VETERAN ROSTER

HEAD COACH—Mike Ditka. Assistant Coaches—Jim Dooley, Dale Haupt, Ed Hughes, Hank Kuhlmann, Jim LaRue, Ted Plumb, Buddy Ryan, Dick Stanfel.

No.	Name	Pos.	Ht.	Wt.	NFL Exp.	College
64	Albrecht, Ted	T-G	6-4	250	6	California
88	Anderson, Marcus	WR	5-11	168	2	Tulane
7	Avellini, Bob	QB	6-2	210	8	Maryland
84	Baschnagel, Brian	WR-KR	6-0	184	7	Ohio State
25	Bell, Todd	S	6-1	207	2	Ohio State
54	Cabral, Brian	LB	6-1	224	4	Colorado
59	Campbell, Gary	LB	6-1	220	6	Colorado
87	Cobb, Mike	TE	6-5	243	5	Michigan State
81	Earl, Robin	TE-P	6-5	240	6	Washington
8	Evans, Vince	QB	6-2	208	6	Southern Calfirnia
67	Fairchild, Greg	G	6-5	254	3	Tulsa
45	Fencik, Gary	S	6-1	192	7	Yale
85	Fisher, Bob	TE	6-3	240	3	Southern Methodist
24	Fisher, Jeff	CB-KR	5-11	188	2	Southern California
21	Frazier, Leslie	CB-S	6-0	189	2	Alcorn State
82	Haines, Kris	WR-KR	5-11	180	3	Notre Dame
99	Hampton, Dan	DE-DT	6-5	255	4	Arkansas
35	Harper, Roland	RB	5-11	210	7	Louisiana Tech
90	Harris, Al	DE	6-5	240	4	Arizona State
73	Hartenstine, Mike	DE	6-3	243	8	Penn State
20	Henderson, Reuben	CB	6-1	200	2	San Diego State
51	Herron, Bruce	LB	6-2	220	5	New Mexico
63	Hilgenberg, Jay	C	6-3	250	2	Iowa
65	Jackson, Noah	G	6-2	265	8	Tampa
62	Jiggetts, Dan	T	6-5	270	7	Harvard
57	Kunz, Lee	LB	6-2	225	4	Nebraska
70	Lick, Dennis	T	6-3	265	7	Wisconsin
82	Margerum, Ken	WR	5-10	170	2	Stanford
37	McClendon, Willie	RB	6-1	205	4	Georgia
76	McMichael, Steve	DE-DT	6-1	245	3	Texas
43	Moorehead, Emery	WR-KR	6-2	210	6	Colorado
58	Muckensturm, Jerry	LB	6-4	220	6	Arkansas State
52	Neal, Dan	C	6-4	255	10	Kentucky
68	Osborne, Jim	DT	6-3	245	11	Southern
86	Parsons, Bob	P	6-5	225	11	Penn State
34	Payton, Walter	RB	5-11	204	8	Jackson State
15	Phipps, Mike	QB	6-3	209	13	Purdue
46	Plank, Doug	S	5-11	202	8	Ohio State
9	Roveto, John	K	6-0	180	2	Southwest Louisiana
44	Schmidt, Terry	CB	6-0	177	9	Ball State
89	Scott, James	WR	6-1	190	5	Henderson College
72	Shearer, Brad	DT	6-3	247	4	Texas
56	Shoate, Rod	LB	6-1	215	7	Oklahoma
50	Singletary, Mike	LB	5-11	230	2	Baylor
30	Skibinski, John	RB	6-0	222	4	Purdue
69	Sorey, Revie	G	6-2	260	8	Illinois
26	Suhey, Matt	RB-KR	5-11	217	3	Penn State
53	Tabor, Paul	C	6-4	241	2	Oklahoma
16	Thomas, Bob	K	5-10	175	7	Notre Dame
78	Van Horne, Keith	T	6-6	265	2	Southern California
23	Walterscheid, Lenny	S-KR	5-11	190	6	South Utah State
80	Watts, Rickey	WR-KR	6-1	203	4	Tulsa
83	Williams, Brooks	TE	6-4	226	5	North Carolina
22	Williams, David	RB-KR	6-2	207	6	Colorado
55	Wilson, Otis	LB	6-2	222	3	Louisville
79	Zanders, Emanuel	G	6-1	248	9	Jackson State

TOP FIVE DRAFT CHOICES

Rd	Name	Sel. No.	Pos.	Ht.	Wt.	College
1	McMahon, Jim	5	QB	6-0	185	Brigham Young
3	Wrightman, Tim	62	TE	6-3	237	UCLA
3	Gentry, Dennis	89	RB	5-9	180	Baylor
5	Hartnett, Perry	116	G	6-5	290	Southern Methodist
5	Tabron, Dennis	134	DB	5-9	182	Duke

Thomas probably will reclaim those chores. Bob Parsons kicks his punts high and accurately and rookie Jeff Fisher averaged 11 yards on punt returns to make that unit dangerous.

THE ROOKIES: The Bears, under GM Jim Finks, never have taken a quarterback on the first round until last April, when they selected the cocky McMahon, who could beat out Evans. Tight end Tim Wrightman of Baylor is another possible starter.

OUTLOOK: Instability in the front office often trickles down to the field, where the Bears need a healthy dose of stability. Ditka isn't that experienced and may be taking on this job before his time. If he can straighten out the offense, especially at quarterback, things would look brighter.

BEAR PROFILES

WALTER PAYTON 28 5–11 204   Running Back

All those carries, all those years of punishment have Payton wondering about his future...Talks of maybe retiring, Bears talk of maybe using him more as a wide receiver...Was hurt last season off the field, falling down stairs trying to stop his daughter from getting hurt...Gained fewest yards since rookie season in 1975, but still ranked seventh in NFC with 1,222 (3.6-yard average)...But decline of offensive line spells punishment for him...Born July 25, 1954, in Columbia, Mo....His uncle is Minnesota's Rickey Young...Many interests include an antique Rolls, condo, Mississippi timberland, convention and shopping centers...After seven seasons, he's NFL's fourth-ranking all-time rusher...Leading scorer in NCAA history with 464 points for Jackson State.

VINCE EVANS 27 6–2 208   Quarterback

Still hasn't had the kind of year the Bears think he is capable of producing...Some days, he plays as if he should be an all-pro...Other games, it seems a struggle to complete even one pass...His size and running ability make him special among league quarterbacks, but how long can the Bears wait for him?...Almost enrolled at North Carolina Central before winding up at USC, where he majored in speech communications... Only a sixth-round draft choice... Born June 14, 1955, in Greensboro, N.C.... Until the Bears find a challenger, he should be able to keep No. 1 spot, though he connected on only 44.7 percent of his passes and had 20 interceptions last year.

GARY FENCIK 28 6-1 192   Safety

Ivy Leaguers aren't supposed to play football this way: bam, bam, bam... Not hard to tell if he is the tackler—just listen for the sound... His background as a receiver at Yale comes in handy... Came back after hurting a knee in 1979 playoffs and undergoing surgery... Studying for master's in business during offseason... In offseason, he also takes vacations in places like Kenya and conducts ski tours to Austria... Has interned as a mortgage banker... Born June 11, 1954, in Chicago... Once took a class from Howard Cosell... A former participant in Pass, Punt and Kick competition.

BRIAN BASCHNAGEL 28 6-0 184   Wide Receiver

Scouting report said he would have a tough time making it, but he didn't believe it... And now he has successful career to prove it... One of those natural athletes who can help even though not blessed with great speed... In pressure situations, Bears throw the ball to him... Former Rhodes Scholarship candidate at Ohio State relies on brains, not brawn, to outfox those defensive backs... Born Jan. 8, 1954, in Kingston, N.Y.... One of those rare players to earn plaudits from Woody Hayes... Wants to become a CPA... Attended 19 different schools between first and 12th grades... Last year's stats were 34 catches for 16.3-yard average.

KEN MARGERUM 23 5-10 170   Wide Receiver

He was the eighth wide receiver taken in the 1981 draft, but Bears found out he should have gone a lot higher during 39-catch pro debut... Flashy player who doesn't mind celebrating the easiest of catches... But he'll make the tough one, too, and take the hardest hits... The scouts were worried about his size, but that didn't seem to slow him down... A consensus All-American at Stanford, where he broke records set by Tony Hill, James Lofton, Gene Washington... Among the best high hurdlers in California as a high school senior... Taught a course for credit at Stanford on wind surfing... Born Oct. 5, 1958, in Fountain Valley, Cal.... Communications major in college.

BOB PARSONS 32 6–5 225   Punter

With his kind of size, probably could have played a number of positions... But Bears are very happy he decided to be punter... For one year, he operated as the team's backup tight end and started some games... Has 19 pro receptions and has attempted 12 passes, completing seven... This from a man drafted originally as a quarterback out of Penn State, where he also played tight end... Conducts health evaluation programs... Likes tennis, golf, basketball, bowling, soap operas... Active in civic affairs... Born June 29, 1950, in Bethlehem, Pa.... Majored in physical education and could go into teaching after retirement... Led league with 114 punts (39.7-yard average) last season.

KEITH VAN HORNE 24 6–6 265   Tackle

Runnerup to Mark May for 1980 Outland Trophy, but his rookie pro year was just the opposite of May's... The Redskin tackle began as a starter and wound up on the bench, while the Bear giant began on the bench and wound up as a starter... Probably has settled into long-term career with the club... An academic all-conference player with Southern California for two years... Arrived at the school as a 230-pound tight end... Weight training helped make him heavier and stronger... Majored in broadcasting... Born Nov. 6, 1957, in Mt. Lebanon, Pa.... Would like to be a disc jockey... Brother Peter was drafted by Chicago Cubs.

DAN HAMPTON 24 6–5 255   Defensive End

If he was on the open market, his price would be very high... Considered one of the very best young linemen in the league... One of those dominating, intimidating rushers who should be a star for years to come, if he can stay healthy... Was the first rookie to start for the Bears since 1975... Fourth man selected in the 1979 draft, out of Arkansas, where he had 18 sacks his senior season... Born Sept. 9, 1957, in Oklahoma City... Had been a grade-school running back before fall from tree resulted in multiple injuries and end of that career... Plays six instruments and had band in college... Also has pet pig.

JAMES SCOTT 30 6–1 190   Wide Receiver

Returning to Bears after a year in Canada to help already decent corps of wide receivers... He'll add experience and some much-needed speed... Left Bears over a contract dispute and played a year with Montreal in the Canadian Football League, where he was outstanding... Led Chicago with 36 catches for 696 yards in 1980 and has 175 receptions in five NFL seasons... That ranks him 10th on the all-time Bear list... Led club in receiving four times... Former World Football League player with Chicago Fire... Born March 28, 1952, in Longview, Tex.... Once was a foundry worker while waiting for his chance to play in the pros... Attended Henderson County Junior College.

MIKE SINGLETARY 23 5–11 230   Linebacker

Considered too small to play in the big-time, but once in became a starter in the Bears defense, the unit became one of the league's toughest over the second half of the season... His size kept him around until the second round, when the Bears could nab him... Southwest Conference Player of the Year at Baylor for two straight seasons... Heart doesn't compute in a computer... Youngest of 10 children, he knows how to survive... Born Oct. 10, 1958, in Houston, Tex.... Turned his garage in Houston into a summer weight-training facility for neighborhood youth.

COACH MIKE DITKA...

During the middle of last season, this Dallas assistant said he didn't think he was ready for a head coaching job in the NFL... But when one came along and when that job meant returning to the Bears, he got ready in a hurry... Comes into a messed-up situation featuring a split front office, owner George Halas' handpicked assistant coaches and a major problem at quarterback... And now everyone will have to find out if he is qualified to take on his new responsibilities . . . Also, can he control his famous temper well enough to put up with the mistakes of his players? Even he doesn't know for sure . . . Lots of times, great players have difficulty becoming good head coaches . . . They are sometimes such perfectionists they can't adjust to less than the best . . . But you can be sure his players will listen to him . . . Born Oct. 18, 1939, in Carnegie, Pa. . . . One of the all-time greats ever to play tight end in the NFL, he set the standard for that position.

GREATEST LINEBACKER

Perhaps no team in pro football has been blessed with as many outstanding linebackers as the Chicago Bears. Four of the Bears in the Football Hall of Fame were honored for their play at the position, an unprecedented total.

But even among this elite group, one player—Dick Butkus—

QB Vince Evans may be hearing footsteps—Jim McMahon's.

stands alone. As Rodney Dangerfield might say, look up the definition of linebacker in the dictionary and Butkus' picture would be there. Butkus, 6-3, 245, exemplified the aggressiveness, and sometimes viciousness, of the game. He was brutal and unyielding, a strong, quick, talented man who brought a new dimension to a position once played by slow hulks. When Butkus made a tackle, running backs didn't go forward. His growl alone kept opponents awake at night. His ability earned him all-pro honors eight times, eight Pro Bowl appearances and the respect of his peers during a career that ran nearly a decade, starting in 1965.

· But no one could argue with those who would pick Bill George or George Connor or Bulldog Turner as the team's best-ever linebacker.

INDIVIDUAL BEAR RECORDS

Rushing

Most Yards Game:	275	Walter Payton, vs Minnesota, 1977
Season:	1,852	Walter Payton, 1977
Career:	9,608	Walter Payton, 1975–81

Passing

Most TD Passes Game:	7	Sid Luckman, vs N.Y. Giants, 1943
Season:	28	Sid Luckman, 1943
Career:	137	Sid Luckman, 1939–50

Receiving

Most TD Passes Game:	4	Harlon Hill, vs San Francisco, 1954
	4	Mike Ditka, vs Los Angeles, 1963
Season:	13	Dick Gordon, 1970
	13	Ken Kavanaugh, 1947
Career:	50	Ken Kavanaugh, 1940–41, 1945–50

Scoring

Most Points Game:	36	Gale Sayers, vs San Francisco, 1965
Season:	132	Gale Sayers, 1965
Career:	541	George Blanda, 1949–58
Most TDs Game:	6	Gale Sayers, vs San Francisco, 1965
Season:	22	Gale Sayers, 1965
Career:	78	Walter Payton, 1975–81

DALLAS COWBOYS

TEAM DIRECTORY: Chairman: Clint Murchison Jr.; Pres./GM: Tex Schramm; VP-Player Development: Gil Brandt; VP-Administration: Joe Bailey; Pub. Rel. Dir.: Doug Todd; Head Coach: Tom Landry. Home field: Texas Stadium (65,101). Colors: Royal blue, metallic blue and white.

SCOUTING REPORT

OFFENSE: Few teams in the league move the ball more efficiently than the Cowboys, but quarterback Danny White says he thinks the team needs to develop a more consistent short passing game. If that is accomplished, the Dallas machine may be impossible to control.

Danny White looks to lead Cowboys back to the playoffs.

As is, it's a pretty impressive unit. White feels more comfortable every season as Roger Staubach's replacement. He was the league's fifth-rated passer last year and is becoming more of an on-field leader. And the running of Tony Dorsett makes him even more effective. Dorsett almost won his first rushing title last season, his best ever as a pro. He can get better, especially if Tom Landry can decide on a fullback from among Ron Springs, Tim Newsome and James Jones.

The trio of Butch Johnson, Drew Pearson and Tony Hill return at receiver. Since Pearson is starting to show some age, Doug Donley could see more time in his place. Billy Joe DuPree, Jay Saldi and Doug Cosbie are a solid trio at tight end.

The Cowboys have developed impressive depth along the line, especially in the middle, where Robert Shaw returns from an injury to battle ex-guard Tom Rafferty. If Shaw wins the job, Rafferty will vie with Kurt Petersen for a guard spot.

DEFENSE: The 49ers were able to control the Dallas front four when it mattered in the NFC title game and that was the main reason the Cowboys didn't get to the Super Bowl once again. That front four remains the best in the league, although Landry would like Harvey Martin to become more aggressive and more consistent. He doesn't have to say anything to Randy White and Too Tall Jones, and John Dutton improved considerably at tackle last season.

Landry has to fill in holes in both the secondary and at linebacker. D.D. Lewis has retired and one of three players—Guy Brown, Anthony Dickerson or Angelo King—could wind up in his place. Dickerson is the most talented. Bob Breunig is solid in the middle and Mike Hegman continues to improve on the outside, but this will be the least experienced linebacking trio in recent Cowboy history.

With Charlie Waters retired, the Cowboys will look to veteran Benny Barnes as their strong safety. Cornerback Dennis Thurman is most likely to assume Waters' leadership role. Free agents Mike Downs (free safety) and Everson Walls (cornerback) had superlative rookie years to shore up what had been a very questionable unit and now rookie Rod Hill will be on hand, too.

KICKING GAME: Landry still wants to find a punter to relieve Danny White of those chores. But, he isn't looking for anyone to take over for all-pro kicker Rafael Septien. But the Cowboys do have to improve their return teams, which did not do as well as their coverage units in 1981.

COWBOYS VETERAN ROSTER

HEAD COACH—Tom Landry. Assistant Coaches—Jim Myers, Ermal Allen, Neill Armstrong, John Mackovic, Al Lavan, Alan Lowry, Dick Nolan, Gene Stallings, Ernie Stautner, Jerry Tubbs, Bob Ward.

No.	Name	Pos.	Ht.	Wt.	NFL Exp.	College
31	Barnes, Benny	CB	6-1	203	11	Stanford
76	Bethea, Larry	DT	6-5	249	5	Michigan State
53	Breunig, Bob	LB	6-2	225	8	Arizona State
59	Brown, Guy	LB	6-4	228	6	Houston
18	Carano, Glenn	QB	6-3	198	6	Nevada-Las Vegas
47	Clinkscale, Dextor	S	5-11	189	2	South Carolina State
61	Cooper, Jim	T	6-5	263	6	Temple
84	Cosbie, Doug	TE	6-6	226	4	Santa Clara
51	Dickerson, Anthony	LB	6-2	222	3	Southern Methodist
83	Donley, Doug	WR	6-0	175	2	Ohio State
67	Donovan, Pat	T	6-4	259	8	Stanford
33	Dorsett, Tony	RB	5-11	192	6	Pittsburgh
26	Downs, Michael	S	6-3	198	2	Rice
89	DuPree, Billy Joe	TE	6-4	228	10	Michigan State
78	Dutton, John	DT	6-7	263	9	Nebraska
27	Fellows, Ron	CB	6-0	170	2	Missouri
71	Frederick, Andy	T	6-6	265	6	New Mexico
58	Hegman, Mike	LB	6-1	225	7	Tennessee State
80	Hill, Tony	WR	6-2	198	6	Stanford
14	Hogeboom, Gary	QB	6-4	200	3	Central Michigan
42	Hughes, Randy	S	6-4	207	7	Oklahoma
86	Johnson, Butch	WR	6-1	180	7	California-Riverside
72	Jones, Ed	DE	6-9	270	7	Tennessee State
23	Jones, James	RB	5-10	196	3	Mississippi State
57	King, Angelo	LB	6-1	220	2	South Carolina State
79	Martin, Harvey	DE	6-5	250	10	East Texas State
44	Newhouse, Robert	FB	5-10	220	11	Houston
30	Newsome, Timmy	FB	6-1	232	3	Winston-Salem State
88	Pearson, Drew	WR	6-0	185	10	Tulsa
65	Petersen, Kurt	G	6-4	266	3	Missouri
64	Rafferty, Tom	G	6-3	258	7	Penn State
70	Richards, Howard	T	6-6	248	2	Missouri
56	Roe, Bill	LB	6-3	230	2	Colorado
87	Saldi, Jay	TE	6-3	223	7	South Carolina
68	Scott, Herbert	G	6-2	258	8	Virginia Union
1	Septien, Rafael	K	5-9	171	6	Southwest Louisiana
52	Shaw, Robert	C	6-4	260	4	Tennessee
60	Smerek, Don	DT	6-7	256	2	Nevada-Reno
55	Spradlin, Danny	LB	6-1	221	2	Tennessee
20	Springs, Ron	FB	6-1	216	4	Ohio State
77	Thornton, Bruce	DE	6-5	262	4	Illinois
32	Thurman, Dennis	CB	5-11	180	5	Southern California
63	Titensor, Glen	G	6-4	257	2	Brigham Young
24	Walls, Everson	CB	6-1	189	2	Grambling
66	Wells, Norm	G	6-5	261	2	Northwestern
11	White, Danny	QB	6-2	192	7	Arizona State
54	White, Randy	DT	6-4	250	8	Maryland
45	Wilson, Steve	CB	5-10	193	4	Howard
73	Wright, Steve	T	6-5	250	2	Northern Iowa

TOP FIVE DRAFT CHOICES

Rd.	Name	Sel. No.	Pos.	Ht.	Wt.	College
1	Hill, Rod	25	DB	6-0	180	Kentucky State
2	Rohrer, Jeff	53	LB	6-3	228	Yale
3	Eliopulos, Jim	81	LB	6-3	221	Wyoming
4	Carpenter, Brian	101	DB	5-11	166	Michigan
5	Hunter, Monty	109	DB	6-0	201	Salem

THE ROOKIES: The best cornerback coming out of college last year, Kentucky State's Hill, is now a Cowboy. Despite the maturation of the secondary last year, Hill could be an instant factor. Otherwise, no rookie appears good enough to do much more than play on special teams this season.

OUTLOOK: There is some sign of age, but the Cowboys keep bringing in new blood that performs well immediately. Injuries at receiver and along the defensive front could prove troublesome, but Dallas has enough talent to finally get past the NFC title game and return once again to the Super Bowl.

COWBOY PROFILES

DANNY WHITE 30 6–2 192   Quarterback

Another outstanding season, taking his team to within one win of the Super Bowl . . . No doubt now that he rates among the top quarterbacks in the league after only two seasons as a starter . . . Threw for 22 touchdowns and 3,098 yards with 57 percent accuracy in '81 . . . Continues as a first-rate punter (40.8-yard average) even though coach Tom Landry keeps trying to relieve him of his extra duties . . . Probably wonders if outcome of the NFC title game would have been different if he had been allowed to throw more to his wide receivers . . . Born Feb. 9, 1952, in Mesa, Ariz. . . . Attended Arizona State, where he played infield well enough to be drafted by four major-league baseball teams . . . Good piano player.

TONY DORSETT 28 5–11 192   Running Back

New attitude and stronger body produced best season . . . No runner in the NFL is more feared, especially for his explosive burst through the line . . . Credits maturity, marriage as reasons for new dedication . . . All-pro choice for first time in his career, even though he never has been below 1,000 yards since leaving Pitt . . . Born April 7, 1954, in Rochester, Pa . . . Jim Brown calls him "the epitome of an artist" . . . No other NFL back has ever gained 1,000 yards in each of his first five seasons . . . His totals for last season: 1,646 yards, 32 receptions, 4.8 yards a carry... Partner in firm that sells burglar and fire alarms.

RANDY WHITE 29 6–4 250   Defensive Tackle

Another ho-hum year for this best of all present defensive tackles... Was all-pro and the Pro Bowl pick again, drew two blockers a game again, gained the accolades of coaches everywhere again... The prototype combination of brawn and quickness mixed with desire and endurance... He never is sure how good he really plays, so won't evaluate himself... But others search for the proper adjectives to describe his play.... One of the few Cowboys who lives away from Dallas in the offseason.... He likes the peace of his Pennsylvania farm.... Born Jan. 15, 1953, in Wilmington, Del.... Outland Trophy winner at Maryland is now highest-paid defensive lineman in the NFL.

ED JONES 31 6–9 270   Defensive End

His coaches say he never played better than last season... Was the dominating force that everyone once thought he would be... Just ask Tampa Bay quarterback Doug Williams about trying to pass with Jones always in your face... The way he plays, wonder how he could have ever left for that stint as boxer in 1979.... Partner in Dallas investment firm ... Lead singer on that non-hit, "Do the Dip '81/Funkin' on Your Radio"... If he asks you to sing the words, make some up in a hurry... Born Feb. 2, 1951, in Jackson, Tenn.... College teammate at Tennessee State dubbed him Too Tall... Has acted in two movies and on TV show.

DENNIS THURMAN 26 5–11 180   Cornerback

His aggressiveness has earned him a mixed reputation throughout the league... He's either a bit on the dirty side or just playing the way football is supposed to be played... He says he has never intentionally tried to hurt anyone... His nine interceptions as a cornerback topped by one his total interceptions for his previous three years as a Cowboy.... Probably isn't quick enough to handle the position, but how can you argue with the results?...Interceptions are nothing new for him... He led the nation in interception return yards with 180 as a senior at USC...Born April 13, 1956, in Santa Monica, Cal....Hopes for a career in broadcasting.

TONY HILL 26 6-2 198   Wide Receiver

Even though an early-season injury got him off to a slow start, he still wound up with 46 catches for 953 yards to lead team in both categories...Remains the Cowboys' most dangerous long threat and has athletic ability to catch in traffic, too...Rebounded after teammates questioned his desire during end of 1980 season...Has political science degree, but wants to attend graduate school in business...Born June 23, 1956, in San Diego...Former high school quarterback was record-setting receiver at Stanford.

RAFAEL SEPTIEN 28 5-9 171   Kicker

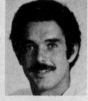

This standout athlete is close to being the top kicker in the league, if he isn't already...Had a marvelous season, scoring 121 points, mainly by converting 27 of 35 field-goal attempts ...Was perfect on 40 conversion tries...Had never scored more than 97 points before since joining the Cowboys...Now has missed only one extra point in his last 100 tries...Two-time NFL Players Association racquetball champion...Born Dec. 12, 1953, in Mexico City, where he is sports hero...Attended Southwest Louisiana...His wife is an opera singer and his father played on two Mexican World Cup soccer teams.

DREW PEARSON 31 6-0 185   Wide Receiver

For some reason, lately he's not catching as many passes as someone this talented should...Part of the problem may be the emergence of Butch Johnson as a quality receiver who needs playing time...But seems like a waste of great ability to see him limited to 38 catches last year...No one plays better in pressure moments...Succeeded Joe Theismann as high-school quarterback in South River, N.J., where he was born, Jan. 12, 1951...Tulsa grad was signed as free agent in 1973 . . . Partner with Harvey Martin in local barbeque restaurant . . . Works for Dallas TV station and has radio program during season.

BOB BREUNIG 29 6–2 225   Linebacker

One of those players who goes about his business quietly and diligently, gets it done right and hardly gets noticed . . . But you never hear Cowboys complaining about any problems in the middle . . . Probably isn't quick enough to be among the elite at his position, but has the intelligence to execute Cowboys' intricate defenses . . . A two-time Pro Bowl participant and the man who replaced Dallas legend Lee Roy Jordan . . . Works for Roger Staubach's real estate firm . . . Born July 4, 1953, in Phoenix and attended Arizona State . . . His wife compiled two editions of Cowboys Wives' Cookbook . . . He wrote children's religious album, "Color Him Love."

HARVEY MARTIN 31 6–5 250   Defensive End

Hitting a happy consistency late in his career . . . Has learned to compensate for loss of some quickness with smarts that come from experience . . . Has his own personal secretary to help manage his business and public affairs . . . Once the most vocal of players, he's toned down his act a bit . . . An open, friendly guy in the locker room, he is one of the few colorful personalities on a team that doesn't promote individuality . . . Born Nov. 16, 1950, in Dallas and played for East Texas State . . . Does some national television commercials.

COACH TOM LANDRY . . . He should go straight into the Pro

Football Hall of Fame . . . Dallas is almost as consistent as death and taxes, and he is the man responsible . . . Yet there is no air of coldness about him . . . Down to earth, consistent, approachable . . . And he doesn't claim to have any miracles in his bag of tricks . . . There was some talk of him possibly retiring, but he doesn't seem to be ready for that yet . . . So his potential replacement will just have to wait...Still has the fire and the desire, which sometimes show through on the sidelines beneath that calm exterior...Not true that he only wears an outfit or a hat once...Born Sept. 11, 1924, in Mission, Tex....Thought he had a Super Bowl team last year and, despite two losses to eventual champ San Francisco, believes the Cowboys are better than 49ers...That didn't win him any friends in the city by the bay...Entering 23rd season as coach...Has compiled 171–59–2 record since 1966 and has led Dallas to record five Super Bowl appearances (winning VI and XII).

GREATEST LINEBACKER

It had never happened before in Super Bowl history. A player from a losing team had been named Most Valuable Player. This was in Super Bowl V, when Baltimore beat Dallas. But even with that unprecedented award, Chuck Howley never became a glamor figure, not even in Dallas, where Cowboys are treated with special care.

But that was Howley's style: quiet, uncontroversial, business-

Randy White is one of NFL's premier defensive tackles.

like. He wasn't fond of bright lights, fast company or the probing eye of publicity. He was Tom Landry's kind of player. He showed up on time, did his job, kept his mouth shut and produced.

And how he produced! Over a 14-year career, he was one of the best linebackers around. He started when the Cowboys were a struggling franchise, he ended when they were at the top of the league. Along the way, he was a six-time Pro Bowler, a frequent all-pro selection and a big-play man of awesome dimensions. He made long fumble returns and interception runs commonplace, which was easy for a 6-2, 225-pounder who still could run a 4.9 40 at age 39. And to think he was a No. 1 round choice of the Bears, who traded him away for a second-round pick after he hurt his knee his rookie season.

INDIVIDUAL COWBOY RECORDS

Rushing

Most Yards Game:	206	Tony Dorsett, vs Philadelphia, 1978
Season:	1,646	Tony Dorsett, 1981
Career:	6,270	Tony Dorsett, 1977–81

Passing

Most TD Passes Game:	5	Eddie LeBaron, vs Pittsburgh, 1962
	5	Don Meredith, vs N.Y. Giants, 1966
	5	Don Meredith, vs Philadelphia, 1966
	5	Don Meredith, vs Philadelphia, 1968
	5	Craig Morton, vs Philadelphia, 1969
	5	Craig Morton, vs Houston, 1970
Season:	28	Danny White, 1980
Career:	153	Roger Staubach, 1969–79

Receiving

Most TD Passes Game:	4	Bob Hayes, vs Houston, 1970
Season:	14	Frank Clarke, 1962
Career:	71	Bob Hayes, 1965–74

Scoring

Most Points Game:	24	Dan Reeves, vs Atlanta, 1967
	24	Bob Hayes, vs Houston, 1970
	24	Calvin Hill, vs Buffalo, 1971
	24	Duane Thomas, vs St. Louis, 1971
Season:	122	Rafael Septien, 1981
Career:	456	Bob Hayes, 1965–74
Most TDs Game:	4	Dan Reeves, vs Atlanta, 1967
	4	Bob Hayes, vs Houston, 1970
	4	Calvin Hill, vs Buffalo, 1971
	4	Duane Thomas, vs St. Louis, 1971
Season:	16	Dan Reeves, 1966
Career:	76	Bob Hayes, 1965–74

DETROIT LIONS

TEAM DIRECTORY: Pres.: William Clay Ford; Exec. VP/GM: Russ Thomas; Dir. Football Operations/Head Coach: Monte Clark; Dir. Player Personnel: Tim Rooney; Dir. Pub. Rel.: Don Kremer. Home field: Pontiac Silverdome (80,638). Colors: Honolulu blue and silver.

SCOUTING REPORT

OFFENSE: Detroit had one of the league's most balanced offenses last year. Defenses never could figure out what to stop first, the pass or the run, even with inexperienced quarterback Eric Hipple replacing the injured Gary Danielson. But when the Lions failed to make the playoffs for the 11th straight year, offensive coordinator Bob Schnelker was fired. Maybe his unit shouldn't have finished first in the NFC.

Clark has to make a quarterback decision and most likely will go with Hipple, who played so well despite so little experience last year. Even Danielson has forecast a benchwarming role for himself. Any indecision could ruin team morale. Certainly, the running game is solid, with halfback Billy Sims gaining 1,437 yards last year to place third in the NFC. And receiver Fred Scott had his first 1,000-yard season while catching 52 passes.

The Lions likewise have a first-rate offensive line that should get better with more experience. With Sims as the big-play man, this can be an exciting offense, one that is capable of carrying the Lions into the playoffs.

DEFENSE: Floyd Peters, the defensive coordinator, has left for St. Louis, which creates a question about this unit's continuity. With Peters in control, the Lions were fourth in the league overall and first against the rush. It will be hard for anyone to improve on those rankings.

The most important man in the unit probably is tackle Doug English, who came back from a year in the oil business to earn Pro Bowl and all-pro honors. He lends stability to a fearsome pass rush that features the quickness of end Al Baker, who was hurt frequently last year. Only a few teams had success generating consistent offense against this club, even though Garry Cobb, Ken Fantetti and Stan White aren't considered the league's most formidable linebackers. Rookie Jimmy Williams may help here.

If the defense has a weakness, it is in the secondary, where the team proved vulnerable to big-play touchdowns late in the season.

KICKING GAME: Robbie Martin gives the Lions stable if not spectacular play as their No. 1 return man. He might look better if the special-teams people around him weren't so good, especially punter Tom Skladany, one of the conference's best, and kicker Ed Murray, who led the league in scoring with 121 points.

THE ROOKIES: The Lions needed defensive help, so they used their first five draft selections on defensive players, starting with

Despite injuries, Billy Sims ran for 13 touchdowns in '81.

LIONS VETERAN ROSTER

HEAD COACH—Monte Clark. Assistant Coaches—Maxie Baughan, John Brunner, Don Doll, Fred Hoaglin, Joe Madden, Ed Khayat, Mel Phillips, Ted Marchibroda, Larry Seiple.

No.	Name	Pos.	Ht.	Wt.	NFL Exp.	College
40	Allen, Jimmy	S	6-2	194	9	UCLA
60	Baker, Al	DE	6-6	250	5	Colorado State
76	Baldischwiler, Karl	T	6-5	265	5	Oklahoma
73	Bolinger, Russ	G	6-5	255	6	Long Beach State
24	Bussey, Dexter	FB	6-1	210	9	Texas-Arlington
31	Callicutt, Ken	RB	6-0	190	5	Clemson
53	Cobb, Garry	LB	6-2	220	4	Southern California
77	Culp, Curley	DT	6-1	265	14	Arizona State
16	Danielson, Gary	QB	6-2	195	6	Purdue
72	Dieterich, Chris	T	6-3	269	3	North Carolina State
70	Dorney, Keith	T	6-5	265	4	Penn State
74	Ehrmann, Joe	DT	6-3	250	10	Syracuse
61	Elias, Homer	G	6-3	255	5	Tennessee State
78	English, Doug	DT	6-5	260	6	Texas
57	Fantetti, Ken	LB	6-2	230	4	Wyoming
65	Fowler, Amos	C	6-3	250	5	Southern Mississippi
71	Furness, Steve	DT	6-4	248	11	Rhode Island
79	Gay, William	DT-DE	6-3	250	5	Southern California
66	Ginn, Tommie	G	6-3	255	3	Arkansas
26	Gray, Hector	CB	6-1	197	2	Florida State
62	Green, Curtis	DE-DT	6-3	256	2	Alabama State
35	Hall, Alvin	CB	5-10	193	2	Miami (O)
51	Harrell, James	LB	6-2	215	4	Florida
81	Hill, David	TE	6-2	230	7	Texas A&I
17	Hipple, Eric	QB	6-1	196	3	Utah State
28	Hunter, James	CB	6-2	195	7	Grambling
32	Kane, Rick	RB	6-0	200	6	San Jose State
25	King, Horace	FB	5-10	210	8	Georgia
19	Komlo, Jeff	QB	6-2	200	4	Delaware
64	Lee, Larry	G-C	6-2	274	2	UCLA
83	Martin, Robbie	WR-KR	5-8	179	2	Cal Poly-SLO
3	Murray, Ed	K	5-9	170	3	Tulane
86	Nichols, Mark	WR	6-2	213	2	San Jose State
80	Norris, Ulysses	TE	6-4	230	4	Georgia
23	Oldham, Ray	S	5-11	192	10	Middle Tennessee
89	Porter, Tracy	WR	6-1	196	2	Louisiana State
75	Pureifory, Dave	DE	6-1	255	11	Eastern Michigan
87	Scott, Fred	WR	6-2	180	9	Amherst
20	Sims, Billy	RB	6-0	210	3	Oklahoma
1	Skladany, Tom	P	6-0	195	4	Ohio State
44	Smith, Wayne	CB	6-0	170	3	Purdue
50	Tautolo, Terry	LB	6-2	235	7	UCLA
84	Thompson, Jesse	WR	6-1	185	3	California
39	Thompson, Leonard	WR	5-11	190	8	Oklahoma State
38	Thompson, Vince	FB	6-0	230	2	Villanova
54	Towle, Steve	LB	6-2	233	7	Kansas
55	Turnure, Tom	C	6-3	243	3	Washington
52	White, Stan	LB	6-1	223	11	Ohio State
30	Williams, Ray	KR	5-9	173	2	Washington State

TOP FIVE DRAFT CHOICES

Rd.	Name	Sel. No.	Pos.	Ht.	Wt.	College
1	Williams, Jimmy	15	LB	6-2	221	Nebraska
2	Watkins, Bobby	42	DB	5-11	186	Southwest Texas State
3	Doig, Steve	69	LB	6-3	235	New Hampshire
4	McNorton, Bruce	96	DB	5-11	172	Georgetown (Ky.)
5	Graham, William	127	DB	5-11	188	Texas

Williams, a mobile Nebraska linebacker, and Bobby Watkins, a little-known cornerback from Southwest Texas who may be able to break into the starting lineup.

OUTLOOK: On paper, the Lions probably should have been in the Super Bowl last year. Every part of the team played well, yet they couldn't break the .500 mark. And coach Monte Clark probably doesn't have the answer that will turn all this talent into a consistent winner.

LION PROFILES

AL BAKER 25 6–6 250   **Defensive End**

Remains one of the elite pass rushers in the league...Hampered at times by injuries last season...When he is healthy, he can alter an opponent's offensive game plan...Blessed with unusual quickness for a man his size...Made to harass quarterbacks...A three-time Pro Bowl performer...Call him Bubba if you dare...Despite all his sacks, his most memorable play probably was deflection and catch of Jim Hart pass two years ago...His peers voted him Defensive Lineman of the Year in 1980...Born Dec. 9, 1956, in Jacksonville, Fla....His football playground as a youngster in Newark, N.J., was a graveyard...Later attended Colorado State.

GARY DANIELSON 30 6–2 195   **Quarterback**

By the time he recovered from broken left wrist suffered early in the season, he no longer was starting quarterback...Has to win back the job from surprising Eric Hipple in training camp...Has accepted competition gracefully after momentarily considering a request to be traded...Had best season of his career in 1980 and team had expected big things out of him last season....Second major injury of his short career suggests questions about his durability...Born Sept. 10, 1951, in Detroit ...Prepared for the pros at Purdue...Was working on a car assembly line when the Lions signed him as a free agent.

KEITH DORNEY 24 6–5 265   Tackle

Coach Monte Clark calls him a lineman "you can build your offense around" and Lions did just that... Consistently opens up huge holes for Billy Sims... Made 10 All-American teams his senior season at Penn State, where he was also an All-Academic choice... Drafted in first round of 1979 draft, he's been a starter whenever he's been healthy... Born Dec. 3, 1957, in Allentown, Pa.... Registered a 3.33 grade-point average while majoring in insurance and real estate in college... Voted to the All-Rookie team in 1979... Played center his first year at Penn State, but switched to tackle his junior season... Lions are glad he did for he's now one of the best.

BILLY SIMS 26 6–0 210   Running Back

Had a spectacular rookie season in 1980 and was even better second time around... Combines surprising strength with great quickness... In the open field, no one in the league looks better or runs more spectacularly... Gained 1,437 yards and scored 13 touchdowns despite a number of nagging injuries... Every bit what the No. 1 pick in the draft should be... No one is talking about his age any more... Born Sept. 18, 1955, in St. Louis... Caught 28 passes, but should improve as a receiver with experience... Won 1978 Heisman Trophy after leading country in rushing... Averaged seven yards a carry during his college days at Oklahoma... Likes to tinker with trucks.

ERIC HIPPLE 25 6–1 196   Quarterback

Eric who? He made sure everyone knew who he was by season's end... Came from nowhere to give the Lions a solid performance at quarterback... Got his break when Gary Danielson was hurt and Jeff Komlo couldn't do the job... Wound up being voted the team's offensive MVP by his teammates... Not bad for a fourth-round 1980 pick from Utah State who didn't throw a pass his rookie season... Instead, he was placekicker Eddie Murray's holder.... Lion scouts rated him a first-round pick and he certainly made them look good... Passed for 2,358 yards and 14 touchdowns... Born Sept. 16, 1957, in Lubbock, Tex.... Has a degree in business administration from Utah State.

DOUG ENGLISH 29 6–5 260   Defensive Tackle

This man sat out the 1980 season to take advantage of business opportunities with a Texas oil company because he didn't think he could do two jobs justice . . . Then he came back and played so spectacularly last year that he was named to the Pro Bowl and was considered by some the best at his spot in the league . . . Traveled the world with his oil job and should be set after he finally retires . . . Had a fine 1979 season in which he had 6½ sacks and 90 solo tackles . . . Born Aug. 25, 1953, in Dallas . . . Once was Lions' player representative . . . Helped Texas to three Southwestern Conference titles.

ED MURRAY 26 5–10 170   Kicker

What could he do for an encore after a stunning rookie year? Would you believe he had an even better second season? . . . Scored 121 points after racking up 116 in his first year . . . Made 25 of 35 field-goal attempts . . . Still couldn't break Doak Walker's club record of 128 . . . But of course, Walker scored touchdowns as well as doing the kicking . . . A seventh-round choice from Tulane who replaced Benny Ricardo and wound up in the Pro Bowl in 1980 . . . Born Aug. 29, 1956, in Halifax, Nova Scotia . . . Had a 54-yarder in college and is school record holder in all the main kicking categories . . . Wanted to be pro soccer player.

DAVID HILL 28 6–2 230   Tight End

Dependable player who will always come up with sufficient season . . . Contributed 33 catches, second-best on the team, last year, and now has 223 in six years in the league . . . A Pro-Bowl caliber player who doesn't always feel he is appreciated by management . . . But that is a complaint of a lot of Lions . . . A second-round pick out of Texas A&I in 1976 . . . He scored 21 TDs in his college days there and he's added 19 scores in his pro career . . . His brother is Jim Hill, who played safety for San Diego and Green Bay . . . Born Jan. 1, 1954, in San Antonio . . . Stepped into shoes of a legend in Detroit by replacing Charlie Sanders.

FRED SCOTT 30 6–2 180   Wide Receiver

Despite being the Lions' only legitimate outside threat, he has continued to excel . . . Added team-high 53 receptions last year and now has 168 in three years after hardly catching anything his first four years in the league . . . Was a starter for one of four seasons in Baltimore before coming to Lions prior to 1978 season . . . Doubled his pass-receiving production his first year in Motown, and he's been the Lions' best WR the last three campaigns . . . Born Aug. 5, 1952, in Grady, Ark. . . . Teammates call him Doc because he's enrolled in medical school at Michigan . . . A cum laude graduate of Amherst . . . Has scored 19 TDs in eight-year career.

STAN WHITE 32 6–1 223   Linebacker

Putting off law career so he can keep playing football . . . Already had magna cum laude law degree . . . Baltimore thought he was finished two years ago and traded him for lowly eighth-round draft choice . . . But this Ohio State alumnus has anchored Lion linebackers and calls defensive signals . . . Bright, sharp, articulate . . . One of the leaders of the National Football League Players Association . . . Born Oct. 24, 1949, in Dover, Ohio. . . . Led NFL linebackers with eight interceptions in 1975 . . . Has worked most of his career with defensive coordinator Maxie Baughan . . . "He's like having another coach on the field," Baughan says.

COACH MONTE CLARK . . .

Came within one win of having the Lions in the playoffs again . . . But for the second straight season, Detroit fell short when it was beaten by Tampa Bay . . . Fact it occurred in Superdome made the loss even harder to take . . . Still, remember this was a 2–14 team in 1979, so he has brought this team a long way . . . The Lions haven't been this good since 1970, which probably isn't saying that much . . . Gained coaching fame with the job he did at San Francisco in 1976 . . . Has pedigree as assistant coach, serving for six years under Don Shula at Miami, where he developed those great Dolphin offensive lines . . . This is no-nonsense disciplinarian who is known as a player's coach . . . Has had problems with general manager Russ Thomas and may not last for duration of his contract . . . Born Jan. 24, 1937, in Fillmore, Cal. . . . Played 11 years in the NFL as offensive lineman for San Francisco, Dallas and Cleveland.

GREATEST LINEBACKER

His teammates talked about his "sixth sense," his ability to sniff out potential plays and be there ahead of time to make the tackle or break up the pass. And never did that sixth sense serve

Stingy Lion defense stopped the run better than anyone.

Joe Schmidt better than against San Francisco in a 1957 game that put the Lions in the NFL championship game against Cleveland.

San Francisco was trying desperately to rally in the final quarter when Y. A. Tittle called a favorite play. He drifted to his right, then threw back to his left, where Hugh McElhenny was waiting. "I had one of those instinctive feelings at the snap," Schmidt said. He hung near McElhenny, made the interception and set up an insurance field goal. And the Lions went on to win the title game.

It was that type of play that put the six-foot, 217-pound Schmidt in the Hall of Fame after being selected All-NFL eight times and making the Pro Bowl eight times. He was a pioneer middle line-backer, switching to that position early in his career when NFL teams abandoned seven-man defensive lines. Not bad for a college fullback (Pittsburgh) who was drafted in the seventh round because there were questions about his banged-up knees. Those knees held up well enough to let him play 13 NFL seasons.

INDIVIDUAL LION RECORDS

Rushing

Most Yards Game:	198	Bob Hoernschemeyer, vs N.Y. Yanks, 1950	
Season:	1,437	Billy Sims, 1981	
Career:	4,629	Dexter Bussey, 1974–81	

Passing

Most TD Passes Game:	5	Gary Danielson, vs Minnesota, 1978
Season:	26	Bobby Layne, 1951
Career:	118	Bobby Layne, 1950–58

Receiving

Most TD Passes Game:	4	Cloyce Box, vs Baltimore, 1950
Season:	15	Cloyce Box, 1952
Career:	35	Terry Barr, 1957–65

Scoring

Most Points Game:	24	Cloyce Box, vs Baltimore, 1950
Season:	128	Doak Walker, 1950
Career:	636	Errol Mann, 1969–76
Most TDs Game:	4	Cloyce Box, vs Baltimore, 1950
Season:	16	Billy Sims, 1980
Career:	38	Terry Barr, 1957–65

GREEN BAY PACKERS

TEAM DIRECTORY: Chairman: Dominic Olejniczak; Pres: Judge Robert Parins; Sec.: John Torinus; Corp. GM: Bob Harlan; Bus. Mgr.: Tom Miller; Dir. Player Personnel: Dick Corrick; Dir. Pub. Rel.: Lee Remmel; Head Coach: Bart Starr. Home fields: Lambeau Field (56,189) and County Stadium, Milwaukee (55,958). Colors: Green and gold.

SCOUTING REPORT

OFFENSE: Much to coach Bart Starr's embarrassment, the Packers slipped drastically on offense last year. After all, this supposedly is his strength as a coach. So Starr hired ex-Lion assistant coach Bob Schnelker as his offensive coordinator in hopes of

John Jefferson leaves many a defender goggle-eyed.

improving Green Bay's attack, which ranked 23rd in the league last year.

If a couple of key things fall into place, the Packers could be among the league's most dangerous teams. In quarterback Lynn Dickey, coming off two good seasons, and receivers John Jefferson and James Lofton, they have a impressive passing offense. As a pair, the two receivers can't be matched by any combination in the NFL. And tight ends Paul Coffman and Gary Lewis are competent.

But Starr must produce a better running offense, and that prospect hinges on the knee of halfback Eddie Lee Ivery, who has missed much of the last two years with injuries. With a healthy Ivery and a good fullback in Gerry Ellis, Starr has decent backs.

Green Bay also needs improvement along its offensive line, which played well in six of the team's final seven games. Center Larry McCarren and tackle Greg Koch are set, but Starr is hoping tackle Karl Swanke will become a starter and give the line stability and that rookie guard Ron Hallstrom will be of immediate help.

DEFENSE: The irony of 1981 for Green Bay was that while the offense deteriorated statistically, the defense improved from 25th to ninth. Now it is up to defensive coordinator John Meyer to maintain that level with a relatively young and still improving unit.

The key to the defensive climb was the play of the Pack's linebackers, all of whom got through the year without major injuries. Mike Douglass is a Pro Bowler and George Cumby is a potential future star and they get plenty of help from John Anderson and Rich Wingo, who came back from a major back operation. Depth, however, could be a problem if injuries strike this year.

Mike Butler settled down and played well at end to lead the team in sacks, and now Starr hopes another gifted lineman, Ezra Johnson, does the same this season. Terry Jones surprised by excelling at nose tackle, but will be pushed by Rich Turner.

The Pack overcame injury problems to pick off 30 passes, their highest total since 1962. There is going to be plenty of competition for starting spots at safety among Mo Harvey, Johnnie Gray, Mark Murphy and Mike Jolly. Mark Lee came on at cornerback and will start along with veteran Mike McCoy.

KICKING GAME: Jan Stenerud led an upsurge in the special teams, which had been among the league's worst. Stenerud was the most accurate kicker in the league and the Pack was No. 1 in kickoff coverage. But Starr isn't pleased with young Ray Stachowicz's punting consistency and is looking for improvement.

PACKERS VETERAN ROSTER

HEAD COACH—Bart Starr. Assistant Coaches—Bob Schnelker, John Meyer, Lew Carpenter, Ross Fichtner, Pete Kettela, John Marshall, Ernie McMillan, Bill Meyers, Dick Rehbein, Richard Ulrich.

No.	Name	Pos.	Ht.	Wt.	NFL Exp.	College
60	Allerman, Kurt	LB	6-2	222	6	Penn State
	Anderson, Gary	G	6-4	255	3	Stanford
59	Anderson, John	LB	6-3	221	5	Michigan
61	Ane, Charlie	C	6-1	237	8	Michigan State
62	Aydelette, Buddy	T	6-4	250	2	Alabama
73	Braggs, Byron	DT	6-4	290	2	Alabama
77	Butler, Mike	DE	6-5	265	6	Kansas
19	Campbell, Rich	QB	6-4	224	2	California-Berkeley
88	Cassidy, Ron	WR	6-0	185	4	Utah State
82	Coffman, Paul	TE	6-3	218	5	Kansas State
52	Cumby, George	LB	6-1	230	3	Oklahoma
12	Dickey, Lynn	QB	6-4	220	12	Kansas State
53	Douglass, Mike	LB	6-0	224	5	San Diego State
31	Ellis, Gerry	FB	5-11	216	3	Missouri
98	Godfrey, Chris	G	6-3	250	2	Michigan
57	Gofourth, Derrel	G	6-3	260	6	Oklahoma State
24	Gray, Johnnie	FS	5-11	185	7	California-Fullerton
69	Harris, Leotis	G	6-1	267	5	Arkansas
23	Harvey, Maurice	S	5-10	190	4	Ball State
38	Hood, Estus	CB	5-11	180	3	Illinois State
25	Huckleby, Harlan	RB	6-1	199	3	Michigan
74	Huffman, Tim	T	6-5	277	2	Notre Dame
40	Ivery, Eddie Lee	RB	6-1	210	3	Georgia Tech
83	Jefferson, John	WR	6-1	198	5	Arizona State
33	Jensen, Jim	RB	6-3	235	6	Iowa
90	Johnson, Ezra	DE	6-4	240	6	Morris Brown
21	Jolly, Mike	S	6-3	185	2	Michigan
63	Jones, Terry	DT	6-2	259	5	Alabama
64	Kitson, Syd	G	6-4	252	2	Wake Forest
68	Koch, Greg	T	6-4	265	6	Arkansas
79	Koncar, Mark	T	6-5	268	6	Colorado
22	Lee, Mark	CB	5-11	187	3	Washington
56	Lewis, Cliff	LB	6-1	226	2	Southern Mississippi
81	Lewis, Gary	TE	6-5	234	2	Texas Arlington
	Livers, Virgil	CB-KR	5-9	183	7	Western Kentucky
80	Lofton, James	WR	6-3	187	5	Stanford
54	McCarren, Larry	C	6-3	238	10	Illinois
29	McCoy, Mike	CB	5-11	183	7	Colorado
78	Merrill, Casey	DE	6-4	255	4	California-Davis
34	Middleton, Terdell	RB	6-0	195	6	Memphis State
37	Murphy, Mark	FS	6-2	199	2	West Liberty State
84	Nixon, Fred	WR	5-11	191	3	Oklahoma
72	Oates, Brad	T	6-6	275	4	Brigham Young
51	Prather, Guy	LB	6-2	230	2	Grambling
58	Rudzinski, Paul	LB	6-1	220	4	Michigan State
55	Scott, Randy	LB	6-1	220	2	Alabama
16	Stachowicz, Ray	P	5-11	185	2	Michigan State
10	Stenerud, Jan	K	6-2	187	16	Montana State
76	Stokes, Tim	T	6-5	252	9	Oregon
67	Swanke, Karl	T-C	6-6	251	3	Boston College
71	Thompson, Arland	G	6-4	265	2	Baylor
87	Thompson, John	TE	6-3	228	3	Utah State
26	Torkelson, Eric	RB	6-2	210	9	Connecticut
75	Turner, Rich	DT	6-2	260	2	Oklahoma
30	Whitaker, Bill	S-CB	6-0	182	2	Missouri
17	Whitehurst, David	QB	6-2	204	6	Furman
50	Wingo, Rich	LB	6-1	230	4	Alabama

TOP FIVE DRAFT CHOICES

Rd.	Name	Sel. No.	Pos.	Ht.	Wt.	College
1	Hallstrom, Ron	22	G	6-6	286	Iowa
3	Rodgers, Del	71	RB	5-9	200	Utah
4	Brown, Robert	98	LB	6-2	238	Virginia Tech
5	Meade, Mike	126	RB	5-10	228	Penn State
6	Parlavecchio, Chet	152	LB	6-2	225	Penn State

THE ROOKIES: The Packers made Iowa's Hallstrom a surprising first-round choice, passing up some better-known linemen. They might have better success with No. 2 pick Del Rogers, a scatback from Utah who could be good enough to step in if Ivery's knees act up again.

OUTLOOK: Despite the optimism coming out of the Green Bay camp, any predictions about the Pack, as long as Starr is the coach, have to be made with caution. Certainly, if Green Bay's youngsters continue to mature, the Packers finally could reward their fans' patience with a long-awaited winning season.

PACKER PROFILES

LYNN DICKEY 32 6–4 220   Quarterback

Came on strong at end of season . . . Got better as his offensive line improved . . . His yardage total of 2,593 dropped from 1981, but his touchdown passes (17) were up and his interceptions (15) were down . . . He threw 25 interceptions in 1981 . . . Playing with the confidence and skill of an all-pro . . . Packers placed future of franchise on his shoulders when they acquired him from Houston in 1976 . . . Born Oct. 19, 1949, in Paola, Kan., where the high school stadium is named after him . . . Set Big Eight passing records while at Kansas State . . . Favorite hobby is golf.

JAMES LOFTON 26 6–3 187   Wide Receiver

Second straight season in which he has caught 71 passes, second-best total in the history of the Packers . . . His 1,294 yards was his personal best and put him rightfully among the league's elite . . . Benefitted from the presence of John Jefferson, who relieved him of much double coverage . . . Scored eight touchdowns last season, including a 75-yarder . . . Was an Olympic-class long jumper at Stanford, with leaps of more than 26 feet . . . An all-pro and his best years are still ahead . . . Born July 5, 1956, in Los Angeles . . . He somehow lasted until the second round of the 1978 draft.

JOHN JEFFERSON 26 6–1 198   Wide Receiver

Chargers ended his contract holdout by sending him to the cold north, as far removed from San Diego as you can get...But that didn't stop his smiling or dampen his positive attitude..."He was a big emotional boost," says linebacker Mike Douglass...By time he grew accustomed to the Packer offense, his receiving totals dropped to 39, but he still averaged 16 yards a catch...Packers can't wait to see how he and James Lofton perform together over an entire season...Hasn't got the greatest speed in the league, but is wonderfully gifted and can leap and catch in the best Lynn Swann style...Born Feb. 3, 1956, in Dallas...Former All-American at Arizona State says he is happy in Green Bay.

MIKE DOUGLASS 27 6–0 224   Linebacker

One of the league's best little-known players...Had an outstanding season, but he didn't get the recognition he deserves...It's the penalty he pays for playing on a little-publicized team..."He was the most effective outside linebacker we played against all year," says 49er assistant Bobb McKittrick...But Packers know that they have a gem...He was defensive MVP in 1980 after leading unit in tackles...Born March 15, 1955, in St. Louis...Nicknamed Mad Dog...When he's not tackling people, he likes to bowl, skate and mess around with cars...A fifth-round 1978 draft choice...Was a shot putter and high jumper at San Diego State.

RICH CAMPBELL 23 6–4 224   Quarterback

Packers pulled surprise when they took him on first round last season...Quarterback of the future who won't get a lot of playing time until Lynn Dickey slows down...But Green Bay is convinced it has a gem in this guy...Ended Bart Starr's six-year quest for a quarterback he wanted to draft...Only question mark is bad knee, which he hurt his senior year at California...Otherwise he is the perfect size and has the great arm you look for at the QB position...Completed 70 percent of his passes his senior year...A religious studies major...Plans to become a minister...Born Dec. 22, 1958, in Oakland.

JAN STENERUD 38 6–2 187   Kicker

Just when everyone thought he was ready for retirement, he produced a quality season...Should have been unanimous all-pro, considering his accuracy and consistency...Made 22 of 24 field-goal attempts and 35 of 36 extra points...You're not going to do much better than that...Didn't become a Packer until near end of 1980 season, when he was signed as free agent in a desperation move...His 101 points last year stand as his highest output since 1971, when he was in the prime of his career at Kansas City...Six points from going ahead of Lou Groza and moving into fifth spot among all-time kickers...Born Nov. 26, 1943, in Fetsund, Norway...Attended Montana State on skiing scholarship.

GERRY ELLIS 24 5–11 216   Running Back

The Packers got lucky with him...And are they glad they did...- Signed as free agent early in 1980, he has shored up questionable running game...Without him, when Eddie Lee Ivery was hurt, Packers would have been in desperate shape...Led team in rushing last year with 860 yards after finishing No. 2 in 1980....Seventh-round choice of Rams out of Missouri, where he was leading scorer and No. 2 rusher as a senior...Played year for Ft. Scott Junior College...Born Nov. 12, 1957, in Columbia, Mo....Compensates for lack of height with quickness and determination.

GEORGE CUMBY 26 6–0 230   Linebacker

Came back after injury-plagued rookie year to establish himself as starter...Showed Packers he could play linebacker after college career as rover back...An exceptional athlete who was an almost unanimous All-American selection as a senior at Oklahoma, where he terrorized offenses with his speed and daring...Major rap on him was his lack of height...Beefed up from 215 with offseason weight-lifting program...Born July 5, 1956, in La Rue, Tex....Hurt knee in preseason of 1980, came back to start two games before hurting it again and missing rest of year.

EDDIE LEE IVERY 25 6–1 210   Running Back

One of those athletes whose middle name should be "If"... If he could stay healthy, he'd be an all-star... If he could stay healthy, Packers' running game would go from so-so to wonderful... His constant injuries have both teased and wounded Green Bay and its fans... Gained 1,302 yards two years ago after being hurt in first game of rookie year in 1979... Then gained 72 yards last year before going down again for the season... Born July 30, 1957, in Thomson, Ga.... Attended Georgia Tech, where he ran for an NCAA-record 356 yards in one game.

RICH WINGO 26 6–1 230   Linebacker

Another comeback star... Missed 1980 season and left Pack without competent inside linebacker... But with both he and Cumby healthy and Mike Douglass playing so well on the outside in 1981, the Packers didn't complain about their linebacking anymore... Only a seventh-round draft choice out of Alabama in 1979... Now plays like a true-blood 'Bama star... A relentless player who uses enthusiasm to make up for lack of special quickness... A fierce tackler in the best Bear Bryant mold... Born July 16, 1956, in Elkhart, Ind.... Been a football captain since he was in elementary school.

COACH BART STARR ... Keeps surviving despite track record

that would have got most men fired long ago... His reputation as player in Green Bay is probably only thing that is saving him and he is at the end of the line with that, too... Has a new two-year contract, only because the Packers didn't want to make him look like a lame duck... But this time, if he doesn't win, he is out... Fast finish by team to salvage 8–8 mark saved him from firing last season... Has coached now for two seasons with reports of his imminent departure circulating around him... Has answered by flaring at the press and barring some members of the media... Some of his players have been known to call him "J.R." . . . Criticized for his coldness and lack of ability to communicate . . . Born Jan. 9, 1934, in Montgomery, Ala. . . . Calls plays for his quarterbacks and Pack has little trouble moving the ball in most games . . . Quarterbacked Packers to six playoff appearances in eight years, but record as head coach is 39–65–2 since taking over in 1975.

GREATEST LINEBACKER

It was bitterly cold, with a wind clocked at 35 miles per hour that created a wind-chill factor of minus 20 degrees. It was a day for defense, and no one was more ready than the immortal Ray

Free-agent Gerry Ellis perked up Packer running game.

Nitschke, the heart of the Green Bay Packers' famed championship defense. On this day in Yankee Stadium, Dec. 30, 1962, Nitschke and his mates were never better, limiting Y. A. Tittle and the New York Giants to only seven points and 94 rushing yards as Green Bay won its second straight NFL title, 16–7. Nitschke was so devastating that he was named the game's Most Valuable Player.

Few linebackers have equalled Ray Nitschke, a 6-4, 250-pounder who for 15 years was one of the game's most crushing tacklers. A Hall of Famer, he was named to the NFL's All-50-Year team. He was an all-pro three times and a member of five world title teams and the first two Super Bowl winners.

He was deceptively quick, a big man who was still mobile enough to intercept 25 passes and recover 20 fumbles, one short of the Packers' all-time record. And even today, almost a decade after his retirement, he looks tough enough to suit up and dominate a game once again.

INDIVIDUAL PACKER RECORDS

Rushing

Most Yards Game:	186	Jim Taylor, vs N.Y. Giants, 1961
Season:	1,474	Jim Taylor, 1962
Career:	8,207	Jim Taylor, 1958–66

Passing

Most TD Passes Game:	5	Cecil Isbell, vs Cleveland, 1942
	5	Don Horn, vs St. Louis, 1969
	5	Lynn Dickey, vs New Orleans, 1981
Season:	24	Cecil Isbell, 1942
Career:	152	Bart Starr, 1956–71

Receiving

Most TD Passes Game:	4	Don Hutson, vs Detroit, 1945
Season:	17	Don Hutson, 1943
Career:	99	Don Hutson, 1935–45

Scoring

Most Points Game:	33	Paul Hornung, vs Baltimore, 1961
Season:	176	Paul Hornung, 1960
Career:	823	Don Hutson, 1935–45
Most TDs Game:	5	Paul Hornung, vs Baltimore, 1961
Season:	19	Jim Taylor, 1962
Career:	105	Don Hutson, 1935–45

LOS ANGELES RAMS

TEAM DIRECTORY: Pres.: Georgia Frontiere; VP/GM: Don Klosterman; Dir. Operations: Dick Bean; Dir. Marketing: Les Marshall; Dir. Player Personnel: John Math; Asst. GM: Jack Faulkner; Dir. Pub. Rel.: Jerry Wilcox; Head Coach: Ray Malavasi. Home field: Anaheim Stadium (69,007). Colors: Royal blue, gold and white.

SCOUTING REPORT

OFFENSE: The Rams knew that until they straightened out their quarterback derby, they wouldn't be a legitimate Super Bowl con-

Rams' Wendell Tyler broke loose for 17 TDs last season.

tender again. And no one recognized the problem caused by the quarterback shuffle better than coach Ray Malavasi, who tried to play three at varous times in '81 with decreasing success.

Former Colt Bert Jones, liberated from Baltimore for first- and second-round draft picks, has the job now, and he won't have any opposition from Pat Haden, the Rhodes Scholar whom Malavasi didn't deem good enough to be the permanent starter. Jones' arrival encouraged Haden to give up his $200,000-a-year salary in favor of a CBS college football commentator role and a law degree.

Malavasi has other concerns, especially the offensive line. Injuries destroyed one of the league's best units last year. Doug Smith needs to play guard, not tackle, but his fate will depend on the return of Doug France and Jackie Slater from injuries. And center Rich Saul has retired, leaving another gap.

With Wendell Tyler, the running game is more than adequate, but Preston Dennard is the lone deep threat at receiver. Mike Barber, veteran tight end obtained from Houston, where he lost his job to Dave Casper, vies with Henry Childs for starting tight end.

DEFENSE: Even with the Fred Dryer retirement controversy swirling around their heads, the Rams' defense was able to survive intact the team's decline to a losing record last year, no small accomplishment considering the morale of the club by the end of December.

The unit could get better, if cornerback Pat Thomas can finally shake off his stubborn leg problems and if Mel Owens, last year's No. 1 draft choice, comes around to shape up a linebacking corps that sorely missed middle man Jack Reynolds. Carl Ekern, the new middle linebacker, played well enough to share the honors as leading tackler with safety Nolan Cromwell, but he doesn't have Reynolds' leadership traits.

Somehow, Jack Youngblood keeps playing with dignity and quality despite advancing age. His performance sets the tempo for the front four, where end Cody Jones and tackle Mike Fanning lend great consistency. And there are youngsters behind them to supply good depth. Cromwell, safety Johnnie Johnson and cornerback Rod Perry all have Pro Bowl talent, and Malavasi can turn to LeRoy Irvin and Ivory Sully as replacements in case of injuries.

KICKING GAME: Los Angeles had the unique distinction of leading the league in punt returns last year, thanks to Irvin, while finishing last in kickoff returns. Frank Corral handles both the punting and the field-goal work and does his double duty well,

RAMS VETERAN ROSTER

HEAD COACH—Ray Malavasi. Assistant Coaches—Jack Snow, Fred Whittingham, Fritz Shurmur, Jim Vechiarella, Jim Ringo, John Hadl, Herb Pattera, Paul Lanham.

No.	Name	Pos.	Ht.	Wt.	NFL Exp.	College
52	Andrews, George	LB	6-3	221	4	Nebraska
84	Arnold, Walt	TE	6-3	230	3	New Mexico
62	Bain, Bill	G	6-4	285	7	Southern California
	Barber, Mike	TE	6-3	233	6	Louisiana Tech
81	Battle, Ron	TE	6-3	225	2	North Texas State
90	Brooks, Larry	DT	6-3	255	11	Virginia State-Petersburg
32	Bryant, Cullen	FB	6-1	236	10	Colorado
54	Carson, Howard	LB	6-2	230	2	Howard Payne
57	Celotto, Mario	LB	6-3	228	4	Southern California
83	Childs, Henry	TE	6-2	220	9	Kansas State
97	Cobb, Bob	DE	6-4	250	2	Arizona
50	Collins, Jim	LB	6-2	230	2	Syracuse
42	Collins, Kirk	CB	5-11	183	2	Baylor
3	Corral, Frank	K-P	6-2	227	5	UCLA
21	Cromwell, Nolan	S	6-1	197	6	Kansas
88	Dennard, Preston	WR	6-1	183	5	New Mexico
71	Doss, Reggie	DE	6-4	263	5	Hampton Institute
55	Ekern, Carl	LB	6-3	222	6	San Jose State
79	Fanning, Mike	DT	6-6	255	8	Notre Dame
77	France, Doug	T	6-5	270	8	Ohio State
44	Guman, Mike	RB	6-2	218	3	Penn State
60	Harrah, Dennis	G	6-5	250	8	Miami
51	Harris, Joe	LB	6-1	230	7	Georgia Tech
87	Hill, Drew	WR-KR	5-9	170	4	Georgia Tech
72	Hill, Kent	G	6-5	260	4	Georgia Tech
47	Irvin, LeRoy	CB-PR	5-11	184	3	Kansas
20	Johnson, Johnnie	S	6-1	185	3	Texas
7	Jones, Bert	QB	6-3	209	10	Louisiana State
76	Jones, Cody	DT	6-5	255	8	San Jose State
9	Kemp, Jeff	QB	6-0	201	2	Dartmouth
69	Meisner, Greg	DE	6-3	253	2	Pittsburgh
82	Miller, Willie	WR	5-9	173	7	Colorado State
86	Moore, Jeff	WR	6-1	188	3	Tennessee
95	Murphy, Phil	DT	6-5	300	3	South Carolina State
58	Owens, Mel	LB	6-2	224	2	Michigan
75	Pankey, Irv	T	6-4	267	3	Penn State
22	Penaranda, Jairo	FB	5-11	215	2	UCLA
49	Perry, Rod	CB	5-9	185	8	Colorado
8	Rutledge, Jeff	QB	6-2	187	4	Alabama
78	Slater, Jackie	T	6-4	271	7	Jackson State
56	Smith, Doug	C-G	6-3	253	5	Bowling Green
23	Smith, Lucious	CB	5-10	190	3	California-Fullerton
37	Sully, Ivory	S	6-0	201	4	Delaware
33	Thomas, Jewerl	FB	5-10	228	3	San Jose State
27	Thomas, Pat	CB	5-9	180	7	Texas A&M
26	Tyler, Wendell	RB	5-10	196	5	UCLA
80	Waddy, Billy	WR	5-11	190	6	Colorado
85	Youngblood, Jack	DE	6-4	245	12	Florida
53	Youngblood, Jim	LB	6-3	231	10	Tennessee Tech

TOP FIVE DRAFT CHOICES

Rd.	Name	Sel. No.	Pos.	Ht.	Wt.	College
1	Redden, Barry	14	RB	6-0	215	Richmond
3	Bechtold, Bill	67	C	6-4	245	Oklahoma
4	Gaylord, Jeff	88	DT	6-3	240	Missouri
5	Kersten, Wally	117	T	6-6	285	Minnesota
5	Barnett, Doug	118	DE	6-3	250	Azusa Pacific

although the Rams would like him to be a bit more consistent with his field-goal accuracy.

THE ROOKIES: With the Rams souring on fullback Cullen Bryant, first-round pick Barry Redden of Richmond will be given every chance to start. And center Bill Bechtold of Oklahoma, drafted on the third round, is a possible replacement for the retiring all-pro Saul.

OUTLOOK: One of the league's puzzles, the Rams have more talent than all but a handful of clubs. With the addition of Jones and a break from the front-office turmoil and the atmosphere of informality that have plagued the club, this could be a turnaround year for the Rams.

RAM PROFILES

BERT JONES 30 6–3 209   **Quarterback**

Unhappy in Baltimore and wanted out desperately...Colts gave him his wish and shipped him to Rams on day of draft...Should step right in as No. 1 quarterback, Pat Haden notwithstanding...When healthy, one of the game's classic throwers...He lost almost all of two seasons with a shoulder injury, but came back last year to toss 21 touchdown passes while playing catchup in virtually every game...Born Sept. 7, 1951, in Ruston, La....Stayed close to home to register 20 school records at LSU...Second player taken in 1973 draft...Led Colts into playoffs three straight years from 1975 through 1977 and threw for over 8,200 yards in that span...Then he got hurt and the franchise fell apart...Still has tendency to blame teammates for mistakes.

NOLAN CROMWELL 27 6-1 197   Safety

Another steady season from the man recognized as one of the elite players in the league . . . Even when rest of the team struggled, he remained consistent and separated himself from the turmoil . . . A gifted athlete who probably broke 90 the first time he tried golf . . . No better safety in the league . . . An all-pro and Pro Bowl performer . . . Along with Randy White, one of those names you automatically write down on the all-star ballot . . . Born Jan. 30, 1955, in Smith Center, Kan. . . . As soon as he can, Kansas alumnus gets away from the bright lights and returns to his farm in Lawrence, where he lives and works in offseason.

JACK YOUNGBLOOD 32 6-4 245   Defensive End

Nothing seems to slow him down—not age, not opponents, not even bad health . . . Came back from serious illness and operation to play another superior season . . . Still one of the league's most consistent performers and a pass-rushing threat on every down . . . Born Jan. 26, 1950, in Jacksonville, Fla., he was a three-year letterman at Florida, where he was named All-American in his senior season . . . Played with a broken leg in 1979 playoffs . . . Had career-high 16 sacks that season . . . Owns a western clothing store in Orange, Cal., and a sports club in Huntington Beach.

FRANK CORRAL 27 6-2 227   Kicker

One of the few in the league who both punts and placekicks for his team . . . Has handled the chores well now for two seasons . . . Saves a roster spot, something the coaches cherish . . . In his first year as a two-way man, averaged almost 40 yards a punt and had a good season placekicking . . . But he is used to double duty . . . Did both in junior college and then at UCLA, where he was first-team all-conference pick as punter and second-team selection as placekicker . . . Broke his jaw his senior year and missed most of the season . . . Born June 16, 1955, in

Chihuahua, Mex.... In his rookie season, he was recognized as perhaps the best kicker in the league.

JOHNNIE JOHNSON 25 6–1 185   Safety

Came in with a high-priced contract his rookie year that upset all the veterans... But they quickly fell silent when they found out this guy can play... Since, in the process, the Rams were prodded to renegotiate a lot of the vets' contracts, now everyone is happy—except maybe the people who have to sign those paychecks... With Nolan Cromwell alongside him, no team in the league is stronger at safety, which was why the Rams drafted him No. 1 in the first place... Born Oct. 8, 1956, in La Grange, Tex.... An All-American his senior year at Texas, where he returned punts... Working toward sociology degree.

PAT THOMAS 28 5–9 180   Cornerback

Can't seem to stay healthy anymore... Had another season ruined by nagging leg problems that could cost him starting position... Yet he came up with four interceptions, one short of Nolan Cromwell's team high... So the talent and the quickness still are there, if he only could be on the field more... The experts recognize his ability... An all-pro at times... Lester Hayes of Oakland credits Thomas, a former teammate at Texas A&M, with teaching him the fundamentals of secondary play... Picked off 13 passes in outstanding college career... Born Sept. 1, 1954, in Plano, Tex.... Became a starter midway through '77 season and no one's pushed him out of job yet.

WENDELL TYLER 27 5–10 196   Running Back

Perhaps the only positive development for Rams last year was his full return from dislocated hip suffered in auto mishap two seasons ago... Gained 1,074 yards, second-best total in an ailment-filled career... He also scored a whopping 17 touchdowns on a team that had trouble developing any offense... After that accident in the summer of 1980, he didn't play until the ninth game of the season and then hurt his elbow...Missed most of the 1978 season with a knee injury...When he is healthy, UCLA grad provides much-needed outside speed and a breakaway threat...Born May 20, 1955, in Shreveport, La....Vice president of local land corporation.

HENRY CHILDS 31 6–2 220   Tight End

Hallelujah Henry, the big-play tight end who has made the clutch catch his trademark ...Acquired from the Saints via the Redskins in a strange three-corner deal...His production in New Orleans had slumped and Bum Phillips decided to change some faces...Never gave the Rams the kind of production they were looking for, but stability at quarterback could help him, too...Left New Orleans near the top of the list in all major receiving categories...Drafted in fifth round by Atlanta out of Kansas State and signed by the Saints as a free agent...Born April 16, 1951, in Thomasville, Ga....Has undergraduate degrees in home economics and child development.

DENNIS HARRAH 29 6–5 250   Guard

Has the distinction of reaching the Pro Bowl in 1980 even though he didn't start until the ninth week...That's how good his peers think he is...Has been hindered by injuries and contract disputes in his seven-year pro career...Second of three first-round picks in 1975...Became a starter in 1976, but a knee injury kept him out of most of 1977...Miami (Fla.) alumnus is strong, determined player who loves contact...When he's healthy, he's one of the best...Born March 9, 1953, in Charleston, W.Va....Owns a night spot in Long Beach...Herk (for Hercules) is his Rams' nickname.

CULLEN BRYANT 31 6–1 236   Running Back

Was the second-leading rusher last season, but didn't end up very happy...Played second string for last part of schedule behind Mike Guman, and he doesn't know why...Claims no one ever told him the reason for the benching...Remains one of the purest power runners in the business...If you need a yard, give him the ball...And don't think he is one-way in ability...He has good enough hands to catch 53 passes in 1980 and 22 last year...Born May 20, 1951, in Ft. Still, Okla....All-American defensive back at Colorado his senior year...Didn't get a chance to show true running ability until his third season in the NFL.

COACH RAY MALAVASI...He survived dismal 6–10 season but half of his assistants didn't...Choice between making changes or finding out what it feels like to be unemployed...Major problem this season will be motivating a team in disarray...A survivor who probably never will be considered a top-flight coach...Once you get a reputation for being a non-genius, it sticks...Doesn't particularly enjoy the spotlight and reveals little in public interviews, but is good companion and popular among his players...But his decision to side with management in some contract disputes in 1980 hurt him in latter area...Born Nov. 8, 1930, in Passaic, N.J....Learned his football at West Point under Red Blaik and Vince Lombardi...Put in long apprenticeship as assistant coach in the NFL before getting No. 1 job...A favorite of owner Georgia Frontiere...Once known strictly as a defensive specialist, but now is calling all the offensive plays...Led Rams to first NFC title in 1979 and has 38–26 overall record since taking job as successor to Chuck Knox in 1978.

GREATEST LINEBACKER

On pure ability, the Rams have never produced a better linebacker than Les Richter, the graceful, hard-nosed star of those very talented Los Angeles teams during the 1950s. Richter made the Pro Bowl eight straight times in a career that ended in 1962, and he was the team's leading tackler in all but two. Yet even someone as talented as Richter has to at least share half the honor with one of the most colorful personalities in the team's history, Jack (Hacksaw) Reynolds.

If nothing else, Reynolds has had the best nickname, obtained after he took out his frustrations over a college loss by sawing an old car in half. Took him 13 saw blades to do it, too, and a whole night's work. So you can imagine how easy it must seem to him to play a boy's game for a few hours every fall weekend.

Reynolds, a first-round choice out of Tennessee, led the Rams in tackles five times before being released following the 1980 season. Reynolds overcame that insult by signing with San Francisco and helping the 49ers win Super Bowl XVI.

INDIVIDUAL RAM RECORDS

Rushing

Most Yards Game:	247	Willie Ellison, vs New Orleans, 1971
Season:	1,238	Lawrence McCutcheon, 1977
Career:	6,186	Lawrence McCutcheon, 1973–79

Passing

Most TD Passes Game:	5	Bob Waterfield, vs N.Y. Bulldogs, 1949
	5	Norm Van Brocklin, vs Detroit, 1950
	5	Norm Van Brocklin, vs N.Y. Yanks, 1951
	5	Roman Gabriel, vs Cleveland, 1965
	5	Vince Ferragamo, vs New Orleans, 1980
Season:	30	Vince Ferragamo, 1980
Career:	154	Roman Gabriel, 1962–72

Receiving

Most TD Passes Game:	4	Bob Shaw, vs Washington, 1949
	4	Elroy Hirsch, vs N.Y. Yanks, 1951
	4	Harold Jackson, vs Dallas, 1973
Season:	17	Elroy Hirsch, 1951
Career:	53	Elroy Hirsch, 1949–57

Scoring

Most Points Game:	24	Elroy Hirsch, vs N.Y. Yanks, 1951
	24	Bob Shaw, vs Washington, 1949
	24	Harold Jackson, vs Dallas, 1973
Season:	130	David Ray, 1973
Career:	573	Bob Waterfield, 1945–52
Most TDs Game:	4	Elroy Hirsch, vs N.Y. Yanks, 1951
	4	Bob Shaw, vs Washington, 1949
	4	Harold Jackson, vs Dallas, 1973
Season:	17	Elroy Hirsch, 1951
	17	Wendell Tyler, 1981
Career:	55	Elroy Hirsch, 1949–57

MINNESOTA VIKINGS

TEAM DIRECTORY: Pres.: Max Winter; GM: Mike Lynn; Administrative Coordinator: Harley Peterson; Coordinator FB Oper.: Jerry Reichow; Dir. Pub. Rel.: Merrill Swanson; Head Coach: Bud Grant. Home field: Hubert H. Humphrey Metrodome (62,202). Colors: Purple, white and gold.

Tommy Kramer is key to Vikes' ball-control offense.

SCOUTING REPORT

OFFENSE: Bud Grant won't say it, but 1981 might have been the most disappointing season in his tenure at Minnesota, mainly because it was so hard to explain how the Vikings could fall out of playoff contention with a five-game losing streak, the longest ever by one of his teams. The offense has to absorb a great deal of the blame.

Quarterback Tommy Kramer, now that he has his personal life squared away, is expected to bounce back from a bad stretch run last year. He threw 26 touchdown passes, but also had 24 passes picked off, far too many for a player with his talents.

Grant's one-back offense, which has been copied by so many other teams, also has been coming under criticism from those who think it is too easy to defense. Certainly, the nucleus for a good offense is still present. Halfback Ted Brown is coming off his best year as a pro, wide receivers Ahmad Rashad and Sammy White are highly capable and tight end Joe Senser is a budding star. But Grant could face a problem with a so-so offensive line that didn't always protect the not-that-mobile Kramer as well as might be expected last season.

DEFENSE: The Vikings found themselves giving up too many big plays and not making enough of their own last year, and that has to be remedied this time around. But one problem continues to be a lack of quickness throughout the entire unit, a weakness that can be troublesome in this era of pitch-and-run.

Matt Blair continues to play with the league's linebacking elite, but sometimes has to all but carry his teammates with him. Grant used a 3–4 last year, which eliminated a spot for pass rusher Doug Martin, who has too much potential to sit on the bench for long. He could be the key to improving the pass rush, which depended too much on blitzing. Jeff Siemon, at one inside linebacking spot, is beginning to show his age and will be pressed to keep his starting spot.

The Vikings had eight fewer interceptions last year than in 1980. The trouble is: how do you increase the interception number when you already are starting your best players? Willie Teal, who had four at his cornerback spot, can get better, and his improvement could bolster the entire secondary.

KICKING GAME: The Vikings have a middle-of-the-road bunch of special teams, except when it comes to blocking kicks. Then no one in the league is better. Field-goal man Rick Danmeier

VIKINGS VETERAN ROSTER

HEAD COACH—Bud Grant. Assistant Coaches—Jerry Burns, Bob Hollway, Jed Hughes, John Michels, Bus Mertes, Les Steckel, Tom Cecchini, Floyd Reese.

No.	Name	Pos.	Ht.	Wt.	NFL Ex.	College
59	Blair, Matt	LB	6-5	230	9	Iowa State
62	Boyd, Brent	G	6-3	260	3	UCLA
23	Brown, Ted	RB	5-10	198	4	North Carolina State
82	Bruer, Bob	TE	6-5	235	4	Mankato State
8	Coleman, Greg	P	6-0	178	6	Florida A&M
7	Danmeier, Rick	K	6-0	183	5	Sioux Falls
12	Dils, Steve	QB	6-1	190	4	Stanford
65	Elshire, Neil	DE	6-6	250	2	Oregon
32	Galbreath, Tony	RB	6-0	230	7	Missouri
61	Hamilton, Wes	G	6-3	255	7	Tulsa
45	Hannon, Tom	S	5-11	193	6	Michigan State
36	Harrell, Sam	RB	6-2	213	2	East Carolina
75	Holloway, Randy	DE	6-5	245	5	Pittsburgh
51	Hough, Jim	C	6-2	267	5	Utah State
56	Huffman, Dave	C	6-6	255	4	Notre Dame
76	Irwin, Tim	T	6-6	275	2	Tennessee
52	Johnson, Dennis	LB	6-3	230	3	Southern California
53	Johnson, Henry	LB	6-2	235	3	Georgia Tech
25	Knoff, Kurt	S	6-2	188	7	Kansas
9	Kramer, Tommy	QB	6-2	200	6	Rice
58	Langer, Jim	C	6-2	253	13	South Dakota State
80	LeCount, Terry	WR	5-10	172	5	Florida
87	Lewis, Leo	WR	5-8	170	2	Missouri
79	Martin, Doug	DE	6-3	258	3	Washington
88	McDole, Mardye	WR	5-11	195	2	Mississippi State
54	McNeill, Fred	LB	6-2	229	9	UCLA
77	Mullaney, Mark	DE	6-6	242	8	Colorado State
49	Nord, Keith	S	6-0	197	4	St. Cloud State
40	Paschal, Doug	RB	6-2	219	2	North Carolina
36	Payton, Eddie	KR	5-6	179	6	Jackson State
28	Rashad, Ahmad	WR	6-2	200	10	Oregon
22	Redwine, Jarvis	RB	5-10	198	2	Nebraska
78	Riley, Steve	T	6-6	253	9	Southern California
57	Sendlein, Robin	LB	6-3	224	2	Texas
81	Senser, Joe	TE	6-4	238	3	West Chester State
50	Siemon, Jeff	LB	6-3	237	11	Stanford
55	Studwell, Scott	LB	6-2	224	6	Illinois
29	Swain, John	CB	6-1	195	2	Miami
67	Swilley, Dennis	C	6-3	241	6	Texas A&M
37	Teal, Willie	CB	5-10	195	3	Louisiana State
27	Turner, John	DB	6-0	199	5	Miami
72	White, James	DT	6-3	263	7	Oklahoma State
85	White, Sammy	WR	5-11	189	7	Grambling
44	Williams, Walt	CB	6-1	185	6	New Mexico State
11	Wilson, Wade	QB	6-3	212	2	East Texas State
91	Yakavonis, Ray	DE	6-4	243	2	East Stroudsburg State
73	Yary, Ron	T	6-6	255	15	Southern California
34	Young, Rickey	RB	6-2	195	8	Jackson State

TOP FIVE DRAFT CHOICES

Rd.	Name	Sel. No.	Pos.	Ht.	Wt.	College
1	Nelson, Darrin	7	RB	5-9	185	Stanford
2	Tausch, Terry	39	T	6-4	265	Texas
4	Fahnhorst, Jim	92	LB	6-4	224	Minnesota
6	Storr, Greg	147	LB	6-2	224	Boston College
7	Jordan, Steve	179	TE	6-3	228	Brown

made 21 of 25 kicks last year and finished with 97 points, but punter Greg Coleman will never make anyone forget Ray Guy.

THE ROOKIES: Grant's wide-open passing offense should be aided by the presence of halfback Darrin Nelson, who proved to be a dangerous receiver and runner at Stanford. Tackle Terry Tausch of Texas will be groomed to take over for the aging Ron Yary, perhaps before this season is over.

OUTLOOK: The Vikings have lost three more games than they have won over the last four years. And there is no reason to believe they are capable of doing much better than .500 this season. This team, without superstars, just can't keep pace in the talent catagory anymore.

VIKING PROFILES

TOMMY KRAMER 27 6–2 200   Quarterback

Treated for alcoholism in the offseason . . . Club officials praised his maturity and recognition of personal problems . . . Maybe those problems were reason for his mysterious late-season slump that helped plunge the Vikings from the league elite . . . Still threw for 26 touchdowns, but his interception total (24) was way too high . . . Other 1981 stats: 322 completions, 3,912 yards . . . So much of what the Vikings do on offense depends on his accuracy . . . Born March 7, 1955, in San Antonio, Tex. . . . One of 11 children . . . His father coached at Texas Lutheran for six years . . . Rice grad still has the ability to be a Pro Bowler.

MATT BLAIR 31 6–5 230   Linebacker

This most consistent of linebackers actually stumbled a bit last season . . . His interception total fell to one after three straight seasons of having at least three . . . But that doesn't indicate a decline in talent . . . Remains perennial All-NFC choice, even though you don't hear a whole lot about him . . . If he played in high-exposure city, he would be worshipped by the football world . . . Once liked photography as a hobby, but now it's a business, along with being a partner in a trucking company . . . Born Sept. 20, 1950, in Honolulu . . . Graduated from Iowa State . . . Has seven dogs.

TED BROWN 25 5–10 198   Running Back

Accidentally shot himself in freak accident and his recovery is being closely watched by the Vikings . . . Had one of the best all-around seasons of any player in the NFL as he took on more and more of the offensive load . . . Wound up with 1,063 yards rushing, his best-ever total, and 83 catches, again a career high . . . Those numbers are two seasons work for many players . . . Now critics realize why the Vikings picked him No. 1, to the surprise of many, after standout career at North Carolina State . . . Born Feb. 2, 1957, in High Point, N.C. . . . Finished four on the NCAA all-time career rushing list.

TONY GALBREATH 28 6–0 230   Running Back

One of the mysteries of the year . . . Here is one of the most talented players in the league, once thought to be a potential superstar, playing second-string for team that doesn't have wealth of talent . . . But why did New Orleans give up on him in the first place? . . . Vikings say he will be utilized better once he learns system and goes through a training camp . . . Gained a mere 198 yards last year, still second-best on team that doesn't run much . . . Once part of Saints' backfield that included Chuck Muncie, who also was traded away . . . Born Jan. 19, 1954, in Fulton, Mo. . . . Plays bass guitar and is good tennis player . . . A Missouri alumnus.

SAMMY WHITE 28 5–11 189   Wide Receiver

This happy man keeps performing at a high level, though he rarely is mentioned among the elite receivers in the league . . . But there are a lot of teams that would take someone who has caught 53 and 66 passes the last two seasons . . . When he slumped to 42 receptions in 1979, he wondered what had happened, but those doubts have now disappeared . . . Once there was a question of whether he would be good enough to make it on this level, even though he had a standout career at Grambling, where he played wingback and got a chance to run the ball . . . Born March 16, 1954, in Winnsboro, La. . . . Earned a teaching credential in the offseason and now spends time as substitute teacher.

AHMAD RASHAD 32 6–2 200   Wide Receiver

No wide receiver in pro football has caught more passes in the last six years (377) than this extraordinarily talented, consistent athlete . . . Holds just about all the Viking club records, wiping out Chuck Foreman's career reception total last season . . . Remember, Seattle gave him up for only a fourth-round draft choice . . . Born Nov. 19, 1949, in Portland, Ore. . . . Starred at the University of Oregon, where he was known as Bobby Moore . . . Originally a first-round draft choice of the St. Louis Cardinals in 1972, then traded to Buffalo in 1973 . . . Has worked as TV reporter in the offseason.

GREG COLEMAN 28 6–0 178   Punter

Enjoyed his best season as a pro . . . Averaged 41 yards on 89 kicks . . . That's two yards higher than best previous total . . . And he had 28 more attempts than in any other season . . . One reason for high total was a booming 73-yard kick . . . Still good at getting kicks to die inside the 20, even with increased distance . . . Signed as a free agent midway into 1978 season . . . A 14th-round choice of Cincinnati in 1976 . . . Punter and placekicker at Florida A&M . . . Has degree in criminology . . . Born Sept. 9, 1954, in Jacksonville, Fla. . . . Investigator for state's attorney office in Florida.

JOE SENSER 26 6–4 238   Tight End

Becoming one of the most consistent, dangerous tight ends in the business . . . Ideal for Vikings' throw, throw, throw offense, which uses the tight end as safety valve, instead of a running back . . . Every time it seems play is over, somehow he gets free for a catch . . . Had 79 last season, which was club record for tight ends . . . He held the old mark, 49, which he set the year before . . . And that was when he was splitting time with Bob Tucker . . . Not anymore . . . He's the starter and should be for years to come...A four-year starter at West Chester State, where he also excelled at basketball...Born Aug. 18, 1956, in Philadelphia.

EDDIE PAYTON 31 5–6 179   Kick Returner

Walter Payton's big brother enjoyed another fine season...Averaged 23 yards on 39 kickoff returns and eight yards on 38 punt returns...Erased memory of playoff goof against Philadelphia two years ago that helped lose game for Vikings...Surviving in young man's business, and will do so as long as quickness holds up...Signed as free agent after year in Canadian Football League...All-conference running back at Jackson State, where he also participated in baseball, track, golf and intramural swimming...Born Aug. 3, 1951, in Columbia, Mo....Umpires college baseball in offseason.

STEVE DILS 26 6–1 190   Quarterback

Vikings feel he is legitimate quarterback material, although he had rocky moments playing against Oakland last year in place of injured Tommy Kramer...He was hurt in that game and that forced Kramer to take over starting duties again sooner than expected...Another Bill Walsh product out of Stanford, where he led nation in passing as a senior...Has economics degree...Works for real estate firm in offseason in Sunnyvale, Cal....Born Dec. 8, 1955, in Vancouver, Wash....Three-sport captain in high school.

COACH BUD GRANT...When the Vikings tumbled last season, he started to hear some pointed questions about his coaching from people who once considered him almost untouchable...For years, he has done more with less than any other coach in the league...But now the Vikings seem to be going nowhere...But he'll probably come up with some solution, since he always does...Like inflation, he never stops growing and never changes his personality . . . Dual face is well known: unsmiling on the field, a practical joker off . . . Can't really say he is conservative, considering the way his club has tossed the ball around the last two years . . . In fact, he is one of the most adaptable, imaginative coaches around . . . Recognized trend toward more passing and found way to take advantage of new rules before most . . . Born May 20, 1927, in Superior, Wis. . . . Real first name is Harry . . . Played for two seasons for world-champion Minneapolis Lakers teams in NBA, then moved on to career as wide receiver with Philadelphia Eagles and Winnipeg of CFL . . . His 25-year record as Vikings' head coach is 138–75–5 and his teams have won 15 championships—11 Central Division, one NFL and three NFC—but no Super Bowls.

GREATEST LINEBACKER

Matt Blair is aging well, like a fine wine. Even after nine seasons of being a superb outside linebacker, he has managed to

Matt Blair (59) has blocked 18 kicks in his career.

change with the times, adapt to new rules and still perform up to his high level of quality.

Consider this: perhaps the best game of his career came during the middle of last season, against Philadelphia, when the Vikings recorded a stunning 35–23 win over the then-undefeated Eagles. Until the fourth quarter, Philadelphia was stymied on offense, thanks mainly to Blair who had 14 (FOURTEEN) unassisted tackles, five assists, an interception, a fumble recovery and, for good measure, a blocked conversion. That performance outshone even another gem, this one against Miami, when he had 10 tackles, six assists, an interception, a fumble recovery and a blocked kick in a 1979 loss.

Blair now has blocked 18 kicks, a Viking regular-season record, over his nine seasons. He also has 15 interceptions and 14 recovered fumbles while scoring two touchdowns. In the process, he has been selected to the last five Pro Bowls.

INDIVIDUAL VIKING RECORDS

Rushing

Most Yards Game:	200	Chuck Foreman, vs Philadelphia, 1976
Season:	1,155	Chuck Foreman, 1976
Career:	5,879	Chuck Foreman, 1973–79

Passing

Most TD Passes Game:	7	Joe Kapp, vs Baltimore, 1969
Season:	26	Tommy Kramer, 1981
Career:	239	Francis Tarkenton, 1961–66, 1972–78

Receiving

Most TD Passes Game:	4	Ahmad Rashad, vs San Francisco, 1979
Season:	11	Jerry Reichow, 1961
Career:	32	Sammy White, 1976–79

Scoring

Most Points Game:	24	Chuck Foreman, vs Buffalo, 1975
	24	Ahmad Rashad, vs San Francisco, 1979
Season:	132	Chuck Foreman, 1975
Career:	1,365	Fred Cox, 1963–77
Most TDs Game:	4	Chuck Foreman, vs Buffalo, 1975
	4	Ahmad Rashad, vs San Francisco, 1979
Season:	22	Chuck Foreman, 1975
Career:	76	Bill Brown, 1962–74

NEW ORLEANS SAINTS

TEAM DIRECTORY: Owner: John Mecom, Jr.; Pres.: Eddie Jones; VP-Administration: Fred Williams; Dir. FB Oper.: Harry Hulmes; GM/Head Coach: Bum Phillips; Controller: Bob Landry; Dir. Pub. Rel.: Greg Suit. Home field: Superdome (71,330). Colors: Old gold, black and white.

SCOUTING REPORT

OFFENSE: Bum Phillips says he wants none of this sixth-story rebuilding. "You start at the foundation," he claims, and that's what he tried to do in his first season with the Saints last year. The result wasn't all that impressive, either in the standings or on the stat sheet, but even a little progress in New Orleans is welcomed with open arms.

At least the Saints proved they could run. In George Rogers, they found a solid, durable, talented runner who led the league in rushing his rookie year, no easy feat. The problem was the Saints could do only one thing—hand off the ball to Rogers and block straight ahead.

After casting off receiver Wes Chandler and seeing quarterback Archie Manning struggle with injuries, Phillips found his passing attack was almost non-existent, the worst in the league. His top receiver, fullback Jack Holmes, caught only 38 passes. Better receivers have to be found and Phillips has to decide whether he wants to stay with Manning or go with youngster Dave Wilson, who performed well at times last season, his rookie year.

DEFENSE: Phillips decided last year his team would learn how to stop the run. And the Saints did, never once giving up 100 yards on the ground to an individual rusher last season. Of course, NFL teams aren't that dumb. If you can't run against someone, try to pass. The result: the Saints were ranked 20th against the pass in the league. Foes completed 61 percent of their passes and threw for 27 touchdowns on New Orleans, which Phillips admits used only three coverages all year.

"We'll get fancier this time around," he says, but whether Phillips has the personnel to accomplish that is another question. He was starting five rookies on the unit by the final game, including two in the secondary, cornerback Johnnie Poe and strong safety Russell Gary. In linebackers Rickey Jackson and Glen Redd, he came up with two young standouts, but the Saints will have to do equally as well with newcomers this season. Ex-Steeler linebacker

Dennis Winston could help, playing behind the Saints' solid front three—Derland Moore, Jerry Boyarsky and Elois Grooms.

KICKING GAME: Considering the Saints' dismal 4–12 record, their special teams held up well. Jeff Groth was fourth in the league in punt returns, Wayne Wilson was 10th in kickoff returns and punter Russell Erxleben had a solid year. Phillips needs a better year from placekicker Benny Ricardo, who made only 13 of 25 field-goal tries.

George Rogers topped all rushers with 1,674 yards.

SAINTS VETERAN ROSTER

HEAD COACH—O. A. (Bum) Phillips. Assistant Coaches—King Hill, John Levra, Lamar McHan, Carl Mauck, Russell Paternostro, Wade Phillips, Harold Richardson, Joe Spencer, Lance Van Zandt, John Paul Young, Willie Zapalac, Andy Everest.

No.	Name	Pos.	Ht.	Wt.	NFL Exp.	College
61	Adams, Sam	G	6-3	260	11	Prairie View A&M
63	Bennett, Barry	DT	6-4	257	5	Concordia (Minn.)
91	Bennett, Monte	DT	6-3	260	2	Kansas State
50	Bordelon, Ken	LB	6-4	226	6	Louisiana State
77	Boyarsky, Jerry	DT	6-3	290	2	Pittsburgh
85	Brenner, Hoby	TE	6-4	240	2	Southern California
67	Brock, Stan	T	6-6	275	3	Colorado
14	Erxleben, Russell	P	6-4	218	3	Texas
59	Evans, Chuck	LB	6-3	235	3	Stanford
20	Gary, Russell	SS	5-11	195	2	Nebraska
78	Grooms, Elois	DE	6-4	250	8	Tennessee Tech
48	Groth, Jeff	WR	5-10	172	4	Bowling Green
87	Hardy, Larry	TE	6-3	230	5	Jackson State
82	Harris, Ike	WR	6-3	210	8	Iowa State
62	Hill, John	C	6-2	246	11	Lehigh
45	Holmes, Jack	FB	6-0	210	5	Texas Southern
69	Hudson, Nat	G	6-3	270	2	Georgia
57	Jackson, Rickey	LB	6-2	230	2	Pittsburgh
52	Kovach, Jim	LB	6-2	225	4	Kentucky
64	Lafary, Dave	T	6-7	280	6	Purdue
8	Manning, Archie	QB	6-3	200	12	Mississippi
86	Martini, Rich	WR	6-2	185	4	California-Davis
56	Mathis, Reggie	LB	6-2	220	3	Oklahoma
84	Mauti, Rich	WR	6-0	190	5	Penn State
19	Merkens, Guido	WR	6-1	195	5	Sam Houston State
74	Moore, Derland	DT	6-4	253	10	Oklahoma
37	Myers, Tommy	FS	5-11	180	11	Syracuse
55	Nairne, Rob	LB	6-4	227	6	Oregon State
83	Owens, Tinker	WR	5-11	170	6	Oklahoma
53	Pelluer, Scott	LB	6-2	215	2	Washington State
76	Pietrzak, Jim	C	6-5	260	8	Eastern Michigan
25	Poe, Johnnie	CB	6-1	182	2	Missouri
58	Redd, Glen	LB	6-1	225	2	Brigham Young
1	Ricardo, Benny	K	5-10	170	6	San Diego State
38	Rogers, George	RB	6-2	220	2	South Carolina
41	Rogers, Jimmy	RB	5-10	190	3	Oklahoma
54	Ryczek, Paul	C	6-2	245	8	Virginia
12	Scott, Bobby	QB	6-1	197	11	Tennessee
47	Spivey, Mike	CB	6-0	198	6	Colorado
32	Stauch, Scott	FB	5-11	204	2	UCLA
68	Sturt, Fred	G	6-4	235	8	Bowling Green
71	Taylor, James	T	6-4	265	5	Missouri
89	Thompson, Aundra	WR	6-1	186	6	East Texas State
42	Tyler, Toussaint	FB	6-2	220	2	Washington
73	Warren, Frank	DE	6-4	275	2	Auburn
49	Wattelet, Frank	FS	6-0	185	2	Kansas
44	Waymer, Dave	CB	6-1	195	3	Notre Dame
94	Wilks, Jim	DT	6-4	252	2	San Diego State
18	Wilson, Dave	QB	6-3	195	2	Illinois
30	Wilson, Wayne	RB	6-3	208	4	Shepherd
	Winston, Dennis	LB	6-0	228	6	Arkansas

TOP FIVE DRAFT CHOICES

Rd.	Name	Sel. No.	Pos.	Ht.	Wt.	College
1	Scott, Lindsay	13	WR	6-1	190	Georgia
2	Edelman, Brad	30	C	6-6	255	Missouri
3	Lewis, Rodney	58	DB	5-11	190	Nebraska
3	Goodlow, Eugene	66	WR	6-2	190	Kansas State
3	Duckett, Ken	68	WR	6-0	187	Wake Forest

THE ROOKIES: Wide receiver Lindsay Scott of Georgia is just what the Saints need—a speedy deep threat to replace Chandler. Center Brad Edelman of Missouri was the best at his spot last year, but many thought Nebraska cornerback Rodney Lewis was overrated.

OUTLOOK: Small steps—that's the Saints' approach. Phillips can't expect to make up for years of bad drafting and turmoil that quickly, and he is trying to take his time. But he has to show he can coach an offense that includes a good passing game, something that was also missing from his Houston teams.

SAINT PROFILES

ARCHIE MANNING 33 6-3 200   **Quarterback**

More and more talk about Saints getting rid of their long-time starting quarterback...And Manning doesn't hide fact he'd love to play on winning team before retiring...Whether Saints can get better before he gets too old is the question...Highest-paid quarterback in the league, so he isn't suffering in the grocery line...Had injury problems at times last season, but still connected on 57.8 percent of passes for 1,447 yards...But miseries are nothing new for him...Has thrown for more than 20,000 yards for his career...Born May 19, 1949, in Cleveland, Miss....Mississippi grad's first name is really Elisha.

GEORGE ROGERS 23 6-2 220   **Running Back**

How about putting the Heisman Trophy jinx to rest after the rookie season this man had?...Led entire NFL in rushing (1,674 yards, 4.4 avg, 13 TDs), despite presence of many veteran superstars...Now Saints have to give him some more help...There were doubts about how good he would be, but those were put to rest...Has that wonderful combination of power and speed...Even his high school has retired his jersey...Born Dec. 8, 1958, in Duluth, Ga....Left South Carolina as NCAA's fourth all-time ground gainer with 4,958 yards...Also South Carolina's first consensus All-American.

RUSSELL ERXLEBEN 25 6-4 218   Punter

Finally has silenced whispers he was not a capable NFL player... Had trouble adjusting to doing both placekicking and punting. Now that he only has to worry about the latter, he is much more consistent and much more dangerous... With the strength in that powerful leg, he should be among the top punters for years to come... But wouldn't mind getting back to placekicking, which he did so well at Texas (14 field goals from 50 yards or more)... Spent 1979 season on injured reserve... One of only four kickers ever chosen on first round... Has degrees in business and finances... Born Jan. 13, 1957, in Seguin, Tex.

RICH MAUTI 28 6-0 190   Wide Receiver

Even with 1981 injury, he is still considered one of the best special teamers around... But ailment ruined bid to make a name for himself as a receiver, too... Doesn't like his future if he has to rely only on suicide-squad work... Not very healthy for the body, either... A tailback at Penn State who was signed as a free agent and moved immediately to the outside... Born May 25, 1954, in Hollis Place, N.Y.... Gives $1 per return yard and $10 per tackle to American Cancer Society.

ELOIS GROOMS 29 6-4 250   Defensive End

The kind of player coach Bum Phillips loves... Never complains, never slacks off and always seems to be improving... Little-known throughout the league, but is just really learning how to play and should get better with this new coaching staff... Has weight room in his garage and takes pride in increased strength... Born May 30, 1953, in Tompkinsville, Ky.... Champion trapshooter, one reason he loves to hunt and fish... Only Saints' defensive lineman to start every game in last four years... Only a third-round draft choice in the 1975 pickings, out of Tennessee Tech.

TOMMY MYERS 31 5-11 180   Safety

Lends defensive mates stability and brains, along with a lot of big plays . . . Talks about retiring and pursuing some of his many off-the-field interests . . . Manages rental property and farms Filbert nuts, among other pursuits . . . An All-American at Syracuse, where he broke Floyd Little's punt return records . . . Has physical education degree . . . Born Oct. 24, 1950, in Cohoes, N.Y., but now lives in Oregon . . . Plays the guitar and piano and has worked as a counselor of juveniles.

JIM KOVACH 26 6-2 230   Linebacker

Here is one of the most intriguing stories in the NFL . . . While he was playing his senior year at Kentucky, he also was attending medical school . . . Try that on for mental wear . . . Was second on club in tackles with 115 last year . . . Phi Beta Kappa . . . And still has become a fine player in the pros . . . Born May 1, 1956, in Parma Heights, Ohio . . . He's the type of athlete that the NCAA likes to brag about when it is criticized for overemphasis on athletics vs. academics . . . When he has time, he plays golf to relax.

JACK HOLMES 29 6-0 210   Running Back

Who would have thought that this free-agent pick-up would become a Saints' offensive mainstay last season? . . . Led the team in receptions with 38 to help bail out depleted passing attack . . . Also finished second on team to George Rogers in rushing in Holmes' fourth year in the league . . . Previously he had been known for his special-team play . . . Had started seven games in 1980, catching 29 passes . . . Product of Texas Southern, where he was all-conference for two years . . . Born June 20, 1953, in Rolling Fork, Miss. . . . Enjoys fishing and playing basketball and tennis in the offseason.

RICKEY JACKSON 24 6–2 230   Linebacker

The Saints knew they had a good one in George Rogers, but got added bonus when this active linebacker walked into a starting role and played outstanding football all season...He was a defensive end at Pittsburgh opposite Hugh Green, but didn't receive the same publicity...Both made transition to linebacker in the pros with flying colors...His main college duty was pass defense, which made transition to linebacker that much easier for him...All-star three times in football and twice in basketball in Florida...Born March 20, 1958, in Pahokee, Fla....Hobbies are checkers and fishing.

BENNY RICARDO 27 5–10 170   Placekicker

Didn't become a Saint until after second game of the 1980 season, but team is very happy with the decision to sign him...Taken a lot of pressure off Russell Erxleben, allowing him to do the punting chores...Established school records for most field goals in a game, season and career at San Diego State...Born Jan. 4, 1954, in Asuncion, Paraguay...Began career with Lions, but when he wanted more money, Detroit just released him...An accomplished racquetball player...Appeared in the film "North Dallas Forty" in 1978...Majored in accounting and journalism...Last year he hit 13 of 25 field-goal attempts and 24 of 24 PATs.

COACH BUM PHILLIPS

...After only one season, the fans in New Orleans worship him...Has given the franchise stability and hope for the future...Didn't promise that much success in first season, but wound up exceeding expectations...Now the Saints are competitive, but he wants them to become contenders...All he did was win in Houston (59–31), and that got him fired...Don't look for same fate here if he can get above .500...Instead he may become mayor of the city...A player's coach...Oilers loved him and a lot of guys would love to be traded to his team...Has a marvelous dry wit and remains down to earth, despite his increasing fame...Been

Bum ever since his baby sister tried to pronounce brother instead of his infinitely more difficult name, Oail...Son, Wade, is now Saints' defensive coordinator...Born Sept. 29, 1923, in Orange, Tex....Noted defensive coach before getting his first head coaching job.

GREATEST LINEBACKER

When the Saints were playing coach Dick Nolan's flex defense, Joe Federspiel was known as the sheriff of Flex County. Outside of New Orleans, few recognized his skills. That's one of the problems playing for a bad team for so many years. But amid seasons of mediocrity, he was a rare gem.

For nine seasons, until he was released in 1981, Federspiel was the heart of the Saints' defense. He led the club in tackles five years and had over 150 for three straight seasons, including an unofficial record of 157 in 1978. During that time, he missed only

Archie Manning hopes for injury-free year this time around.

one game despite the constant battering inherent in his middle linebacker position.

Coming out of college, no one could have predicted that the 6-2, 230-pound Federspiel would last so long and play so well in the pros. Although he was All-Southeastern Conference pick at Kentucky, he lasted until the fourth round of the 1972 draft. But he made the all-rookie team his first year to become a fixture in the middle of the Saints' defense.

INDIVIDUAL SAINT RECORDS

Rushing

Most Yards Game:	162	George Rogers, vs Los Angeles, 1981
Season:	1,674	George Rogers, 1981
Career:	3,218	Chuck Muncie, 1976–79

Passing

Most TD Passes Game:	6	Billy Kilmer, vs St. Louis, 1969
Season:	23	Archie Manning, 1980
Career:	115	Archie Manning, 1971–81

Receiving

Most TD Passes Game:	3	Dan Abramowicz, vs San Francisco, 1971
Season:	9	Henry Childs, 1977
Career:	37	Dan Abramowicz, 1967–72

Scoring

Most Points Game:	18	Walt Roberts, vs Philadelphia, 1967
	18	Dan Abramowicz, vs San Francisco, 1971
	18	Archie Manning, vs Chicago, 1977
	18	Chuck Muncie, vs San Francisco, 1979
	18	George Rogers, vs Los Angeles, 1981
Season:	99	Tom Dempsey, 1969
Career:	243	Charlie Durkee, 1967–68, 1971–72
Most TDs Game:	3	Walt Roberts, vs Philadelphia, 1967
	3	Dan Abramowicz, vs San Francisco, 1971
	3	Archie Manning, vs Chicago, 1977
	3	Chuck Muncie, vs San Francisco, 1979
	3	George Rogers, vs Los Angeles, 1981
Season:	13	George Rogers, 1981
Career:	37	Dan Abramowicz, 1967–72

NEW YORK GIANTS

TEAM DIRECTORY: Pres.: Wellington Mara; VP-Treasurer: Timothy Mara; GM: George Young; Dir. Pro Personnel: Jim Trimble; Dir. Pub. Rel.: Ed Croke; Head Coach: Ray Perkins. Home field: Giants Stadium (76,500). Colors: Blue, red and white.

SCOUTING REPORT

OFFENSE: If you just look at what the Giants did in the playoffs, it's hard to remember how lackluster this offense was last season,

Rob Carpenter helped make Giants a postseason entry.

ranking dead last in the league. Among the NFC teams, only Chicago scored less points, which means that coach Ray Perkins still hasn't brought New York all the way back to a point where it is a consistent force every weekend.

But getting Rob Carpenter in trade from Houston has taken the offensive rebuilding plans a major step forward. He provides the team with its first legitimate rusher in years, but if he gets hurt or worn down, the same old running troubles will resurface. This team needs a better fullback, more running depth and a decision on a starting quarterback. Perkins is well aware that a delay in choosing between Scott Brunner and Phil Simms could divide the team and ruin its momentum.

Jim Clack has retired again, leaving the center spot for Ernie Hughes. The rest of the line performed well down the stretch, once Perkins moved Jeff Weston ahead of Brad Benson at tackle. At one receiver, Earnest Gray has great speed, but not the consistency the Giants would like. They'd also like to find someone to replace him.

DEFENSE: For years, even when they were losing, the Giants could take pride in one area—their linebacking. Their pride is really showing now, with the addition of Lawrence Taylor. Taylor still has to learn some of his position's more subtle ways, but when he goes after a quarterback there seems little need for more experience.

Taylor's presence turned this unit into a big-play, tough, tough outfit. Only two other teams in the league ranked higher and, with so many youngsters aboard, there could be better days ahead. Remember, the Giants played well at season's end, even with linebacker Brad Van Pelt injured. Harry Carson had a Pro Bowl season, and Mark Haynes improved dramatically at cornerback to become one of the best around. Gary Jeter plays like a roller coaster at defensive end, the pass rush isn't always the best and Bill Neill is an awfully young middle guard, but who's quibbling?

Terry Jackson isn't a Haynes at the other cornerback, but he's good and safeties Bill Currier and Beasley Reece don't hurt you with too many mistakes. That's important on a unit that lives by causing turnovers and not giving up big plays.

KICKING GAME: If CFL import Leon Bright stays healthy, the Giants would have a much improved return game. By ridding themselves of Alvin Garrett, New York made its commitment to Bright. Punter Dave Jennings and placekicker Joe Danelo are among the league's best.

GIANTS VETERAN ROSTER

HEAD COACH—Ray Perkins. Assistant Coaches—Bill Austin, Ernie Adams, Bill Belichick, Romeo Crennel, Fred Glick, Pat Hodgson, Lamar Leachman, Bob Lord, Bill Parcells, Ron Erhardt.

No.	Name	Pos.	Ht.	Wt.	NFL Exp.	College
	Anderson, Anthony	RB	6-0	200	3	Temple
67	Ard, Billy	G	6-3	250	2	Wake Forest
60	Benson, Brad	T	6-3	258	5	Penn State
45	Bright, Leon	RB	5-9	192	2	Florida State
12	Brunner, Scott	QB	6-5	200	3	Delaware
64	Burt, Jim	DT	6-1	255	2	Miami
26	Carpenter, Rob	RB	6-1	230	6	Miami (O.)
53	Carson, Harry	LB	6-2	235	7	South Carolina State
29	Currier, Bill	S	6-0	195	6	South Carolina
18	Danelo, Joe	K	5-9	166	8	Washington State
46	Dennis, Mike	CB	5-10	190	3	Wyoming
37	Flowers, Larry	S	6-1	190	2	Texas Tech
35	Forte, Ike	RB	6-0	210	7	Arkansas
88	Friede, Mike	WR	6-3	205	3	Indiana
83	Gray, Earnest	WR	6-3	195	4	Memphis State
79	Hardison, Dee	DE	6-4	269	5	North Carolina
36	Haynes, Mark	CB	5-11	185	3	Colorado
27	Heater, Larry	RB	5-11	205	3	Arizona
61	Hughes, Ernie	C	6-3	265	4	Notre Dame
57	Hunt, Byron	LB	6-4	230	2	Southern Methodist
21	Jackson, Louis	RB	5-11	195	2	California Poly-SLO
24	Jackson, Terry	CB	5-11	197	5	San Diego State
13	Jennings, Dave	P	6-4	205	9	St. Lawrence
70	Jeter, Gary	DE	6-4	260	6	Southern California
	Johnson, Dennis	RB	6-3	220	5	Mississippi State
55	Kelley, Brian	LB	6-3	222	10	California-Lutheran
72	King, Gordon	T	6-6	275	5	Stanford
44	Kotar, Doug	RB	5-11	205	9	Kentucky
71	Lapka, Myron	DT	6-4	260	2	Southern California
54	Lloyd, Dan	LB	6-2	225	5	Washington
51	Marion, Frank	LB	6-3	228	6	Florida A&M
75	Martin, George	DE	6-4	245	8	Oregon
59	McGlasson, Ed	C	6-4	248	4	Youngstown State
76	McGriff, Curtis	DE	6-5	265	3	Alabama
52	McLaughlin, Joe	LB	6-1	235	4	Massachusetts
81	Mistler, John	WR	6-2	186	2	Arizona State
81	Mullady, Tom	TE	6-3	232	4	Southwest at Memphis
77	Neill, Bill	DT	6-4	255	2	Pittsburgh
86	Perkins, Johnny	WR	6-2	205	6	Abilene Christian
30	Perry, Leon	RB	5-11	224	3	Mississippi
82	Pittman, Danny	WR	6-2	205	3	Wyoming
28	Reece, Beasley	S	6-1	195	7	North Texas State
87	Shirk, Gary	TE	6-1	220	7	Morehead State
69	Simmons, Roy	G	6-3	264	4	Georgia Tech
11	Simms, Phil	QB	6-3	216	4	Morehead State
65	Sinnott, John	T	6-4	275	3	Brown
80	Tabor, Paul	DE	6-4	255	4	Oklahoma
56	Taylor, Lawrence	LB	6-3	242	2	North Carolina
68	Turner, J. T.	G	6-3	250	6	Duke
10	Van Pelt, Brad	LB	6-5	235	10	Michigan State
73	Weston, Jeff	T	6-5	280	4	Notre Dame
62	Whittington, Mike	LB	6-2	220	3	Notre Dame
	Wyatt, Kervin	LB	6-1	235	3	Maryland
89	Young, Dave	TE	6-6	242	2	Purdue

TOP FIVE DRAFT CHOICES

Rd.	Name	Sel. No.	Pos.	Ht.	Wt.	College
1	Woolfolk, Butch	18	RB	6-2	207	Michigan
2	Morris, Joe	45	RB	5-7	182	Syracuse
4	Raymond, Gerry	102	C	6-3	256	Boston College
5	Umphrey, Rich	129	C	6-3	253	Colorado
6	Nicholson, Darrell	156	LB	6-2	234	North Carolina

THE ROOKIES: Even though Carpenter was so good last season, the Giants still felt they needed more runners, so they drafted Michigan's Butch Woolfolk and Syracuse's Joe Morris on the first two rounds. Morris, the little scatback, could surprise. Center Rich Umphrey of Colorado may press for starting time.

OUTLOOK: A team on the move, but one that already has had its coming-out party in the playoffs. That will put more pressure on the players and Perkins this year. If he can straighten out his quarterback crowd, then the Giants have enough ability, especially on defense, to reach the playoffs again.

GIANT PROFILES

PHIL SIMMS 26 6–3 216   **Quarterback**

For the second straight year, he finished season on the sidelines with an injury (collarbone) while Scott Brunner did the quarterbacking... Burnner played so well that Simms will have to win job back in training camp... Until he was hurt against the Redskins, he was maturing into kind of quarterback Giants expected when he was drafted on first round three years ago... Threw for 11 touchdowns and 54.4 completion percentage ... "I'd love to see the average person get back there and have the Dallas Cowboys rush at them," he says... Born Nov. 3, 1955, in Lebanon, Ky.... He's done pretty good job of handling media pressure after coming from low-key program at Morehead State.

SCOTT BRUNNER 25 6–5 200   **Quarterback**

Made the most of his chance last season... Was the quarterback during the Giants' year-end rush to a playoff berth... Did wonderful job in playoff win over the Eagles... Quiet, confident although he comes from small-time college football program at Delaware, where he replaced Detroit's Jeff Komlo at quarterback... A sixth-round pick, he was chosen for insurance... Born March 24, 1957, in Lawrence, N.J.... His father is offensive backfield coach with Detroit Lions... Former participant in Pass, Punt and Kick contest.

DAVE JENNINGS 30 6-4 205   **Punter**

He was Houston's property for 2½ weeks and now ranks as one of the Giants' prime free-agent pickups of all-time...Articulate, outspoken, whimsical....Not one of the biggest backers of the NFL Players Association ...Among the very best at his trade in the league, he averaged 43.3 yards a kick last season...A budding radio and TV announcer, he is a gifted athlete who won the Superstars competition and is a star on the club's offseason basketball team...Sets a club or conference record almost with every punt...Born June 8, 1952, in New York City...Attended St. Lawrence...Third cousin of White Sox' Carlton Fisk...Father is former college president.

ROB CARPENTER 27 6-1 230   **Running Back**

He made the Giants into a playoff contender after coming over from Houston for a third-round draft choice...Gave the team a much-needed running threat...Giant fans will long remember his virtuoso performance in playoffs against the Eagles...He called it "the greatest thrill of my career, because for the first time I made the difference in an important game"...Grew tired of being Earl Campbell's caddy with the Oilers...Says he found out, however, that a team can't win by relying just on one offensive threat...Born April 20, 1955, in Lancaster, Ohio...Gained prominence when, as an Oiler, he played well against San Diego in playoffs after being on crutches day of the game...Attended Miami of Ohio.

LAWRENCE TAYLOR 23 6-3 242   **Linebacker**

Came in highly touted and exceeded his clippings...Only standout season by George Rogers prevented him from running away with Rookie of the Year honors...Given freedom in the Giant defense to ad-lib and rush the passer (9½ sacks)...Proved to be almost unstoppable ...Opponents would pull a guard and hope that would stop his blitzes...A superb physical specimen who is blessed with extraordinary quickness...Didn't play football until his junior year in high school...Began career at North Carolina as a nose guard...Born Feb. 4, 1959, in Williamsburg, Va....ACC Player of the Year as a senior.

HARRY CARSON 28 6-2 235   Linebacker

Came back from injury-riddled season to once again rank among the best in the league... With Lawrence Taylor thriving on the outside, Carson was able to roam more freely inside... No one really controlled him throughout the season... Rest of team finally caught up to his level... Once threatened to quit and join the Air Force—that's how frustrating things had gotten with the Giants... Loves music, fishing and target shooting and he's also devoted to watching soap operas on TV... Even appeared in one TV tear jerker... Born Nov. 23, 1953, in Florence, S.C.... Former South Carolina State star still has many quality years ahead of him.

JOE DANELO 28 5-9 166   Kicker

Enjoyed by far his best season as a pro last year... His 103 points were 13 more than his previous high.... Twenty-four successful field goals also were personal best... Getting into the spotlight finally allowed him to tell everyone that he doesn't really play the concertina anymore... "Haven't in 10 years," he says... But he loves to run waist-deep in ocean water, remodel apartments, build patios and furniture and work as a stevedore... His 55-yarder against New Orleans was a club record, breaking standard that stood since 1970... Traded from Green Bay for a seventh-round pick after a three-year career at Washington State... Born Sept. 2, 1953, in Spokane, Wash.

BRAD VAN PELT 31 6-5 235   Linebacker

Finally had thrill of seeing team make the playoffs after all his years of personal success while the club floundered.... Had another fine season, helped in part by the emergence of Lawrence Taylor on the other side... Which way do opponents run their sweeps?... The Giants picked him No. 1 in 1973, but could have lost the Michigan State star to major-league baseball, where he probably would have been a star pitcher.... A perennial Pro Bowl performer... Born April 5, 1951, in Owosso, Mich., where he became one of the town's most fabled athletes... Turned down $100,000 bonus to become St. Louis Cardinal baseball player... Former Pass, Punt and Kick winner.

GARY JETER 27 6–4 260   Defensive End

Will be haunted by his personal foul call against San Francisco that all but ended the Giants' chances of winning that playoff game... Marred an otherwise fine season as the team's best pass rusher (7 sacks)... Can be a highly quotable, accessible person... Has been in-and-out player as pro despite glowing reputation he earned at USC... Took him two seasons to win a starting job, but should hold on to spot for years to come... Born Jan. 24, 1955, in Weirton, W.Va., but grew up in Cleveland, where he had an outstanding athletic career... Uncles Tony and Bob Jeter are former NFL players... Probably will become lawyer eventually.

MARK HAYNES 23 5–11 185   Cornerback

After a disappointing rookie year, he more than lived up to expectations in 1981... Became one of the best corners in the conference, if not the league... Suddenly, the Giants seem very solid at this troublesome position... Gives credit to added maturity and confidence... Giant coaches never panicked and stuck with him... They also helped by putting him at left cornerback after slow start his rookie year at the right side... Born Nov. 6, 1958, in Kansas City, Mo.... Legendary high-school athlete in Kansas City, where he was three-sport star... Attended Colorado, where he switched from running back to cornerback.

COACH RAY PERKINS... When Giants made the playoffs last

season, suddenly he wasn't being criticized as much... Now he is considered miracle worker for the way he has turned around this down-trodden franchise... Not very open and friendly with the press, which has contributed to his image as a sour, serious type... But he sure does know his offensive football... Working with inexperienced quarterbacks and makeshift line, but got the most he could out of the whole bunch... Leads the league in no-quotes and no comments about surprise moves... Puts in long, long hours and is completely dedicated to winning... May burn himself out in the process... Born Nov. 6, 1941, in Mt. Olive, Miss.... Played for Bear Bryant at Alabama, where he was a star receiver... Another product of Don

Rookie Lawrence Taylor was NFL Defensive Player of the Year.

Coryell's offensive philosophy . . . Went 6–10 and 4–12 first two seasons with Giants before last year's 9–7 and first-round upset of Eagles.

GREATEST LINEBACKER

Long before New York's Sam Huff turned linebacker into a glamor position by making it his own personal violent world, the

Giants had another special player at that position, Mel Hein, a 6-3, 235-pound iron man who never missed a game during his 15-year career.

Hein played both ways from 1931–45, and was an All-NFL selection 10 times, including eight straight from 1933 to 1940. That string began the season that included perhaps his best-ever game, a 23–21 NFL title-game loss to the Bears.

On that memorable afternoon, Hein played both center and linebacker. On one trick play, he lined up on the end of the line as a center, snapped the ball, then got it back and rushed for 18 yards and a big first down. On defense, he was the leading tackler, harassing Red Grange and Bronco Nagurski and leading goal-line stands which stopped three long drives and forced the Bears to kick field goals.

It took that kind of play for Hein to overshadow even the likes of Huff, whose modern-day jousts with Jimmy Brown led to his inclusion, like Hein's, in the Hall of Fame.

INDIVIDUAL GIANT RECORDS

Rushing

Most Yards Game:	218	Gene Roberts, vs Chi. Cardinals, 1950
Season:	1,182	Ron Johnson, 1972
Career:	4,638	Alex Webster, 1955–64

Passing

Most TD Passes Game:	7	Y. A. Tittle, vs Washington, 1962
Season:	36	Y. A. Tittle, 1963
Career:	173	Charley Conerly, 1948–61

Receiving

Most TD Passes Game:	4	Earnest Gray, vs St. Louis, 1980
Season:	13	Homer Jones, 1967
Career:	48	Kyle Rote, 1951–61

Scoring

Most Points Game:	24	Ron Johnson, vs Philadelphia, 1972
	24	Earnest Gray, vs St. Louis, 1980
Season:	107	Pete Gogolak, 1970
Career:	646	Pete Gogolak, 1966–74
Most TDs Game:	4	Ron Johnson, vs Philadelphia, 1972
	4	Earnest Gray, vs St. Louis, 1980
Season:	17	Gene Roberts, 1949
Career:	78	Frank Gifford, 1952–60, 1962–64

PHILADELPHIA EAGLES

TEAM DIRECTORY: Pres.: Leonard Tose; GM: Jim Murray; Bus. Mgr.: Jim Borden; Dir. Player Personnel: Carl Peterson; Dir. Pub. Rel.: Jim Gallagher; Head Coach: Dick Vermeil. Home field: Veterans Stadium (72,200). Colors: Kelly green, white and silver.

SCOUTING REPORT

OFFENSE: Dick Vermeil found that life without Sid Gillman wasn't very enjoyable last season, so he has coaxed his offensive guru back to Philly to watch over quarterback Ron Jaworski and try to add some spice to the Eagles' bland diet.

Jaworski was blamed for much of the Eagles' offensive inconsistency and predictability last year. When Philadelphia lost six of its last 10, including four straight, the Eagles couldn't come up with the big plays on offense, something Vermeil wants to correct by adding more quickness and upgrading the skills of some of his offensive specialists.

The most glaring area that he needs to improve is wide receiver, where Harold Carmichael just isn't enough. There is a lack of speed that defenses long ago recognized, and now Vermeil has found out that execution alone is not enough. His offensive line allowed only 22 sacks, fourth fewest in the NFL, and it blocked well enough for Wilbert Montgomery to gain 1,402 yards. But tackle Stan Walters could be on the downside of his career.

Vermeil would be happy if he could find more backfield speed to give the overworked Montgomery a break.

DEFENSE: Vermeil loves to point out that he has used most of his best draft choices to pick defensive players, so maybe that's why the Eagles have the best defense in the league and the offense is struggling. Even if that emphasis changes in future years, Philadelphia should remain a constant defensive force for seasons to come, under the instruction of coordinator Marion Campbell.

The Eagles allowed the fewest points (221) and the least amount of yards (277.9 per game) in the league. They are a fine example of how the sum can be better than the individual parts. Other than cornerback Roynell Young, linebacker Jerry Robinson and linemen Carl Hairston and Charlie Johnson, this is not a team of great personnel. But Campbell has them playing so well together that it's difficult for offenses to concentrate on any particular weakness.

Even the loss of linebacker Bill Bergey last year hardly caused a problem, with youngster Al Chesley stepping in to tie Frank

LeMaster for most tackles. And the team could be even stronger if end Leonard Mitchell asserts himself after an injury-prone freshman year.

KICKING GAME: Tony Franklin got out of Vermeil's doghouse last season and kicked with the ability he showed in college. Max

Tony Franklin's accurate kicking kept the Eagles soaring.

EAGLES VETERAN ROSTER

HEAD COACH—Dick Vermeil. Assistant Coaches—John Becker, Fred Bruney, Marion Campbell, Chuck Clausen, Dick Coury, George Hill, Ken Iman, Lynn Stiles, Jerry Wampfler, Sid Gillman.

No.	Name	Pos.	Ht.	Wt.	NFL Exp.	College
38	Atkins, Steve	FB	6-0	219	4	Maryland
63	Baker, Ron	G	6-4	250	5	Oklahoma State
27	Blackmore, Richard	CB	5-10	174	4	Mississippi State
	Brown, Aaron	LB	6-2	235	4	Ohio State
98	Brown, Gregory	DE	6-5	240	2	Kansas State
95	Bunting, John	LB	6-1	220	11	North Carolina
37	Campfield, Billy	RB	6-0	205	5	Kansas
17	Carmichael, Harold	WR	6-8	225	12	Southern
59	Chesley, Al	LB	6-3	240	4	Pittsburgh
71	Clarke, Ken	DT	6-2	255	5	Syracuse
57	Curcio, Mike	LB	6-1	237	2	Temple
46	Edwards, Herm	CB	6-0	194	6	San Diego State
24	Ellis, Ray	CB-S	6-1	192	2	Ohio State
86	Folsom, Steve	TE	6-4	230	2	Utah
1	Franklin, Tony	K	5-8	182	4	Texas A&M
33	Giammona, Louie	RB-KR	5-9	180	6	Utah State
79	Giddens, Frank	T	6-7	300	2	New Mexico
78	Hairston, Carl	DE	6-3	260	7	Maryland State
35	Harrington, Perry	FB	5-11	210	3	Jackson State
20	Harris, Leroy	FB	5-9	230	4	Arkansas State
89	Henry, Wally	WR-PR	5-8	180	6	UCLA
	Hooks, Alven	WR	5-11	170	2	California-Northridge
87	Humphrey, Claude	DE	6-5	258	15	Tennessee State
7	Jaworski, Ron	QB	6-2	185	8	Youngstown State
	Johnson, Charles	DT	6-1	262	4	Maryland
65	Johnson, Charlie	DT	6-3	265	6	Colorado
73	Kenney, Steve	G	6-4	262	3	Clemson
	King, Jerome	S-CB	5-10	175	2	Purdue
84	Krepfle, Keith	TE	6-3	230	8	Iowa State
55	LeMaster, Frank	LB	6-2	238	9	Kentucky
41	Logan, Randy	S	6-1	195	10	Michigan
99	Mitchell, Leonard	DE	6-7	272	2	Houston
31	Montgomery, Wilbert	RB	5-10	195	6	Abilene Christian
50	Morriss, Guy	C	6-4	255	10	Texas Christian
42	Murray, Calvin	RB	5-11	185	2	Ohio State
34	Oliver, Hubert	FB	5-10	212	2	Arizona
83	Parker, Rodney	WR	6-1	190	3	Tennessee State
62	Perot, Pete	G	6-2	261	4	Northwest Louisiana
52	Phillips, Ray	LB	6-4	230	6	Nebraska
9	Pisarcik, Joe	QB	6-4	220	6	New Mexico State
56	Robinson, Jerry	LB	6-2	216	4	UCLA
4	Runager, Max	P	6-1	189	4	South Carolina
32	Russell, Booker	FB	6-2	235	5	Southwest Texas State
21	Sciarra, John	S	5-11	185	5	UCLA
76	Sisemore, Jerry	T	6-4	265	10	Texas
61	Slater, Mark	C	6-2	257	5	Minnesota
85	Smith, Charles	WR	6-1	185	9	Grambling
81	Smith, Ron	WR	6-0	185	5	San Diego State
88	Spagnola, John	TE	6-4	240	4	Yale
	Steptoe, Jack	WR	6-1	175	3	Utah
42	Wagner, Steve	LB	6-2	208	6	Wisconsin
75	Walters, Stan	T	6-6	275	11	Syracuse
51	Wilkes, Reggie	LB	6-4	230	5	Georgia Tech
22	Wilson, Brenard	S	6-0	175	4	Vanderbilt
43	Young, Roynell	CB	6-1	181	3	Alcorn State

TOP FIVE DRAFT CHOICES

Rd.	Name	Sel. No.	Pos.	Ht.	Wt.	College
1	Quick, Mike	20	WR	6-2	186	North Carolina State
2	Sampleton, Larry	47	TE	6-6	230	Texas
3	Kab, Vyto	78	TE	6-4	246	Penn State
4	Griggs, Anthony	105	LB	6-2	221	Ohio State
5	DeVaughan, Dennis	132	DB	5-10	175	Bishop

Runager is not spectacular as a punter, but he gives Vermeil the consistency he wants. Not so with Wally Henry, who struggled as a return man and might lose his job this year.

THE ROOKIES: Vermeil's quest for more quickness led him to draft receiver Mike Quick of North Carolina State as his No. 1 pick. Quick has the talent, but had an off year his senior season. Tight end Lawrence Sampleton of Texas could be awesome or, if not motivated, a bust.

OUTLOOK: The Eagles' late-season decline casts them as an unpredictable team this season. But with Gillman around again and a year to shake off those post-Super Bowl blues, Vermeil could have them contending for the NFL title once again. If not, he will wear out his players from too much work.

EAGLE PROFILES

RON JAWORSKI 31 6–2 185   Quarterback

Not the most popular athlete in Philadelphia ... Took the brunt of the criticism last season when the Eagles stumbled down the stretch ... Wasn't as sharp as in 1980 but didn't do as badly as the fans seemed to think. ... Claims he has learned to live with the booing, but don't believe it ... Missed the help of retired assistant Sid Gillman ... Jaworski threw for 3,095 yards and 23 touchdowns, both down from his totals of the year before ... Born March 23, 1951, in Lackawanna, N.Y. ... Partner in business that represents other pro athletes for promotional activities ... Youngstown State alumnus lends name to scholarship fund for deserving students.

TONY FRANKLIN 25 5–8 182   Kicker

Maybe has finally grown up and become mature player after bumpy early years with the Eagles ... Raised his point total to 101, making 20 of 31 field goals ... Much more reliable toward end of 1981 season than he was during comparable stretch in 1980 ... The better he kicked, the less coach Dick Vermeil criticized him ... Was the first kicker at Texas A&M to receive a full scholarship... Only player in NCAA history to kick two field goals of more than 60 yards in one game (64, 65 yards vs. Baylor)... Born Nov. 18, 1956, in Big Springs, Tex.... Halfback in high school before switching strictly to kicking.

WILBERT MONTGOMERY 27 5–10 195 Running Back

Entering the critical part of his career... How long can this very physical runner stand up to battering?... Limped off the field during first half of one game last year and looked as if he would be out for a couple of weeks, but wound up playing in the second half... While rest of offense slumped, Montgomery had his second-best year as a pro, gaining 1,402 yards and scoring eight touchdowns... Played at Abilene Christian, where there now is $60,000 Wilbert Montgomery scholarship fund ... Named Mississippi's Pro Athlete of the Year in 1980... Born Sept. 16, 1954, in Greenville, Miss.

HAROLD CARMICHAEL 32 6–8 225 Wide Receiver

After his record consecutive-game pass-catching streak was snapped at 127 in 1980, the tallest of receivers had a quiet season last year... Still caught 61 passes, which remarkably was the second-highest total of his career... For some reason, the Eagles don't throw to him that much... Just ask opponents for a list of receivers they fear the most and he'd be ranked highly.... Winner of NFL Man of the Year Award in 1980 for many community services... Was star basketball player at Southern, where he played both center and forward... Born Sept. 22, 1949, in Jacksonville, Fla... Would benefit if Eagles could improve quality of rest of receiving corps.

JERRY ROBINSON 25 6–2 216 Linebacker

With Bill Bergey sidelined, he became the team's premier linebacker in only his third season... The better he plays, the better it makes Dick Vermeil look, since it was Vermeil who insisted on drafting him No. 1 out of UCLA... Not bad progress for a former wide receiver... He once rushed for 350 yards and scored five touchdowns in a high-school game....Had track bests of 9.9 for the 100, 6–5 for the high jump, 23–2 for long jump...Born Dec. 18, 1956, in San Francisco ...Hopes for a post-football career in sports broadcasting...Warning to opponents: his best years are still ahead.

CARL HAIRSTON 29 6-3 260   Defensive End

One of the most intriguing players in the league...He's good, but he has unusual habit of being injured in almost every game...Usually necessitates injury timeout, then he's helped off the field and, within minutes, he returns ...Happens week after week...Still not recognized for being as good as he is...Can be one of the most dominating ends in the conference...Only a seventh-round pick from Maryland-Eastern Shore...Born Dec. 15, 1952, in Martinsville, Va....Drove a truck for a while before entering college...Now he drives quarterbacks crazy.

JOHN BUNTING 32 6-1 220   Linebacker

One of the steadiest and most inspiring linebackers in the game...Honest, friendly, a model player...A 10th-round 1972 draft pick who has paid off handsomely for Philly...Has an uncanny knack for being around the ball, but hasn't intercepted a pass the last two seasons...Born July 15, 1950, in Portland, Me....Has a B.S. in education from North Carolina, where he made honorable mention All-American...A veteran of four Bowls: Senior, Gator, Peach and Super...A big Baltimore Oriole fan...Took over starting job in 1974 and has held it since, except half of '78 season, when he suffered knee injury...Active in Philadelphia charities.

AL CHESLEY 25 6-3 240   Linebacker

The man who replaced Bill Bergey...Played well enough so Eagle defense never missed a step...An aggressive, talented hitter who still is learning the position...Not bad start, however, for an 11th-round draft choice...Prior to last season he was mostly special teams player...Majored in communications at Pittsburgh...Was a standout in college as a senior, but the pros weren't sure about his quickness...But he certainly has ample size... Could have played pro baseball out of high school... Born Aug. 23, 1957, in Washington, D.C.

HERMAN EDWARDS 28 6-0 194   Cornerback

Steady Herman anchors one of the most consistent secondaries in the league... No one plays more zone than Eagles, and no one plays zone better than Edwards... Articulate and outgoing, one of the best interviews around ... Added three more interceptions last year and now has 22 in five-year career.... Biggest play of career came in 1978, when he scooped up fumble and ran 26 yards for winning touchdown in final seconds to beat Giants... Born April 27, 1954, in Fort Monmouth, N.J.... Had a 3.5 grade-point average at San Diego State, where he majored in criminal justice... Active in boys' club work.

CHARLIE JOHNSON 30 6-3 265   Middle Guard

One of the premier defensive linemen in the game... Once people started recognizing his ability, he has won accolade after accolade ... And to think in 1977 he was only a seventh-round pick out of Colorado, where he was all-conference... Began his college career as All-American tight end in junior college... Usually leaves the game in passing situations... Born Jan. 17, 1952, in West Columbia, Tex.... Spent two years after high school in the Army, including tour in Vietnam, as a military policeman... Career almost cut short by a knee injury and operation late in his rookie season.

COACH DICK VERMEIL

... His invincibility crumbled last year as the Eagles stumbled en route to trying to get into the Super Bowl again... Astonished his critics by coming clean after the season and admitting team needed some help... Usually not that open... Probably has gotten more out of the talent available than he should have... Eagles never had been quick enough to be a top contender, but always exceeded expectations—until last season... Drives his players so hard that sometimes it backfires... Laid off practicing them in pads during season this year and says he won't make that mistake again . . . Defended use of Ron Jaworski in face of heavy criticism, but who else could he have used? . . . Missed the help of super assistant Sid Gillman, who had retired for a year . . . Born Oct. 30, 1936, in Calistoga, Cal. . . . Considered big risk when he came into the league, but he could go anywhere now after leading Philadelphia to Super Bowl in 1980.

GREATEST LINEBACKER

As long as Eagle and Giant fans can breathe and remember and argue, they will debate The Tackle.

It came late in the 1960 season, with elimination from the NFL title chase at stake. The Giants' Frank Gifford had the ball and was trying for extra yardage. Suddenly he was smashed by Eagle linebacker Chuck Bednarik. "It was one of the hardest tackles I

Ron Jaworski was booed despite 23 touchdown passes.

ever made but it was a clean shot," Bednarik said. Gifford lay unconscious on the field. He would be away from the game for a year. And the Eagles, winners over the Giants by a touchdown, would continue on to the league championship game, where their victory over Green Bay was insured by two other marvelous Bednarik plays: a crumbling tackle of Paul Hornung to stop one scoring threat and a tackle of Jim Taylor at the five as time ran out.

Bednarik's marvelous career was climaxed by that 1960 season, when he played both center and linebacker every game, including 58 minutes against Green Bay. The 6-3, 230-pounder was all-pro eight times, a Pro Bowler eight times and the last of the two-way performers. He played in 169 out of a possible 172 league games during his career, missing only one after his rookie season.

INDIVIDUAL EAGLE RECORDS

Rushing

Most Yards Game:	205	Steve Van Buren, vs Pittsburgh, 1949
Season:	1,512	Wilbert Montgomery, 1979
Career:	5,680	Steve Van Buren, 1944–51

Passing

Most TD Passes Game:	7	Adrian Burk, vs Washington, 1954
Season:	32	Sonny Jurgensen, 1961
Career:	111	Norman Snead, 1964–70

Receiving

Most TD Passes Game:	4	Joe Carter, vs Cincinnati, 1934
	4	Ben Hawkins, vs Pittsburgh, 1969
Season:	13	Tommy McDonald, 1960 and 1961
Career:	72	Harold Carmichael, 1971–81

Scoring

Most Points Game:	25	Bobby Walston, vs Washington,
Season:		1954
Career:	114	Bobby Walston, 1954
Most TDs Game:	881	Bobby Walston, 1951–62
	4	Joe Carter, vs Cincinnati, 1934
	4	Clarence Peaks, vs St. Louis, 1958
	4	Tommy McDonald, vs N.Y. Giants, 1959
	4	Ben Hawkins, vs Pittsburgh, 1969
	4	Wilbert Montgomery, vs Washington, 1978
	4	Wilbert Montgomery, vs Washington, 1979
Season:	18	Steve Van Buren, 1945
Career:	77	Steve Van Buren, 1944–51

SAN FRANCISCO 49ERS

TEAM DIRECTORY: Pres.: Edward J. DeBartolo, Jr.; GM/Head Coach: Bill Walsh; Administrative VP: John McVay; Dir. Pub. Rel.: George Heddleston. Home field: Candlestick Park (61,185). Colors: 49er Gold and scarlet.

SCOUTING REPORT

OFFENSE: After years as a little-known assistant coach and unsuccessful head coach, Bill Walsh received his rightful recognition as an offensive innovator last year. The 49ers don't really have the personnel to match up with the league's best teams, yet Walsh maneuvered his players and altered his tactics enough from week to week to outfox even Tom Landry.

Ray Wersching booted for 81 points, plus 14 in Super Bowl.

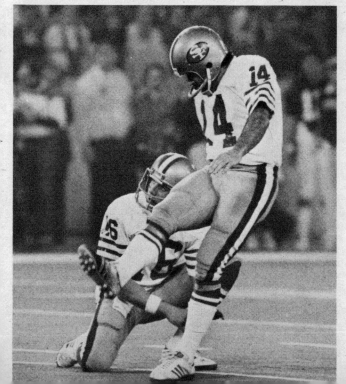

The question now is: can he maintain the same level of excellence over another season, a year after the team won 15 of its last 16 games? After all, the 49ers had only the 13th-best offense in the league, climbing that high on the performances of quarterback Joe Montana and receivers Dwight Clark and Fred Solomon. Those three are superb and now they will be joined by Russ Francis, former all-pro tight end from New England who was obtained for two draft picks and returns after a year in retirement. But unless second-year Amos Lawrence develops or a rookie comes through, the 49ers lack a standout running back.

A preseason trade for Dan Audick patched up the offensive line, which has top guards in Randy Cross and John Ayers. Ken Bungarda could push Audick for a starting spot at tackle. Fred Quillan is improving at center and Keith Fahnhorst is one of the league's most underrated tackles.

DEFENSE: With veteran Jack Reynolds providing leadership and aggressiveness, the 49er defense was the second-best in the league, and third-best against the pass. Even with Reynolds' presence, this is an extremely young and quick unit and could be a dominating force for years, especially considering that it got better faster than even Walsh anticipated.

No secondary can match the hitting force of San Francisco's, which incorporated three rookie starters last season. In cornerbacks Ronnie Lott and Eric Wright, the 49ers have a fine combination of tackling ability and defensive talent. Safeties Carlton Williamson and Dwight Hicks were consistent, producing big plays all season.

The 49ers shuffle linebackers, moving from a 3-4 to a 4-3 depending on situations. Reynolds probably can't match his 1981 performance, but Craig Puki, Dan Bunz, Willie Harper, Keena Turner and Bobby Leopold are good enough to cover up if Reynolds' play falls off a bit.

Walsh wants end Fred Dean to expand beyond a pass-rush specialist this season. He'll need to beat out Jim Stuckey, Lawrence Pillars or Dwaine Board for those extra minutes. Archie Reese had a standout season, and Walsh expects more from youngster John Harty.

KICKING GAME: Jim Miller finally showed some improvement in his punting last year to reward Walsh's faith. Field-goal man Ray Wersching is one of the most solid pressure kickers around. The 49er special teams are competent, but not destined to rewrite football history.

49ERS VETERAN ROSTER

HEAD COACH—Bill Walsh. Assistant Coaches—Norb Hecker, Milt Jackson, Billie Matthews, Bobb McKittrick, Bill McPherson, Ray Rhodes, George Seifert, Chuck Studley, Al Vermeil, Sam Wyche.

No.	Name	Pos.	Ht.	Wt.	NFL Exp.	College
61	Audick, Dan	T	6-3	253	5	Hawaii
68	Ayers, John	G	6-5	260	6	West Texas State
7	Benjamin, Guy	QB	6-3	210	5	Stanford
76	Board, Dwaine	DE	6-5	250	4	North Carolina A&T
72	Bungarda, Ken	T	6-6	270	2	Missouri
57	Bunz, Dan	LB	6-4	225	5	Cal State-Long Beach
60	Choma, John	G-C	6-5	261	2	Virginia
33	Churchman, Ricky	S	6-1	193	3	Texas
87	Clark, Dwight	WR	6-3	205	4	Clemson
49	Cooper, Earl	FB	6-2	227	3	Rice
51	Cross, Randy	G	6-3	250	7	UCLA
38	Davis, Johnny	FB	6-1	235	5	Alabama
74	Dean, Fred	DE	6-2	230	8	Louisiana Tech
62	Downing, Walt	C-G	6-3	254	5	Michigan
31	Easley, Walt	FB	6-1	226	2	West Virginia
71	Fahnhorst, Keith	T	6-6	263	9	Minnesota
48	Francis, Phil	FB	6-1	215	3	Stanford
81	Francis, Russ	TE	6-6	242	6	Oregon
24	Gervais, Rick	S	5-11	190	2	Stanford
59	Harper, Willie	LB	6-2	215	9	Nebraska
75	Harty, John	DT	6-4	253	2	Iowa
22	Hicks, Dwight	S	6-1	189	4	Michigan
66	Kennedy, Allan	T	6-7	275	2	Washington State
77	Kugler, Peter	DT	6-4	255	2	Penn State
20	Lawrence, Amos	RB	5-10	179	2	North Carolina
52	Leopold, Bobby	LB	6-1	215	3	Notre Dame
42	Lott, Ronnie	CB	6-0	199	2	Southern California
29	Martin, Saladin	CB	6-1	180	3	San Diego State
53	McColl, Milt	LB	6-6	220	2	Stanford
3	Miller, Jim	P	5-11	183	3	Mississippi
16	Montana, Joe	QB	6-2	200	3	Notre Dame
32	Patton, Ricky	RB	5-11	192	5	Jackson State
65	Pillers, Lawrence	DE	6-4	260	7	Alcorn State
54	Puki, Craaig	LB	6-1	231	3	Tennessee
56	Quillan, Fred	C	6-5	260	5	Oregon
80	Ramson, Eason	TE	6-2	234	4	Washington State
78	Reese, Archie	DT	6-3	262	5	Clemson
64	Reynolds, Jack	LB	6-1	232	13	Tennessee
30	Ring, Bill	RB	5-10	215	2	Brigham Young
84	Shumann, Mike	WR	6-0	175	5	Florida State
88	Solomon, Freddie	WR	5-11	181	8	Tampa
79	Stuckey, Jim	DE	6-4	251	3	Clemson
28	Thomas, Lynn	CB	5-11	181	2	Pittsburgh
58	Turner, Keena	LB	6-2	219	3	Purdue
14	Wersching, Ray	PK	5-11	210	10	California
27	Williamson, Carlton	S	6-0	204	2	Pittsburgh
85	Wilson, Mike	WR	6-3	210	2	Washington State
21	Wright, Eric	CB	6-1	180	2	Missouri
86	Young, Charle	TE	6-4	234	10	Southern California

TOP FIVE DRAFT CHOICES

Rd.	Name	Sel. No.	Pos.	Ht.	Wt.	College
2	Paris, Bubba	29	T	6-6	293	Michigan
5	Williams, Newton	139	RB	5-10	204	Arizona State
6	Williams, Vince	151	RLB	6-0	231	Oregon
7	Ferrari, Ron	195	QB	6-0	212	Illinois
9	Clar, Bryan	251	WR	6-2	196	Michigan State
*	Nehemiah, Renaldo			6-1	180	Maryland

* Signed as free agent

THE ROOKIES: With Francis serving as the No. 1 choice, the 49ers didn't need much more help from their rookies. But tackle Bubba Paris of Michigan could help shore up a rare weakness in the 49er lineup within a couple of years. World-class track star Renaldo Nehemiah, signed as a free agent, will be playing his first football since high school. If he makes the grade, he looms as a devastating deep threat.

OUTLOOK: Was it a fluky year or are the 49ers on the verge of becoming the league's next dynasty? Walsh must continue to be enthusiastic for the team to succeed. Now that he's got a couple more offensive weapons, there could be no stopping this group.

49ER PROFILES

JOE MONTANA 26 6–2 200   Quarterback

Big Sky...The glamor player of the season...Came out of nowhere to capture the NFL spotlight...NFC's top-ranked passer last season, hitting 63.7 percent for 3,565 yards, 19 TDs...Was on just about every cover of the sports and non-sports magazines the week of the Sugar Bowl...But even with the hype, he never seemed to change...Tried to fulfill all interview requests and be as cooperative as possible...Not gifted with all the attributes of superstar quarterback, but is proven winner...Made the Pro Bowl for the first time...And he was only a third-round draft choice in 1979...Born June 11, 1956, in Monongahela, Pa....Raises horses on ranch above San Francisco hills...Led Notre Dame to 1977 national title.

DWIGHT CLARK 25 6–3 205   Wide Receiver

No one seems to be able to figure out how he is so good...Not very quick and defensive backs think they can cover him...But every time you look up, he is open and catching another pass...Pulled in NFL-high 85 (13-yard average) last year after making 82 the season before...This 10th-round pick in the 1979 draft "is a much better football player than any of us could have anticipated," says coach Bill Walsh...Born Jan. 8, 1957, in Charlotte, N.C....Who will ever forget his game-winning TD catch against Dallas in the NFC title game?...Played in Jerry Butler's shadow at Clemson... Outgoing personality could mean future in television.

JACK REYNOLDS 34 6–1 232   Linebacker

Rams didn't think enough of him to give him a decent contract... But he helped the 49ers win Super Bowl after signing as free agent last summer... Some of 49er coaches told Bill Walsh he was making a mistake, since they wanted to build with youth... The man they call Hacksaw was a highlight of Super Bowl week, where he handed out a mimeographed sheet explaining how he got his nickname... Didn't want to keep repeating the story... Deals with how he cut a car in half once during college days at Tennessee, giving vent to frustration caused by losing... Born Nov. 22, 1947, in Cincinnati... Lives on Bahamas island in offseason.

RUSS FRANCIS 29 6–6 242   Tight End

A welcome addition to the 49ers' receiving corps... Sat out last season in retirement and said he'd only come back with a West Coast team... Signed by San Francisco on day of NFL draft... Howard Cosell called him "all-world" when Francis toiled at New England, but you'd never call him that if you looked at his stats... Had his finest season in 1980 when he caught 41 passes for 664 yards... That's hardly Kellen Winslow material... But he has one of the great bodies in the game and the 49ers' short-pass attack should be made to order for him... Born April 3, 1953, in Seattle... A quarterback in high school, he switched to tight end as a freshman at U. of Oregon... Didn't play his senior year but still was Patriots' No. 1 pick in '75.

FRED SOLOMON 29 5–11 181   Wide Receiver

One of the best game-breakers in the league... The man the 49ers rely on to come up with the big play... Once the subject of trade rumors, but that talk has long since past... With the emergence of Dwight Clark, he was able to function a lot more freely... Redskins' GM Bobby Beathard said Solomon was the quickest college player he has ever seen, as a quarterback at the University of Tampa...Born Jan. 11, 1953, in Sumter, S.C....Involved in a commercial film production company...Once had a 252-yard, three-touchdown game against Buffalo, when he scored on a 79-yard punt return, 59-yard flanker reverse and 53-yard pass...Made 59 catches last season for 16.4-yard average.

RONNIE LOTT 23 6–0 199   Cornerback

Even before he had put on a 49er uniform, he was being hailed as the team's best athlete...And he proved it with outstanding first season, considered by many to be the best in the league...But he had plenty of competition for top rookie honors from Saints' George Rogers and Giants' Lawrence Taylor...His aggressiveness and vicious hitting set the tone for the 49ers' improved secondary...Wasn't afraid of any receiver, but there were a few that feared him, especially when they came across the middle...Had seven interceptions for the season...Born May 8, 1959, in Albuquerque, N.M....All-American at USC, where he was a safety.

KEITH FAHNHORST 30 6–6 263   Tackle

If there is a most respected player on the team, then it is this man...Team captain, player representative, and a longtime standout, even when the 49ers were struggling...Probably no one was happier when the Super Bowl was over...Had been waiting for years just to see team become winner, much less win the NFL title...A tenacious and aggressive player who has fine speed and strength...Got little recognition before now...Born Feb. 6, 1952, in St. Paul, Minn....A tight end at the University of Minnesota, where he caught only 28 passes in three seasons.

RANDY CROSS 28 6–3 250   Guard

Made the transition from center to guard so well that he now is considered one of the best in the business...Had a wonderful season leading the 49ers' revitalized offense...Got into the Pro Bowl as a reward...Strongest player on the line, but once wasn't as consistent as necessary on pass blocking...Played all three line spots at UCLA, often in the same game

...How's that for versatility?...Second-round pick in 1976 immediately became the starting center...Born April 25, 1954, in Encino, Cal.

RAY WERSCHING 32 5–11 210   Placekicker

The 49ers refer to him as Mr. Clutch...One of those athletes who seems to function best when there is the most pressure...Has won numerous games for the team, especially when the 49ers were struggling...Warm, friendly guy who is very popular with 49er fans...Bounced around from Atlanta to San Diego and, finally, to San Francisco before finding permanent home—for now...Extremely accurate and consistent...Born Aug. 21, 1950, in Mondsee, Austria...Graduate of University of California-Berkeley...A CPA who works for one of the big accounting firms...Last year he converted 17 of 23 field-goal tries and was perfect on 30 PATs.

DWIGHT HICKS 26 6–1 189   Safety

A former health store manager who couldn't get a job in the NFL after failing tryouts with Detroit and Philadelphia...Now he is the anchor of the most exciting and perhaps most talented secondary in the league...Dwight Hicks and the Hot Licks...Aggressive style set the tone for the rest of his mates...And it paid off for him, as he made nine interceptions—the third-best total in the league—including one for touchdown...His 239 yards on those interceptions were tops in the league...Born April 5, 1956, in Mount Holly, N.J....Former Michigan star works with youth during offseason.

RICKY PATTON 28 5–11 192   Running Back

In 1980, he gained one yard on one carry...In 1981, he was key figure in drive to Super Bowl...With Paul Hofer injured and Earl Cooper inconsistent, he became the team's No. 1 rusher...Gained 543 yards and also caught 27 passes, although he came out on many passing downs...Picked up many important yards during March that led to Super Bowl-winning field goal...A 10th-round Atlanta draft choice who also was cut by Green Bay... Once gained 99 yards in a game for the Pack... Jackson State standout... Born April 6, 1954, in Birmingham, Ala.... Related to Walter Payton.

COACH BILL WALSH... No one disputes the fact that this man is a football miracle worker... Look what he has done with the 49ers in just three seasons (2–14, 6–10, 13–3)... No one can match his success in such a short time... An offensive genius who tears up defenses with his carefully plotted game plans... Can tell you almost exactly what plays he will call... Put in a long apprenticeship as a pro assistant coach and college head coach before finally getting 49ers' job... Resents the long wait, but feels he at least has the maturity to handle it once it came his way... Why he was passed over by the Bengals when Paul Brown retired is one of the major mysteries in football and one of the biggest blunders... His special talent is developing quarterbacks... And no one has come along better than Joe Montana... Born Nov. 30, 1931, in Los Angeles... Was an end at San Jose State and holds a master's degree in education... Very bright and articulate.

GREATEST LINEBACKER

A decade before the 49ers won the Super Bowl, they had three teams that almost were good enough to be league champions. Those clubs had some outstanding stars, including quarterback John Brodie, but 49er fans also worshipped another player, a crafty, consistent, outside linebacker who dominated his position during the early years of the 1970s.

Dave Wilcox, at least in the 49ers' eyes, was the best around. Certainly, his peers and those who cast votes for all-star teams agreed. He was named to the Pro Bowl seven times during an eight-year span starting in 1966. He was all-league five times, including 1973, the season before he retired.

His teammates called him "the intimidator" for his toughness, which enabled him to intercept 13 career passes. This is how good

Dave Wilcox was: an average grade score for a 49er linebacker off 1973 game films was 750. His average that season was 1,306. Maybe the fact he was a rodeo performer in his younger days made playing football that much easier for him.

INDIVIDUAL 49ER RECORDS

Rushing

Most Yards Game: 194 Delvin Williams, vs St. Louis, 1976
Season: 1,203 Delvin Williams, 1976
Career: 8,689 Joe Perry, 1948–60, 1963

Passing

Most TD Passes Game: 5 Frank Albert, vs Cleveland (ACC), 1949
5 John Brodie, vs Minnesota, 1965
5 Steve Spurrier, vs Chicago, 1972
Season: 30 John Brodie, 1965
Career: 214 John Brodie, 1957–73

Receiving

Most TD Passes Game: 3 Alyn Beals, vs Brooklyn (AAC), 1948
3 Alyn Beals, vs Chicago (AAC), 1949
3 Gordy Soltau, vs Los Angeles, 1951
3 Bernie Casey, vs Minnesota, 1962
3 Dave Parks, vs Baltimore, 1965
3 Gene Washington, vs San Diego, 1972
Season: 14 Alyn Beals (AAC), 1948
Career: 54 Gene Washington, 1969–76

Scoring

Most Points Game: 26 Gordy Soltau, vs Los Angeles, 1951
Season: 114 Gordy Soltau, 1953
Career: 738 Tommy Davis, 1959–69
Most TDs Game: 4 Bill Kilmer, vs Minnesota, 1961
Season: 14 Alyn Beals (AAC), 1948
Career: 80 Joe Perry, 1948–60

ST. LOUIS CARDINALS

TEAM DIRECTORY: Pres.: William Bidwill; Dir. Pro. Personnel: Larry Wilson; Dir. Pub. Rel.: Marty Igel; Head Coach: Jim Hanifan. Home field: Busch Memorial Stadium (51,392). Colors: Cardinal red, white and black.

SCOUTING REPORT

OFFENSE: The hope of the Cardinal offense can be pinpointed in two words: Neil Lomax. The youngster from tiny Portland State was handed the starting quarterback spot midway through last season, after veteran Jim Hart was benched, and the Cards promptly went on a four-game winning streak that salvaged a potentially horrid season.

Now Lomax will go through a whole training camp as the No. 1 quarterback—Hart was signed to be a backup—and with his emergence, the club has a scrambling quarterback for the first time in memory. But Lomax lacks Hart's experience and leadership.

Ottis Anderson had another 1,000-plus season, but did not gain more than 28 yards on one carry the whole year. He has to improve his breakaway skills. With the trading of Theotis Brown to Seattle, Wayne Morris once more is the fullback, but is on the downside of his career. Pat Tilley had his best year as a pro, but Mel Gray is ready to be replaced, if someone is available.

The once-proud offensive line gave up 48 sacks last year and its best player, Dan Dierdorf, is almost ready for medicare. Coach Jim Hanifan is counting on fresh input in this area from first-round pick Luis Sharpe, a UCLA tackle.

DEFENSE: St. Louis has hired Floyd Peters as an assistant coach in charge of defense. It was an acknowledgement that the Cards' woeful defensive problems couldn't continue without some major attempt to bring about a change.

Peters is a self-proclaimed expert in developing pass rushes. He can point to the Detroit Silver Rush as his prime accomplishment. The Cards would welcome similar surgery. He'll start his operation with end Curtis Greer, who was quick enough to register 12½ sacks last year, but was very inconsistent. The defensive line is, for the most part, young and willing, so maybe Peters can get something going.

E.J. Junior had offseason problems with the law, which clouds the linebacker situation, something the Cards thought would be a

Old pro Dan Dierdorf is still stalwart on Cards' line.

strength. Junior came on at the end of the season, as did Dave Ahrens, a promising middle linebacker. Hanifan calls cornerback Jeff Griffin a "buzzbomb", because of the way Griffin belts people around. He adds some aggressiveness to a secondary that will miss Roy Green, who will concentrate strictly on offense this year, possibly as Gray's replacement.

KICKING GAME: This is an area of strength. Stump Mitchell brought excitement to both kickoff and punt returns last year, the coverage teams were solid, rookie Carl Birdsong was the NFC's No. 5 punter and kicker Neil O'Donoghue missed only two of 16 attempts from inside the 40.

CARDINALS VETERAN ROSTER

HEAD COACH—Jim Hanifan. Assistant Coaches—Chuck Banker, Tom Bettis, Rudy Feldman, Harry Gilmer, Dick Jamieson, Tom Lovat, Leon McLaughlin, Floyd Peters, Emmitt Thomas, Don Brown.

No.	Name	Pos.	Ht.	Wt.	NFL Exp.	College
58	Ahrens, Dave	LB	6-3	230	2	Wisconsin
27	Allen, Carl	CB	6-0	188	6	Southern Mississippi
32	Anderson, Ottis	RB	6-2	220	4	Miami
52	Baker, Charlie	LB	6-2	218	3	New Mexico
18	Birdsong, Carl	P	6-0	192	2	Southwest Oklahoma State
71	Bostic, Joe	G	6-3	265	4	Clemson
51	Brahaney, Tom	C	6-2	247	10	Oklahoma
69	Brown, Rush	DT	6-2	257	3	Ball State
43	Carpenter, Steve	S-CB	6-2	205	2	Western Illinois
64	Clark, Randy	C-G	6-3	254	3	Northern Illinois
86	Clayton, Ralph	WR	6-3	222	2	Michigan
61	Coder, Ron	G	6-4	260	5	Penn State
44	Collier, Tim	CB	6-0	176	7	East Texas State
66	Collins, George	T	6-2	265	5	Georgia
80	Combs, Chris	TE	6-4	249	3	New Mexico
60	Cotton, Barney	G	6-5	265	4	Nebraska
63	Criswell, Kirby	DE	6-5	242	2	Kansas
73	Dawson, Mike	DT	6-4	275	7	Arizona
72	Dierdorf, Dan	T	6-3	280	11	Michigan
59	Favron, Calvin	LB	6-1	227	4	Southeast Louisiana State
50	Field, Doak	LB	6-2	227	2	Baylor
57	Gillen, John	LB	6-3	228	2	Illinois
85	Gray, Mel	WR	5-9	175	12	Missouri
25	Green, Roy	WR-S	6-0	195	4	Henderson State
37	Greene, Ken	S	6-3	205	5	Washington State
75	Greer, Curtis	DE	6-4	258	3	Michigan
35	Griffin, Jeff	CB	6-0	185	2	Utah
39	Harrell, Willard	RB	5-8	182	8	Pacific
17	Hart, Jim	QB	6-0	210	17	Southern Illinois
46	Johnson, Charles	S-CB	5-10	180	4	Grambling
54	Junior, E. J.	LB	6-3	237	2	Alabama
56	Kearney, Tim	LB	6-2	227	11	Northern Michigan
89	LaFleur, Greg	TE	6-4	236	2	Louisiana State
16	Lisch, Rusty	QB	6-3	215	3	Notre Dame
15	Lomax, Neil	QB	6-3	215	2	Portland State
40	Love, Randy	RB	6-1	205	4	Houston
62	Markham, Dale	T	6-8	280	2	North Dakota
82	Marsh, Doug	TE	6-3	238	3	Michigan
76	Mays, Stafford	DE	6-2	250	3	Washington
30	Mitchell, Stump	RB	5-9	188	2	The Citadel
24	Morris, Wayne	RB	6-0	210	7	Southern Methodist
38	Nelson, Lee	S	5-10	185	7	Florida State
11	O'Donoghue, Neil	K	6-6	210	6	Auburn
70	Plunkett, Art	T	6-7	262	2	Nevada-Las Vegas
79	Radford, Bruce	DE	6-5	260	4	Grambling
48	Schwartz, Don	S-CB	6-1	194	5	Washington State
21	Stief, Dave	S-CB	6-3	195	5	Portland State
68	Stieve, Terry	G	6-2	265	6	Wisconsin
83	Tilley, Pat	WR	5-10	171	7	Louisiana Tech
74	Times, Ken	DT	6-2	248	2	Southern U.
22	Wehrli, Roger	CB	6-0	194	14	Missouri
55	Williams, Eric	LB	6-2	235	6	Southern California
42	Williams, Herb	S-CB	6-0	200	3	Southern U.

TOP FIVE DRAFT CHOICES

Rd.	Name	Sel. No.	Pos.	Ht.	Wt.	College
1	Sharpe, Luis	16	T	6-4	250	UCLA
2	Galloway, David	38	DT	6-3	274	Florida
3	Perrin, Benny	65	DB	6-2	175	Alabama
3	Guilbeau, Rusty	73	DE	6-4	250	McNeese State
4	Robbins, Tootie	90	T	6-5	270	East Carolina

THE ROOKIES: Sharpe is Dierdorf's heir apparent, filling the Cards' greatest need. David Galloway, a defensive end from Florida, needs to hustle more than he did in college to give any quick help to the Cards' defensive line.

OUTLOOK: Bit by bit, the Cards are adding young talent. So much of their development, however, hinges on Lomax's play at quarterback and how well Peters does with an undisciplined defense that sometimes was borderline inept. Playing in the league's toughest division doesn't make things easier, either.

CARDINAL PROFILES

OTTIS ANDERSON 25 6–2 220   **Running Back**

Even with offense playing inconsistently, he still managed to shine...Came through with 1,376-yard season...Maintains his standing as one of the league's elite runners...No one laughs anymore when they call him O.J....Already holds club all-time rushing mark after just three seasons...But breaking records is nothing new to him...He shattered all of Chuck Foreman's marks at University of Miami...Unusual spelling of first name resulted when doctor who delivered him misspelled it on birth certificate...Born Jan. 19, 1957, in West Palm Beach, Fla....Already has own local radio program.

NEIL LOMAX 23 6–3 215   **Quarterback**

Won starting job from Jim Hart after Cardinal offense sputtered...Justified high draft selection by playing creditably despite lack of experience...Threw for 1,575 yards and four touchdowns on 119 completions...Making the transition from sprint and rollout passer at Portland State to dropback passer in pros...Member of Cardinals' fine 1981 draft class...His boyhood idol was Roman Gabriel...An extremely physical quarterback with very strong arm...Set all types of NCAA records at pass-happy Portland State...Finished seventh in the Heisman voting his senior season...Born Feb. 17, 1959, in Lake Oswego, Ore....Began college career as fifth-string quarterback.

DAN DIERDORF 33 6-3 280   Tackle

One of the remaining old veterans on what is becoming a very young team... Few defensive linemen have ever been able to beat him consistently, even before he could benefit from liberalized rules on holding... Once member of one of the finest offensive lines in recent NFL history... Came off serious knee injury two years ago to resume high standard of play... Active in numerous local charitable organizations.... Been in TV commercials and films... Part-owner of printing company ... Born June 29, 1949, in Canton, Ohio... Voted to NFL Team of the Decade for the 1970s... Second-round 1971 draft choice out of Michigan.

JIM HART 38 6-0 210   Quarterback

Most likely will fill unfamiliar role of backup this season... Lost his starting job to Neil Lomax midway through the schedule... Cardinals surprised almost everyone by deciding to sign him to another one-year contract... Merely the best quarterback in team history and one of the most prolific in league history... Nearing the top in almost every league passing statistic... Won NFL's top humanitarian award in 1976... Born April 29, 1944, in Evanston, Ill.... A long time ago, he was star at Southern Illinois before signing as free agent with St. Louis ... Remembered most for his characteristic hot streaks during certain games.

E. J. JUNIOR 22 6-3 237   Linebacker

Cardinals broke him in carefully, but once he got chance to play, he showed why he was one of the most sought-after players in last year's draft... Will get a chance to play on the left side this year, which should get him more involved than ever... Real name is Ester James Junior III... Father is college administrator, mother is high school principal... He has degree in public relations and later will get one in civil engineering... Voted to Alabama team of the 1970s... Born Dec. 8, 1959 in Nashville, Tenn.... Wore red and white uniforms in high school, college and now, the pros.

ROY GREEN 25 6-0 195   Wide Receiver

A year ago, he was a defensive back and relatively unknown around the league...Now he is slated for starting wide receiver spot after a spectacular 1981 season in which he revived memories of the two-way player...Against the Redskins, he caught a TD pass, intercepted a pass, recovered a fumble on special teams...Kept up iron-man duties for most of season, but Cardinals feel he'd help them the most by concentrating on one position...Says going both ways is no sweat, he did it in high school and sometimes in college, at Henderson State...Born June 30, 1957, in Magnolia, Ark....Ottis (Anderson), Theotis (Brown) and Roy's brother Leotis were groomsmen in his wedding.

STUMP MITCHELL 23 5-9 188   Kick Returner

Another one of the Cardinals' bright draft choices last year...One of the league's best kick-returners, averaging 23.5 yards on kickoff returns and 10.6 on punt returns last year, including one he brought back for a touchdown...Still around in the ninth round when the Cardinals decided to take a chance...Didn't get his nickname because he is a giant...Real name is Lyvonia Albert, but was rechristened Stump at early age by a brother...Standout running back at The Citadel, where he gained 1,647 yards as a senior, second in nation to George Rogers...Was Southern Conference Player of the Year as a senior ...Born March 15, 1959, in St. Mary's, Ga.

JOE BOSTIC 25 6-3 265   Guard

Part of a rare brother act in the NFL...Brother Jeff is the starting center for the Redskins...When two teams played for the first time this year, Joe suffered a bad ankle injury...A third-round pick in 1979 out of Clemson...Got a quick initiation into the NFL, when he had to start for injured Dan Dierdorf at tackle his rookie season...Became fixture at guard last year....Didn't get much recognition outside the south in college, but won ACC's top blocking award two straight years...Born April 20, 1957, in Greensboro, N.C....Was state wrestling champion in high school.

WAYNE MORRIS 28 6–0 210   Running Back

Was replaced at start of the year by Theotis Brown as the No. 1 fullback, but when Brown was sent to Seattle, he became a regular again... Won't dazzle anyone with his speed, but is steady, reliable and gets the tough yardage. Fifth-round 1976 pick from SMU holds on to the ball, too, as he carried ball 190 consecutive times without fumbling in 1980 ... Gained 417 yards and scored five touchdowns last season... Caught 19 passes, too... Born May 5, 1954, in Dallas.

PAT TILLEY 29 5–10 171   Wide Receiver

Has changed from being a question mark because of his speed to being one of the league's steadiest receivers... Caught 66 passes for 1,040 yards last year, the first time he has gone over the 1,000-yard mark in his career... Had 68 receptions the year before... Gifted with wonderful concentration and soft hands... Jack Pardee once called him the most dangerous receiver in the NFC... He credits eye-to-ball concentration for his success ... Born Feb. 15, 1953, in Marshall, Tex.... Played at Louisiana Tech and still resides in Shreveport, La.

COACH JIM HANIFAN... This is the kind of season he had

in 1981: some of his players complained about his foul language in the locker room while giving pep talks... That's a new gripe, even in this modern era... Remains optimistic, however, even though his team is showing turtle-slow progress... Has yet to establish his personality with the Cardinals in first two years as head coach but, even with his outbursts, is known as a decent guy... A Don Coryell protege who coached in high school and was a long-time assistant in college and pros (St. Louis and San Diego) before getting this opportunity... Born Sept. 21, 1922, in Compton, Cal. ... Considered one of the league's top head coaching prospects before he got this job... Always can get a spot as someone's offensive line coach, since that is his strength... As long as he is with the Cardinals, he will never have job security... Owner Bill Bidwell's unpredictable behavior dictates anxiety for every employee.

GREATEST LINEBACKER

Larry Stallings had a problem faced by few other players in the history of the NFL. He was on active military duty for a time during his career, but the Army said he could still play on Sundays. But how would he prepare for games?

The solution came in the form of film. He would take game films of his upcoming opponents with him to the base and study them. He would get a copy of the game plan through the mail or, if necessary, have it dictated to him over the phone. He couldn't practice with the team during this span, yet he would show up on Sundays and produce the kind of intelligent, steady performances that made him the Cardinals' best-ever linebacker.

For 14 years, Stallings and safety Larry Wilson were the heart and soul of the Cardinals' sometimes wobbly defense. Stallings, 6-1, 230, played in 180 games from 1963 to 1976, fourth-most in club history. He was a Pro Bowler in 1970, although if he had been on better teams he probably would have received that honor more frequently.

INDIVIDUAL CARDINAL RECORDS

Rushing

Most Yards Game:	203	John David Crow, vs Pittsburgh, 1960
Season:	1,605	Ottis Anderson, 1979
Career:	4,333	Ottis Anderson, 1978–81

Passing

Most TD Passes Game:	6	Jim Hardy, vs Baltimore, 1950
	6	Charley Johnson, vs Cleveland, 1965
	6	Charley Johnson, vs New Orleans, 1969
Season:	28	Charley Johnson, 1963
Career:	204	Jim Hart, 1966–81

Receiving

Most TD Passes Game:	5	Bob Shaw, vs Baltimore, 1950
Season:	15	Sonny Randle, 1960
Career:	60	Sonny Randle, 1959–66

Scoring

Most Points Game:	40	Ernie Nevers, vs Chicago, 1929
Season:	117	Jim Bakken, 1967
Career:	1,380	Jim Bakken, 1962–78
Most TDs Game:	6	Ernie Nevers, vs Chicago, 1929
Season:	17	John David Crow, 1962
Career:	60	Sonny Randle, 1959–66

TAMPA BAY BUCCANEERS

TEAM DIRECTORY: Pres.: Hugh Culverhouse; VP/Head Coach: John McKay; VP: Joy Culverhouse; Dir. Administration: Herb Gold; Dir. Player Personnel: Ken Herock; Dir. Pro Personnel: Jack Bushofsky; Dir. Pub. Rel.: Bob Best. Home field: Tampa Stadium (72,128). Colors: Florida orange, white and red.

SCOUTING REPORT

OFFENSE: What part of last season do Bucs' fans remember— that embarrassing loss to Dallas in the playoffs or the final stretch drive during which they won four of their last five games? The an-

Bucs' Jimmie Giles hauled in 45 passes last season.

swer to that question probably will be determined by how well the team and particularly the offense, which is coming off the best season in Tampa's history, performs early this season.

The Bucs scored 315 points last year and improved as quarterback Doug Williams improved. Williams is beginning to mature and is emerging as a good quarterback, sometimes overzealous backing from coach John McKay notwithstanding. It also helps that his receiving corps has been upgraded, with the addition of Theo Bell and the improvement of Kevin House. Jimmie Giles continues as one of the league's best tight ends and a favorite Williams target.

With Ricky Bell in San Diego, Jerry Eckwood is clearly established as the No. 1 runner, although James Owens might prove to be better this year. But no one will really play well unless McKay gets a more consistent offensive line and installs a more sophisticated offense.

DEFENSE: One other team, the Eagles, allowed fewer touchdowns last year than Tampa Bay, which is an indication of the Buc unit's strength and determination. With a fine blend of youth and experience, there is no reason to think the Bucs can't keep improving.

Their linebacking is so good that McKay could send two talented players, Dave Lewis and Dewey Selmon, to San Diego. But with Hugh Green coming on and Cecil Johnson playing like an all-pro in Selmon's inside-linebacker's spot, who's to worry? There has never been a more consistent Buc than linebacker Richard Wood, unless it's end Lee Roy Selmon, who made another Pro Bowl appearance despite so-so knees. And how's this for a statistic? Nose guard David Logan broke up 13 passes, not bad work for a cornerback, much less a down lineman.

Injuries threw the secondary off kilter early in the season, but free safety Cedric Brown came back to intercept 13 passes and cornerback Mike Washington six. With everyone healthy, the secondary play could rival the linebacking as a team strength.

KICKING GAME: McKay's gamble early in the season—going with kicker Bill Capece instead of Garo Yepremian—paid off when Capece kicked five of the seven longest field goals in team history. Newcomer Larry Swider was also third in the NFC in punting. But the Bucs were next to last in punt returns, an area that has to be strengthened.

THE ROOKIES: The Bucs hope guard Sean Farrell of Penn State will strengthen an offensive line that is still shaking off its em-

BUCCANEERS VETERAN ROSTER

HEAD COACH—John McKay. Assistant Coaches—Wayne Fontes, Abe Gibron, Howard Tippett, Boyd Dowler, Bill Johnson, Jim Gruden, Bill Nelson, Frank Emanuel.

No.	Name	Pos.	Ht.	Wt.	NFL Exp.	College
69	Austin, Darrell	G-T	6-4	255	7	South Carolina
83	Bell, Theo	WR	5-11	180	6	Arizona
52	Brantley, Scot	LB	6-1	230	3	Florida
34	Brown, Cedric	S	6-2	205	6	Kent State
79	Campbell, Joe	DE	6-6	250	6	Maryland
3	Capece, Bill	K	5-7	170	2	Florida State
87	Carter, Gerald	WR	6-1	185	3	Texas A&M
44	Cesare, Billy	S	5-11	190	4	Miami
20	Colzie, Neal	S	6-2	200	8	Ohio State
33	Cotney, Mark	S	6-0	205	7	Cameron State
71	Crowder, Randy	DT	6-3	250	6	Penn State
27	Davis, Tony	RB	5-11	210	7	Nebraska
43	Eckwood, Jerry	RB	6-0	200	4	Arkansas
10	Ford, Mike	QB	6-3	220	2	Southern Methodist
14	Fusina, Chuck	QB	6-1	195	4	Penn State
88	Giles, Jimmie	TE	6-3	241	6	Alcorn State
53	Green, Hugh	LB	6-2	225	2	Pittsburgh
73	Hannah, Charley	T	6-6	255	6	Alabama
59	Hawkins, Andy	LB	6-2	230	3	Texas A&I
21	Holt, John	CB	5-11	180	2	West Texas State
89	House, Kevin	WR	6-1	175	3	Southern Illinois
70	Hutchinson, Scott	DE	6-3	245	5	Florida
56	Johnson, Cecil	LB	6-2	230	6	Pittsburgh
84	Jones, Gordon	WR	6-0	190	4	Pittsburgh
77	Kollar, Bill	DE	6-4	250	9	Montana State
62	Leonard, Jim	C-G	6-3	250	3	Santa Clara
76	Logan, David	DT	6-2	250	4	Pittsburgh
55	Melontree, Andrew	LB	6-3	225	2	Baylor
45	Mitchell, Aaron	S	6-1	195	4	Nevada-Las Vegas
51	Nafziger, Dana	LB	6-1	225	5	California Poly-SLO
86	Obradovich, Jim	TE	6-2	230	8	Southern California
26	Owens, James	RB	5-11	190	4	UCLA
75	Reavis, Dave	T	6-5	265	8	Arkansas
61	Roberts, Greg	G	6-3	255	4	Oklahoma
80	Samuels, Tony	TE	6-4	235	5	Bethune-Cookman
74	Sanders, Gene	T	6-3	270	4	Texas A&M
63	Selmon, Lee Roy	DE	6-3	260	7	Oklahoma
64	Short, Laval	DT	6-3	250	3	Colorado
72	Snell, Ray	G	6-3	260	3	Wisconsin
65	Stalls, Dave	DE	6-4	250	6	Northern Colorado
9	Swider, Larry	P	6-2	195	4	Pittsburgh
41	Thomas, Norris	CB	5-11	185	6	Southern Mississippi
40	Washington, Mike	CB	6-2	200	7	Alabama
90	White, Brad	DT	6-2	250	2	Tennessee
32	Wilder, James	RB	6-2	220	2	Missouri
12	Williams, Doug	QB	6-4	214	5	Grambling
50	Wilson, Steve	C	6-3	265	7	Georgia
54	Wood, Richard	LB	6-2	230	8	Southern California
68	Yarno, George	G	6-2	255	4	Washington State

TOP FIVE DRAFT CHOICES

Rd.	Name	Sel. No.	Pos.	Ht.	Wt.	College
1	Farrell, Sean	17	G	6-3	266	Penn State
2	Reese, Booker	32	DE	6-7	260	Bethune-Cookman
3	Bell, Jerry	74	TE	6-5	224	Arizona State
3	Cannon, John	83	DE	6-4	245	William & Mary
4	Barrett, Dave	103	RB	6-0	215	Houston

barrassing play in the playoffs. He's a good one, way ahead of tight end Jerry Bell of Arizona, the third-round choice. But defensive ends Booker Reese of Bethune-Cookman and John Cannon of William & Mary could help.

OUTLOOK: If the Bucs have an edge in the Central Division, it is a slight one. They have to remain relatively injury free and they have to become much more consistent on offense. It remains to be seen if McKay's offseason talent purge will wind up hurting his team.

BUCCANEER PROFILES

DOUG WILLIAMS 27 6-4 214　　　　　Quarterback

Had his best season yet as a pro (3,568 yards passing, 50.5 completion percentage, 19 TDs), but all fans will remember is that awful day he had against Dallas in the playoffs . . . Not all his fault, because offensive line couldn't control Cowboy front four, which meant he spent the afternoon throwing with Too Tall Jones and Co. in his face . . . Coach John McKay remains very defensive about him, but now he doesn't have to stand up for his quarterback as much . . . Still learning to throw the ball better short . . . His arm could be the strongest in the league and, with better receivers, he is becoming more versatile . . . Born Aug. 9, 1955, in Baton Rouge, La. . . . Still talks frequently with his college coach, Grambling's Eddie Robinson.

LEE ROY SELMON 27 6-3 260　　　　　Defensive End

Probably as good as he ever was, but for some reason, you don't hear as much about him anymore . . . Doesn't have the overwhelming height or strength of other defensive linemen in the league . . . But who can knock his consistency? . . . Personable, gracious and intelligent . . . Extremely active in community and charity work . . . Works for bank . . . Born Nov. 20, 1954, in Eufaula, Okla. . . . For pleasure, he plays the drums and listens to music . . . Youngest of nine children . . . Brother Dewey, one-time teammate with Bucs, now plays for San Diego and brother Lucious is now assistant at Oklahoma, where all three Selmons played together.

JIMMIE GILES 27 6–3 241   Tight End

Bounced back to have fine season (45 catches, 17.5-yard average) after critics were wondering if he would be a bust...They forgot he has superstar ability...Consistency, however, sometimes takes time...Joined Tampa after 1977 rookie season with Houston as part of trade that helped Oilers land Earl Campbell...Played football for only two seasons at Alcorn State...Concentrated on baseball his first two years until a chance to play Grambling in the Superdome motivated him to try football...Works for bank and does some radio work...Born Nov. 8, 1954, in Greenville, Miss....Played pro ball in 1976 after being drafted by the Los Angeles Dodgers.

HUGH GREEN 23 6–2 225   Linebacker

People wondered if he could make transition from defensive end at Pitt to linebacker in the pros...He proved he could with wonderful rookie year...Has all the quickness and aggressiveness you could ever want in a defensive player...Even adapted well to defending on pass plays, the area he needed to work on most...Came to Tampa as one of the most honored players in college football...Won Lombardi Trophy as best lineman in country his senior year...Had 52 sacks in four years...Born July 27, 1959, in Natchez, Miss....Orphaned at age six, raised by his grandparents...Cooks and sews like an expert.

KEVIN HOUSE 24 6–1 175   Wide Receiver

After showing signs of becoming a good pro receiver, he really blossomed last year...Became one of the league's most consistent deep threats...Why? Because the Bucs started throwing to him more and Doug Williams got more time to pass...Caught 56 passes and averaged an outstanding 21 yards a reception...Became a specialist in the long-touchdown catch...For some reason, some defensive backs thought he was slow...They didn't know about his 4.3 clocking at Southern Illinois...Some have compared him to Paul Warfield ...A baseball draftee of the St. Louis Cardinals...An outfielder who batted .307 his sophomore year...Born Dec. 20, 1957, in St. Louis.

CHARLEY HANNAH 27 6-6 255   Tackle

The Chicken Man...Earned nickname because he has owned a chicken farm since his college days at Alabama...His value to the team became obvious last year after he was injured and had to watch play of offensive line diminish...When he returned, things perked up...Still making the transition from defensive line to offensive tackle, but has enough natural ability to become a success...But there remains plenty of room for improvement, as he found out against Dallas in the playoffs...Brother John is the best guard in the league, with New England...Born July 26, 1955, in Canton, Ga....Finishing up work on degree...Enjoys tennis, golf and fishing.

JERRY ECKWOOD 27 6-0 200   Running Back

With the exile of Ricky Bell to San Diego, he has emerged as the Bucs' major running threat...That makes for much brighter future than he had when he first joined team in 1979 as a third-round pick out of Arkansas...Gained 651 yards to lead the club last season...Always has been a standout, even since he was Player of the Year in Arkansas as a high-school senior...Fifth-leading career rusher at Arkansas...Graduated with degree in political science and minor in journalism...Worked for TV station in college and now works for video production company in offseason...Born Dec. 26, 1954, in Brinkley, Ark....Also has decent receiving hands on a team that doesn't throw to its backs all that much.

GREG ROBERTS 25 6-3 255   Guard

For someone who wasn't supposed to have ability to be a front-line NFL player, he is carving out a decent pro career for himself...Once a blocker for Billy Sims, his old college roommate at Oklahoma...Won the Outland Trophy his senior year in college, yet was still around when Tampa's second-round pick came up...Always has been hurt that he wasn't taken in the first round, where top-quality offensive linemen usually are chosen...Born Nov. 19, 1956, in Nacogdoches, Tex....Says he is "just a dull guy" who works as a salesman in the offseason...A high-school linebacker.

CECIL JOHNSON 27 6–2 230 Linebacker

What a difference a year made for this man...Bucs moved him from outside linebacker to inside linebacker and suddenly they had an all-pro caliber player on their hands...The move was made possible by the emergence of Hugh Green...Not that he played that badly on the outside, but he used his strength and positioning to better advantage inside...Overlooked in the draft and signed as a free agent...Born Aug. 19, 1955, in Miami, Fla....Was in Tony Dorsett's class at Pitt...Owns home improvement firm...Brother is a professional drummer.

GORDON JONES 25 6–0 190 Wide Receiver

One of the reasons Doug Williams has come along as a passer is the improvement of his receivers...And none have improved more than this man, another of the Pittsburgh products now in a Buc uniform...Not very tall, but set club record in 1980 with 48 receptions...A second-round pick...Was an All-American at Pittsburgh...Majored in administration of justice...Was also a punt returner in college, but hasn't had to perform those duties in the pros...Was a three-sport star in high school...Born July 25, 1957, in Buffalo.

COACH JOHN McKAY

...Remains one of the most outspoken and controversial coaches in the league...Some thought he might step down after last season and concentrate on administrative duties...But he says he might coach five more years...Had the Bucs back into the playoffs for the second time in three years...About the only coach who openly criticizes his players, but if someone takes an unwarranted potshot at one of his athletes, he'll defend him vigorously...Just ask Doug Williams... For years, he poked fun at the pros from his mountaintop at USC, then finally lived up to his boasts with Bucs, after some very lean years (0–14, 2–12) with expansion club...Has one of the more relaxed approaches in the league...Doesn't believe in burning the midnight oil, especially in the offseason...Born July 5, 1924, in Everettsville, W. Va....Can be one of the funniest men in football when he gets warmed up.

GREATEST LINEBACKER

After one so-so season, the New York Jets decided that Richard Wood was never going to be a quality pro. "They were looking for some fool to take him off their hands and I was that fool," said Tampa Bay's John McKay, who sent a seventh-round pick to the Jets to obtain his former Southern California player. It was one of the Bucs' best-ever trades.

Wood has started 88 straight games since coming over in the 1976 season. In that period, he has made 813 tackles, more than 200 above any other Buc. Four times in six years, he has led in tackles and he recorded 140 and 141 in the years he finished second. He also has nine interceptions, has caused 12 fumbles and has scored three touchdowns. In 37 games, he has recorded 10 or more tackles.

But Wood's claim as the Bucs' best-ever linebacker may be short-lived. Hugh Green already has established himself as a potential all-pro after just one season. Give him another year or two of experience and there may be only a few better linebackers in all of pro football.

INDIVIDUAL BUCCANEER RECORDS

Rushing

Most Yards Game:	167	Ricky Bell, vs Green Bay, 1979
Season:	1,263	Ricky Bell, 1979
Career:	3,057	Ricky Bell, 1977–81

Passing

Most TD Passes Game:	4	Doug Williams, vs Minnesota, 1980
	4	Doug Williams, vs Detroit, 1981
Season:	20	Doug Williams, 1980
Career:	64	Doug Williams, 1978–81

Receiving

Most TD Passes Game:	3	Morris Owens, vs Miami, 1976
Season:	9	Kevin House, 1981
Career:	19	Jimmie Giles, 1978–81

Scoring

Most Points Game:	18	Morris Owens, vs Miami, 1976
Season:	79	Garo Yepremian, 1980
Career:	127	Neil O'Donoghue, 1978–79
Most TDs Game:	3	Morris Owens, vs Miami, 1976
Season:	9	Ricky Bell, 1979
	9	Kevin House, 1981
Career:	19	Ricky Bell, 1977–81
	19	Jimmie Giles, 1978–81

WASHINGTON REDSKINS

TEAM DIRECTORY: Chairman: Jack Kent Cooke; Pres.: Edward Bennett Williams; GM: Bobby Beathard; Dir. Pub. Rel.: Joe Blair; Head Coach: Joe Gibbs. Home field: Robert F. Kennedy Memorial Stadium (55,045). Colors: Burgundy and gold.

SCOUTING REPORT

OFFENSE: Once Joe Gibbs settled on a one-back, two-tight-end offense last year, the Redskins shook off a 0–5 start and won eight of their last 11 games—thanks mainly to an attack that became one of the most efficient in the league. But Washington has to be stronger physically before it can move the ball steadily against the league's top defenses.

Still, Gibbs says his club has only scratched the surface of his multi-faceted offense. Quarterback Joe Theismann produced the best statistics of his career and should improve as he is exposed to more of Gibbs' thinking. Joe Washington won the hearts of Redskin fans by leading in both receiving and rushing, but there is no quickness behind him. Look for Wilbur Jackson, if he can stay healthy, to have more playing time than John Riggins, who came back after a year's retirement to produce in pressure situations. Art Monk needs more help at receiver, where there is little speed, and Gibbs wants improved receiving at his tight end spot, held down by Don Warren.

A remade offensive line was the league's youngest. Tackle Joe Jacoby, guard Russ Grimm and center Jeff Bostic are solid and rookie flop Mark May could push out veteran George Starke at tackle.

DEFENSE: The Redskins scrambled and patched and made lineup changes almost every week, but their defense was less than respectable for most of the 1981 season. If the team is going to improve, this unit will have to be shored up quickly.

The main problem is the front four, where there is no consistent pass rush. Tackle Dave Butz can be awesome against the run, but he gets little help. Ends Dexter Manley and Mat Mendenhall started the last half of the season and the Redskins hope Manley can become a sack specialist. More youngsters could be worked into starting roles before the end of training camp.

The most spirited preseason position battle will be between veteran Neal Olkewicz and youngster Larry Kubin for the middle linebacker spot. Kubin is quicker and stronger, but Olkewiez has

Joe Washington was Capitol improvement in Skins' attack.

the experience edge. Monte Coleman still is trying to live up to his potential on the outside, and Brad Dusek and Rich Milot probably will share time again on the other side.

The Redskins once again had impressive pass defense statistics, but the secondary showed its age, especially at cornerback, so Lemar Parrish was traded to Buffalo following an injury-prone year. Free safety Mark Murphy led in tackles, interceptions and fumble recoveries, while strong safety Tony Peters showed flashes of excellence amid inconsistency.

KICKING GAME: Mike Connell had the best average for a Redskin punter in years, but he still was in the bottom fourth of the league and wasn't as steady as Gibbs would like. Mark Moseley had leg miseries and had fewer attempts, but when healthy, he still ranks as one of the league's best field-goal kickers.

REDSKINS VETERAN ROSTER

HEAD COACH—Joe Gibbs. Assistant Coaches—Dan Henning, Joe Bugel, Don Breaux, Richie Petitbon, LaVern Torgeson, Larry Peccatiello, Wayne Sevier, Charley Taylor, Bill Hickman, Warren Simmons.

No.	Name	Pos.	Ht.	Wt.	NFL Exp.	College
	Batton, Bobby	RB	6-0	190	2	Nevada-Las Vagas
53	Bostic, Jeff	C	6-2	246	2	Clemson
69	Brooks, Perry	DT	6-3	260	5	Southern
65	Butz, Dave	DT	6-7	295	10	Purdue
82	Caster, Rich	TE	6-5	230	13	Jackson State
35	Claitt, Rickey	RB	5-10	206	3	Bethune-Cookman
75	Clark, Mike	DE	6-4	240	2	Florida
51	Coleman, Monte	LB	6-2	230	4	Central Arkansas
10	Connell, Mike	P	6-1	200	4	Cincinnati
28	Crissy, Cris	CB-WR	5-11	195	2	Princeton
65	Cronan, Peter	LB	6-2	238	5	Boston College
63	Dean, Fred	G	6-3	253	5	Texas Southern
59	Dusek, Brad	LB	6-2	223	9	Texas A&M
12	Flick, Tom	QB	6-1	190	2	Washington
89	Garrett, Alvin	WR	5-7	178	3	Angelo State
30	Giaquinto, Nick	RB	5-11	204	3	Connecticut
77	Grant, Darryl	G	6-1	230	2	Rice
68	Grimm, Russ	G	6-3	258	2	Pittsburgh
38	Harmon, Clarence	RB	5-11	209	6	Mississippi State
78	Hickman, Dallas	DE-LB	6-6	242	7	California-Berkeley
40	Jackson, Wilbur	RB	6-1	219	8	Alabama
66	Jacoby, Joe	T	6-7	290	2	Louisville
22	Jones, Melvin	G	6-2	260	2	Houston
22	Jordan, Curtis	CB-S	6-2	205	6	Texas Tech
55	Kaufman, Mel	LB	6-2	214	2	Cal Poly-SLO
50	Kubin, Larry	LB	6-2	230	2	Penn State
71	Lavender, Joe	CB	6-4	185	10	San Diego State
71	Lorch, Karl	DE	6-3	258	7	Southern California
56	Lowry, Quentin	LB	6-2	225	2	Youngstown State
72	Manley, Dexter	DE	6-3	240	2	Oklahoma State
73	May, Mark	T	6-6	270	2	Pittsburgh
84	McCrary, Gregg	TE	6-2	235	7	Clark
45	McDaniel, LeCharls	CB	5-9	169	2	Cal Poly-SLO
76	Mendenhall, Mat	DE	6-6	253	2	Brigham Young
26	Metcalf, Terry	RB	5-10	183	7	Long Beach State
57	Milot, Rich	LB	6-4	230	3	Penn State
81	Monk, Art	WR	6-3	209	3	Syracuse
3	Moseley, Mark	K	6-0	205	11	Stephen F. Austin
29	Murphy, Mark	S	6-4	210	6	Colgate
21	Nelms, Mike	S	6-1	185	3	Baylor
79	Ogrin, Pat	DT	6-5	265	2	Wyoming
52	Olkewicz, Neal	LB	6-1	227	4	Maryland
23	Peters, Tony	S	6-1	177	8	Oklahoma
86	Raba, Bob	TE	6-4	235	5	Maryland
44	Riggins, John	RB	6-2	235	11	Kansas
64	Saul, Ron	G	6-3	254	13	Michigan State
	Scanlan, Jerry	T	6-5	270	3	Hawaii
80	Seay, Virgil	WR	5-8	170	2	Troy State
74	Starke, George	T	6-5	250	10	Columbia
7	Theismann, Joe	QB	6-0	195	9	Notre Dame
83	Thompson, Ricky	WR	6-0	177	7	Baylor
88	Walker, Rick	TE	6-4	235	6	UCLA
85	Warren, Don	TE	6-4	236	4	San Diego State
25	Washington, Joe	RB	5-10	185	6	Oklahoma
58	Weaver, Charlie	LB	6-2	225	12	Southern California
45	White, Jeris	CB	5-10	188	9	Hawaii
39	Wonsley, Otis	RB	5-10	214	2	Alcorn State

TOP FIVE DRAFT CHOICES

Rd.	Name	Sel. No.	Pos.	Ht.	Wt.	College
2	Dean, Vernon	49	DB	5-11	180	San Diego State
3	Powell, Carl	61	WR	5-11	182	Jackson State
4	Liebenstein, Todd	99	DE	6-7	232	Nevada-Las Vegas
5	Williams, Michael	133	TE	6-4	220	Alabama A&M
6	Jeffers, Lemont	153	LB	6-3	205	Tennessee

THE ROOKIES: The Redskins think their top two choices, cornerback Vernon Dean of San Diego State and receiver Carl Powell of Jackson State, can be starters this season. And tight end Michael Williams of Alabama A&M has the hands and speed to earn some immediate playing time.

OUTLOOK: Gibbs cautions that the Redskins' finish last year could be misleading, especially in the face of a difficult schedule. In such an evenly balanced league, a healthy Washington team could climb over .500, but the loss of any key players could lead to another losing season.

REDSKIN PROFILES

JOE THEISMANN 32 6-0 195   **Quarterback**

Bitter contract squabble with management has left him puzzled about his role on the team... "I don't know what else I have to do to please them," he says... Threw for 3,568 yards and 19 TDs with 59.1 percent accuracy, but suffered 20 INTs. Still, it was his best season statistically... Wasn't comfortable with coach Joe Gibbs' system until one-third of the season had elapsed... Man with a thousand business interests... Owns two restaurants, has numerous investments, does national ads for camera company... Born Sept. 9, 1949, in New Brunswick, N.J.... Former Notre Dame star plans to play three more years, then don't be surprised if he campaigns heavily for spot in Hollywood movie industry.

MARK MURPHY 27 6-4 210   **Safety**

In ticklish spot as team's player representative and member of NFLPA negotiating team... If anyone can keep the peace in that role, this former free agent from Colgate is the man... Scholarly, mild-mannered and respected both by his teammates and management... Studying for master's in economics and takes a class during every season... Led the Redskins in tackles from his free safety spot... Also was tops in interceptions (7) and among the leaders in every other defensive category... Born July 14, 1955, in Fulton, N.Y.... One of the league's most underrated players, probably because he doesn't have outstanding quickness.

JOE WASHINGTON 28 5–10 185　　　**Running Back**

A spectacular debut season with the Redskins... Became the added offensive dimension the team had been lacking... If he hadn't missed parts of the season with injuries probably would have enjoyed his best-ever year... Still, led the club in rushing (916 yards, 4.4 per carry) and receiving (70 catches for 558 yards)... Became instant fan favorite... Finally happy after going through prolonged contract dispute with Colts, who surrendered him for second-round selection... Born Sept. 4, 1953, in Crocket, Tex., and attended Oklahoma, where he accounted for nearly 4,000 yards.

RUSS GRIMM 23 6–3 258　　　**Guard**

Hadn't even put on a Redskin uniform and already was a much-talked-about figure ... Stepped right into starting left guard spot although he played center at Pitt... Made most of the major all-rookie teams and was the man the team was running behind for most of its key yardage... Down-to-earth straight shooter who tells it like it is... After going up against all-world Randy White, he said, "They said he was quick, but not that quick"... Troubled by knee injury throughout most of the season, but refused operation until after the final game... Born May 2, 1959, in Pittsburgh... Played quarterback in high school.

JOHN RIGGINS 33 6–2 235　　　**Fullback**

Never a dull moment when Riggins is involved... His controversial career took another turn when he came back last season after a year's layoff and contributed heavily to improved Redskin running game... Expected to be booed by the fans, but instead was cheered with every appearance... When Redskins went to one-back offense, he had limited playing time behind Joe Washington, but still gained 714 yards and scored 13 TDs...Once one of the NFL's most accessible players, he declined interview requests while his grievance with the Redskins was being decided...Drives a motorcycle, lives on a farm outside Lawrence, Kan., where he was born Aug. 4, 1949, but don't mistake him for some country bumpkin...Broke Gale Sayers' records at Kansas...Redskins owe him $1 million in deferred salary.

MARK MOSELEY 34 6–0 205   Kicker

League's highest-paid kicker...Came back from so-so 1980 season to have improved year with 95 points on 19 of 30 field-goal accuracy...Hindered by leg pulls, but healed enough to win a couple of games with his late field goals...Didn't get as much work as usual once the Redskins started moving the ball better and were more successful working for touchdowns...Figures he is nowhere near retirement if he can keep away from those leg injuries...Changed his off season conditioning program, cutting down on weightlifting...Born March 12, 1948, in Laneville, Tex....Started college at Texas A&M before finishing up at Stephen F. Austin.

ART MONK 24 6–3 209   Receiver

Has to put up with constant double teaming...Would be helped greatly if the Redskins could add second quality wide receiver, especially if newcomer was a speedburner ...Didn't have the statistics last year that he or the team wanted (56 catches, 894 yards), particularly in view of all the throwing done by the Redskins...Admits he has to improve on his takeoff from the line and on work against the bump-and-run...Remarkable receiver who has the guts to run patterns over the middle and not drop the ball....Born Dec. 5, 1957, in White Plains, N.Y....The highest-paid rookie in Redskin history as 1980 first-round pick out of Syracuse, he keeps to himself and does his job without complaining.

NEAL OLKEWICZ 25 6–1 227   Linebacker

Until late-season injury, he was leading the team in tackles and gutty plays ... Pushes himself to perform well above the level indicated by his natural talent ... Worked hard on being a better pass defender although quickness problems hinder him in this area.... Has served as a jail guard in the offseason ... Teammates call him Mole ... First free agent signed after 1979 draft ... Born Jan. 30, 1957, in Phoenixville, Pa.... Set single-game school tackling record at Maryland with 27 against Penn State his senior year ... Mr. Pleasant off the field, with the brightest smile on the team.

MIKE NELMS 27 6–1 185   Safety

Pro Bowl kick returner for second year in a row ... When he was out with broken arm at start of season, the Redskins couldn't win a game ... When he came back, they got untracked ... He is one of the team's few big-play athletes ... Probably will be tried as a wingback-wide receiver to see if he can add more to Redskin offense ... Has great balance and has deceiving quickness ... His size and strength make him difficult to tackle ... After leaving Baylor, he played in the Canadian Football League before signing with the Redskins ... Born April 8, 1955, in Ft. Worth, Tex.... Does wonderful bird calls.

DAVE BUTZ 32 6–7 295   Defensive Tackle

One of the league's biggest players ... When he is playing well, it takes two opponents to control him ... His strength is containing the run, not rushing the passer ... Had thrill of a career last year when he intercepted pass against Chicago and lumbered toward goal line ... "I thought I'd never get there," he said.... Has to be steadying force on constantly changing defensive front ... Wears 12½ shoes, 7EEEEEEE in width ... Shattered a backboard during a basketball game in high school ... Offseason banker ... When he calls in a loan, you pay it off quickly ... Born June 23, 1950, in Lafayette, Ala.... Attended Purdue ... Serves as Santa Claus at team's annual Christmas party for needy kids.

COACH JOE GIBBS... Wondered when he would ever win his

first game as a head coach... Lost five straight before finally beating Chicago... Stood up well under tremendous fan and media pressure ... Admits he didn't know how deep the team's problems were until after training camp... Made some rookie coaching mistakes, particularly in staying with a passing offense too long... By season's end, Redskins were one of the league's most efficient teams... Member of the league's new wave of offensive thinkers... Prides himself on developing new plays and changing offense from week to week to sabotage opponents' scouting reports... Born Nov. 25, 1943, in Mocksville, N.C.... Likes to ski, plays an outstanding game of racquetball, is determined to run a marathon... Absent-minded, once forgetting where he parked his car after he couldn't find it in team parking lot... Gained reputation as innovator while he was offensive coordinator for San Diego Chargers... Things got so hectic last season that he started sleeping at Redskin Park two nights a week on pullout sofa bed given to him by his wife.

GREATEST LINEBACKER

Even though Chris Hanburger had made All-Atlantic Coast Conference his senior year at North Carolina, the pro scouts were hardly enthusiastic about the skinny, awkward, not-that-aggressive linebacker. No prospect, they said. So when he still was available on the 18th round of the 1964 draft, the Redskins hesitated to take him even then. But it was getting late, so they called out his name. It was a selection they came to cherish.

Over 14 years, Hanburger established himself as the team's best-ever linebacker. George Allen called him a coach on the field who was so intelligent that he would invariably call almost-perfect defensive signals. Hanburger wound up playing in nine Pro Bowls and was voted the NFC Defensive Player of the Year in 1972, the season the Redskins went to the Super Bowl.

He was especially nifty on pass defense, where he picked off 19 passes, returning an impressive five for touchdowns. And despite his modest 218 pounds, he was durable. At one point, he played in 135 straight games before an appendix operation sidelined him.

Joe Theismann's 19 TDs highlighted a fine season.

INDIVIDUAL REDSKIN RECORDS

Rushing

Most Yards Game:	195	Mike Thomas, vs St. Louis, 1976
Season:	1,216	Larry Brown, 1972
Career:	5,812	Larry Brown, 1969–72

Passing

Most TD Passes Game:	6	Sam Baugh, vs Brooklyn, 1943
	6	Sam Baugh, vs St. Louis, 1947
Season:	31	Sonny Jurgensen, 1967
Career:	209	Sonny Jurgensen, Eagles 1957–63, Redskins 1964–74

Receiving

Most TD Passes Game:	3	Hugh Taylor (5 times)
	3	Jerry Smith, vs Los Angeles, 1967
	3	Jerry Smith, vs Dallas, 1969
	3	Hal Crisler (once)
	3	Joe Walton (once)
	3	Pat Richter, vs Chicago, 1968
	3	Larry Brown, vs Philadelphia, 1973
	3	Jean Fugett, vs San Francisco, 1976
Season:	12	Hugh Taylor, 1952
	12	Charley Taylor, 1966
	12	Jerry Smith, 1967
Career:	79	Charley Taylor, 1964–77

Scoring

Most Points Game:	24	Dick James, vs Dallas, 1961
	24	Larry Brown, vs Philadelphia, 1973
Season:	114	Curt Knight, 1971
	114	Mark Moseley, 1979
Career:	722	Mark Moseley, 1974–81
Most TDs Game:	4	Dick James, vs Dallas, 1961
Season:	15	Charley Taylor, 1966
Career:	90	Charley Taylor, 1964–77

INSIDE THE AFC

By DAVE NEWHOUSE

PREDICTED ORDER OF FINISH		
EAST	**CENTRAL**	**WEST**
New York Jets	Cincinnati	Kansas City
Miami	Pittsburgh	San Diego
Buffalo	Cleveland	Denver
New England	Houston	Oakland
Baltimore		Seattle

AFC Champion: New York Jets

The winds that blow inside Shea Stadium and the dust that swirls on the Missouri plains represent elements of change in the American Football Conference.

The New York Jets, who last year saw the ghost of Joe Willie come to life in the form of Richard Todd, are ready to seize control of the AFC East.

Out in Kansas City, the Chiefs have grown slowly into a definite force under Marv Levy's methodical guidance and are now prepared to stand the AFC West on its head.

It will be the first return to power for the Jets and Chiefs since their Super Bowl heydays in the old American Football League, and the Jets will land in Super Bowl XVII.

So where does this leave the Cincinnati Bengals, you ask? In first place in the Central Division, as expected, though Cincinnati isn't invincible, which San Francisco proved twice last season.

The Jets have Super weaponry in Todd—as good a quarterback as there was in football at the tail end of last year—as well as pass protection, receivers, loads of backs and a sack-happy defense that will be even better in 1982.

It won't be a cakewalk for New York—it never is in the East.

Dave Newhouse of the Oakland Tribune *is, among other things, an authority on pro football.*

Terry Bradshaw's burden: To bring back Steeler glory.

Miami will be tough again, but the Jets have the Dolphins' number. Buffalo would look better if it didn't let Tom Cousineau get away. New England could surprise under new coach Ron Meyer, but Baltimore's embarrassing defense will keep Frank Kush rebuilding for a while.

Ken Anderson can't be expected to repeat his spectacular '81 season and the Bengals can't expect to remain so injury-free. However, the competition isn't much. Pittsburgh will only be strong with its passing game intact, but it isn't the Pittsburgh of old. Cleveland's defense looks better with Cousineau. Houston hasn't been the same since Bum left.

The AFC West will be as tight, or tighter, than the East. The Chiefs could win with a 10–6 record, like San Diego a year ago. Kansas City's only question mark is quarterback Steve Fuller, but he might be ready to put it all together this year. The Chargers have mortgaged their future to win at all costs now through heavy trading. This philosophy eventually backfires; this could be San Diego's last hurrah.

Denver depends heavily on Craig Morton, but at his age (39) this is risky. Coming off its first losing season in 16 years, Oakland is an unlikely playoff candidate, but Al Davis has fooled us before. Seattle? Nice place to go boating.

BALTIMORE COLTS

TEAM DIRECTORY: Pres./Treas.: Robert Irsay; VP: Harriet Irsay; VP/Gen. Counsel: Michael Chernoff; Asst. GM: Ernie Accorsi; Dir. Player Personnel: Fred Schubach; Dir. Pub. Rel.: Walt Gutowski; Head Coach: Frank Kush. Home field: Memorial Stadium (60,763). Colors: Royal blue and white.

SCOUTING REPORT

OFFENSE: Bert Jones' long and bitter struggle with owner Robert Irsay finally reached an end when the Colts sent him to Los Angeles for the second pick overall in the draft and a second-round choice. Jones' great passing ability will be missed, but not his immaturity in singling out teammates for their mistakes.

Jones' departure will leave the QB chores to one of three candidates—rookies Art Schlichter and Mike Pagel and veteran Greg Landry. Schlichter, the fifth pick overall, was a standout at Ohio State and is probably the best bet to step in for Jones.

The Colts have two promising young running backs in Curtis Dickey and Randy McMillan, two fine wide receivers in Roger Carr and Raymond Butler and a solid tight end in Reese McCall. The offensive line has top guards in Robert Pratt and Ken Huff, a good center in Ray Donaldson. The best tackles may be the backups, Tim Foley and Randy Van Divier.

Baltimore's offense would improve if the defense would just cooperate and put the ball in the Colts' hands more frequently. The Colts ran 957 plays to 1,111 for opponents in '81. Schlichter may make Baltimore fans forget Jones in time but, while he learns the NFL ropes, the Colts' suffering will continue.

DEFENSE: The pits. The absolute worst. Baltimore had the only defense in the league that gave up more than 500 points (533) and 6,000 yards (6,793). That averages out to 33.3 points and 424.6 yards. It's amazing the Colts won two games with a defense so porous.

Frank Kush had better have rosary beads on hand for every game. One pre-draft report said of the Colts' needs: "If Bert Jones is traded, a quarterback. Then, anything on defense, especially a linebacker."

The front three of Donnell Thompson, Bubba Green and Hosea Taylor produced only 13 sacks—the only NFL team that didn't record at least 20. The Colts don't need linebackers; they need linemen.

Sanders Shiver, Joe Federspiel and Barry Krauss are satisfactory, but rookie Johnnie Cooks, picked No. 2 overall, is the mean stud this linebacking unit has been lacking.

The secondary intercepted only 16 passes, the third worst mark in football. However, Derrick Hatchett, Larry Braziel and Nesby Glasgow are young players. Only Bruce Laird is truly experienced. This group could get better through osmosis, if it recovers from the shell-shock of '81.

KICKING GAME: So-so punter Mike Garrett (39.4, 11 punts inside 20) may lose job to rookie Rohn Stark. Kicker Mike Wood

Curtis Dickey is bright spot for new coach Frank Kush.

COLTS VETERAN ROSTER

HEAD COACH—Frank Kush. Assistant Coaches—Dick Bielski, George Boutselis, Bobby Boyd, John Idzik, Ed Khayat, Clyde Powers, John Symank, Chuck Weber, Ray Wietecha, Joe Vitt.

No.	Name	Pos.	Ht.	Wt.	NFL Exp.	College
26	Anderson, Kim	CB	5-11	182	3	Arizona State
47	Braziel, Larry	CB	6-0	184	4	Southern California
84	Burke, Randy	WR	6-2	198	5	Kentucky
80	Butler, Ray	WR	6-3	190	3	Southern California
81	Carr, Roger	WR	6-2	193	9	Louisiana Tech
87	DeRoo, Brian	WR	6-3	200	4	Redlands
27	Dickey, Curtis	RB	6-0	201	3	Texas A&M
31	Dixon, Zachary	RB	6-1	204	4	Temple
53	Donaldson, Ray	C	6-3	263	3	Georgia
50	Federspiel, Joe	LB	6-2	230	11	Kentucky
78	Foley, Tim	T	6-6	275	2	Notre Dame
66	Foote, Chris	C	6-3	247	3	Southern California
28	Franklin, Cleveland	FB	6-2	220	5	Baylor
72	Fultz, Mike	DT	6-5	278	6	Nebraska
9	Garrett, Mike	P	6-1	184	2	Georgia
25	Glasgow, Nesby	S	5-11	185	4	Washington
91	Green, Bubba	DT	6-4	278	2	North Carolina State
69	Griffin, Wade	T	6-5	278	6	Mississippi
68	Hart, Jeff	T	6-5	272	6	Oregon State
42	Hatchett, Derrick	CB	6-0	186	3	Texas
58	Heimkreiter, Steve	LB	6-2	226	3	Notre Dame
44	Henry, Steve	S	6-2	190	3	Emporia State
62	Huff, Ken	G	6-5	253	8	North Carolina
10	Humm, David	QB	6-2	190	8	Nebraska
51	Jones, Ricky	LB	6-2	222	6	Tuskegee
55	Krauss, Barry	LB	6-4	238	4	Alabama
40	Laird, Bruce	S	6-1	194	11	American International
11	Landry, Greg	QB	6-4	210	15	Massachusetts
86	McCall, Reese	TE	6-6	243	5	Auburn
23	McCauley, Don	RB	6-1	206	12	North Carolina
32	McMillan, Randy	FB	6-1	226	2	Pittsburgh
65	Moore, Jimmy	G	6-5	268	2	Ohio State
88	Orvis, Herb	DT	6-5	255	11	Colorado
71	Ozdowski, Mike	DE	6-5	243	5	Virginia
37	Pinkey, Reggie	S	6-0	187	6	East Carolina
61	Pratt, Robert	G	6-4	250	9	North Carolina
83	Sherwin, Tim	TE	6-5	239	2	Boston College
54	Shiver, Sanders	LB	6-2	230	7	Carson-Newman
85	Shula, Dave	WR	5-11	182	2	Dartmouth
	Simmons, Dave	LB	6-4	220	2	North Carolina
56	Simonini, Ed	LB	6-0	206	7	Texas A&M
39	Sims, Marvin	FB	6-4	324	3	Clemson
52	Smith, Ed	LB	6-3	216	3	Vanderbilt
90	Taylor, Hosea	DE	6-5	250	2	Houston
99	Thompson, Donnell	DE	6-5	252	2	North Carolina
79	Van Divier, Randy	T	6-5	282	2	Washington
21	Williams, Kevin	RB-S	5-8	168	2	Southern California
16	Wood, Mike	K	5-11	199	4	Southeast Missouri State
59	Woods, Mike	LB	6-2	237	4	Cincinnati

TOP FIVE DRAFT CHOICES

Rd.	Name	Sel. No.	Pos.	Ht.	Wt.	College
1	Cooks, Johnie	2	LB	6-4	240	Mississippi State
1	Schlichter, Art	4	QB	6-3	208	Ohio State
2	Wisniewski, Leo	28	DT	6-1	251	Penn State
2	Stark, Rohn	34	P	6-3	195	Florida State
3	Burroughs, Jim	57	DB	6-1	190	Michigan State

(10–18, but can do better) is steady, while return men Dave Shula and Zachary Dixon are average.

THE ROOKIES: Cooks should bring the Colts 10 years of solid linebacking, but the most interesting draft pick is Schlichter. If he's the quarterback he was as an Ohio State sophomore, he could possibly start as an NFL rookie. If he's the quarterback he was the last two years, he could fail. Ohio State is no QB factory. Michigan State cornerback Jim Burroughs is a sleeper.

OUTLOOK: Kush has been a coaching magician for years. If he can get this bunch to win six games, Baltimore should rename its stadium after him at once. The Colts will never surpass .500 until that defense improves, which may take two or three years.

COLT PROFILES

GREG LANDRY 35 6–4 210   Quarterback

The go-between . . . With Bert Jones gone, Landry goes between Art Schlichter and the day he is ready to become an NFL starter, when and if that happens . . . Early in his career, Landry was anything but a fill-in . . . Ten years ago he was the best pass-run quarterback in the pros, at Detroit, until the battering took its toll . . . He came to Baltimore in '79 as a stand-in for the injured Jones, but threw only 29 passes last year, completing 14 for no scores, as Jones regained his health and job . . . Landry's now in his 15th year . . . Born Dec. 18, 1946, in Nashua, N.H. . . . Quarterback star at Massachusetts, then a top draft pick of the Lions in '68 . . . Wife Jeannine a top gymnast; both were installed in Massachusetts Hall of Fame.

CURTIS DICKEY 25 6–0 201   Running Back

Texas lightning . . . Dickey has scored 23 touchdowns, more than any Colt in first two seasons . . . His 1,579 yards rushing is second only to Alan Ameche's 1,819 (1956–57) . . . Dickey has incredible speed and tremendous potential. All he really needs is a good team around him . . . Ran 67 yards for a touchdown against Dallas. It was like trying to catch

Secretariat...Dickey was a world-class sprinter at Texas A&M, running 100 yards in 9.2 and 100 meters in 10.05, a half-second off the world record...Born Nov. 27, 1956, in Madisonville, Tex....All-time leading rusher at Texas A&M and three-time NCAA 60-yard indoor sprint champ...Rushed for 779 yards (4.8) last year and caught 37 passes, including 11 in one game.

RANDY McMILLAN 23 6–1 226   Running Back

Mr. Inside...Rushed for 597 yards (4.0) as a rookie and most of it was between the tackles...Caught 50 passes to lead the team, setting a club record for rookies...McMillan served notice of what was to come by pounding for 146 yards against New England in his pro debut...Solid, compact fullback, built low to the ground with strong legs...The Colts losing 14 games was a new experience for McMillan, whose college record was 42–2. He transferred from Harford (Md.) Community College to Pittsburgh...Colts drafted him No. 1, the 12th player taken in the entire draft...Born in Havre de Grace, Md., on Dec. 17, 1958...Has good speed despite his bulky frame and is a good blocker, too...Ask Curtis Dickey.

RAYMOND BUTLER 26 6–3 190   Wide Receiver

This Butler isn't silent...Rang up nine touchdowns last year and now has 80 receptions in two seasons—the most ever by a second-year Colt...Another of Baltimore's fine young players at skilled positions...Only this one arrived with few press clippings...Butler played two years at USC, caught 28 passes and reminded no one of Lynn Swann...The Colts put a bunch of names in a hat during the fourth round of the 1980 draft, reached in and picked out a name: Raymond Butler. Raymond Who?...Started all 16 games and had the best year of any Colts' rookie wide receiver ever. Raymond What?...Born June 28, 1956, in Port Larace, Tex....Transferred to USC from Wharton County (Tex.) JC and sat around watching Charles White carry the ball.

ROGER CARR 30 6–2 193   Wide Receiver

Long-distance runner... Carr's game is speed, and speed means the bomb, and he doesn't like to fool around with anything in between... Has scored on touchdown passes of 90, 89, 79 and 78 yards for Baltimore... His career average per catch is 18.0... Though Carr hasn't lost much speed, his longest catch the last three years has been 43 yards... He is Bert Jones' favorite receiver, but Jones' injury problems two of the last three years have cut down on Carr's statistics. Young Raymond Butler has had something to do with it, too... Carr was born July 1, 1952, in Seminole, Tex.... Small-college All-American at Terry Bradshaw Tech, otherwise known as Louisiana Tech... Carr was a first-round pick in 1974... Has history of injuries.

DON McCAULEY 33 6–1 216   Running Back

Traded for Don Shula... When Miami signed Shula as its head coach, the Dolphins had to give Baltimore a No. 1 draft pick, which turned out to be McCauley... Getting Shula for a No. 1 is a bargain, but McCauley has given the Colts 11 years of dependable service at running back... He's the Bill Brown, Pete Banaszak type—not spectacular, but durable, smart and productive... Need a first down, send in McCauley. That occurs more in passing situations now... Preston Pearson and Jim Kiick functioned in similar roles for years in Dallas and Miami... McCauley was born May 12, 1949, in Garden City, N.Y.... Broke O. J. Simpson's single-season collegiate rushing record while at North Carolina, where he was a dean's list student.

REESE McCALL 26 6–6 243   Tight End

Big 'un... McCall doesn't catch many passes. At his size, who needs to? He should be playing tackle, but in a way he is. Colts stick him at tight end and say, "Block, Reese, block."... So Reese blocks. Does a pretty good job, too, clearing the way for Curtis Dickey and Randy McMillan... On occasion last year the Colts fooled Reese. They sent him out to catch a football, which he did 21 times. Twice, he made it to the end zone, once from 65 yards away...Long run for Reese, but he was so happy to get there, he didn't mind...In fact, he'd like to catch 40–50 passes just to show the Colts he can do other things but block...Born June 16, 1956, in Bessemer, Ala....No. 1 pick ('78) out of Auburn.

ROBERT PRATT 31 6–4 250   Offensive Guard

Robert Pratt eats no fat, and so he stays so lean...Keeping enough fat on Pratt has been a problem. The Colts list him at 250, but he could be 240 midway through the season...Yet he is the Colts' most consistent offensive lineman, for he is lean and mean...Graduate of North Carolina, as is Baltimore's other offensive guard, Ken Huff...In fact, he and Huff lined up together in college as well...Pratt earned a degree in business administration and now is a stockbroker in the offseason. Member of Wall Street's all-pro team...Born May 25, 1951, in White Plains, N.Y....Scored 20 touchdowns as a high school fullback...Switched to tackle in college, then to guard in the pros.

DERRICK HATCHETT 24 6–0 186   Cornerback

Hatchett was buried by the bomb last year...Denver's Steve Watson burned him three times for touchdowns last September... However, Hatchett has speed and ability. In time, he may be doing the burning... Colts' second pick of the first round in the 1980 draft behind Curtis Dickey...Has been a starter ever since, getting his baptism the hard way...All-American at Texas who ran on the Longhorns' record-setting sprint relay team with Johnny (Lam) Jones, etc....Born Aug. 14, 1958, in Bryan, Tex....Sociology major at Texas, where younger brother Mike also was a cornerback...Derrick was named to NFL's all-rookie team, then intercepted two passes last year...Regarded as a good tackler.

BRUCE LAIRD 32 6–1 194   Strong Safety

Like a strong coat of wax: apply once and it protects for a long time... This is Laird's 11th year with the Colts and he has seen it all: play-offs, the cellar, Joe Thomas, Robert Irsay, etc.... Laird continues to remain one of the staples holding this crazy, mixed-up team together... Reliable strong safety and holder of Colts' career marks for kickoff return yardage... Played in two Pro Bowls and named to Sports Illustrated's all-pro team in '80.... Born May 23, 1950, in Lowell, Mass.... Played at American International, rushed for 1,402 yards as a senior and was named All-New England... Colts found him just about the same time they found American International. Drafted him No. 6 in 1972... Sales rep in offseason.

COACH FRANK KUSH...

"I believe the Colts organization is in a rebirth... We need to reinstill the burning desire to excel. I love to see people have success. I don't like to be around losers."... With those words, Frank Kush, 53, the one-time Desert Fox, took over football's clownish organization, the Baltimore Colts... Kush is used to winning, which the Colts haven't been lately... His 22-year record of 176–54–1 at Arizona State computed into a .764 winning percentage, ranking him second behind Bear Bryant among active coaches... But Kush's rough coaching tactics—an Arizona State punter took him to court on charges that the coach slapped him during a game; Kush was acquitted—led to his ouster... Born Jan. 20, 1929, in Windber, Pa., he was an All-American defensive guard at Michigan State... He coached the Hamilton Tiger Cats of the Canadian Football League to an 11–4–1 record last year and first place in the Eastern Conference... The National Football League is a lot tougher place to win, but Kush has won everywhere he has gone. It's safe to assume he will win in the NFL, too, eventually... How long he can put up with the eccentric owner, Robert Irsay, and vice versa, is the question... Kush can't be physical with the Colts like he was at Arizona State, either... He'll need to inspire them in other ways.

GREATEST LINEBACKER

Don Shinnick was a character. He once entered a game for the Baltimore Colts while munching on a sandwich and with his helmet tied to his belt. He handed the sandwich to a surprised Colts tackle at the line of scrimmage, hurriedly snapped on his helmet and made the tackle.

Even with his shenanigans, he intercepted 37 passes—the career high for NFL linebackers to this day—in 12 seasons with Baltimore.

Key to Colts' passing game: The Butler (Ray) does it.

Shinnick was an accomplished pass thief even though he was out of position on a number of those interceptions. Somehow he marched to his own game plan and still managed to get the job done.

Shinnick was a fullback at UCLA before he was shifted permanently to linebacker. The Colts drafted him No. 2 behind Jim Parker in 1957 and Shinnick remained with the team until 1968. His interceptions are the second-largest total by a Colt behind Bobby Boyd's 57.

There have been some great Baltimore linebackers—Mike Curtis, Bill Pellington, etc.—but none with better statistics or a more unique playing style than Don Shinnick.

INDIVIDUAL COLT RECORDS

Rushing

Most Yards Game:	198	Norm Bulaich, vs N.Y. Jets, 1971
Season:	1,200	Lydell Mitchell, 1976
Career:	5,487	Lydell Mitchell, 1972–77

Passing

Most TD Passes Game:	5	Gary Cuozzo, vs Minnesota, 1965
Season:	32	John Unitas, 1959
Career:	287	John Unitas, 1956–72

Receiving

Most TD Passes Game:	3	Jim Mutscheller, vs Green Bay, 1957
	3	Raymond Berry, vs Dallas, 1960
	3	Raymond Berry, vs Green Bay, 1960
	3	Jimmy Orr, vs Washington, 1962
	3	Jimmy Orr, vs Los Angeles, 1964
	3	Roger Carr, vs Cincinnati, 1976
Season:	14	Raymond Berry, 1959
Career:	68	Raymond Berry, 1955–67

Scoring

Most Points Game:	24	Lenny Moore, vs Chicago, 1958
	24	Lenny Moore, vs Los Angeles, 1960
	24	Lenny Moore, vs Minnesota, 1961
	24	Lydell Mitchell, vs Buffalo, 1975
Season:	120	Lenny Moore, 1964
Career:	678	Lenny Moore, 1956–67
Most TDs Game:	4	Lenny Moore, vs Chicago, 1958
	4	Lenny Moore, vs Los Angeles, 1960
	4	Lenny Moore, vs Minnesota, 1961
	4	Lydell Mitchell, vs Buffalo, 1975
Season:	20	Lenny Moore, 1964
Career:	113	Lenny Moore, 1956–67

BUFFALO BILLS

TEAM DIRECTORY: Pres.: Ralph Wilson; VP/Football Oper.-Head Coach: Chuck Knox; VP/GM: Stew Barber; VP: Patrick McGroder; VP/Pub. Rel.: L. Budd Thalman. Home field: Rich Stadium (80,020). Colors: Scarlet red, royal blue and white.

SCOUTING REPORT

OFFENSE: Not a great offense, but a very good one. Joe Ferguson isn't the classic quarterback, but he gets the job done in his own way. Joe Cribbs' versatility helps Ferguson, because Shreve-

Buffalo's version of the one-man offense is Joe Cribbs.

port Joe now has a dangerous back to slip into the passing routes. Cribbs is the biggest threat Buffalo has had since O. J. Simpson.

The Bills are satisfactory at fullback. The emergence of Booker Moore, who was ill during his rookie year, would be a big plus here. Tight end Mark Brammer is dependable, but no game-breaker. The wide receivers are outstanding, though Frank Lewis is 35 with possibly only one good year left.

The offensive line appears in transition. Reggie McKenzie and Conrad Dobler are listed as starting guards. But Jim Ritcher has been shifted from center to Dobler's spot. McKenzie has ex-Seahawk Tom Lynch and Jon Borchardt to contend with at left guard. Borchard is also on the depth chart at both tackles behind starters Ken Jones and Joe Devlin. Borchardt may break through somewhere before the year is out. Will Grant is a stable center; otherwise, why would Ritcher be moved to guard?

DEFENSE: Strong throughout, but weakest at linebacker and at the safeties. The Bills' linebacking foursome of Lucius Sanford, Jim Haslett, Shane Nelson and Isiah Robertson is experienced and adequate. But if Buffalo could have satisfied the contract demands of Tom Cousineau instead of dealing the rights to the former Alouette to Cleveland, the Bills' linebacking would have been greatly upgraded.

Free safety Bill Simpson made a game-saving interception against the Jets in the playoffs, but he can be beaten on the deep pass. Strong safety Steve Freeman led the defense in total tackles, but he didn't have an interception. Former Redskin Lemar Parrish joins adequate backups Jeff Nixon and Rod Kush. The cornerbacks, Mario Clark and Charles Romes, are good ones.

The strength of the defense is the front three: Fred Smerlas, Ben Williams and Sherman White. They supply enough pressure on the passer that the secondary isn't under constant siege. Buffalo ranked No. 1 in the AFC against the pass, but only ninth against the run. With better linebacking, Freeman wouldn't have to make all those tackles at strong safety.

KICKING GAME: Weakest part of the team. Nick Mike-Mayer is better than his brother, Steve, but adequate (14–24) at best—only 5-of-10 between 40–49 yards. Greg Cater (39.7) improved a yard over his '80 punting average, but he's not a great one either. Buffalo's longest return last year was 36 yards.

THE ROOKIES: Clemson's Perry Tuttle is the heir apparent to Lewis whenever Old Bones finally slows down. Tuttle and Jerry Butler together could take some of the receiving burden off the

BILLS VETERAN ROSTER

HEAD COACH—Chuck Knox. Assistant Coaches—Tom Catlin, Jack Donaldson, George Dyer, Chick Harris, Ralph Hawkins, Miller McCalmon, Steve Moore, Ray Prochaska, Kay Stephenson.

No.	Name	Pos.	Ht.	Wt.	NFL Exp.	College
87	Alvers, Steve	TE	6-4	240	2	Miami
84	Barnett, Buster	TE	6-5	225	2	Jackson State
28	Bess, Rufus	CB	5-9	180	4	South Carolina State
73	Borchardt, Jon	T	6-5	255	4	Montana State
86	Brammer, Mark	TE	6-3	225	3	Michigan State
47	Brown, Curtis	RB	5-10	203	6	Missouri
80	Butler, Jerry	WR	6-0	171	4	Clemson
7	Cater, Greg	P	6-0	191	3	Tennessee-Chattanooga
29	Clark, Mario	CB	6-2	195	7	Oregon
20	Cribbs, Joe	RB	5-11	190	3	Auburn
70	Devlin, Joe	T	6-5	250	7	Iowa
69	Dobler, Conrad	G	6-3	255	11	Wyoming
12	Ferguson, Joe	QB	6-1	195	10	Arkansas
85	Franklin, Byron	WR	6-1	179	2	Auburn
22	Freeman, Steve	S	5-11	185	8	Mississippi State
53	Grant, Will	C	6-4	248	5	Kentucky
55	Haslett, Jim	LB	6-3	232	4	Indiana, Pa.
25	Hooks, Roland	RB	6-0	195	7	North Carolina State
50	Humiston, Mike	LB	6-3	238	2	Weber State
97	Irvin, Darrell	DE	6-4	255	3	Oklahoma
81	Jessie, Ron	WR	6-0	181	12	Kansas
91	Johnson, Ken	DE	6-5	253	4	Knoxville
72	Jones, Ken	T	6-5	250	7	Arkansas State
71	Kadish, Mike	NT	6-5	250	10	Notre Dame
52	Keating, Chris	LB	6-2	223	3	Maine
42	Kush, Rod	S	6-0	188	3	Nebraska-Omaha
48	Leaks, Roosevelt	RB	5-10	225	8	Texas
82	Lewis, Frank	WR	6-1	196	12	Grambling
61	Lynch, Tom	G	6-5	250	6	Boston College
30	McCutcheon, Lawrence	RB	6-1	205	11	Colorado State
67	McKenzie, Reggie	G	6-5	242	11	Michigan
5	Mike-Mayer, Nick	K	5-9	185	10	Temple
43	Moore, Booker	RB	5-11	229	2	Penn State
59	Nelson, Shane	LB	6-1	225	6	Baylor
38	Nixon, Jeff	S	6-3	190	4	Richmond
62	Parker, Ervin	LB	6-5	240	3	South Carolina State
24	Parrish, Lemar	CB	5-10	170	13	Lincoln
89	Piccone, Lou	WR	5-9	175	9	West Liberty State
40	Riddick, Robb	RB	6-0	195	2	Millersville State
51	Ritcher, Jim	G-C	6-3	251	3	North Carolina State
58	Robertson, Isiah	LB	6-3	225	12	Southern
17	Robinson, Matt	QB	6-2	196	6	Georgia
23	Romes, Charles	CB	6-1	190	6	North Carolina Central
57	Sanford, Lucius	LB	6-2	216	5	Georgia Tech
45	Simpson, Bill	S	6-1	191	8	Michigan State
76	Smerlas, Fred	NT	6-3	270	4	Boston College
41	Villapiano, Phil	LB	6-2	225	12	Bowling Green
65	Vogler, Tim	C	6-3	245	4	Ohio State
83	White, Sherman	DE	6-5	250	11	California
77	Williams, Ben	DE	6-3	245	7	Mississippi

TOP FIVE DRAFT CHOICES

Rd.	Name	Sel. No.	Pos.	Ht.	Wt.	College
1	Tuttle, Perry	19	WR	6-0	180	Clemson
2	Kofler, Matt	48	QB	6-3	185	San Diego State
3	Marve, Eugene	59	LB	6-3	230	Saginaw Valley
4	Williams, Van	93	RB	5-11	190	Carson-Newman
6	Chivers, DeWayne	160	TE	6-5	232	South Carolina

overworked Cribbs. San Diego State's Matt Kofler threw the football well in all-star games, but he's a long-range project. With Cousineau in Cleveland, Saginaw Valley's Eugene Marve will get a good look at linebacker.

OUTLOOK: Bills are playoff material and some improved play by the special teams could take them all the way to the Super Bowl. With Chuck Knox, Buffalo will always be in contention for the AFC East title. Other teams may have better personnel than Buffalo's, but not better coaching.

BILL PROFILES

JOE FERGUSON 32 6–1 195   Quarterback

Natchitoches Joe...The Louisiana kid who flew to Buffalo (no one shuffles there anymore) nine years ago and began the long, slow, development process that turned him into one of football's better quarterbacks...Ferguson's not among the best in pure throwing ability, but he makes up for it with experience and an intense competitive drive...He set Buffalo records last year for passing attempts, completion and yardage as the Bills set a club mark for total yardage...Born April 23, 1950, in Alvin, Tex....Ferguson grew up in Shreveport and went to the same high school (Woodlawn) as Terry Bradshaw...Ferguson broke numerous passing records at Arkansas...No. 3 draft choice of Buffalo in 1973.

JOE CRIBBS 24 5–11 190   Running Back

The Greg Pruitt of the '80s...The perfect little back who can scoot, catch passes, throw an occasional block and play with pain...Cribbs, at times, is a one-man show for Buffalo in the same manner that Pruitt was for Cleveland in the '70s...He has rushed for 1,185 and 1,097 yards in two pro seasons. He has scored 22 touchdowns—14 by land...Born Jan. 5, 1958, in Sulligent, Ala....Set an Auburn rushing record career with 3,368 yards, teaming in the same backfield with Atlanta's William Andrews...Bills drafted him in 1980 in the second round, the sixth running back chosen overall..."Joe is a big-play performer who gives defensive coaches nightmares," said Chuck Knox.

JERRY BUTLER 24 6–0 171   Wide Receiver

Jerry-built for speed... Scored on eight touchdown passes, giving him 18 in three pro seasons... The man can motor. Defeated world sprint star Harvey Glance in a qualifying race for the 1977 NCAA indoor championships, then won the '78 Atlantic Coast Conference 60-yard dash... All-American receiver at Clemson, where he broke records in football and track... First-round pick of Bills in 1979, scored four touchdowns in one game against the Jets as a rookie, ironically his only touchdowns of the season... Caught touchdown bombs of 75, 69, 67 yards in brief pro career... Born Oct. 10, 1957, in Greenwood, S.C.... A high school quarterback and basketball star at Ware Shoals, S.C.... Loves the outdoor life.

FRANK LEWIS 35 6–1 196   Wide Receiver

Old Folks... Caught more passes (70) for more yards (1,244) at the age of 34 than he had in 10 previous NFL seasons... Both figures were Buffalo records... Lewis tied Denver's Steve Watson for the AFC lead in receiving yardage and ranked third overall in the league... "He's such a fluid, smooth athlete. It looks like he's not going that fast, then all of a sudden he's by you," said Chuck Knox... Lewis scored twice in the playoffs, including a 50-yard reception where he outran two younger Jets... Caught 10 passes in the two playoff games... Born July 4, 1947, in Houma, La.... Scored 42 touchdowns and ran the 100 in 9.4 at Grambling... Pittsburgh drafted him No. 1 in 1971, traded him to Buffalo in 1978.

REGGIE McKENZIE 32 6–5 242   Offensive Guard

Last bulb in the Electric Company... Remember how the E.C. used to light up the Juice?... Well, the Juice is gone and so is the Electric Company, except for McKenzie... Now Reggie's hanging tough in Buffalo himself. He missed 10 games with a knee injury, thereby ending his consecutive-game streak at 140... Tom Lynch played well in McKenzie's absence and

Big Mac must fight to get his job back . . . Born in Detroit on July
27, 1950 . . . Consensus All-American at Michigan . . . "He's the
glue behind this team. He's a winner," Conrad Dobler said of
McKenzie . . . "The best way to lead is by showing. You go out
there Sunday after Sunday and do your best, and you don't have
to say anything," McKenzie said of McKenzie.

CONRAD DOBLER 31 6–3 255   Offensive Guard

The nasty one in repose . . . Lost his starting job
to Jon Borchardt, which could mean trouble for
Conrad . . . It appears that he will be a backup
this fall, but will he accept it? . . . How can one
who is used to biting, scratching and leg-whip-
ping opponents, sit meekly on the bench? . . . The
Bills may ask him to become a reserve. If he
says no, it could be the end of the line for
football's most hated player . . . A good football player, not a great
one, but his antics have brought him more attention than his
ability . . . Born Oct. 10, 1950, in Chicago . . . Went to high school
in Twenty-Nine Palms, Cal., then earned a political science degree
from Wyoming . . . St. Louis drafted him fifth in 1972 . . .
Played for Saints in 1978–79.

MARK BRAMMER 24 6–3 225   Tight End

Good now and getting better . . . In a year or
two might be one of the top tight ends in the
NFL . . . Drafted third by Buffalo in 1980 out
of Michigan State, Brammer beat out Reuben
Gant to become a fulltime starter in
'81 . . . Caught 33 passes for 365 yards and two
touchdowns, plus five more receptions in the
two playoff games . . . "Mark is dependable at
catching the football and we probably should have gotten it to him
more, especially in the latter stages of the season," said Chuck
Knox . . . Brammer could be a big threat this year if Knox practices
what he preaches . . . Born May 3, 1958, in Traverse City,
Mich. . . . All-Big Ten at Michigan State, where he once caught
eight passes for 129 yards against Notre Dame.

BEN WILLIAMS 28 6–3 245   Defensive End

Nobody knows his name...But quarterbacks know his number (77)...Williams led the Bills' defensive line in sacks (10½) and tackles for the second straight year, but was overlooked for postseason honors once again...Though not large, he is quick off the ball and tough to stop once he gets moving...Williams has worked over some of the best offensive tackles in the game, then sat home and watched them in the Pro Bowl...Born Sept. 1, 1954, in Yazoo City, Miss....Played nose guard at Mississippi, making all-conference...Bills drafted him in '76 in the third round and he was a starter the next year...Had 12 sacks in '80 for a personal high...Good chess player, he works in a bank handling loans in offseason.

FRED SMERLAS 25 6–3 270   Nose Tackle

The cookie monster..."Sometimes people ask me, 'How'd you get so big, by lifting weights?' I tell them, 'Naw, I wrapped cookies,'" said Fred Smerlas...He has wrapped up a few centers and running backs as well...Possibly the best nose tackle in the game right now...Made the Pro Bowl twice in three NFL seasons... Tremendously strong and agile, he was a championship wrestler in high school and remains hard to "take down"...Born April 8, 1957, in Waltham, Mass....Started three years at Boston College, winning All-New England honors...Buffalo drafted him second in 1979. He exploded on the NFL scene the following year...Had 73 tackles and 2½ sacks last fall...Hobbies are weightlifting and camping.

SHERMAN WHITE 33 6–5 250   Defensive End

Model of consistency...White has played a decade in the NFL, without many headlines and no honors...He just does his job steadily week in and week out, seldom making the spectacular play, but never making the colossal mistake, either...He has been around, he knows the game and he plays it like out of a textbook ...Cincinnati treated White as the Second

Coming by making him the second player taken in the 1972 draft . . . Bengals traded him to Buffalo four years later for a No. 1 . . . Born Sept. 6, 1948, in Manchester, N.H. . . . Played only basketball in high school, then developed into a Sherman tank at California, making consensus All-America . . . Degree in social science . . . Eight sacks and 63 tackles in '81.

COACH CHUCK KNOX . . . Nine seasons as an NFL head coach, seven seasons with 10 or more victories. And with two different teams! . . . The stuff of greatness . . . That's Chuck Knox . . . After two rebuilding years in Buffalo (5–11 and 7–9), Knox returned to the playoffs for the sixth and seventh times . . . The man is a tremendous coach, though there isn't an iota of flamboyance in him. He doesn't seem to have an ego, either . . . "I try," he said, "never to get too low or too high. I have a saying that regardless of whatever is written about you or your team, no one is as good or as bad as he is made out to be." . . . Knox has a whirlpool of pride inside him, plus an affinity for detail that has made him one of football's most efficient coaches . . . Born April 27, 1932, in Sewickley, Pa. . . . Only had head-coaching experience at Elwood City (Pa.) High School before the late Carroll Rosenbloom gave him the Rams' job in 1973 . . . A tackle at tiny Juniata College in Huntington, Pa., Knox went on to become line coach of the New York Jets and Detroit Lions . . . Criticized in Los Angeles as too conservative a coach, he has been much more liberal in Buffalo. The Bills are throwing the ball like crazy . . . Knox isn't inflexible.

GREATEST LINEBACKER

In Buffalo, it is still regarded as The Hit.

Keith Lincoln caught a swing pass for San Diego in the 1964 AFL championship game. Then Lincoln caught Buffalo linebacker Mike Stratton under his chin. Exit Lincoln. Exit Chargers. Buffalo won, 20–7.

Stratton was a fantastic hitter for Buffalo in the days when the AFL was about as popular as a fat girl on a blind date. His tackles didn't get much attention.

Tennessee is regarded, along with Penn State, as a school for linebackers. Stratton was one of the Vols' first top linebackers and then played for Buffalo from 1962–72.

The Bills of the early '60s played in three straight AFL title games, capturing the first two. This was when Jack Kemp was Buffalo's quarterback and not a Congressman.

Stratton was all-league first-team four times and all-league second-team twice during the pre-merger period. He set a Buffalo record for consecutive games, since broken by Reggie McKenzie. Stratton was one of the AFL's greatest linebackers—and greatest players.

But he left his mark on the game—and Keith Lincoln—with one tackle.

INDIVIDUAL BILL RECORDS

Rushing

Most Yards Game:	273	O. J. Simpson, vs Detroit, 1976
Season:	2,003	O. J. Simpson, 1973
Career:	10,183	O. J. Simpson, 1969–77

Passing

Most TD Passes Game:	5	Joe Ferguson, vs N.Y. Jets, 1979
Season:	25	Joe Ferguson, 1975
Career:	136	Joe Ferguson, 1973–81

Receiving

Most TD Passes Game:	4	Jerry Butler, vs N.Y. Jets, 1979
Season:	10	Elbert Dubenion, 1964
Career:	35	Elbert Dubenion, 1960–67

Scoring

Most Points Game:	30	Cookie Gilchrist, vs New York, 1963
Season:	138	O. J. Simpson, 1975
Career:	420	O. J. Simpson, 1969–77
Most TDs Game:	5	Cookie Gilchrist, vs New York, 1963
Season:	23	O. J. Simpson, 1975
Career:	70	O. J. Simpson, 1969–1977

CINCINNATI BENGALS

TEAM DIRECTORY: Chairman: Austin E. Knowlton; Pres.: John Sawyer; VP/GM: Paul Brown; Asst. GM: Michael Brown; Dir. Player Personnel: Pete Brown; Dir. Pub. Rel.: Allan Heim; Bus. Mgr.: John Murdough; Head Coach: Forrest Gregg. Home field: Riverfront Stadium (59,754). Colors: Orange, black and white.

SCOUTING REPORT

OFFENSE: Loaded. Ken Anderson is in his prime and should have two great seasons ahead, though perhaps not as spectacular as 1981. He has one of football's best tight ends in Dan Ross, a great young receiver in Cris Collinsworth and perhaps another one in David Verser, who was drafted ahead of Collinsworth a year

Ken Anderson passed his way to Player-of-Year award.

ago. Verser is listed behind Collinsworth on the Bengals' depth chart, but he could be shifted over to challenge the aging, slowed-down Isaac Curtis.

Pete Johnson is the battering-ram fullback that is in such short supply in this day and age. What the Bengals could use would be a big year from halfback Charles Alexander, who hasn't had nearly the effect in the pros as he had at LSU. Nevertheless, Anderson is surrounded by depth and protected by a great line.

Anthony Munoz is an all-pro tackle, while the rest of the interior line—Dave Lapham, Blair Bush, Max Montoya and Mike Wilson—is a talented bunch as well.

The Bengals have so much firepower, it's difficult to conceive of them not scoring in bunches, unless injuries occur. The only missing ingredient is a breakaway back.

DEFENSE: The Bengals can be passed on. That, in fact, is the way to beat Cincinnati, which San Francisco proved by controlling the ball through the air in Super Bowl XVI. The 49ers used the pass to set up the run instead of the opposite, customary manner.

Cincinnati is stronger against the run with Eddie Edwards, Wilson Whitley and Ross Browner controlling the line of scrimmage. These three provide much of the pass defense with their strong rush, forcing quarterbacks to throw prematurely.

The Bengals' linebacking is dependable. Reggie Williams is the biggest threat with his ability to blitz. Jim LeClair is not as active as he was several years ago. Glenn Cameron and Bo Harris man the left side well, but not with Pro Bowl ability.

Louis Breeden and Ken Riley are very good at the corners, though Riley is 35 and near the end of his all-star career. That's all right, for Breeden should take up where Riley leaves off. Safeties Bryan Hicks and Bobby Kemp are tough tacklers, but didn't have an interception between them during the regular season.

KICKING GAME: Top quality. Jimmy Breech hit 22 of 32 field goals. He doesn't have the strongest leg, but is great under pressure. Pat McInally (45.5) led all of football in punting. Mike Fuller isn't fast, but he's a smart punt returner. Verser returned a kickoff 78 yards last year.

THE ROOKIES: Bengals drafted Mississippi State defensive lineman Glen Collins possibly for four-man fronts or as a replacement for nose tackle Whitley, who was buried in Super Bowl XVI by 49er center Fred Quillan. No. 2 pick Emanuel Weaver, another defensive tackle, from South Carolina, may be a threat to Gary

BENGALS VETERAN ROSTER

HEAD COACH—Forrest Gregg. Assistant Coaches—Lindy Infante, George Sefcik, Jim McNally, Hank Bullough, Dick Modzelewski, Dick LeBeau, Bruce Coslet, Kim Wood.

No.	Name	Pos.	Ht.	Wt.	NFL Exp.	College
40	Alexander, Charles	RB	6-1	221	4	Louisiana State
14	Anderson, Ken	QB	6-3	208	12	Augustana, Ill.
84	Bass, Don	WR	6-2	220	5	Houston
10	Breech, Jim	K	5-6	161	4	California
34	Breeden, Louis	CB	5-11	185	5	North Carolina Central
79	Browner, Ross	DE	6-3	261	5	Notre Dame
74	Bujnoch, Glenn	G	6-6	265	7	Texas A&M
67	Burley, Gary	DE	6-3	274	7	Pittsburgh
58	Bush, Blair	C	6-3	252	5	Washington
50	Cameron, Glenn	LB	6-2	228	8	Florida
80	Collinsworth, Cris	WR	6-5	192	2	Florida
85	Curtis, Isaac	WR	6-1	192	10	San Diego State
21	Davis, Oliver	S	6-1	205	6	Tennessee
52	Dinkel, Tom	LB	6-3	237	5	Kansas
73	Edwards, Eddie	DE	6-5	261	6	Miami
49	Frazier, Guy	LB	6-2	215	2	Wyoming
42	Fuller, Mike	S	5-10	182	8	Auburn
45	Griffin, Archie	RB	5-9	184	7	Ohio State
44	Griffin, Ray	CB	5-10	186	5	Ohio State
36	Hargrove, Jim	RB	6-2	228	2	Wake Forest
53	Harris, Bo	LB	6-3	226	8	Louisiana State
83	Harris, M.L.	TE	6-5	238	3	Kansas State
27	Hicks, Bryan	S	6-0	192	3	McNeese
30	Jauron, Dick	S	6-0	190	9	Yale
46	Johnson, Pete	RB	6-0	249	6	Ohio State
26	Kemp, Bobby	S	6-0	186	2	Cal-State Fullerton
86	Kreider, Steve	WR	6-3	192	4	Lehigh
62	Lepham, Dave	G	6-4	262	9	Syracuse
55	LeClair, Jim	LB	6-3	234	11	North Dakota
87	McInally, Pat	P-WR	6-6	212	7	Harvard
65	Montoya, Max	G	6-5	275	4	UCLA
60	Moore, Blake	C	6-5	267	3	Wooster
78	Munoz, Anthony	T	6-6	278	3	Southern California
68	Obrovac, Mike	T	6-6	275	2	Bowling Green
51	Razzano, Rick	LB	5-11	227	3	Virginia Tech
13	Riley, Ken	CB	6-0	183	14	Florida A&M
89	Ross, Dan	TE	6-4	235	4	Northeastern
72	St. Clair, Mike	DE	6-5	254	7	Grambling
15	Schonert, Turk	QB	6-1	185	3	Stanford
59	Schuh, Jeff	LB	6-2	228	2	Minnesota
25	Simmons, John	CB	5-11	192	2	Southern Methodist
56	Simpkins, Ron	LB	6-1	235	2	Michigan
12	Thompson, Jack	QB	6-3	217	4	Washington State
81	Verser, David	WR	6-1	200	2	Kansas
75	Whitley, Wilson	NT	6-3	265	6	Houston
57	Williams, Reggie	LB	6-0	228	7	Dartmouth
77	Wilson, Mike	T	6-5	271	5	Georgia

TOP FIVE DRAFT CHOICES

Rd.	Name	Sel. No.	Pos.	Ht.	Wt.	College
1	Collins, Glen	26	DE	6-6	260	Mississippi State
2	Weaver, Emanuel	54	DT	6-4	255	South Carolina
3	Holman, Rodney	82	TE	6-3	230	Tulane
4	Tate, Rodney	110	RB	5-11	190	Texas
5	Sorensen, Paul	138	DB	6-0	189	Washington State

Burley, a former starter in the 4–3 (before Cincinnati went to a 3–4), who has a weight problem.

OUTLOOK: Cincinnati's as good as its offense. Anderson was incredible last year, bringing the Bengals back time after time. If he can't do it as often this year, Cincinnati's defense will have to carry more of its weight. Regardless, the Bengals have the AFC's strongest roster.

BENGAL PROFILES

KEN ANDERSON 33 6–3 208   Quarterback

F. Lee Bailey of quarterbacks... Earned law degree last summer, planned to take the bar this summer... Won't get into fulltime practice just yet, not after the greatest year of his 11-year career... Threw 29 touchdown passes and only 10 interceptions. Passed more times (479) with more completions (300) for more yards (3,754) than ever before... Voted NFL Player of the Year... Strong, fast athlete who finished second on Bengals in rushing with 320 yards (7.0)... Born Feb. 15, 1949, in Batavia, Ill.... The pride of Augustana (Ill.) College... Third-round draft pick in 1971, Year of the Quarterbacks... Anderson has the best statistics out of that bunch, including history's lowest interception percentage.

PETE JOHNSON 28 6–0 249   Running Back

Elephant in a china shop... The prototype full-back: big, bullish, carries tacklers with him ... Only line he couldn't crunch was the 49ers' in the Super Bowl... Johnson has a weight problem. He balloons to 270 in the offseason. The Sam Hunt of fullbacks... The day he can't get below 250, the Bengals should make him a guard... Had best year in '81, rushing for 1,077 yards (3.9) and 12 touchdowns besides catching 46 passes for another four touchdowns... Born March 2, 1954, in Peach County, Ga.... Rumor is he was 200 at birth... Set an Ohio State and Big Ten record with 58 touchdowns, though he did some blocking for Archie Griffin as well... No. 2 draft pick of Bengals in 1977... Scored 49 touchdowns in five seasons.

CRIS COLLINSWORTH 23 6–5 192   Wide Receiver

The new media star...Rookie pass-catching sensation who had 67 receptions for 1,009 yards and eight touchdowns...Pro Bowl selection...Long and lean with a deceptive gait; he's much faster than he looks...Entertained the media all year with his unaffected manner, boyish charm..."In my dreams, I make some amazing catches," he told the Super Bowl press corps. "My greatest? I jump up, catch the ball and Ronnie Lott low-bridges me. I do a complete flip and land on my feet, then run 80 yards for a touchdown."...Born Jan. 27, 1959, in Dayton, Ohio...Threw a 99-yard pass as a Florida freshman, tying an NCAA record...Switched to wide receiver the next year and caught 120 career passes...Bengals' No. 2 draft pick in '81.

DAN ROSS 25 6–4 235   Tight End

Bengals' best player in Super Bowl XVI ...Caught Super Bowl-record 11 passes, two for touchdowns...Even more impressively, Ross would line up against the 49ers' best pass rusher, Fred Dean, chop him down at the line of scrimmage, then get up and make the reception...One of the NFL's best tight ends, Ross has caught 168 passes in three seasons, including a personal-high 71 last fall...Extremely adept at breaking away from tight coverage and catching the ball in crowds...Born Feb. 9, 1957, in Malden, Mass....Played college ball at Northeastern, which could beat Northwestern any day...Holds numerous Northeastern and NCAA Division II receiving records...Second-round draft pick in '79...Hobbies are fishing, water skiing, snowmobiling.

ANTHONY MUNOZ 24 6–6 278   Offensive Tackle

Mt. Munoz...Became an all-pro in two years...Tremendous agility for a man his size. Has the footwork of a 210-pound running back..."He's a rare specimen," said Bengals' coach Forrest Gregg. "He moves better than any big man I've ever seen."..."The best young offensive lineman I've ever played against," said Tampa Bay's Leroy Selmon...Born Aug. 19, 1958, in Ontario, Cal....All-American tackle at USC and a pitcher on the Trojans' baseball team... Had knee problems in college and sat out most of senior year, returning to play the entire Rose Bowl game against Ohio State as USC rallied to win... The Bengals gambled on his knees by making Munoz the second player chosen in the 1980 draft... No knee problems since.

ROSS BROWNER 28 6-3 261   Defensive End

A perfect 10... Browner led all Super Bowl defenders with 10 tackles, all unassisted... Had the Bengals' only sack against former Notre Dame teammate Joe Montana... After the game, in a class gesture, Browner gave Montana a big bear hug... One of four football-playing Browners, two of whom are at USC... Jim Browner was a Bengals' safety for awhile... Ross was a fantastic performer at Notre Dame, a consensus All-American who received the Outland Trophy and Lombardi Trophy... Born March 22, 1954, in Warren, Ohio... The thinking man's defensive end: likes chess and backgammon... Cincinnati drafted Browner No. 1 in 1978 and he became a starter his rookie year... Seventeen sacks last two years.

EDDIE EDWARDS 28 6-5 261   Defensive End

Sack man... Led the Bengals in sacks the last two years (22)... Once sacked Brian Sipe five times... Was the most consistent Cincinnati defensive lineman all last year, but was held to only two tackles by 49er tackle Keith Fahnhorst in the Super Bowl... Edwards has all-pro ability, possibly this year... Cincinnati began rebuilding its defense in 1977 by drafting Edwards in the first round... All-American at the University of Miami (Fla.)... Has everything a defensive end needs to be great—size, speed, quickness, strength and the ability to make the great play... Born April 25, 1954, in Sumter, S.C.... Edwards and Browner give the Bengals the best pair of defensive ends in the AFC and possibly in football.

REGGIE WILLIAMS 27 6–0 228   Outside Linebacker

The blitzer... Tremendous speed makes him ideal on the blitz... Holds club record for solo tackles in a game with 13... Started all six years in the pros after graduating from Dartmouth... Third-round pick in 1976... Williams had a speech impediment that he worked to overcome as a youth... Soft-spoken, articulate young man whose hobbies include charcoal drawing, pets and music... Actively engaged in community and charitable causes... Born Sept. 19, 1954, in Flint, Mich.... Chose Dartmouth over other schools because of the educational challenge. All Ivy-League three straight years... Made six tackles and knocked down a pass in Super Bowl XVI.

LOUIS BREEDEN 28 5–11 185   Cornerback

Cover man... One of the best cornerbacks when it comes to man-on-man coverage... The Saran Wrap of defensive backs—he sticks that close to a receiver... Broke into prominence in 1980 when he saved Bengal victories over Chicago and Pittsburgh with last-minute interceptions... Picked off three that day against the Bears and led Cincinnati for the season with seven... Intercepted four passes last year, returning one 102 yards... Born Oct. 26, 1953, in Hamlet, N.C.... Attended that non-football factory, North Carolina Central... Seventh-round draft pick in 1977, spent that season on injured reserve list... Missed half the '79 season with shoulder injury. Following surgery, became a permanent starter the next autumn.

PAT McINALLY 29 6–6 212   Punter

The boomer... Dominated pro football's punters in 1981, averaging 45.4 yards, two yards better than the NFL runnerup, Ray Guy... It was also two yards better than McInally had averaged in five previous NFL seasons... His previous best year was 1978, when he averaged 43.1 yards and led the NFL... Born May 7, 1953, in Villa Park, Cal.... Standout wide re-

ceiver and Rhodes Scholar candidate from Harvard
...Fifth-round draft pick of Bengals in '75...Has caught 57
passes as a spot receiver in pros...One of the NFL's more interesting players, he's a songwriter who has two tunes that are
being recorded...The Hal David of punters...Very interested
in travel.

COACH FORREST GREGG...Take that, Cleveland!...Run

out of Cleveland, Gregg returned to the NFL
with Cincinnati...In two years he coached the
Bengals to their first Super Bowl...This made
two former Browns who found new success in
Cincinnati: Gregg and Paul Brown...Gregg
coached Cleveland to 3–11, 9–5, and 6–7 records and was named AFC Coach of the Year
in 1976. The following year he was bounced
after the Browns players found him too rigid and uncompromis-
ing...He spent a year in exile in Toronto, coaching the Argonauts
to a forgettable 5–11 season...Brown beckoned Gregg to come
home in '80 and he coached the Bengals to a 6–10 record, getting
the team prepared for the 12–4 season that followed...Bengal
players have found Gregg to be all business, but fair...He is one
of the great offensive linemen of all time, an eight-time all-pro
for the Green Bay Packers and a Pro Football Hall of Fame selection..."Forrest Gregg is the finest player I ever coached," said
Vince Lombardi, the ultimate compliment...One year Gregg
made all-pro at both guard *and* tackle...Played 14 years for Green
Bay and another season with Dallas...Born Oct. 18, 1933, in
Birthright, Tex., he was a two-way tackle at SMU.

GREATEST LINEBACKER

Paul Brown's bullheadedness cost him this time. When Bill
Bergey signed with the World Football League, this was tantamount to treason in Brown's mind and the Cincinnati owner ban-
ished Bergey to Philadelphia.

In only five seasons in Cincinnati, Bergey firmly established himself as the greatest of Bengal linebackers. It was after he joined the Eagles that he became one of football's greatest middle linebackers.

Bergey is a bear of a man at 6–3, 245 pounds who hit like a grizzly during his prime. Remarkably mobile for someone his size, Bergey was as much a threat to intercept a pass as he was to plug a hole at the line.

He reached the end of his brilliant career in 1981. After damaging his knee two years ago, Bergey went through an exhaustive, painful rehabilitation that allowed him to play in his only Super Bowl, but his 1981 season was ruined.

He is a future Hall of Famer, though certainly more Philadelphia's candidate than Cincinnati's. Paul Brown has only himself to blame.

INDIVIDUAL BENGAL RECORDS

Rushing

Most Yards Game:	160	Pete Johnson, vs Cleveland, 1978
Season:	1,077	Pete Johnson, 1981
Career:	3,070	Essex Johnson, 1968–75

Passing

Most TD Passes Game:	4	Greg Cook, vs Houston, 1969
	4	Ken Anderson, vs Cleveland, 1976
Season:	29	Ken Anderson, 1981
Career:	160	Ken Anderson, 1971–81

Receiving

Most TD Passes Game:	3	Bob Trumpy, vs Houston, 1969
	3	Isaac Curtis, vs Cleveland, 1973
	3	Isaac Curtis, vs Baltimore, 1979
Season:	10	Isaac Curtis, 1974
Career:	50	Isaac Curtis, 1973–81

Scoring

Most Points Game:	19	Horst Muhlmann, vs Buffalo, 1970
	19	Horst Muhlmann, vs Houston, 1972
Season:	115	Jim Breech, 1981
Most TDs Game:	3	Paul Robinson, vs Miami, 1968
	3	Bob Trumpy, vs Houston, 1969
	3	Doug Dressler, vs Houston, 1972
	3	Isaac Curtis, vs Cleveland, 1973
Season:	16	Pete Johnson, 1981
Career:	50	Isaac Curtis, 1973–81

CLEVELAND BROWNS

TEAM DIRECTORY: Pres: Art Modell; VP/Gen. Counsel: James Bailey; Asst. to the Pres.: Paul Warfield; Personnel Dir.: Bill Davis; Dir. Operations: Dennis Lynch; VP/Dir. Pub. Rel.: Nathan Wallack; Dir. Publicity: Kevin Byrne; Head Coach: Sam Rutligliano. Home field: Cleveland Stadium (80,322). Colors: Seal brown, orange and white.

SCOUTING REPORT

OFFENSE: Did the Browns' offense suffer permanent cardiac arrest last year? They had so many heart-stopping comebacks two years ago that Cleveland fans thought it was all part of the game plan. The Browns' players thought they could fool around for 58 minutes, then win the game in the last two.

Ozzie Newsome made 69 catches to earn trip to Pro Bowl.

Cleveland actually finished third in AFC passing even though Brian Sipe had an off year. The problem was with the running game, which wound up 10th in the conference. Fullback Mike Pruitt went over the 1,000-yard mark again, but there wasn't any noise from the halfback position. Greg Pruitt, still a capable receiver but no longer a top-quality rusher, was sent to Oakland, so Charles White will get another chance to impress.

Reggie Rucker and Dave Logan are capable receivers, though the Browns need more of a home-run threat. Ricky Feacher could add this dimension. Tight end Ozzie Newsome should be used more often than he is as a deep threat.

The offensive line, led by Joe DeLamielleure and Doug Dieken, permitted 40 sacks and didn't block well enough on running plays. They should have bought the backfield dinner after the season.

DEFENSE: There's the Browns' defense, sinking in Lake Erie. Tenth in the AFC against the run, 27th in the NFL in interceptions. This is a team with definite defensive holes.

First of all, they need a dominating linebacker. A defensive tackle wouldn't hurt, either. Then while they're at it, the secondary could use some patching.

Cleveland hopes Tom Cousineau, the first player in the draft three years ago, will be the dominant linebacker now that he's returned from the CFL. USC's Chip Banks, the third player chosen in the 1982 draft, may be an immediate help, too. Robert L. Jackson was dealt to Denver, leaving holdovers Clay Matthews and Don Goode.

Aging Lyle Alzado, the best of a sorry lot on the line, was sent to Oakland. So, rookie DE Keith Baldwin will get a shot at joining Henry Bradley and Marshall Harris, neither of whom distinguished himself last year.

The secondary? Clarence Scott's not bad. Who else is there? Hoooo, do the Browns need a talent infusion.

KICKING: The Browns haven't had a breakaway return man in years. Dino Hall is a great name and likable kid, but he doesn't remind anyone of White Shoes Johnson. Matt Bahr hit 15 of 26 field goals, but he's no Don Cockroft. Rookie Steve Cox punted for a 42.4 average, fourth in the AFC.

THE ROOKIES: Banks was spectacular as a USC junior, but so-so as a senior when he was shifted to inside linebacker. He's back on the outside for the Browns, though his 4.8 speed makes him vulnerable on pass coverage. Cleveland has a terrible record

BROWNS VETERAN ROSTER

HEAD COACH—Sam Rutigliano. Assistant Coaches—Dave Adolph, Jim Garrett, Len Fontes, Paul Hackett, Rod Humenuk, Rich Kotite, John Petercuskie, Tom Pratt, David Redding, Joe Scannella, Marty Schottenheimer.

No.	Name	Pos.	Ht.	Wt.	NFL Exp.	College
80	Adams, Willis	WR	6-2	194	4	Houston
52	Ambrose, Dick	LB	6-0	228	8	Virginia
9	Bahr, Matt	K	5-10	165	4	Penn State
28	Bolton, Ron	CB	6-2	170	11	Norfolk State
91	Bradley, Henry	DT	6-2	260	4	Alcorn State
97	Brown, Thomas	DE	6-4	240	3	Baylor
49	Burrell, Clinton	S	6-1	192	3	Louisiana State
53	Cowher, Bill	LB	6-3	225	2	North Carolina State
15	Cox, Steve	P-K	6-4	195	2	Arkansas
21	Davis, Gary	RB	5-10	210	7	Cal Poly-SLO
64	DeLamielleure, Joe	G	6-3	245	10	Michigan State
54	DeLeone, Tom	C	6-2	248	11	Ohio State
73	Dieken, Doug	T	6-5	252	12	Illinois
29	Dixon, Hanford	CB	5-11	182	2	Southern Mississippi
83	Feacher, Ricky	WR	5-10	174	7	Mississippi Valley
20	Flint, Judson	CB	6-0	201	3	Memphis State
94	Franks, Elvis	DE	6-4	238	3	Morgan State
86	Fulton, Dan	WR	6-2	186	3	Nebraska-Omaha
50	Goode, Don	LB	6-2	240	9	Kansas
26	Hall, Dino	RB-KR	5-7	165	4	Glassboro State
90	Harris, Marshall	DE	6-6	261	3	Texas Christian
58	Huther, Bruce	LB	6-1	220	6	New Hampshire
68	Jackson, Robert E.	G	6-5	260	8	Duke
51	Johnson, Eddie	LB	6-1	210	2	Louisville
48	Johnson, Lawrence	CB	5-11	204	3	Wisconsin
85	Logan, Dave	WR	6-4	216	7	Colorado
57	Matthews, Clay	LB	6-2	230	5	Southern California
16	McDonald, Paul	QB	6-2	185	3	Southern California
30	Miller, Cleo	RB	5-11	214	9	Arkansas-Pine Bluff
71	Miller, Matt	T	6-6	270	3	Colorado
82	Newsome, Ozzie	TE	6-2	232	5	Alabama
84	Oden, McDonald	TE	6-4	215	3	Tennessee State
69	Patten, Joel	T	6-6	240	2	Duke
43	Pruitt, Mike	RB	6-0	225	7	Purdue
63	Risien, Cody	T	6-7	255	4	Texas A&M
92	Robinson, Mike	DE	6-4	260	2	Arizona
33	Rucker, Reggie	WR	6-2	190	13	Boston University
22	Scott, Clarence	S	6-0	190	12	Kansas State
65	Sheppard, Henry	G	6-6	263	7	Southern Methodist
17	Sipe, Brian	QB	6-1	195	9	San Diego State
79	Sullivan, Gerry	C-T	6-4	250	9	Illinois
12	Trocano, Rick	QB	6-0	188	2	Pittsburgh
55	Weathers, Curtis	LB	6-5	220	4	Mississippi
25	White, Charles	RB	5-10	183	3	Southern California
89	Wright, Keith	WR-KR	5-9	175	4	Memphis State

TOP FIVE DRAFT CHOICES

Rd.	Name	Sel. No.	Pos.	Ht.	Wt.	College
1	Banks, Chip	3	LB	6-5	230	Southern California
2	Baldwin, Keith	31	DE	6-4	245	Texas
4	Walker, Dwight	87	WR	5-10	185	Nicholls State
5	Babb, Mike	115	C	6-4	270	Texas
6	Whitwell, Mike	162	WR	6-0	175	Texas A&M
*	Cousineau, Tom		LB	6-3	232	Ohio State

* Played with Montreal of CFL, 1979–81

on No. 1 picks. Defensive end Keith Baldwin, from Texas A&M, will bolster the defensive line, which needs bolstering badly.

OUTLOOK: On paper, Cleveland isn't as good as Cincinnati and Pittsburgh in the AFC Central. If the Browns don't answer some defensive needs, they are in serious trouble. The offense figures to play better than last year, but not as well as two years ago. The Browns are a third-place team.

BROWN PROFILES

BRIAN SIPE 33 6–1 195　　　　　　　Quarterback

What a difference a year makes...Sipe fell from the NFL's top-rated quarterback in 1980 to 22nd last season...From NFL Player of the Year to a non-invitee at Pro Bowl time...Sipe dropped in touchdown passes from 30 to 17 and climbed in interceptions from 14 to 25...What happened? Well, how could anyone repeat Sipe's '80 season where everything went right in a series of cardiac comebacks?...Cleveland has no reason to panic unless Sipe strings two average seasons together...Still one of the best money quarterbacks in football, though he isn't surrounded by one of the great teams. Browns are mediocre on defense...Born Aug. 8, 1949, in San Diego...San Diego State star and Browns' No. 13 draft pick in 1972.

TOM COUSINEAU 25 6–3 232　　　　　　Linebacker

At last, the NFL will find out just how good this former Ohio State linebacker is...The first player taken in the 1979 draft, Cousineau spurned the Bills' offers and instead headed north to Montreal and the CFL...He said "au revoir" to the Alouettes when his contract expired and he signed with the Browns in April...Should step right in as replacement for Robert L. Jackson, who was shipped to Denver...Born May 6, 1957, in Indianapolis...Talk about strength: at age 10, he won a trophy for bench-pressing 100 pounds ten times in a row...Starred at OSU, where Woody Hayes called him "the best-conditioned athlete I've ever coached."...Runs the 40 in 4.7...Question is, can he adjust from three downs to four?

MIKE PRUITT 28 6-0 225   Running Back

He's now Do It Pruitt No. 1 . . . Two-dimensional fullback: Third straight 1,000-yard rushing season (1,103) ranked him fourth in the conference . . . Sixty-three receptions tied him for 10th . . . Scored eight touchdowns, seven on the ground . . . Sprinter's speed inside a strong body makes him an ideal back . . . Scored 31 touchdowns in six years with Browns, some from short yardage, plus two from 71 and 77 yards . . . Born April 3, 1954, in Chicago . . . Purdue's Most Valuable Player in 1975 . . . Cleveland saw his 4.4 speed in the 40 and drafted him first in 1976 . . . "Mike proves there is nothing more important than self-confidence," said Sam Rutigliano. "He's a big-play guy." . . . Last year his longest run was 21 yards—an off year for all the Browns.

OZZIE NEWSOME 26 6-2 232   Tight End

Ozzie found Oz last season . . . Newsome was named to his first Pro Bowl after a career-high 69 receptions . . . One of the game's best tight ends, built into one from a wide receiver at Alabama . . . Now 230 pounds, he still runs like the 200-pounder he was under the Bear . . . Could still play wide receiver if the Browns needed him there . . . Cleveland first-round choice in '78, he was named the Cleveland Touchdown Club's Browns' Offensive Player of the Year that same season, the only time a Cleveland rookie has been thus honored . . . Born March 15, 1956, in Muscle Shoals, Ala. . . . . "The finest receiver we've ever had at Alabama," said Bryant, who played end at 'Bama with a kid named Don Hutson.

DOUG DIEKEN 33 6-5 252   Offensive Tackle

Rodney Dangerfield of Cleveland . . . "Doug keeps the team loose with one-liners," said Sam Rutigliano, "but he also performs." . . . Without respect . . . "He is the most underrated offensive tackle in the league," Rutigliano continued. "Year after year he faces many of the best defensive ends and just keeps every rusher over there quiet." . . . Eleven seasons of no respect haven't destroyed his confidence or his determination. He continues to play with painful injury that would drive others to the bench...Born Feb. 12, 1949, in Streator, Ill....Split end and tight end at Illinois...Drafted No. 6 by Browns in 1971...Caught a touchdown pass on a fake field-goal play with Browns in 1978 preseason game.

DAVE LOGAN 28 6–4 216   Wide Receiver

The man who defies computers...A third-round draft pick in 1976 because he neither looked nor ran like a wide receiver, Logan continues to play in the NFL, and play well, though last year was an off season for Logan as well as the Browns...Caught only 31 passes for four touchdowns, though he was right around his career yardage average (16.0)...Rare athlete who was drafted in three different sports—by Cincinnati in baseball and Kansas City in basketball...Born Feb. 2, 1954, in Fargo, N.D....Earned four letters in football and three in basketball at Colorado (the Reds drafted him as a pitcher-first baseman out of high school; he didn't play baseball in college)...Known in Cleveland as "a Gary Gollins with speed." Not a burner, however.

CHARLES WHITE 24 5–10 198   Running Back

Third year the charm?...White hasn't done much but sit his last two years with the Browns, starting rumors of another Heisman bust...White was brought in to replace Greg Pruitt, but hasn't done it yet...The former USC star has talked about going elsewhere, but no trades have materialized...Enigmatic type who walked out of Browns' camp, then came back. Says everything is OK now. Hmmmmmmm...Born Jan. 22, 1958, in Los Angeles...Broke the career rushing record at USC, closing out his career with a Rose Bowl-record 247 yards against Ohio State...Browns drafted him No. 1 in '80...Since that time, nothing...This may be White's last chance to oust Pruitt, who is 31...Two raps against White: small body, big head.

REGGIE RUCKER 34 6-2 190   Wide Receiver

The receiver they love to replace, but never do... This is Rucker's 13th year in the NFL and few football "experts" thought he would last this long... Signed as a free agent by Dallas in '68 after starring at Boston University... Cowboys and New York Giants released him, but he caught on with New England, where Sam Rutigliano was an assistant coach... Rucker moved on to Cleveland, where Rutigliano would become the head coach... "Sam saved my career," Rucker said, thinking back on New England. "I owe him so much."... Rucker has 447 career catches and could qualify for the exclusive "500 Club"... Born Sept. 21, 1947, in Washington, D.C.... Calls himself the Bionic Man for his having overcome operations on both knees, a shoulder, wrist and foot.

CLAY MATTHEWS 26 6-2 230   Outside Linebacker

Two-hundred and thirty pounds of Clay make a fine linebacker... "He'll be a Jack Ham-type, a Pro Bowler, before it's all over with," said Sam Rutigliano... There's only one Ham, but not many are compared to him, either ... Matthews isn't spectacular, but steady and efficient... In the long run, these are the best kind of athletes to have... Born March 15, 1956, in Palo Alto, Cal.... His father, who has the same name, played end for the San Francisco 49ers... Young Clay went to USC, where he played middle linebacker... Browns rated him as the fifth-best player in the nation in 1978 behind Earl Campbell, Wes Chandler, Terry Miller and Steve Little... Matthews loves to fly those radio-control planes.

DINO HALL 26 5-7 165   Return Specialist

Dino Who?... It's the story that asks the question: can a little kick-returner from Glassboro State find happiness in the National Football League?... Apparently so, because Hall has played three years in Cleveland... Last year he finished seventh in the AFC in kickoff returns and 12th in punt returns... He's the kind of player the Browns keep trying to replace, but can find no one to replace him...."I don't think about size," said Dino. "When you do that, you start running scared. I just try to outquick opponents. If I can get a step on them, they're not going to get me."...Born Dec. 6, 1955, in Atlantic City, N.J....NCAA Division III rushing champ and baseball star at Glassboro...Browns signed him as a free agent.

COACH SAM RUTIGLIANO...The players' coach... Compassionate, philosophical, practical ...That's Sam...Pushed Cleveland past Pittsburgh to win the AFC Central title two years ago...The Browns dropped from first to last in a year's time...Now comes another rebuilding job—rebuilding the areas where the Browns are weak, but, more importantly, rebuilding the team's confidence...This is where Rutigliano stands out. His players believe in him, respond to him...He learned of players' habits and needs in 11 years as an NFL assistant...Improved the Browns from 8–8 to 9–7 to 11–6 in his three years with the franchise before last year's collapse...Rutigliano was born in Brooklyn on July 1, 1932, and played college ball at Tennessee and Tulsa...Has a master's degree from Columbia...After losing to Oakland in the playoffs two years ago, Rutigliano was asked if this was his most bitter defeat. He answered with something about death being the worst thing in life...Everyone knew what he meant...After Brian Sipe threw the interception that lost that game, Sam told him, "I love you," then patted him on the helmet.

GREATEST LINEBACKER

Walt Michaels coached the New York Jets back into the playoffs last year. But the playoffs are nothing new to Michaels, who made a steady habit of reaching them with the Cleveland Browns a few decades ago.

Michaels was a tremendous linebacker with Cleveland from 1952–61. He played on two NFL championship teams, five divisional winners and made the Pro Bowl four straight years from 1957–60.

He was born in Pennsylvania coal mining country and recognized early that football was a one-way ticket out of a life in the mines.

"My father died when he was 54 and he understood two things about football," Michaels recalled. "If you hit, you won. And if you won, you were successful."

Young Walt Michaels played fullback, guard and linebacker at Washington & Lee. Cleveland drafted him No. 7 in '51, traded him to Green Bay that same year for Dan Orlich, then reacquired Michaels in '52 for Richard Logan, Elmer Costa and Forrest Grigg. That's Forrest Grigg, not Forrest Gregg.

Michaels missed only two games in 10 years with Cleveland. He scored two touchdowns. He was successful.

INDIVIDUAL BROWN RECORDS
Rushing

Most Yards Game:	237	Jim Brown, vs Los Angeles, 1957
	237	Jim Brown, vs Philadelphia, 1961
Season:	1,863	Jim Brown, 1963
Career:	12,312	Jim Brown, 1957–65

Passing

Most TD Passes Game:	5	Frank Ryan, vs N.Y. Giants, 1964
	5	Bill Nelson, vs Dallas, 1969
	5	Brian Sipe, vs Pittsburgh, 1979
Season:	30	Brian Sipe, 1980
Career:	134	Frank Ryan, 1962–68

Receiving

Most TD Passes Game:	3	Mac Speedie, vs Chicago, 1951
	3	Darrell Brewster, vs N.Y. Giants, 1953
	3	Ray Renfro, vs Pittsburgh, 1959
	3	Gary Collins, vs Philadelphia, 1963
	3	Reggie Rucker, vs N.Y. Jets, 1976
	3	Larry Poole, vs Pittsburgh, 1977
	3	Calvin Hill, vs Baltimore, 1978
Season:	13	Gary Collins, 1963
Career:	70	Gary Collins, 1962–71

Scoring

Most Points Game:	36	Dub Jones, vs Chicago Bears, 1951
Season:	126	Jim Brown, 1965
Career:	1,349	Lou Groza, 1950–59, 1961–67
Most TDs Game:	6	Dub Jones, vs Chicago Bears, 1951
Season:	21	Jim Brown, 1965
Career:	126	Jim Brown, 1957–65

DENVER BRONCOS

TEAM DIRECTORY: Chairman: Edgar F. Kaiser, Jr.; GM: Grady Alderman; Dir. Player Personnel: John Beake; Dir. Pub. Rel.: Charlie Lee; Pub. Dir.: Jim Saccomano; Head Coach: Dan Reeves. Home Field: Mile High Stadium (75,123). Colors: Orange, blue and white.

SCOUTING REPORT

OFFENSE: It's not Craig Morton's arm, but his body. Morton has knocked all raps against his courage in the pocket in recent years by taking a terrible pounding week after week and refusing to leave the lineup.

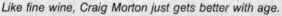

Like fine wine, Craig Morton just gets better with age.

How much longer can this go on? Morton is 39, an age when quarterbacks are selling insurance or working as TV analysts. It doesn't figure that Morton can play a 16-game schedule. If not, then it will have to be Steve DeBerg, whose arm isn't as good and who had a tendency in San Francisco to throw fourth-quarter interceptions in win-or-lose situations. Get ready, Mark Herrmann.

Rick Parros gave Denver its most dangerous back since Otis Armstrong was in one piece. But Parros isn't a dominant back. Maybe rookie Gerald Willhite will be.

Steve Watson, Rick Upchurch and Riley Odoms make up a capable receiving corps. The offensive line nearly got its quarterbacks killed last year with 61 sacks. Morton, who can't run from trouble, was nailed 54 times. A harbinger of things to come?

DEFENSE: Year after year, it doesn't change: the Broncos play great defense. If their offense was as good as their defense, the Broncos would have several Super Bowl trophies by now.

Denver has possibly the best "back eight" in football. With linebackers like Bob Swenson, Tom Jackson, Randy Gradishar and Larry Evans, and a secondary of Louis Wright, Aaron Kyle, Bill Thompson and Steve Foley, who couldn't win?

The Broncos use six players up front, with Barney Chavous, Rubin Carter and Rulon Jones as starters. Jones is the club's best pass rusher, but keep an eye on fifth-year pro Greg Boyd, who keeps getting better.

Denver ranked second in the AFC against the pass, picking off 23 passes. The team can improve its seventh-place ranking against the run. With Evans and Jones each having a full year as starters, the Broncos' rushing defense should be even better.

One area to watch for possible change: strong safety. This is Bill Thompson's 14th year. Dennis Smith, a second-year man from USC with great promise, should play more for Thompson this season.

KICKING GAME: Great shape. Fred Steinfort, after a horrendous start last year, then regained his placekicking form of 1980. Punter Luke Prestridge averaged 40.4 and dropped 20 inside the 20-yard line. Wade Manning isn't a Rick Upchurch on returns, but then Upchurch has slipped some as a returner.

THE ROOKIES: San Jose State's Willhite gives Denver a new dimension, a strong receiver coming out of the backfield. He will be a third-down player, a situation back, unless he can put on weight. He's 195 pounds now after weighing 100 as a high school

BRONCOS VETERAN ROSTER

HEAD COACH—Dan Reeves. Assistant Coaches—Joe Collier, Stan Jones, Richie McCabe, Bob Zeman, Rod Dowhower, Jerry Frei, Nick Nicolau, Fran Polsfoot, Marvin Bass.

No.	Name	Pos.	Ht.	Wt.	NFL Exp.	College
54	Bishop, Keith	C-G	6-3	260	2	Baylor
77	Boyd, Greg	DE	6-6	280	5	San Diego State
64	Bryan, Bill	C	6-2	244	6	Duke
58	Busick, Steve	LB	6-4	227	2	Southern California
35	Canada, Larry	RB	6-2	226	4	Wisconsin
68	Carter, Rubin	DT	6-0	253	8	Miami
79	Chavous, Barney	DE	6-3	245	10	South Carolina State
73	Clark, Kelvin	T	6-3	245	4	Nebraska
17	DeBerg, Steve	QB	6-2	205	6	San Jose State
85	Egloff, Ron	TE	6-5	227	6	Wisconsin
56	Evans, Larry	LB	6-2	220	7	Mississippi College
43	Foley, Steve	S	6-2	190	7	Tulane
62	Glassic, Tom	G	6-3	250	7	Virginia
53	Gradishar, Randy	LB	6-2	231	9	Ohio State
31	Harden, Mike	S	6-1	190	3	Michigan
10	Herrmann, Mark	QB	6-4	184	2	Purdue
60	Howard, Paul	G	6-3	260	9	Brigham Young
65	Hyde, Glenn	C-G	6-3	252	7	Pittsburgh
67	Jackson, Tom	LB	5-11	220	10	Louisville
	Jackson, Robert L.	LB	6-1	230	5	Texas A&M
75	Jones, Rulon	DE	6-6	260	3	Utah State
22	Kyle, Aaron	CB	5-11	185	7	Wyoming
76	Lanier, Ken	T	6-3	269	2	Florida State
72	Latimer, Don	DT	6-2	253	5	Miami
41	Lytle, Rob	RB	5-11	195	6	Michigan
83	Manning, Wade	WR-KR	5-11	190	3	Ohio State
66	Manor, Brison	DE	6-4	248	6	Arkansas
59	Merrill, Mark	LB	6-4	240	4	Minnesota
71	Minor, Claudie	T	6-4	275	9	San Diego State
7	Morton, Craig	QB	6-4	210	18	California
88	Odoms, Riley	TE	6-4	235	11	Houston
24	Parros, Rick	RB	5-11	200	2	Utah State
46	Preston, Dave	RB	5-10	195	5	Bowling Green
41	Prestridge, Luke	P	6-4	235	4	Baylor
32	Reed, Tony	RB	5-10	197	6	Colorado
50	Ryan, Jim	LB	6-1	212	4	William & Mary
49	Smith, Dennis	S	6-3	200	2	Southern California
45	Smith, Perry	CB	6-1	190	10	Colorado State
39	Solomon, Roland	CB	6-0	189	3	Utah
19	Steinfort, Fred	K	5-11	190	7	Boston College
70	Studdard, Dave	T	6-4	255	4	Texas
51	Swenson, Bob	LB	6-3	225	7	California
36	Thompson, Billy	S	6-1	220	14	Maryland State
37	Trimble, Steve	CB	5-10	181	2	Maryland
80	Upchurch, Rick	WR-KR	5-10	176	8	Minnesota
81	Watson, Steve	WR	6-4	195	4	Temple
87	Wright, Jim	TE	6-3	240	4	Texas Christian
20	Wright, Louis	CB	6-2	200	8	San Jose State

TOP FIVE DRAFT CHOICES

Rd.	Name	Sel. No.	Pos.	Ht.	Wt.	College
1	Willhite, Gerald	21	RB	5-10	190	San Jose State
2	McDaniel, Orlando	50	WR	6-1	175	Louisiana State
4	Plater, Dan	106	WR	6-2	188	Brigham Young
5	Winder, Sammy	131	RB	6-0	191	Southern Mississippi
6	Ruben, Alvin	189	DE	6-4	230	Houston

sophomore. With Willhite as a pass catcher who can break the long one, Morton will save wear and tear on his arm. Rest of Denver's draft? Eh.

OUTLOOK: Doesn't look good. While the defense should play well, the offense figures to have rough sledding, starting at quarterback. It will take a super year from Steinfort to keep points on the board. Denver will drop from second to third or fourth in that tight little island, the AFC West.

BRONCO PROFILES

CRAIG MORTON 39 6-4 210   Quarterback

Methuselah of the mountains...Time is slipping away on Morton, but time hasn't been cruel...At 38, Morton tied with Dan Fouts for the NFL's second-highest quarterback efficiency rating behind Ken Anderson...Morton set personal bests in attempts (479), completions (300), passing yards (3,195) and matched his career high in touchdowns (21) set back in Dallas in 1969...Denver brought in other quarterbacks (Norris Weese, Craig Penrose, Matt Robinson) to take Morton's job, but they left without it...Born Feb. 5, 1943, in Flint, Mich....Consensus All-American at California...Cowboys' No. 1 draft pick in 1965...Lost out to Roger Staubach in quarterback battle, went to New York Giants in '74, led Denver to its only Super Bowl in '77.

STEVE WATSON 25 6-4 195   Wide Receiver

NFL's surprise player of 1981...Burst into stardom with 13 touchdown catches and 1,244 receiving yards to lead the AFC in both categories, sharing the yardage title with Buffalo's Frank Lewis...Watson's 60 receptions and 20.7 yards per catch gave him four Denver club marks...He had caught only 12 passes in two previous seasons in Denver before he exploded with five 100-yard games and a starting spot in the Pro Bowl...And to think that Watson came to the Broncos as a free agent from Temple, where he graduated cum laude with a degree in parks administration...Born May 28, 1957, in Baltimore...Nickname is "Blade"...Four-year letterman at Temple and twice a conference long jump champion.

RILEY ODOMS 32 6–4 235   Tight End

Down near the goal line it's the life of Riley..."Riley really produced in the area that is so tough, inside the opponent's 20-yard line, catching five touchdown passes," said Dan Reeves of Odom's 1981 season...It was also a comeback of sorts from the 1980 season when Odoms grew from a Bronco into an overweight plowhorse...He reduced from 260 back to 235 and played back to previous form...Now in his 11th year, Odoms remains a capable receiver and punishing blocker...Born March 1, 1950, in Luling, Tex., he played football and a little basketball at Houston...Fifth player taken in the entire 1972 draft...Bronco starter since his rookie year, he averages 38 catches a season, mostly on third downs and near the end zone.

BILL BRYAN 27 6–2 244   Center

No worries up front...Bryan is an excellent blocker and, perhaps, the most underrated center in the NFL...He doesn't get much attention, but he's one of Denver's most solid fixtures on offense...In a game against Oakland, he knocked down every member of the defensive line...Bryan can pass block and run block equally well...Born June 21, 1955, in Burlington, N.C....Studied economics at Duke...Part-owner of a family sporting goods store in Burlington...Bryan's father was a Little All-American at Elon College and Bill's uncle was an outstanding player at Clemson...Denver drafted Bill No. 4 in 1977...He became a starter two years later...Sailing and target shooting are his hobbies...Denver's offensive MVP in 1980.

DAVE PRESTON 27 5–10 195   Running Back

Mr. Capable...Preston isn't a breakaway back or a Csonka clone, but somewhere in between...He's not tremendously big or fast, but he's hard to knock off his feet, which makes him good on short-yardage situations. And he can catch the ball...Finished second on the Broncos in rushing and receiving, producing a total of 1,147 yards and three touchdowns...Good blocker, too...One of these years, he'll turn in 800 to 1,000 yards rushing...Born May 29, 1955, in Dayton, Ohio...Tailback and Academic All-American at Bowling Green...Free agent signed by Denver in 1978...The type of back who might last 10 years in the game...Had offseason knee surgery, so it will be hard for him to duplicate his all-purpose performance of 1981.

RULON JONES 24 6-6 260   **Defensive End**

Unruly Rulon...Really works himself up for games, especially against division rival Oakland when he is at his best...Has 20 sacks in his first two seasons..."Rulon had an outstanding sophomore year," said Dan Reeves. "He's only going to get better."...The mystery about Jones is how he managed to last until the second round of the 1980 draft, when the Broncos nabbed him...He was a blue-chipper until his senior year at Utah State, when he dropped in the estimation of pro scouts for some unexplained reason...He has played like a No. 1 ever since...Born March 25, 1958, in Salt Lake City...Grew up in Ogden, Utah...At Utah State his best performance was 15 tackles and three quarterback sacks as a senior against Fresno State.

ROBERT L. JACKSON 28 6-1 230   **Inside Linebacker**

Bruise Brother takes his act from Cleveland to the Mile High City...Part of Lake Erie shakeup, Browns shipped him to Broncos in draft-day trade...Reckless player who hits anything that moves...An intimidating tackler who has earned his nickname of "Stonewall"...Had to be referred to with middle initial because Browns have a Robert E. Jackson...Born Aug. 7, 1954, in Houston...Defensive star at Texas A&M and teammate of Oakland's Lester Hayes, though Jackson has never been accused of using Stickum...Browns drafted him first in 1977 after scouts ranked him as fifth-best athlete behind Tony Dorsett, Ricky Bell, Wilson Faumuina and Marvin Powell...But he missed entire rookie season with knee injury...Recovered and became one of game's better linebackers.

BOB SWENSON 29 6–3 225   Outside Linebacker

Fantastic comeback...Swenson missed the 1980 season, then came back in '81 to make the Pro Bowl for the first time...He totaled 145 tackles, three interceptions, three fumble recoveries and three sacks..."At the end of the season Bob was as good a linebacker as I've ever seen," said Dan Reeves...Swenson's strength is against the run. He is adept at stacking up the tight end, shedding the block and making the tackle...Swenson is both strong and intense, a tough combination to overcome...Born July 1, 1953, in Stockton, Cal....Three-year letterman at California, but not a world-beater in college...Signed with Denver as a free agent in 1975 and became a starter right away...Broncos' defensive MVP in 1979.

BILL THOMPSON 35 6–1 200   Strong Safety

Denver's most eligible bachelor...Still single after all these years; he'll be 36 in October...Now in his 14th season in Denver, Thompson has played longer than any other Bronco...And there aren't many Broncos who've ever played better, if any...Despite his advancing years, Thompson was selected to the Pro Bowl last year for the third time...He intercepted four passes, recovered two fumbles and led all Bronco defensive backs in tackles with 91..."He was outstanding," said Dan Reeves. "He didn't miss a game or a practice. For a guy his age, that's incredible."...Born Oct. 10, 1946, in Greenville, S.C....Football and baseball star at Maryland State...Denver's No. 3 pick in 1969.

FRED STEINFORT 29 5–11 190   Kicker

Kicking isn't mental?...Ask Steinfort, who made five of 15 field goals over the first half of the season, then 12 of 14 over the second half...Steinfort had a new holder (Steve DeBerg) and snapper (Glenn Hyde), so it might have had something to do with his slow start...All-pro kicker the previous fall after making 26 of 34 attempts, including five field goals from beyond 50 yards. Longest was 57...Born Nov. 3, 1952, in Wetter/Ruhr, West Germany...Came to the United

States when he was 13 . . . Four-year kicker at Boston College. . . He beat out George Blanda in Oakland as a rookie, then kicked for parts of two seasons in Atlanta before joining Denver for the last game of 1979 . . . Then he beat out Jim Turner.

COACH DAN REEVES. . . Final-game collapse in Chicago cost the Broncos a playoff shot . . . Reeves was 10–6 his first season as a head coach after completing his apprenticeship in Dallas . . . Was a candidate for several NFL jobs, but never connected until new Bronco management fired Red Miller (three playoff appearances in four years) and brought in Reeves . . . Installed Dallas' multiple offense in Denver and gave new ooomph to Craig Morton's statistical chart . . . Reeves was born Jan. 19, 1944, in Americus, Ga., just down the road from Jimmy, Billy and Miss Lillian . . . A quarterback at South Carolina, Reeves was an all-purpose offensive back for the Cowboys, who signed him as a free agent in 1965 . . . He stayed with Dallas until '72, when his knees finally gave out . . . He is the club's fifth all-time leading rusher . . . Went to work immediately for Tom Landry after his retirement as a player . . . Reeves then left the Cowboys for one year to enter private business, but missed football and came back to Dallas, eventually, as offensive coordinator, a position he held for three years . . . Unquotable sort, but a straight shooter . . . Restored harmony on Broncos that was lacking in Miller's last year . . . Restored Broncomania, too.

GREATEST LINEBACKER

Perhaps there is no such thing as a perfect football player, but Randy Gradishar may be the closest thing to one.

There was no Orange Crush in Denver until Gradishar showed up in 1974 from Ohio State. He moved in at middle linebacker, the Broncos later shifted to a 3–4 defense and opponents have been paying for it ever since.

The Broncos perennially rank among the NFL's defensive top teams and Gradishar is the leader. His tackles over the course of a season sometimes double totals of other *teams*. Gradishar was voted the NFL's Defensive Player of the Year in 1978 after leading Denver to its only Super Bowl the year before.

Gradishar is strong (6–3, 230), smart and tough. Although not as fierce as Pittsburgh's Jack Lambert, his competition for all-pro honors, Gradishar is just as immovable in the middle and maybe a tad quicker than Lambert. The Broncos' great linebacker has the acceleration and speed to stop an end run before it gets to the end.

Woody Hayes said Gradishar was the best linebacker he ever coached. John Ralston, Red Miller and Dan Reeves have felt the same way about Gradishar in Denver.

INDIVIDUAL BRONCO RECORDS

Rushing

Most Yards Game:	183	Otis Armstrong, vs Houston, 1974
Season:	1,407	Otis Armstrong, 1974
Career:	6,323	Floyd Little, 1967–75

Passing

Most TD Passes Game:	5	Frank Tripucka, vs Buffalo, 1962
Season:	24	Frank Tripucka, 1960
Career:	74	Craig Morton, 1977–81

Receiving

Most TD Passes Game:	3	Lionel Taylor, vs Buffalo, 1960
	3	Bob Scarpitto, vs Buffalo, 1966
	3	Haven Moses, vs Houston, 1973
	3	Steve Watson, vs Baltimore, 1981
Season:	13	Steve Watson, 1981
Career:	44	Lionel Taylor, 1960–66
	44	Haven Moses, 1972–81

Scoring

Most Points Game:	21	Gene Mingo, vs Los Angeles, 1960
Season:	137	Gene Mingo, 1962
Career:	736	Jim Turner, 1971–79
Most TDs Game:	3	Lionel Taylor, vs Buffalo, 1960
	3	Don Stone, vs San Diego, 1962
	3	Bob Scarpitto, vs Buffalo, 1966
	3	Floyd Little, vs Minnesota, 1972
	3	Floyd Little, vs Cincinnati, 1973
	3	Haven Moses, vs Houston, 1973
	3	Otis Armstrong, vs Houston, 1974
	3	Jon Keyworth, vs Kansas City, 1974
	3	Steve Watson, vs Baltimore, 1981
Season:	13	Floyd Little, 1972
	13	Floyd Little, 1973
	13	Steve Watson, 1981
Career:	54	Floyd Little, 1967–75

HOUSTON OILERS

TEAM DIRECTORY: Pres./Owner: K. S. (Bud) Adams, Jr.; Exec. VP/GM: Ladd Herzeg; Asst. GM: Mike Holovak; Bus. Mgr.: Lewis Mangum; Dir. Media Rel.: Bob Hyde: Dir. Marketing/Promotions: Rick Nichols; Head Coach: Ed Biles. Home field: Astrodome (50,452). Colors: Scarlet, Columbia blue and white.

SCOUTING REPORT

OFFENSE: Ed Biles faces a philosophical question: Does he stay with a good thing—Earl Campbell carrying the football 60 percent of the time—or does he defer to Gifford Nielsen's arm and make the forward pass the dominant factor in Houston's offense?

An easy question to answer, unless Biles wants to run a good quarterhorse (Campbell) into a plowhorse. The Tyler Rose could wear down from overuse, which is why he caught more passes last year than in his previous three NFL seasons.

Nielsen has the arm to give Houston a deep threat. The kid can fire it out there! And he has the receivers in Ken Burrough, Mike Renfro, Mike Holston and Dave Casper.

The Oilers finished last in AFC offense last year, even with Campbell. They have become a conservative, short-yardage team under Ken Stabler, whose arm has lost much of its strength. Nielsen must open things up more to take the pressure off Campbell. Since Nielsen is more mobile than Stabler, he will take the pressure off his line and buy his receivers extra time.

Biles doesn't have much of a choice, does he?

DEFENSE: The Oilers recovered fewer fumbles than anyone in the league (13) and intercepted only 18 passes in 16 games. That snoring sound you hear is from inside the Astrodome.

Houston was known for hard-hitting defense in its heyday. That heyday has turned to hay. Those lumps the Oilers once left on the bodies of opponents are now appearing on their own bodies. Houston is no longer the puncher, but the catcher. What a sad transformation.

Elvin Bethea is now more a technician than a terror. Ken Kennard and Andy Dorris aren't Fred Smerlas and Fred Dean. The Oilers' best defensive line may be the young backups: Jesse Baker, Daryl Skaugstad (if his knee holds up) and Mike Stensrud. Baker and Stensrud certainly are the best pass rushers.

Robert Brazile and Gregg Bingham are top-notch linebackers,

Earl Campbell has averaged 1,600 yards in four pro seasons.

though Art Stringer and Ted Washington aren't. Is it time for Daryl Hunt and Avon Riley?

The secondary was in a stupor. Mike Reinfeldt had only two interceptions. Greg Stemrick and Carter Hartwig led the group with three each. Three? Maybe ex-Lion Luther Bradley will help.

KICKING GAME: Toni Fritsch is as steady as they come and, next to Efren Herrera, football's most colorful kicker. On those rare times he misses, Toni lets us know by how much. Cliff Parsley punts for a 39.7 average, but placed 18 inside the 20-yard line. Carl Roaches and Willie Tullis are the two best return men on any one team.

THE ROOKIES: Penn State's Mike Munchak is a block of granite lineman who will create more running room for Campbell. Munchak had a year of eligibility left at Penn State, but passed it up to go in the first round. In three years, he will be a Pro Bowler. No. 2 choice Oliver Luck, from West Virginia, is a smart Frank

OILERS VETERAN ROSTER

HEAD COACH—Ed Biles. Assistant Coaches—Andy Bourgeois, Ray Callahan, Bob Gambold, Kenny Houston, Elijah Pitts, Dick Selcer, Jim Shofner, Bill Allerheligen, Ralph Staub.

No.	Name	Pos.	Ht.	Wt.	NFL Exp.	College
39	Armstrong, Adger	RB	6-0	222	3	Texas A&M
11	Bailey, Harold	WR-KR	6-2	197	2	Oklahoma State
75	Baker, Jesse	DE	6-5	265	4	Jacksonville State
65	Bethea, Elvin	DE	6-2	254	15	North Carolina A&T
54	Bingham, Gregg	LB	6-1	229	10	Purdue
	Bradley, Luther	S	6-2	195	5	Notre Dame
52	Brazile, Robert	LB	6-4	237	8	Jackson State
88	Brooks, Billy	WR	6-3	196	6	Oklahoma
00	Burrough, Ken	WR	6-3	210	12	Texas Southern
34	Campbell, Earl	RB	5-11	237	5	Texas
58	Carter, David	G-C	6-2	258	6	Western Kentucky
87	Casper, Dave	TE	6-4	249	9	Notre Dame
47	Coleman, Ronnie	RB	5-11	203	9	Alabama A&M
57	Corker, John	LB	6-5	240	3	Oklahoma State
66	Davidson, Greg	C	6-2	249	3	North Texas State
69	Dorris, Andy	DE	6-4	262	10	New Mexico State
78	Eyre, Nick	T	6-5	276	2	Brigham Young
77	Fields, Angelo	T	6-6	319	3	Michigan State
60	Fisher, Ed	G	6-3	260	9	Arizona State
16	Fritsch, Toni	K	5-7	195	11	No College
74	Gray, Leon	T	6-3	260	10	Jackson State
36	Hartwig, Carter	CB-S	6-0	205	4	Southern California
84	Holston, Mike	WR	6-3	184	2	Morgan State
50	Hunt, Daryl	LB	6-3	234	4	Oklahoma
22	Kay, Bill	CB-S	6-1	190	2	Purdue
71	Kennard, Ken	G	6-2	258	6	Angelo State
14	Nielsen, Gifford	QB	6-4	205	5	Brigham Young
18	Parsley, Cliff	P	6-1	223	6	Oklahoma State
32	Perry, Vernon	S	6-2	211	4	Jackson State
37	Reinfeldt, Mike	S	6-2	196	8	Wisconsin-Milwaukee
82	Renfro, Mike	WR	6-0	184	5	Texas Christian
53	Riley, Avon	LB	6-3	211	2	UCLA
85	Roaches, Carl	WR-KR	5-8	165	3	Texas A&M
62	Schuhmacher, John	G	6-3	266	4	Southern California
90	Skaugstad, Daryle	G	6-5	254	2	California
83	Smith, Tim	WR	6-2	192	3	Nebraska
12	Stabler, Ken	QB	6-3	210	13	Alabama
27	Stemrick, Greg	CB	5-11	185	8	Colorado State
67	Stensrud, Mike	DE	6-5	280	4	Iowa State
56	Stringer, Art	LB	6-2	223	5	Ball State
28	Thomaselli, Rich	RB	6-1	196	2	West Virginia Wesleyan
51	Thompson, Ted	LB	6-1	229	8	Southern Methodist
76	Towns, Morris	T-G	6-5	251	6	Missouri
20	Tullis, Willie	CB-S	6-0	190	2	Troy State
59	Washington, Ted	LB	6-2	248	10	Mississippi Valley
33	Wilson, J.C.	CB	6-0	178	5	Pittsburgh
45	Wilson, Tim	RB	6-3	230	6	Maryland

TOP FIVE DRAFT CHOICES

Rd.	Name	Sel. No.	Pos.	Ht.	Wt.	College
1	Munchak, Mike	8	G	6-3	257	Penn State
2	Luck, Oliver	44	QB	6-2	190	West Virginia
3	Edwards, Stan	72	RB	6-0	208	Michigan
3	Abraham, Robert	77	LB	6-1	212	North Carolina State
4	Bryant, Steve	94	WR	6-2	185	Purdue

Ryan-type at quarterback, who will win some games down the road.

OUTLOOK: The Oilers are a team in transition, a team on the way down. It will take time for Nielsen to make his presence truly felt on offense. The defense is in need of numerous changes. The longer Biles sits on this problem, the worse it's going to get. Houston? A last-place shoo-in.

OILER PROFILES

KEN STABLER 36 6-3 210   Quarterback

A wake for the Snake?... Days as a starter are over if Gifford Nielsen stays healthy... Loss of arm strength has hurt Stabler in recent years, though his short-range accuracy remains the best in football... Incredible timing with receivers over years has made him a 60 percent passer... One of gutsiest quarterbacks in football history and one of the best in last two minutes, too... Been the focus of league attention in recent years—both on and off the field... Born Dec. 25, 1945, in Foley, Ala.... Great player at Alabama and with the Oakland Raiders, recording some of the NFL's greatest comeback victories... Good ol' boy at heart, who doesn't mind a drink and doesn't mind saying so... Loves to play football and party.

GIFFORD NIELSEN 27 6-4 205   Quarterback

Ken Stabler in reverse... Nielsen reads his playbook in chapel while Stabler reads his by the juke box... Nielsen lives a pure and simple life. Very religious, father of four... Won the No. 1 quarterback job, then preseason injury shelved him until late November... Started two games and threw three touchdown passes in season-ending victory against Pittsburgh... Born Oct. 25, 1954, in Provo, Utah... Graduate of BYU's quarterback factory that has also produced Marc Wilson and Jim McMahon... Nielsen led the nation in passing as a junior, before injury in the fourth game of his senior year ended his career... Oilers' third-round draft pick in 1978... Can throw the ball deep, which Houston needs... In his one playoff start, 1979, he upset San Diego, 17–14.

EARL CAMPBELL 27 5–11 237   **Running Back**

Trouble in paradise?...Campbell was unhappy in 1981, feeling that the Oilers were interested in changing their offense away from a ball-control game...Rumors of Campbell as trade bait drifted out of the Gulf. Quickly denied by Oilers...Campbell rushed for 1,376 yards (3.9) and 10 touchdowns, his *worst* season as a pro...Now has 6,457 yards rushing in four seasons, an incredible figure...At this rate, he could pass Jim Brown as the all-time rusher by his seventh season...Last year was the first time in four NFL seasons that Campbell didn't lead the league in rushing...Born March 29, 1955, in Tyler, Tex....The Tyler Rose...Won the Heisman at Texas in 1977... First player taken in the NFL's 1978 draft.

DAVE CASPER 30 6–4 249   **Tight End**

Willie Nelson as a tight end...Casper would be just as happy as a country picker and singer than as one of the game's best tight ends...Missed the Pro Bowl for the first time in six years, but led the Oilers in touchdown catches (8) and yards per reception (17.3)...Scored three times in 21–20 win over Pittsburgh...Uninhibited type, Casper talked his way out of Oakland by angering a number of teammates at a 1980 team meeting...Houston got him for two second-round picks...Born Sept. 26, 1951, in Bemidji, Minn....Graduated with All-American and academic honors from Notre Dame...Oakland's No. 2 pick in 1974, he played little for two years before catching 53 passes, 10 for touchdowns, in '76...Caught 318 passes in seven years...Fine blocker.

KEN BURROUGH 34 6–3 210   **Wide Receiver**

Double zero—in jersey number and recognition...Caught 421 passes in 12 NFL seasons as one of the game's best deep threats, but never has been named all-pro...Led Houston in receptions last year for the seventh time in eight seasons with 40 catches...He scored seven touchdowns to raise his career total to 49...Longest touchdown receptions are 85,

80, 77 and 71 yards, the last in '81 . . . Born July 14, 1948, in Jacksonville, Fla. . . . Two-time team MVP at Texas Southern . . . New Orleans' No. 1 pick in '70 . . . Houston stole him from Saints for three players, none of whom did anything in Mardi Gras town . . . Burrough is a thoroughbred with a long, beautiful stride and tremendous speed for his age . . . Superbly conditioned athlete.

LEON GRAY 30 6–3 260   Offensive Tackle

Look, Bucko, see the Oilers laugh . . . Why are they laughing? You know why . . . Bucko Kilroy, in one of the worst trades of the 1970s, sent Leon Gray from New England to Houston . . . Gray has made the Pro Bowl all three years with Oilers . . . One of the NFL's premier linemen for years . . . Great blocker who once teamed with John Hannah on the left side of New England's offensive line . . . Born Nov. 15, 1951, in Olive Branch, Miss. . . . Played at Jackson State, where he was named to Who's Who Among American College Athletes and Students . . . His football nickname at the time was "Big Dog" because of his 295 pounds at the time . . . Miami drafted him No. 3 in 1973. He trimmed down and became a star in New England, which picked him up on waivers from Dolphins.

VERNON PERRY 28 6–2 211   Strong Safety

The ol' perfessor . . . Perry is a school teacher in Mississippi in the offseason . . . Plays his best in the playoffs. He had the greatest playoff game ever by a defensive back in 1979 when he intercepted four passes and blocked a field goal against San Diego . . . One week later, he intercepted a Terry Bradshaw pass and ran 75 yards for a touchdown . . . Born Sept. 22, 1953, in Jackson, Miss. . . . Played with Robert Brazile and Walter Payton at Jackson State . . . Signed by Chicago as a free agent and then was released . . . Played two years with Montreal, leading the Canadian Football League with nine interceptions in 1977 . . . Has 10 interceptions in three seasons with Houston . . . Been with Oilers three years and started every game . . . On Sports Illustrated's all-pro team in '79 . . . Perry's play has since fallen off.

TONI FRITSCH 37 5-7 195   Kicker

Keek the ball, Toni . . . Keek the ball he does, hitting 15 of 22 field-goal attempts last year . . . Career accuracy is 68 percent . . . Colorful player who bought a Houston restaurant and acquired a beer belly in the process, but it didn't hurt his kicking . . . An Austrian, Fritsch played eight years of professional soccer in Europe before signing with the Dallas Cowboys . . . Kicked a field goal in the first American football game he saw . . . Speaks four languages: Austrian, German, French and English . . . Born July 10, 1945, in Vienna . . . Never attended college . . . Spent 1971–75 with Dallas, then was released . . . He kicked for San Diego in '76, then joined the Oilers in the next year . . . NFL's most accurate kicker in 1980.

JESSE BAKER 25 6–5 265   Defensive End

Big, bad Jesse . . . The scourge of quarterbacks for three years with 32 sacks . . . Set a club record with 15½ sacks, also the AFC high, his rookie year of 1979. Followed that up with 6½ and 10 sacks the last two autumns . . . Plays behind Elvin Bethea on Houston's depth chart, although Baker comes in whenever the Oilers switch from a 3–4 to 4–3 defense . . . One of the most dangerous sack specialists in football: the Cedrick Hardman of the '80s . . . Born July 10, 1957, in Conyers, Ga. . . . Three-time all-conference pick at Jacksonville (Ala.) State . . . MVP in 1977 Grantland Rice Bowl . . . Drafted in the second round in '79 along with another Oiler defensive end, Mike Stensrud . . . Baker plays the run fairly well, too.

CARL ROACHES 28 5–8 165   Kick Returner

Mark one up for the little man . . . Roaches led the AFC in kickoff returns last year with a 27.5 average. One of those runbacks was for 96 yards and a touchdown against Cincinnati—the AFC's longest return . . . Little Carl also tied for 10th in conference punt returns with a 7.6 average . . . Great success story: Roaches played for Texas A&M and was drafted in the 14th round by Tampa Bay in 1976...Cut by the lowly Bucs, he spent the next four years out of professional football before Bum Phillips gave him a shot with Houston in '80. Roaches made the club—the oldest rookie in the NFL—as a return specialist...Born Oct. 2, 1953, in Houston...Return man and wide receiver for the Texas Aggies...The Charlie Criss of football.

COACH ED BILES...Still finding it a tough act to follow Bum Phillips...Oilers made playoffs three years in a row under Phillips, who was fired after the third year...Biles, his defensive coordinator, was named to replace him...The Oilers immediately fell to a 7–9 season, including a 27–24 defeat to Phillips and his Saints in Houston...Biles made a strategic mistake last summer in implying that he didn't want Ken Stabler back...Stabler retired, then when Gifford Nielsen was injured, Biles almost had to get down on hands and knees to get Stabler back. The Snake got a new contract to boot...The new coach lost Earl Campbell's favor by tinkering with the offense, though there may now be accord between the two...Born Oct. 18, 1931, in Reading, Ohio, Biles played for Ara Parseghian at the "Cradle of Coaches," Miami (Ohio) University, then coached for 13 years at Xavier, the last seven as head coach...Spent his NFL indoctrination at New Orleans and with the New York Jets before joining the Oilers in 1974...Not big in height at 5–6, Biles can coach some Texas-sized defense—or at least he could until he became head coach. The Oilers gave up 357.9 yards a game...Biles must show improvement this year to keep his job.

GREATEST LINEBACKER

When the all-pro ballots are sent out, voters immediately pencil in the name of Robert Brazile, then start worrying about other positions.

Brazile was voted NFL Defensive Rookie of the Year in 1976 and has been chosen to the all-pro and Pro Bowl teams the last five years. Any questions?

He was the sixth player drafted in '76 and became an instant starter for Houston at outside linebacker. Brazile looks like a linebacker should look—6–4, 238—and plays like a linebacker should play—4.6 speed and a ferocious ability to hit that has earned him the name "Dr. Doom."

Brazile played at Jackson State with Walter Payton. It has been said that Payton became the elusive back that he is from trying to avoid Brazile in practice. Brazile entered college as a tight end, but his toughness was better suited for defense.

Bum Phillips, who drafted Brazile, said not long ago that the Oilers' linebacker "is the same kid now after becoming a genuine star as when he was a rookie. And he has more fun on the field than the rest of the guys."

But, it's no fun to play against Brazile.

INDIVIDUAL OILER RECORDS

Rushing

Most Yards Game:	216	Billy Cannon, vs New York, 1961
Season:	1,934	Earl Campbell, 1980
Career:	6,457	Earl Campbell, 1978–81

Passing

Most TD Passes Game:	7	George Blanda, vs New York, 1961
Season:	36	George Blanda, 1961
Career:	165	George Blanda, 1960–66

Receiving

Most TD Passes Game:	3	Bill Groman, vs New York, 1960
	3	Bill Groman, vs New York, 1961
	3	Billy Cannon, vs New York, 1961
	3	Charlie Hennigan, vs San Diego, 1961
	3	Charlie Hennigan, vs Buffalo, 1963
	3	Willie Frazier, vs New York, 1965
	3	Charles Frazier, vs Denver, 1966 (twice)
	3	Dave Casper, vs Pittsburgh, 1981
Season:	17	Bill Groman, 1961
Career:	51	Charlie Hennigan, 1960–66

Scoring

Most Points Game:	30	Billy Cannon, vs New York, 1961
Season:	115	George Blanda, 1960
Career:	596	George Blanda, 1960–66
Most TDs Game:	5	Billy Cannon, vs New York, 1961
Season:	19	Earl Campbell, 1979
Career:	55	Earl Campbell, 1978–81

KANSAS CITY CHIEFS

TEAM DIRECTORY: Owner: Lamar Hunt; Pres.: Jack Steadman; VP/GM: Jim Schaaf; Dir. Player Personnel: Les Miller; Dir. Research and Development: Ron Waller; Dir. Pub. Rel.: Bob Sprenger; Head Coach: Marv Levy. Home field: Arrowhead Stadium (78,094). Colors: Red and gold.

SCOUTING REPORT

OFFENSE: Marv Levy no longer has to experiment to win. The days of the wing-T in Kansas City are over. The Chiefs don't need gimmicks any longer. They can win with what they have playing the same pro-set offensive formation as everyone else.

The wing-T and Levy arrived in Kansas City the same time, 1978. The Chiefs had more running backs than receivers and a quarterback, Mike Livingston, who was OK, but no Len Dawson.

Rookie Joe Delaney almost vaulted KC into the playoffs.

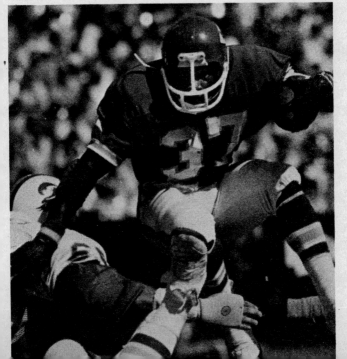

A third running back helped the blocking scheme as well because the tight end, Walter White, couldn't block a Kansas City cheerleader.

The Chiefs now have a quarterback, Steve Fuller, who might someday be as good as Dawson. But first he must supplant Bill Kenney, last year's No. 1. There are good running backs in Ted McKnight, super find Joe Delaney and short-yardage workhorse Billy Jackson, who scored 11 touchdowns as a rookie to finish fourth among AFC non-kick scorers.

Kansas City has good receivers in J. T. Smith, Henry Marshall and Carlos Carson, and rookie Anthony Hancock, from Tennessee, could be the explosive deep threat the Chiefs need. The offensive line is good, but not great. The best players are young guard Brad Budde and aging center Jack Rudnay.

DEFENSE: It's quite possible that the defense everyone will be talking about this year will be Kansas City's.

The two ends, Art Still and Mike Bell, only need a full season of working together. Both of them were the second players taken in their respective drafts, so the talent is there. The Chiefs have used different bodies at nose tackle in recent years, but the best may be Dino Mangiero, who is bulky and rugged in the mold of Lyle Alzado.

Key to the defense is Kansas City's linebacking. Gary Spani became a needed force inside last year. However, there is a question mark at the other inside backer—Frank Manumaleuga or Jerry Blanton? Whitney Paul and Thomas Howard may not have a lock on the outside positions. The linebacking, especially against the pass, will determine how well the Chiefs play defense.

Three talented defensive backs—Eric Harris, Gary Green and Gary Barbaro—intercepted 17 passes among them last year. But who is the strong safety? It seems to be a new one every year.

Regardless, the Chiefs were No. 1 in the AFC against the run last year and they could be No. 1 overall defensively this year.

KICKING GAME: Good and bad. The good is kicker Nick Lowery, the four-time retread who has been tremendous for two seasons. The other good is J. T. Smith, who can bust open a punt return as well as anyone. The bad is punter Bob Grupp, the former NFL leader (1979) who seems to have lost it.

THE ROOKIES: Tennessee's Hancock is a Stanley Morgan type, possibly the missing link that could springboard the Chiefs into the playoffs. Linebacking has been up and down for Kansas City, which explains the drafting of North Carolina's Calvin Daniels

CHIEFS VETERAN ROSTER

HEAD COACH—Marv Levy. Assistant Coaches—Rod Rust, Walt Corey, Don Lawrence, Ted Cotterell, Kay Dalton, J.D. Helm, Tom Bresnahan, Frank Gansz, Ron Waller, Rick Abernethy.

No.	Name	Pos.	Ht.	Wt.	NFL Exp.	College
26	Barbaro, Gary	S	6-4	204	7	Nicholls State
85	Beckman, Ed	TE	6-4	237	6	Florida State
99	Bell, Mike	DE	6-4	255	3	Colorado State
35	Belton, Horace	RB	5-8	200	4	Southeast Louisiana
57	Blanton, Jerry	LB	6-1	236	4	Kentucky
30	Bledsoe, Curtis	RB	5-11	215	2	San Diego State
66	Budde, Brad	G	6-4	255	3	Southern California
34	Burruss, Lloyd	S	6-0	201	2	Maryland
56	Cancik, Phil	LB	6-1	230	3	Northern Arizona
88	Carson, Carlos	WR-KR	5-10	172	3	Louisiana State
42	Carter, M.L.	DE	5-9	173	4	Cal State-Fullerton
95	Case, Frank	DE	6-4	242	2	Penn State
20	Cherry, Deron	S	5-11	185	2	Rutgers
41	Christopher, Herb	S	5-10	202	4	Morris Brown
65	Condon, Tom	G	6-3	272	9	Boston College
37	Delaney, Joe	RB	5-10	186	2	Northwest Louisiana
84	Dixon, Al	TE	6-5	235	6	Iowa State
4	Fuller, Steve	QB	6-4	198	4	Clemson
11	Gagliano, Bob	QB	6-3	193	2	Utah State
21	Gaines, Clark	RB	6-1	212	6	Wake Forest
77	Getty, Charlie	T	6-4	269	9	Penn State
7	Gossett, Jeff	P	6-2	195	2	Eastern Illinois
24	Green, Gary	CB	5-11	184	5	Baylor
1	Grupp, Bob	P	5-11	204	4	Duke
48	Hadnot, James	RB	6-2	244	3	Texas Tech
44	Harris, Eric	CB	6-3	191	3	Memphis State
83	Harvey, Marvin	TE	6-3	220	2	Southern Mississippi
60	Herkenhoff, Matt	T	6-4	270	7	Minnesota
75	Hicks, Sylvester	DE	6-4	252	5	Tennessee State
52	Howard, Thomas	LB	6-2	215	6	Texas Tech
43	Jackson, Billy	RB	5-10	223	2	Alabama
51	Jackson, Charles	LB	6-2	220	5	Washington
9	Kenney, Bill	QB	6-4	210	4	Northern Colorado
55	Klug, Dave	LB	6-4	230	2	Concordia, Minn.
91	Kremer, Ken	NT	6-4	250	4	Ball State
31	Lewis, Will	CB	5-10	195	3	Millersville State
71	Lindstrom, Dave	DE	6-6	257	5	Boston
0	Lowery, Nick	K	6-4	190	3	Dartmouth
74	Mangiero, Dino	T	6-2	265	4	Rutgers
54	Manumaleuga, Frank	LB	6-2	245	4	San Jose State
89	Marshall, Henry	WR	6-2	214	7	Missouri
22	McKnight, Ted	RB	6-1	216	6	Minnesota-Duluth
82	Murphy, James	WR	5-10	177	2	Utah State
61	Parrish, Don	T	6-2	263	5	Pittsburgh
53	Paul, Whitney	LB	6-3	220	7	Colorado
50	Peterson, Cal	LB	6-4	230	4	UCLA
85	Rome, Stan	WR	6-4	218	4	Clemson
70	Rourke, Jim	G-T	6-5	265	3	Boston College
58	Rudnay, Jack	C	6-2	242	13	Northwestern
81	Scott, Willie	TE	6-4	245	2	South Carolina
73	Simmons, Bob	G	6-4	260	6	Texas
86	Smith, J.T.	KR-WR	6-2	186	5	North Texas State
59	Spani, Gary	LB	6-2	230	5	Kansas State
67	Still, Art	DE	6-7	252	5	Kentucky
76	Taylor, Roger	T	6-6	271	2	Oklahoma State
62	Thomas, Todd	C	6-5	262	2	North Dakota
40	Williams, Mike	RB	6-3	222	4	New Mexico

TOP FIVE DRAFT CHOICES

Rd.	Name	Sel. No.	Pos.	Ht.	Wt.	College
1	Hancock, Anthony	11	WR	6-0	187	Tennessee
2	Daniels, Calvin	46	LB	6-3	234	North Carolina
4	Haynes, Louis	100	LB	6-0	206	North Texas State
4	Anderson, Stuart	104	DT	6-1	247	Virginia
5	Thompson, Delbert	130	RB	6-1	204	Texas-El Paso

and North Texas State's Louis Haynes. Howard and Manunaleuga, beware! Stuart Anderson is a long-shot to make it as a nose tackle.

OUTLOOK: Everything's up to date in Kansas City. Well, almost. If the quarterbacking and linebacking improve, the Chiefs look like a playoff team. Their defense is strong enough to get them 10 wins, regardless. Kansas City has drafted well and by 1983 should be one of the AFC's powerhouses.

CHIEF PROFILES

STEVE FULLER 25 6–4 198   Quarterback

The missing link . . . Fuller must live up to his potential or the future of the Chiefs is doubtful . . . Injuries and Bill Kenney have detoured Fuller's career . . . However, he is more athletic than Kenney, who has the mobility of a banana slug . . . Fuller's arm may not be as strong, but it's good enough to make the Chiefs a winner . . . Fuller played sparingly last year for the aforementioned reasons . . . If he wants the job, he must take it away from Kenney . . . Fuller was born Jan. 5, 1957, in Enid, Okla. . . . Set several passing records at Clemson, where he was a Rhodes Scholar candidate . . . Chiefs' first-round draft pick in 1979 . . . Can be as good as he wants, though he better get going . . . Kenney doesn't give up easily.

JOE DELANEY 23 5–10 186   Running Back

Whatta find, whatta back! . . . NFL teams are kicking themselves for letting Delaney slip through the first round of the draft . . . Chiefs are pinching themselves that they came up lucky in the second—Delaney was the 41st player taken, but should have been in the top 15 . . . He finished third in AFC rushing with 1,121 yards (4.8) and caught 22 passes for 246 yards . . . His longest run was 82 yards—second longest in Kansas City history—and his longest reception 61 yards . . . He scored three touchdowns and was as pleasant off the field as he was unpleasant on it . . . Born Oct. 30, 1958, in Henderson, Tex. . . . Football and track star at Northwest Louisiana, setting career rushing record and sprint marks of 10.3 for 100 meters and 20.6 for 200 . . . Ducks under tacklers to prevent injuries.

J. T. SMITH 26 6-2 186　　　　　Wide Receiver

New job title...Smith once was considered a punt returner, though now he listed as a wide receiver...He's a threat at either occupation...J. T. had his best year as a receiver, catching 63 passes, tying him for 10th place in the AFC...He finished third in AFC punt returns with a 10.6 average, though his 62-yard return was second among the leaders...First time in three years he didn't score on a return, however...Smith returned four punts all the way in 1979-80...Holds the club record with an 88-yard runback against Oakland in '79...Born Oct. 29, 1955, in Leonard, Tex....Wasn't drafted out of North Texas State...Washington signed him as a defensive back...Chiefs picked him up after Redskins cut him in '78.

BRAD BUDDE 24 6-4 255　　　　　Offensive Guard

Keeping alive a tradition...Father Ed played guard for the Chiefs from 1963-76...And like his dad, Brad was a first-round draft pick (1980)...Brad wanted to wear Ed's old number, 71, which Brad wore at USC...But Dave Lindstrom already had it, so Brad chose 66...Son may turn out to be as good as father...Brad became a starter late in his rookie year, then held the job last fall...He started all four years at USC, the first freshman to start for the Trojans since World War II...Former Chiefs' water boy...Born May 9, 1958, in Detroit...Helped Ricky Bell and Charles White rush to numerous records and honors at USC...Budde played alongside Anthony Munoz, which had to be the greatest half of a college line ever.

ART STILL 26 6-7 252　　　　　Defensive End

Big Chief...Still has played in last two Pro Bowls and he's still learning how to play defensive end...Hasn't reached his prime yet, though when he does, offensive tackles in the league may call in sick on days when the Chiefs are in town...Lean and mean, still doesn't have the body a defensive lineman is perceived to have—big and bulky...Still has a washboard abdomen and narrow hips, like a prize fighter . . . Pro football players have their best years, normally, between their fourth and eighth seasons . . . This is Still's fifth year, so get ready all you tackles! . . . Born Dec. 5, 1955, in Camden, N.J. . . . Has nine brothers and sisters . . . Started four years at Kentucky . . . Second player taken in '80 draft.

ERIC HARRIS 27 6-3 191   **Cornerback**

Mr. Personality . . . Harris was a candidate to become the Duane Thomas of the '80s until he turned the corner, in terms of maturity, last season . . . In terms of playing ability at cornerback, he may become a perennial Pro Bowler . . . Intercepted seven passes two years ago and seven more last season . . . Great cover man with quick reactions and a pickpocket's hands. Everything he needs to be a fine corner for years . . . Born Aug. 11, 1955, in Memphis, Tenn. . . . Four-year star at Memphis State . . . Chiefs drafted him in the fourth round of a '77 supplemental draft, but he had signed beforehand with Toronto . . . He spent three years in Canada, then joined the Chiefs after they exercised their right of first refusal on an offer tendered by New Orleans.

GARY GREEN 26 5-11 184   **Cornerback**

The quiet corner . . . Nothing much happens at Green's cornerback position. That's because he takes care of it so well . . . His five interceptions last year matched his NFL high. Green's 16 thefts in five seasons is nothing to phone Canton, Ohio, about . . . However, he isn't tested that often, either . . . Eric Harris' 14 interceptions in two seasons are a good indication of where the action is flowing . . . Most NFL scouts would agree that Green is one of the game's best corners . . . Quarterbacks feel the same way, so they throw to the other side of the field where Harris is waiting . . . Either way, you can't win . . . Green was born Oct. 22, 1955, in San Antonio, Tex. . . . All-American as a Baylor senior . . . Chiefs' first-round pick in 1977.

ARY BARBARO 28 6-4 204   Free Safety

Second-story man ... Burglar in the defensive backfield ... Barbaro is the most dangerous free safety in pro football, year in and year out, when it comes to interceptions ... He has 36 in six seasons, just one off the club record ... Although it is premature to think this way, if Barbaro continues his pace for another six years, he could wind up as football's all-time interception leader ... Born Feb. 11, 1954, in New Orleans ... He knocked them dead at Nicholls State, where he was among the first varsity football graduates ... Barbaro came to college as a wide receiver, then shifted to the secondary as a junior ... Third-round pick of Chiefs in 1976 ... Barbaro and Nolan Cromwell consistently are the NFL's best free safeties.

NICK LOWERY 26 6-4 190   Kicker

Senator Lowery? ... Has the proper resume: father served in the U.S. Foreign Service, Nick majored in government at Dartmouth (Hmmmmm, Ivy League background), he worked as an intern on Capitol Hill and spent time working for a Missouri state senator ... Kicking a football might get him a few votes, too ... Throwing a football didn't hurt Jack Kemp ... Lowery replaced Kansas City legend Jan Stenerud in 1980, then kicked a club-record 57-yarder that season ... Lowery tied for AFC scoring lead with Cincinnati's Jim Breech at 115 points ... Lowery has made 20 of 26 and 26 of 36 in two Kansas City seasons ... Born May 27, 1956 in Munich, Germany ... Turned down by Jets, Patriots, Bengals and Redskins before success with K.C.

BOB GRUPP 27 5-11 204   Punter

From fabulous to El Floppo ... Grupp averaged 43.6 yards three years ago and the Chiefs thought they had themselves another Ray Guy ... His 39.5 and 38.0 averages of the last two seasons now have the Chiefs wondering if they have a right-footed Bucky Dilts ... His placements inside the 20-yard line plummeted from 23 to five ... In other words, punter in trouble...Grupp failed in two previous tries with Jets before finding punting guru Ray Pelfrey in Sparks, Nev....With new form and confidence, Cinderella found the right kicking shoe in Kansas City...Since 1979, nothing seems to fit...Grupp was born May 8, 1955, in Philadelphia...Economics major at Duke, where he averaged 40.4 yards a punt and was the baseball team's MVP.

COACH MARV LEVY...Irving Berlin of coaches...Wrote the Chiefs' fight song which is played every game at Arrowhead Stadium...Follow the words on the message board, kiddies...Writing a bigger story on the football field...Chiefs have improved from 4–12 to 7–9 to 8–8 to 9–7 in Levy's four years...Last year was the club's first winning season since 1973...Kansas City has to be considered a playoff contender this season...Levy has built slowly through the draft. "It's the sound way," he said...The gray-haired coach is confident and capable. He's smart, too, a Phi Beta Kappa graduate of Coe College in Cedar Rapids, Iowa, and bearer of a master's degree in English history from Harvard...Levy has experienced highs and lows in coaching...The low point was at California in the early 1960s...The highs were virtually every place else—Coe, New Mexico, William & Mary and Montreal Alouettes...Montreal played in three Grey Cups in Levy's five seasons there, winning twice...Levy also has coached as an NFL assistant at Philadelphia, Los Angeles and Washington...He was born Aug. 3, 1928, in Chicago.

GREATEST LINEBACKER

Choosing between Willie Lanier and Bobby Bell for the title of Kansas City's greatest linebacker is like choosing between Hank Aaron and Babe Ruth for the title of baseball's greatest home-run hitter. Why not say simply that they were both the best?

Lanier and Bell weren't necessarily bookends, because Lanier played middle linebacker and Bell outside linebacker on Kansas

City's Super Bowl IV champions. But they were a perfectly matched set when it came to talent.

Lanier was oddly shaped (6–1, 235), but he could run and hit and cover the pass. His 27 interceptions are the fourth-highest total by a Chief. Drafted in the second round out of Morgan State in 1967, he became the premier middle linebacker in the AFL and later the AFC.

Bell was much bigger (6–4, 240) than Lanier and a tremendous force on the outside. An All-America defensive tackle at Minnesota, Bell wasn't selected until the seventh round of the 1963 draft. But there was never any doubt about his potential greatness after the Chiefs placed him at linebacker. He intercepted 26 passes in his career and stood like a stone wall against the run.

INDIVIDUAL CHIEF RECORDS

Rushing

Most Yards Game:	193	Joe Delaney, vs Houston, 1981
Season:	1,121	Joe Delaney, 1981
Career:	4,451	Ed Podolak, 1969–77

Passing

Most TD Passes Game:	6	Len Dawson, vs Denver, 1964
Season:	30	Len Dawson, 1964
Career:	237	Len Dawson, 1962–75

Receiving

Most TD Passes Game:	4	Frank Jackson, vs San Diego, 1964
Season:	12	Chris Burford, 1962
Career:	57	Otis Taylor, 1965–75

Scoring

Most Points Game:	30	Abner Haynes, vs Oakland, 1961
Season:	129	Jan Stenerud, 1968
Career:	1,231	Jan Stenerud, 1967–79
Most TDs Game:	5	Abner Haynes, vs Oakland, 1961
Season:	19	Abner Haynes, 1962
Career:	60	Otis Taylor, 1965–75

MIAMI DOLPHINS

TEAM DIRECTORY: Pres.: Joseph Robbie; Head Coach: Don Shula; Dir. Pro Scouting: Charley Winner; Dir. Player Personnel: Chuck Connor; Dir. Pub. Rel.: Bob Kearney. Home field: Orange Bowl (75,289). Colors: Aqua and orange.

SCOUTING REPORT

OFFENSE: Miami is the Lon Chaney of football: the offense with a thousand faces. The Dolphins don't have one great offensive threat like a Larry Csonka or Paul Warfield, but they have a number of good players who can hurt an opponent in different ways.

Tony Nathan and Andra Franklin combined for 1,493 yards

Young David Woodley will fight for starting QB job in '82.

rushing and 12 touchdowns by land. Rookie back Tom Vigorito helped the club with his running, receiving and punt returns. The Dolphins could use a Csonka or a Mercury Morris, but they're not in bad shape, with Don Shula mixing up his backfield combinations.

The Dolphins are always a playoff threat because of their head coach, who successfully manipulated two quarterbacks, David Woodley and Don Strock, into 11 victories a year ago. Miami might win more than that if Woodley becomes a 60-minute quarterback instead of a 30-minute quarterback.

There are numerous receivers in Nat Moore, Duriel Harris, Jimmy Cefalo and tight ends Bruce Hardy, Joe Rose and Ronnie Lee. The offensive line, led by Ed Newman and Bob Kuechenberg, is steady and solid in typical Miami tradition.

DEFENSE: Miami can stop the run, but will it ever stop the pass?

The Dolphins could be one of the best defenses in football if they could only stop the forward pass. Even slowing it down would be a help.

Look at the talent in the front seven: Bob Baumhower, Doug Betters, A. J. Duhe, Larry Gordon, Earnest Rhone, Bob Brudzinski and Kim Bokamper. There's some great players in that group and they're young, too.

Miami gave up 275 points last year, fewest in the AFC. With Bill Arnsparger, who is considered the best defensive coach in the game, the Dolphins will be even better this fall.

Cornerback Gerald Small and safety Don Bessillieu are quality players, but the Miami secondary could use a shot in the arm through the draft or via a trade. Another safety might be the team's most glaring need. Oh, if only Jake Scott and Dick Anderson were 23 again.

KICKING GAME: Best it has been in years. Punt returner Vigorito and kick returner Fulton Walker each broke one all the way last year. Free-agent punter Tom Orosz averaged 40.8, but placed 21 punts inside the 20-yard line. Uwe von Schamann had his best year as a placekicker.

THE ROOKIES: USC guard Roy Foster is another Larry Little. Foster will replace Kuechenberg, 34, eventually, though he is big enough to play tackle and may get a look there. Wide receiver Mark Duper is a super athlete from Northwest Louisiana who could suprise. The most interesting Dolphin selection is Yale back Rich Diana. Can Don Shula turn him into another Vigorito?

DOLPHINS VETERAN ROSTER

HEAD COACH—Don Shula. Assistant Coaches—Bill Arnsparger, Wally English, Tom Keane, John Sandusky, Mike Scarry, Carl Taseff, Steve Crosby.

No.	Name	Pos.	Ht.	Wt.	NFL Exp.	College
88	Bailey, Elmer	WR	6-0	195	3	Minnesota
70	Barnett, Bill	DE	6-4	260	3	Nebraska
73	Baumhower, Bob	DT	6-5	260	6	Alabama
34	Bennett, Woody	RB	6-2	222	4	Miami
46	Bessillieu, Don	S	6-1	200	4	Georgia Tech
75	Betters, Doug	DE	6-7	260	5	Nevada-Reno
47	Blackwood, Glenn	S	6-0	186	4	Texas
42	Blackwood, Lyle	S	6-1	188	10	Texas Christian
58	Bokamper, Kim	DE	6-6	250	6	San Jose State
59	Brudzinski, Bob	LB	6-4	230	6	Ohio State
81	Cefalo, Jimmy	WR	5-11	188	5	Penn State
	Cunningham, Eric	G	6-3	257	3	Penn State
	Darby, Paul	WR	5-10	192	3	Southwest Texas State
63	Dennard, Mark	C	6-1	252	4	Texas A&M
77	Duhe, A.J.	LB	6-4	245	6	Louisiana State
37	Franklin, Andra	FB	5-10	225	2	Nebraska
79	Giesler, Jon	T	6-4	260	4	Michigan
50	Gordon, Larry	LB	6-4	230	7	Arizona State
74	Green, Cleveland	T	6-3	262	4	Southern
84	Hardy, Bruce	TE	6-4	230	5	Arizona State
82	Harris, Duriel	WR	5-11	184	7	New Mexico State
31	Hill, Ed	RB	6-2	210	4	Memphis State
36	Howell, Steve	RB	6-2	210	4	Baylor
11	Jensen, Jim	QB	6-4	212	2	Boston University
40	Kozlowski, Mike	S	6-0	198	3	Colorado
67	Kuechenberg, Bob	G	6-2	255	13	Notre Dame
68	Laakso, Eric	T	6-4	265	5	Tulane
86	Lee, Ronnie	TE	6-3	236	4	Baylor
33	Matthews, Bo	RB	6-3	222	9	Colorado
28	McNeal, Don	CB	5-11	192	3	Alabama
89	Moore, Nat	WR	5-9	188	9	Florida
22	Nathan, Tony	RB	6-0	206	4	Alabama
64	Newman, Ed	G	6-2	255	10	Duke
3	Orosz, Tom	P	6-1	204	2	Ohio State
78	Poole, Ken	DE	6-3	251	2	Northeast Louisiana
54	Potter, Steve	LB	6-3	235	2	Virginia
43	Ray, Ricky	CB	5-11	180	4	Norfolk State
55	Rhone, Earnie	LB	6-2	224	7	Henderson, Ark.
38	Robiskie, Terry	FB	6-1	210	5	Louisiana State
80	Rose, Joe	TE	6-3	228	3	California
52	Shull, Steve	LB	6-1	220	3	William & Mary
48	Small, Gerald	CB	5-11	192	5	San Jose State
57	Stephenson, Dwight	C	6-2	255	3	Alabama
10	Strock, Don	QB	6-5	220	9	Virginia Tech
45	Taylor, Ed	CB	6-0	175	8	Memphis State
60	Toews, Jeff	G	6-3	255	4	Washington
32	Vigorito, Tom	RB	5-10	197	2	Virginia
5	von Schamann, Uwe	K	6-0	188	4	Oklahoma
41	Walker, Fulton	CB	5-10	193	2	West Virginia
16	Woodley, David	QB	6-2	204	3	Louisiana State

TOP FIVE DRAFT CHOICES

Rd.	Name	Sel. No.	Pos.	Ht.	Wt.	College
1	Foster, Roy	24	G	6-4	265	Southern California
2	Duper, Mark	52	WR	5-10	180	Northwest Louisiana
3	Lankford, Paul	80	DB	6-1	177	Penn State
4	Bowser, Charles	108	LB	6-3	224	Duke
5	Nelson, Bob	120	DT	6-3	250	Miami

OUTLOOK: The Dolphins are Super Bowl material if Woodley becomes a Bob Griese, take-charge quarterback and the pass defense improves. Everything else seems to be there. The Dolphins are a young team, except for graybeard Kuechenberg up front. It's important that Miami gets the home-field advantage for playoffs because it's not a good cold-weather team.

DOLPHIN PROFILES

DAVID WOODLEY 23 6–2 204   Quarterback

The latest pride of Shreveport...Quarterback capital of America...Terry Bradshaw, Joe Ferguson, Woodley, with Bert Jones just down the road at Rustin...Woodley had a 4–0 record against the other three in '81, beating Jones twice...Miami's quarterback of the future, but he must learn to finish what he starts...Gave way four times to Don Strock in regular season and once during the playoffs...Eighth-round draft pick in '80, Woodley surprised everyone—including Strock— by winning the starting job as a rookie...Woodley wasn't even a fulltime starter at LSU; he shared the job with Steve Ensminger, who wasn't drafted...Born Oct. 25, 1958, in Shreveport, La....Woodley's short on words, like Bob Griese.

DON STROCK 31 6–5 220   Quarterback

How do you spell relief? S-t-r-o-c-k...He "saved" four victories for Dolphins last year during the regular season...Strock's finest moment in nine NFL seasons came in the 41–38 playoff overtime defeat to San Diego...He entered the game with Miami losing 24–0 in the second quarter. He was incredible, completing 29 of 43 passes for 403 yards and four touchdowns. Actually pulled the Dolphins into the lead until the Chargers rallied to win...Strock's performance still leaves him No. 2 because of an inconsistency factor...Born Nov. 20, 1950, in Pottstown, Pa....Led the nation in passing at Virginia Tech, once throwing for 527 yards against University of Houston...Dolphins' No. 5 pick in 1973.

ED NEWMAN 31 6-2 255   Offensive Guard

Good things sometimes take longer to turn out... Take the case of Newman, who spent seven years playing behind Larry Little before getting his chance... "An overpriced insurance policy finally paid off," Newman said of the long wait... He reaped the dividends last year when he was named to the Pro Bowl... Known as the human torpedo for his blocking charge off the line... Strongest Dolphin ever, Newman can bench press 485 pounds and do 10 or more repetitions of 400 pounds... "Working hard has never been an obstacle for me."... Malignant tumor on thyroid gland required two throat operations in January, 1975... "I'm not medical hero. People can overcome problems with determination."... No. 6 draft pick in '73 from Duke... Born June 4, 1951, in Woodbury, N.Y.

BOB BAUMHOWER 27 6-5 260   Defensive Tackle

Nose for the ball... Nose, as in nose tackle... Baumhower's play last year allowed him to nose out Buffalo's Fred Smerlas for starting tackle berth in the Pro Bowl... "Bama" led the Dolphins with nine sacks, four in one game against Houston against another Bama-ite, Ken Stabler... Baumhower was named to The Sporting News' all-pro team... He hasn't missed a game for the Dolphins in the five years he has been with team... Club's second-round pick in '77... Born Aug. 4, 1955, in Portsmouth, Va.... Finished high school in Tuscaloosa, Ala., then played at Alabama... Loves deep sea fishing on his 26-foot Thunderbird Formula... Owns a Bachelors III with Joe Namath and Richard Todd in Fort Lauderdale, Fla.

TONY NATHAN 25 6-0 206   Running Back

Toughest of the pass-catching running backs... Nathan caught 50 passes last year and none of them were dumps or screens. He runs those circling patterns out of the backfield where he has to beat a linebacker... Scored three times through the air, plus five times on the ground as he rushed for 782 yards. His 5.3 per-carry average was tops among NFL leaders . . . Nathan's biggest play last year, however, was the pass lateral from Duriel Harris that went for a touchdown just before halftime against San Diego in the playoffs . . . Born Dec. 14, 1956, in Birmingham, Ala. . . . Full name: Tony Curtis Nathan . . . Great back at Alabama, where he led the Tide to '79 national championship . . . Miami third-round pick in 1979, immediate sensation as kick-returner.

DURIEL HARRIS 27 5–11 184   Wide Receiver

The poor man's spiker . . . Spiked the ball after a touchdown against the Eagles on national TV and when he came down twisted his knee . . . Harris' showboating kept him from a 1,000-yard receiving year and should serve as warning to other receivers. But don't count on it . . . Harris caught 53 passes for 911 yards and two touchdowns . . . Passed the great Paul Warfield on Miami's receiving yardage chart. Now has to overtake Nat Moore . . . Harris was a lonesome end at New Mexico State, which ran the Wishbone . . . Still caught 89 passes, 13 for touchdowns . . . Born Nov. 27, 1954, in Port Arthur, Tex . . . Father a high school football coach in Beaumont . . . Harris was the Dolphins' third-round pick in '76.

A. J. DUHE 26 6–4 245   Inside Linebacker

Duhe thought "Phooey" . . . That was A. J.'s initial reaction when Don Shula suggested he change from defensive end to linebacker . . . Larry Gordon was a holdout and Shula needed help . . . So Duhe reluctantly climbed out of his crouch and now stands up for a living . . . Moved from the outside to the inside, he was spectacular at times in '81, recording 7½ sacks . . . It's still rather new to Duhe, but he's catching on. When he gets the full hang of linebacking, watch out! . . . Actually the idea of Duhe as a linebacker was given Shula by sportswriter Chuck Otterson of the *Palm Beach Post* . . . Adam Joseph Duhe was born Nov. 27, 1955, in New Orleans . . . Standout player at LSU . . . Married Baton Rouge flame, Frances, during her reign as Orange Bowl queen.

JOE ROSE 25 6-3 228   Tight End

Slow Joe . . . Speed doesn't impress anyone, but his moves do . . . The kind of receiver who manages to get open all the time, while faster defensive backs wonder how he did it . . . Miami drafted him in the seventh round in 1980 after one good year at California . . . Entered college as a wide receiver, was redshirted, and finally grew into a tight end's body . . . Has good size and great hands . . . Dolphins occasionally play him as wide receiver . . . He caught two touchdown passes against San Diego in the playoffs . . . Born June 24, 1957, in Marysville, Cal. . . . The pride of Marysville High . . . Can bench press almost 400 pounds and his 4.7 speed isn't exactly sloth-like . . . Woodley's roommate . . . These two practice conservation—of words.

UWE von SCHAMANN 26 6-0 188   Kicker

The little tiemaker's successor . . . Von Schamann replaced Garo Yepremian in Miami, a move that couldn't have been any more unpopular with Dolphin fans . . . In von Schamann's debut, his first field-goal attempt was blocked and returned for a touchdown by Buffalo. Von Schamann missed his first PAT try that game, too . . . "Things couldn't have gotten worse," he recalls . . . Fortunately, Miami won, 9-7, as Uwe (Uva) kicked a field goal . . . Things have gotten better since. He made 24 of 31 field goals last year . . . Miami's No. 7 draft pick in '79 . . . Born Uwe Detlef Walter von Schamann in West Berlin, Germany, April 23, 1956 . . . Moved with his mother to Fort Worth, Tex. . . . Kicked memorable field goal for Oklahoma that beat Ohio State.

EARNEST RHONE 28 6-2 224   Inside Linebacker

Fie on computers! . . . Miami has three No. 1 picks playing linebacker along with one free agent . . . Guess who was voted the team's best linebacker last year? The free agent, Rhone . . . He had six sacks and enough key tackles to make scouts ask themselves: "How did we miss this guy?" . . . Well, if you can't find Arkadelphia, Ark., on the map, it's easy . . . Arkadelphia is where the Henderson State Reddies play. Rhone was an NAIA All-American for the Reddies when they were national runnerup to Texas A&I . . . How did Rhone make the Dolphins as a free agent? "When Coach Shula would run everybody until they passed out," he replied, "I always felt I had to be the last one who passed out." . . . Born Aug. 20, 1953, in Ogden, Ark. . . . Eighth year with Miami.

COACH DON SHULA . . . What can you say about a legend? . . . Shula should win 200th game this season. He has 194 victories, trailing only George Halas (320), Curley Lambeau (231) and Tom Landry (196) . . . The only modern NFL coach with a perfect season under his belt (17–0, 1972) . . . The coaches' coach . . . Most would say he is the best in the game . . . "He can take his'n and beat your'n or he can take your'n and beat his'n," Bum Phillips believes . . . This is Shula's 20th season as an NFL head coach. He may be back in the Super Bowl hunt after another rebuilding plan reached fruition last year . . . Shula has known success and frustration . . . He left Baltimore for Miami to get a bigger slice of the pie, but has had numerous run-ins with owner Joe Robbie . . . Robbie then brought irascible Joe Thomas back to Miami, which only irritated Shula more . . . Shula is close to Monte Clark, whom Thomas got rid of in San Francisco . . . Thomas' duties haven't really been defined, but if he takes away some of Shula's front-office power, the sparks will fly. Stay tuned . . . Born Jan. 4, 1930, in Painesville, Ohio, Shula was an NFL defensive back for seven years with Cleveland, Washington and Baltimore . . . He became the youngest head coach in NFL history at 33 when the Colts picked him in 1963.

GREATEST LINEBACKER

On March 24, 1969, the No-Name Defense got its only name player. Miami traded quarterback Kim Hammond and linebacker John Bramlett to the Patriots for middle linebacker Nick Buoniconti in the most one-sided trade of that era.

Although the Dolphins would become famous in the early '70s for their No-Namers, Buoniconti had, in fact, been voted the AFL's all-time middle linebacker. But, his greatest fame would come in Miami.

Buoniconti was the heart of the Dolphins' defense, flying all over the field and making one key tackle after another. Miami designed its defense to protect him. The Dolphin line would keep blockers off Buoniconti, giving him time to figure where the play was going and move accordingly.

He wasn't very big (5–11, 220), but he was fast and a solid tackler. With Buoniconti in the middle, the Dolphins went to three straight Super Bowls, winning the last two, and enjoyed their perfect 17–0 season in 1972.

Buoniconti played from 1962–68 with the Patriots and from 1969–74 and again in '76 with the Dolphins. He now practices law.

INDIVIDUAL DOLPHIN RECORDS

Rushing

Most Yards Game:	197	Mercury Morris, vs New England, 1973
Season:	1,258	Delvin Williams, 1978
Career:	6,737	Larry Csonka, 1968–74, 1979

Passing

Most TD Passes Game:	6	Bob Griese, vs St. Louis, 1977
Season:	22	Bob Griese, 1977
Career:	192	Bob Griese, 1967–80

Receiving

Most TD Passes Game:	4	Paul Warfield, vs Detroit, 1973
Season:	12	Nat Moore, 1977
Career:	47	Nat Moore, 1974–81

Scoring

Most Points Game:	24	Paul Warfield, vs Detroit, 1973
Season:	117	Garo Yepremian, 1971
Career:	830	Garo Yepremian, 1970–78
Most TDs Game:	4	Paul Warfield, vs Detroit, 1973
Season:	13	Nat Moore, 1977
	13	Larry Csonka, 1979
Career:	57	Larry Csonka, 1968–74, 1979

NEW ENGLAND PATRIOTS

TEAM DIRECTORY: Pres.: William H. Sullivan, Jr.; GM: Bucko Kilroy; Asst. GM: Patrick J. Sullivan; Dir. Media Rel.: Tom Hoffman; Head Coach: Ron Meyer. Home field: Schaefer Stadium (61,297). Colors: Red, white and blue.

SCOUTING REPORTS

OFFENSE: Forget last year. The Patriots scored 322 points even though they won only two games. New England still has the firepower to blow a football team away as well as anyone.

It's important, however, that new coach Ron Meyer establish one quarterback. Either it's Steve Grogan or Matt Cavanaugh. Make one a starter and one a reliever, if necessary, but Meyer must give that position stability.

Texas' Ken Sims: No. 1 pick in the NFL draft.

The Patriots are loaded at running back with Tony Collins, Vagas Ferguson, Don Calhoun, Sam Cunningham, Mosi Tatupu and versatile Andy Johnson. Stanley Morgan and aging, but dangerous Harold Jackson are talented wide receivers. Tight end Don Hasselbeck caught six touchdown passes.

The offensive line has John Hannah, but falls off after that. It's possible that Brian Holloway will replace Dwight Wheeler, who never replaced Leon Gray at left tackle. This is only an average line: the Patriots finished seventh in AFC rushing.

DEFENSE: Couldn't stop the run if the opposing quarterback told the Patriots' defense the play beforehand. Dead last on rushing defense last year in the NFL.

The Patriots are loaded down with defensive linemen who are too old or too suspect in ability. Tony McGee can rush the passer, but the rush passes him by. Nose tackle Richard Bishop didn't play as well last year as he had in previous years; the reason might be his switch from defensive end. Julius Adams is getting so long of tooth, he's having trouble getting down into a stance. Sugar Bear Hamilton once was football's best nose tackle, but he's now second string. John Lee started some at end for New England when he couldn't start anywhere else. Kenneth Sims, this year's No. 1 pick overall, is a defensive end who'll get a chance to live up to the giant reputation he built at Texas. The Pats' other first-round choice, Miami DT Lester Williams, may provide immediate help, too, probably at the other end.

Linebackers Mike Hawkins, Bob Golic and Steve Nelson aren't bad and Mike Haynes, Ray Clayborn and Rich Sanford key a secondary that is among football's best. But if the defensive line isn't better, it could also look like the worst.

KICKING GAME: Baaaaad. That's bad as in bad, not good. Morgan is into receiving, not returning, so the Patriots have no return threat. Rich Camarillo, the team's latest punter, didn't do badly (41.7) after taking over the job midway through 1981, but let's see what he does this year. Kicker John Smith is the only plus mark.

THE ROOKIES: Ron Meyer starts out with an excellent draft. Texas' Sims, and Miami's Williams provide the Patriots' downtrodden front three with a new look. Arizona State's Robert Weathers gives New England enough running backs to stock two franchises, but Weathers could play right away. If Iowa linebacker Andre Tippett and Utah tackle Darryl Haley (bad back) come through, the Pats could turn around fast.

PATRIOTS VETERAN ROSTER

HEAD COACH—Ron Meyer. Assistant Coaches—Tom Brasher, Cleve Bryant, LeBaron Caruthers, Steve Endicott, Lew Erber, Jim Mora, Bill Muir, Dante Scarnecchia, Steve Sidwell, Steve Walters.

No.	Name	Pos.	Ht.	Wt.	NFL Exp.	College
85	Adams, Julius	DE	6-4	263	11	Texas Southern
64	Bishop, Richard	NT	6-1	260	7	Louisville
55	Blackmon, Don	LB	6-3	235	2	Tulsa
58	Brock, Pete	C	6-5	260	7	Colorado
37	Brown, Preston	WR	5-10	184	2	Vanderbilt
63	Buben, Mark	DE	6-3	260	3	Tufts
44	Calhoun, Don	RB	6-0	212	9	Kansas State
3	Camarillo, Rich	P	5-11	189	2	Washington
12	Cavanaugh, Matt	QB	6-1	210	5	Pittsburgh
35	Clark, Allan	RB	5-10	186	3	Northern Arizona
65	Clark, Steve	DE	6-5	260	2	Kansas State
26	Clayborn, Ray	CB	6-1	190	6	Texas
33	Collins, Tony	RB	5-11	202	2	East Carolina
75	Cryder, Bob	G	6-4	265	5	Alabama
39	Cunningham, Sam	RB	6-3	230	9	Southern California
87	Dawson, Lin	TE	6-3	235	2	North Carolina State
47	Dombroski, Paul	CB	6-0	185	3	Linfield
43	Ferguson, Vagas	RB	6-1	194	3	Notre Dame
51	Golic, Bob	LB	6-2	240	3	Notre Dame
14	Grogan, Steve	QB	6-4	208	8	Kansas State
71	Hamilton, Ray	NT	6-1	245	10	Oklahoma
73	Hannah, John	G	6-2	265	10	Alabama
80	Hasselbeck, Don	TE	6-7	245	6	Colorado
59	Hawkins, Mike	LB	6-2	232	5	Texas A&I
40	Haynes, Mike	CB	6-2	195	7	Arizona State
76	Holloway, Brian	T	6-7	273	2	Stanford
29	Jackson, Harold	WR	5-10	175	15	Jackson State
38	James, Roland	CB-S	6-2	189	3	Tennessee
32	Johnson, Andy	RB	6-0	205	8	Georgia
74	Jordan, Shelby	T	6-7	260	7	Washington, Mo.
52	King, Steve	LB	6-4	230	10	Tulsa
66	Lee, John	DE	6-2	260	7	Nebraska
22	Lee, Keith	CB-S	5-11	192	2	Colorado State
67	Lenkaitis, Bill	C	6-4	255	15	Penn State
53	Matthews, Bill	LB	6-2	235	4	South Dakota State
78	McGee, Tony	DE	6-4	250	12	Bishop
50	McGrew, Larry	LB	6-4	231	2	Southern California
86	Morgan, Stanley	WR	5-11	180	6	Tennessee
57	Nelson, Steve	LB	6-2	230	9	North Dakota State
89	Owen, Tom	QB	6-1	194	9	Wichita State
83	Pennywell, Carlos	WR	6-2	180	5	Grambling
77	Puetz, Garry	T	6-4	255	10	Valparaiso
25	Sanford, Rick	CB-S	6-1	192	4	South Carolina
1	Smith, John	K	6-0	185	9	Southampton, Eng.
30	Tatupu, Mosi	RB	6-0	229	5	Southern California
82	Toler, Ken	WR	6-2	195	2	Mississippi
83	Westbrook, Don	WR	5-10	185	6	Nebraska
62	Wheeler, Dwight	T	6-3	225	4	Tennessee State
54	Zamberlin, John	LB	6-2	239	4	Pacific Lutheran

TOP FIVE DRAFT CHOICES

Rd.	Name	Sel. No.	Pos.	Ht.	Wt.	College
1	Sims, Ken	1	DE	6-6	265	Texas
1	Williams, Lester	27	DT	6-3	277	Miami
2	Weathers, Robert	40	RB	6-1	205	Arizona State
2	Tippett, Andre	41	LB	6-3	231	Iowa
2	Haley, Darryl	55	T	6-4	275	Utah

OUTLOOK: It all depends on the coach. If Meyer can inspire the Patriots (Ron Erhardt couldn't), they could have a winning season. But it will take more than inspiration. The defensive line must be rebuilt. New England will not win until its defense stops getting pushed around.

PATRIOT PROFILES

STEVE GROGAN 29 6–4 208   **Quarterback**

Quarterback on the spot...Grogan's fighting for his job...Matt Cavanaugh wants it and so does Tom Owen...All three started at least one game in 1981...Grogan's problems are (1) injuries of late and (2) inconsistency...He has a cannon for an arm, but it often misfires...He can be hot-and-cold in the same game, sometimes the same quarter...Gave his body to surgery by running even more recklessly than he threw...One year he threw 18 touchdown passes and ran for 12 more...Has scored at least one touchdown on the ground in each of seven seasons in the NFL...Born July 24, 1953, in San Antonio, Tex....Reared in Ottawa, Kan., where he still helps out yearly on dad's farm at harvest time...Fifth-round pick in 1976 from Kansas State.

MATT CAVANAUGH 25 6–1 210   **Quarterback**

Started eight games last year, one more than Steve Grogan...Will challenge seriously for quarterback job this fall...His 1981 stats were remarkably similar to Grogan's...Really, nothing much to choose from between the two except consistency...If Cavanaugh shows a steady hand, the job is his...Courageous player who broke a leg at Pitt, then returned a month later to lead the Panthers to Sugar Bowl win over Georgia and capture the game's MVP award...Born Oct. 27, 1956, in Youngstown, Ohio...Broke numerous passing records at Pitt, records that Dan Marino is now about to obliterate...Cavanaugh has a brother, Dan, playing behind Marino and another brother at Youngstown State...Matt was a second-round draft pick of Patriots in 1978.

JOHN SMITH 33 6–0 185   Kicker

Common name, uncommon kicker...Tore a leg muscle in his kicking leg in 1978, then came back to win back-to-back NFL scoring titles...One of the league's best kickers for a half-dozen years...Connected on 15 of 24 field goals, making one out of four from 50 yards and beyond. The one he made was exactly 50 and a personal best...Patriots gave him a tryout in 1973 when he was a visiting soccer camp instructor from England...He was traded to Pittsburgh, waived, then wound up in the semipro ranks...The Patriots brought him back in '74...Born Dec. 30, 1948, in Leafield, England...Career field-goal accuracy: 68 percent...One of many foreign kickers who played in the first American game he ever saw.

JOHN HANNAH 31 6–2 265   Offensive Guard

The very best, so help me Hannah...Sports Illustrated writer Paul Zimmerman last year picked Hannah as the greatest offensive lineman in pro football history...This is subjective thinking, but there are few that would disagree about Hannah's greatness...Year in and year out, his fellow players select him as the NFL's best...Bear Bryant said he has never seen a better lineman in all his years at Alabama...Hannah's an automatic entry on all-pro and Pro Bowl teams...Born April 4, 1951, in Canton, Ga., he climbed out of his crib a week later and bulldogged a steer...Actually has a bull on 250-acre farm in Alabama...Created a stir—Hannah, not his bull—by walking out on the Patriots one season over a contract dispute.

TONY COLLINS 23 5–11 202   Running Back

What's 11 men to run through, Collins figures, when you're one of 16 children at the table fighting for food...Collins comes from that large a family, so he learned to be "offensive" at a young age...He led the Patriots in rushing with 873 yards (4.3) as a rookie, the most yards ever amassed by a first-year Patriot back...Scored seven touchdowns, caught 26 passes, returned three punts, 39 kickoffs and even threw a pass (incomplete)...It was Collins' all-purpose ability that led New England to draft him in the second round, '80...Standout at East Carolina, where he rushed for 2,207 yards and scored 27 touchdowns in his career...Born May 27, 1959, in Sanford, Fla....Attended high school at upstate New York academy.

STANLEY MORGAN 27 5–11 180   Wide Receiver

Dynamite with a long fuse...The Patriots don't use Morgan often, but when they do, the results are explosive...Caught 44 passes in 1981, his average for the last three years, but seven were for touchdowns...Stanley Steamer doesn't bother with anything short; he goes for it all...He has averaged 22 yards per catch over his five-year NFL career and has scored 33 touchdowns on receptions. He has a 34th on a punt return... Born Feb. 17, 1955, in Easley, S.C....Piled up 4,713 all-purpose yards at Tennessee as a running back, wingback and wide receiver...First-round pick of Patriots in 1977...Works in municipal bonds in the offseason...Two-time Pro Bowl selection...Doesn't catch enough passes to make all-pro, but everyone knows Stanley Morgan.

VAGAS FERGUSON 25 6–1 194   Running Back

Ferguson the bandido...Given name is Vasquero Diaz—didn't he ride with Pancho Villa?— but Ferguson's grandmother nicknamed him Vagas...Defenses call him Trouble...Led the Patriots in rushing as a rookie two years ago with 818 yards (3.9). Tailed off last year, though his 340 yards averaged out to 4.4, best on the club...Another Golden Domer from Notre Dame who holds Fighting Irish records for most yards rushing in a game (255) and over a career (3,472)...Patriots drafted him in the first round after he rushed for 17 touchdowns as a senior...Born March 6, 1957, in Richmond, Ind....Started all 16 games as a rookie and five last year, sharing halfback with Tony Collins...Ferguson must improve on his pass-catching ability.

SAM CUNNINGHAM 32 6–3 230   Running Back

Gus Williams of football...Cunningham sat out a full season because of contract difficulties...Came back last year, with lukewarm success...Rushed for 269 yards (3.1) and caught only 12 passes...With younger backs around, the Patriots might consider Cunningham backup material or even expendable...One thing Sam Bam can do is block: none of the young Patriot backs can knock the socks off a tight end or linebacker the way Sam can...One time, Cunningham was the Dr. J. of football with his great leaping ability around the goal line...Born Aug. 15, 1950, in Santa Barbara, Cal....Set a modern-day Rose Bowl record by scoring four times in one game...Pats' first-round draft pick in '73 from USC.

DON HASSELBECK 27 6–7 245   Tight End

Picasso of tight ends...Hasselbeck was a fine arts major at Colorado who is a painter and metal sculptor. He has had a one-man art show in Boston...Patriots' tight end job is his exclusively now that Russ Francis, who retired a year ago, plays for San Francisco...Hasselbeck caught 46 passes for 808 yards (17.6) and six touchdowns in '81...Formerly used in double tight-end situations, and twice caught four touchdown passes in a season...Born April 1, 1955, in Cincinnati...Became a starter at Colorado as a freshman...New England drafted him in the second round in '77...Attended Rhode Island School of Design in offseason...Among hobbies are hitchhiking, though it's tough for him to accept rides in compact cars.

ANDY JOHNSON 29 6–0 205   Running Back

Handy Andy...New passing sensation in Foxboro...Threw nine passes in 1981, completed seven, four for touchdowns...He had never completed a pass in seven years with Patriots until last fall...However, Andy learns quickly...He was a quarterback at Georgia, though he ran much more than he threw...New England drafted him fifth in '74 as a running back, then forgot about his passing until a year ago...Andy threw a 66-yard touchdown pass to Stanley Morgan, demonstrating that he can pass short or long...Born Oct. 18, 1952, in Athens, Ga....Won the NFLPA Tennis Tournament's singles championship in '80...There's nothing, it seems, he isn't good at athletically...Oh, yes, he caught 39 passes last year, one for a touchdown.

COACH RON MEYER..."I spent my life preparing to coach in the National Football League and now have a great opportunity and challenge in coaching the Patriots."...These were Meyer's words in becoming the Patriots' eighth coach in January...Familiar with reconstruction—he rebuilt losing programs at Nevada-Las Vegas and Southern Methodist—Meyer takes over the 2–14 Patriots who've sunk to mediocrity in recent years...He met New England Player Personnel Director Bucko Kilroy when both worked for the Dallas Cowboys, Meyer as a scout...UNLV had won one game the year before Meyer arrived...In his three years there the Rebels finished 8–3, 12–1 and 7–4...Meyer inherited a 4–7 team at SMU in '76. His six-year record there was 34–31–1 as the '81 Mustangs finished 10–1 and won the Southwest Conference...Meyer, 41, is "very bright, an innovator, a workaholic and a no-nonsense guy with one goal in mind—to win," said Kilroy...Born Feb. 17, 1941, in Westerville, Ohio...Meyer excelled in academics and athletics at Purdue after coming in as a walk-on defensive back...Spent six years as a Purdue assistant before moving on to Dallas and Las Vegas..."Ron recruited me. He's the reason I went to Purdue," said Darryl Stingley.

GREATEST LINEBACKER

Steve Nelson. Common name, easy to forget, which is the case yearly when NFL honors are passed out.

Nelson is a steady, heady inside linebacker who unfortunately happens to work in the same conference as Jack Lambert and Randy Gradishar, making it next to impossible for him to get a Pro Bowl invitation or an all-pro vote.

It's too bad because Nelson, when healthy, is a tremendous football player—the best linebacker ever to call himself a Patriot.

New England drafted him in the second round in 1974 out of North Dakota State. The 6–2, 230-pound Nelson led the Patriots in tackles almost immediately and has gone on to become captain of the NFL's All-Unsung Team.

The blond inside linebacker has been bothered in recent years by injuries, but it is tough to keep him out of the lineup. He received a concussion one autumn and it appeared as if he was through for the year. Nelson was back in two weeks and averaged 10 tackles over the last 10 games of the season.

Nelson is a gamer, only not a namer.

INDIVIDUAL PATRIOT RECORDS

Rushing

Most Yards Game:	208	Jim Nance, vs Oakland, 1966
Season:	1,458	Jim Nance, 1966
Career:	5,432	Sam Cunningham, 1973–79, 1981

Passing

Most TD Passes Game:	5	Babe Parilli, vs Buffalo, 1965
	5	Babe Parilli, vs Miami, 1967
	5	Steve Grogan, vs N.Y. Jets, 1979
Season:	31	Babe Parilli, 1964
Career:	132	Babe Parilli, 1961–67

Receiving

Most TD Passes Game:	3	Billy Lott, vs Buffalo, 1961
	3	Gino Cappelletti, vs Buffalo, 1964
	3	Jim Whalen, vs Miami, 1967
	3	Harold Jackson, vs N.Y. Jets, 1979
Season:	12	Stanley Morgan, 1979
Career:	42	Gino Cappelletti, 1960–70

Scoring

Most Points Game:	28	Gino Cappelletti, vs Houston, 1965
Season:	155	Gino Cappelletti, 1964
Career:	1,130	Gino Cappelletti, 1960–70
Most TDs Game:	3	Billy Lott, vs Buffalo, 1961
	3	Billy Lott, vs Oakland, 1961
	3	Larry Garron, vs Oakland, 1964
	3	Gino Cappelletti, vs Buffalo, 1964
	3	Larry Garron, vs San Diego, 1966
	3	Jim Whalen, vs Miami, 1967
	3	Sam Cunningham, vs Buffalo, 1974
	3	Mack Herron, vs Buffalo, 1974
	3	Sam Cunningham, vs Buffalo, 1975
	3	Harold Jackson, vs N.Y. Jets, 1979
Season:	13	Steve Grogan, 1976
	13	Stanley Morgan, 1979
Career:	49	Sam Cunningham, 1973–79, 1981

NEW YORK JETS

TEAM DIRECTORY: Chairman: Leon Hess; Pres.: Jim Kensil; Pro Personnel Dir.: Jim Royer; Dir. Pub. Rel.: Frank Ramos; Head Coach: Walt Michaels. Home field: Shea Stadium (60,000). Colors: Kelly green and white.

SCOUTING REPORT

OFFENSE: The Jets have the division's best quarterback in Richard Todd. This is an advantage in a close title fight, which the AFC East figures to be again this autumn.

Todd had his first super season a year ago and could be ready for all-pro. He has one deep receiver in Wesley Walker and possibly another in Johnny "Lam" Jones. Todd has sure-handed tight ends in Jerome Barkum and Mickey Shuler. The Jets' backs can catch the ball as well. And the offensive line can protect the passer, especially the tackles, Marvin Powell and Chris Ward.

Richard Todd tossed 25 TD passes in Jets' playoff year.

The Jets have seven—count 'em, seven—running backs in Freeman McNeil, Tom Newton, Bruce Harper, Kevin Long, Scott Dierking, Mike Augustyniak and Kenny Lewis (injured reserve). Harper had a combined 852 yards and five touchdowns on rushing and receiving. McNeil is the big horse who must carry the load, however.

Barkum scored seven touchdowns last year, but he will have trouble keeping Shuler on the bench. A strong duo. Wesley Walker is back (nine touchdowns) from his injury problems of '80. The jury is still out on Lam Jones.

The Jets' only area of doubt is at offensive guard. Randy Rasmussen, 37, can't go on forever. Ward may be tried here.

DEFENSE: The best in the AFC statistically a year ago and one of the best in modern times against the pass. No two ends on one team have ever had a season rushing the passer as Joe Klecko and Mark Gastineau had in '81. Forty sacks between them.

In order to reduce the effectiveness of this sack-happy pair, teams should throw quicker patterns against the Jets, testing their linebackers. The longer you set up against the Jets, the worse it's going to be.

Tackles Marty Lyons and Abdul Salaam also contributed to a club-record 66 sacks, one shy of the NFL record set by Oakland in 1967. Lyons should come into his own this year. Salaam is the weakest member of the New York Sack Exchange.

Greg Buttle, Stan Blinka and Lance Mehl are a young linebacking corps with a promising future. However, none of the three is an intimidator.

Cornerback Bobby Jackson and free safety Darrol Ray lead the secondary. Strong safety Ken Schroy and corner Jerry Holmes are replaceable; they better keep their eyes on Johnny Lynn, Jesse Johnson and Kirk Springs. The Jets need a third top defensive back to go with Jackson and Ray.

KICKING GAME: Not too shabby. Punter Chuck Ramsey (40.6) led the AFC in punt placements inside the 20 (27). Kicker Pat Leahy (25–36 in field goals) finished fourth in AFC scoring. Harper had another satisfactory year on returns, even though he didn't score.

THE ROOKIES: Notre Dame's Bob Crable doesn't have great speed, but he is a sure tackler and smart enough to help the Jets right away on pass defense. If Ward moves to guard, West Texas State's Reggie McElroy may have a shot at tackle. Can Iowa State's Dwayne Crutchfield crack the Jets' overloaded running

JETS VETERAN ROSTER

HEAD COACH—Walt Michaels. Assistant Coaches—Billy Baird, Ralph Baker, Bob Fry, Joe Gardi, Bob Ledbetter, Pete McCulley, Larry Pasquale, Dan Sekanovich, Joe Walton.

No.	Name	Pos.	Ht.	Wt.	NFL Exp.	College
60	Alexander, Dan	G	6-4	260	6	Louisiana State
35	Augustyniak, Mike	RB	6-0	220	2	Purdue
83	Barkum, Jerome	TE	6-4	227	11	Jackson State
64	Bingham, Guy	C-G-T	6-3	255	3	Montana
54	Blinka, Stan	LB	6-2	234	4	Sam Houston State
51	Buttle, Greg	LB	6-3	232	7	Penn State
55	Crosby, Ron	LB	6-3	227	5	Penn State
25	Dierking, Scott	RB	5-10	220	6	Purdue
26	Dykes, Donald	CB	5-11	188	4	Southeast Louisiana
65	Fields, Joe	C	6-2	253	8	Widener
81	Gaffney, Derrick	WR	6-1	182	5	Florida
99	Gastineau, Mark	DE	6-5	276	4	East Central Oklahoma
42	Harper, Bruce	RB-KR	5-8	177	6	Kutztown State
47	Holmes, Jerry	CB-S	6-2	175	3	West Virginia
40	Jackson, Bobby	CB	5-10	180	5	Florida State
27	Johnson, Jesse	S-CB	6-3	188	3	Colorado
89	Jones, Bobby	WR	5-11	185	5	No College
80	Jones, Johnny "Lam"	WR	5-11	180	3	Texas
73	Klecko, Joe	DE	6-3	265	6	Temple
5	Leahy, Pat	K	6-0	189	9	St. Louis
20	Lewis, Kenny	RB	6-0	196	3	Virginia Tech
33	Long, Kevin	RB	6-1	218	6	South Carolina
29	Lynn, Johnny	CB	6-0	195	3	UCLA
93	Lyons, Marty	DT	6-5	269	4	Alabama
53	McKibben, Mike	LB	6-3	224	4	Kent State
24	McNeil, Freeman	RB	5-11	225	2	UCLA
56	Mehl, Lance	LB	6-3	235	3	Penn State
77	Neil, Kenny	DE-DT	6-4	244	2	Iowa State
44	Newton, Tom	RB	6-0	220	6	California
79	Powell, Marvin	T	6-5	268	6	Southern California
15	Ramsey, Chuck	P	6-2	189	6	Wake Forest
66	Rasmussen, Randy	G	6-2	260	16	Kearney State
28	Ray, Darrol	S	6-1	206	3	Oklahoma
61	Roman, John	T	6-4	270	7	Idaho State
76	Rudolph, Ben	DT-DE	6-5	271	2	Long Beach State
10	Ryan, Pat	QB	6-3	205	5	Tennessee
74	Salaam, Abdul	DT	6-3	269	7	Kent State
48	Schroy, Ken	S	6-2	198	6	Maryland
82	Shuler, Mickey	TE	6-3	236	5	Penn State
87	Sohn, Kurt	WR-KR	5-11	176	2	Fordham
45	Springs, Kirk	S-CB	6-0	192	2	Miami, Ohio
86	Stephens, Steve	TE	6-3	227	2	Oklahoma State
14	Todd, Richard	QB	6-2	203	7	Alabama
70	Waldemore, Stan	G-C-T	6-4	269	5	Nebraska
85	Walker, Wesley	WR	6-0	177	6	California
72	Ward, Chris	T	6-3	267	5	Ohio State
52	Washington, Al	LB	6-3	235	2	Ohio State
58	Wetzel, Marty	LB	6-3	235	2	Tulane
57	Woodring, John	LB	6-2	230	2	Brown

TOP FIVE DRAFT CHOICES

Rd.	Name	Sel. No.	Pos.	Ht.	Wt.	College
1	Crable, Bob	23	LB	6-3	225	Notre Dame
2	McElroy, Reggie	51	T	6-6	266	West Texas State
3	Crutchfield, Dwayne	79	RB	6-1	225	Iowa State
4	Floyd, George	107	DB	5-11	185	Eastern Kentucky
5	Jerue, Mark	135	LB	6-3	225	Washington

back situation? Darkhorse could be Washington linebacker Mark Jerue, a tough, smart player.

OUTLOOK: Playoff timber. The Jets have offense, defense, special teams. What could really turn the tide would be super seasons from McNeil and Lam Jones on offense and the linebackers on defense. And Klecko and Gastineau must have another big year to keep pressure off the secondary.

JET PROFILES

RICHARD TODD 28 6–2 203   Quarterback

Great right arm... Not a bad right, either... Socked a New York sportswriter last year... Knocked around a few defenses, too... Todd came into his own last year, his sixth NFL season, with a personal high in passing percentage (56.1) and touchdown passes (25), plus only 13 interceptions... Instead of the next Joe Namath, he might be Joe Willie II right now... Rallied the Jets from a 24–0 second-quarter deficit against Buffalo in the playoffs to almost overtake the Bills at the end. Bill Simpson's goal-line interception preserved Buffalo's 31–27 win... Todd was born Nov. 19, 1953, in Birmingham, Ala.... Last of the great Alabama quarterbacks... Jets' No. 1 pick in 1976... Father has doctorate, mother working on one... Richard a licensed pilot.

WESLEY WALKER 27 6–0 177   Wide Receiver

Walker by name, sprinter by trade... Wesley Whoosh returned from a year of nagging injuries to record his most productive season— nine touchdown catches... His yardage-per-catch average slipped from a career 23.0 mark to 16.4, but that could change this year with his body having had another winter to get well... Holds NCAA record with 25.7 yards per catch at California... And he's legally blind in one eye, too... Born May 26, 1955, in San Bernardino, Cal.... Jets rated him the 10th-best player in the draft his senior year at Cal, but because he had knee surgery that season, they were able to get him in the second round... With the Jets, he has touchdown catches of 87, 77 and 71 yards... Has 4.38 speed in the 40.

JOHNNY (LAM) JONES 24 5–11 180   Wide Receiver

Lam a lamb or tiger?... Two seasons now and he hasn't lived up to his advanced billing... We're talking here about the second player taken in the 1980 draft... Caught 25 passes as a rookie, 20 last year, six touchdowns total... Yawn... So far has had better feet than hands. Drops a pass now and then... When it all comes together—Jets feel that it will—he could be the scourge of the league... Born April 4, 1958, in Lawton, Okla.... Reared in Lampasas, Tex., hence Lam... Texas teammate Johnny (Ham) Jones was from Hamlin, Tex.... Coach Darrell Royal gave out nicknames to keep the two players straight... Lam was part of victorious U.S. 400-meter relay in 1976 Olympics... Donated his gold medal to Special Olympics.

FREEMAN McNEIL 23 5–11 225   Running Back

Freight-train Freeman... Rushed for 623 yards (4.5) his rookie season despite missing five complete games and parts of three others... Caught 18 passes and wound up the year with three touchdowns... Strong back with powerful legs... His only weakness is lack of breakaway speed... "My ambitions are high and I'll really compete," McNeil says... Competed well at UCLA, setting single-season and career rushing records... So great a prep prospect in Wilmington, Cal., Woody Hayes spoke at his high school awards banquet, but couldn't land McNeil for Ohio State... Born April 22, 1959, in Jackson, Miss.... Third player chosen in the 1981 draft... McNeil enjoys tinkering with automobiles... "I can tear down and rebuild a bus," he said.

MICKEY SHULER 26 6–3 236   Tight End

Mickey come lately... Missed the entire 1981 regular season with the Jets, but came back spectacularly for the playoffs... Made many a key catch as New York struggled valiantly to erase Buffalo's 24-point first-half lead... Shuler surprised the Bills with his play, and maybe even the Jets as well... Tough player, but who could have expected that kind of performance after so long a layoff?... You can bet the Jets will have him playing every down this fall... Born Aug. 21, 1956, in Harrisburg, Pa.... Father Bob was a high school coach who retired before Mickey could play for him... Joe Paterno calls Shuler "the most consistent" tight end he has ever coached at Penn State... Jets' third draft pick in 1978... Punishing blocker.

MARVIN POWELL 27 6–5 268   Offensive Tackle

President Powell?... He has presidential aspirations for 2004... Campaigned for the Reagan-Bush team in '80... Quotes Shakespeare, Faulkner and Churchill, his idol... Voracious reader, vicious blocker... "Marvin is harder to get around or through than a swamp in Mississippi," said Baltimore end Fred Cook... Powell might be the best offensive tackle in the game... All-pro the last two years... Born Aug. 30, 1955, at Fort Bragg, N.C.... Father a career Army combat medical specialist who fought in World War II, Korea and Vietnam... Marvin an All-American at USC... Jets' No. 1 pick in 1977, fourth player taken in the draft... Attends law school in the offseason... Raps with William Buckley... Powell's a "Churchillian conservative."

MARK GASTINEAU 25 6–5 276   Defensive End

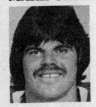

Blown-gasket Gastineau... Jets' defensive end goes bonkers every time he makes a sack... Jumps up and down, as if he's on a trampoline, shaking his fists and screaming wildly... "It's an exciting feeling to tackle the quarterback," he explains. "It's fantastic. It must be the way Richard Todd feels when he throws a 60-yard touchdown pass or Wesley Walker when he catches it."... Maybe, but Todd and Walker don't even begin to get *that* excited... Gastineau had 20 sacks last year, second in the league and also on the Jets to Joe Klecko... Gastineau was born screaming Nov. 20, 1956, in Ardmore, Okla.... First player from East Central (Okla.) State selected to the Senior Bowl, where he starred... Jets' No. 2 pick, in 1979.

JOE FIELDS 28 6–2 253   Center

White Shoes Fields?... Played at tiny Widener (Pa.) College with Billy (White Shoes) Johnson, but is only now beginning to get some of Johnson's publicity... Fields made two all-pro teams and was selected to the Pro Bowl... Self-made player who put on 25 pounds between his junior and senior years of college because he wanted to be a pro center... Jets drafted him 14th in 1975 when he was nothing more than baby fat and determination... Got on the weights and practiced snaps to his wife and father... Made the roster, then made first-string, then became a star. That is, if centers will ever be considered stars... Born Nov. 14, 1953, in Woodbury, N.J.

JOE KLECKO 28 6–3 265   Defensive End

Super Joe... Had a dream year, leading the NFL in sacks (20½) and winning about every honor a defensive end can win... Sports Illustrated's NFL Player of the Year, Pro Football Weekly's NFL Defensive Player of the Year, all-pro, Pro Bowl... Leader of The New York Sack Exchange... Klecko hits like a truck and drove one for two years before entering college... All-East middle guard at Temple... Amateur heavyweight boxer, lost only once in 35 fights... No. 6 draft pick of Jets in 1977, had eight sacks even though he didn't start until the ninth game... Fifty-four sacks in five seasons... Born Oct. 15, 1953, in Chester, Pa.... Started own trucking firm... Appeared in two Burt Reynolds' movies—about truckers, naturally.

DARROL RAY 24 6–1 206   Free Safety

Quick hands, quick feet... Ray has 13 interceptions in only two years and 359 yards in interception return yardage—the latter a Jets' *career* record... Ray has three touchdowns, too, the longest return 71 yards as a rookie. He brought one back 64 yards last year... "Darrol seems to be a natural centerfielder out there," said Walt Michaels. "When the quarterback's cocking his arm, he seems to be moving to the ball. Some people have that knack."... Son of an Army career man, Darrol was born June 25, 1958, in San Francisco... Lived in Paris, Belgium and Southern California before settling in Killeen, Tex.... Four-year letterman at Oklahoma... Can punt and kick off, if Jets ever get in a pinch... New York second-round pick in '80.

COACH WALT MICHAELS... "I think now we have the foun-

dation on which to continue building," said Walt Michaels after the 1981 season. "The players learned about winning. They got a taste of what it means to win. They learned how 'warm' New York can be in December and January."... It has been a long uphill climb for Michaels, who was a Jets' assistant coach for more than a decade, but left when he was passed

up in favor of Charley Winner for head coach... After three seasons in Philadelphia, he rejoined the Jets under Lou Holtz. He became the head coach when Holtz unexpectedly resigned in 1976... After a 3–11 start, Michaels fashioned back-to-back 8–8 records. The Jets fell to 4–12 in '80, when talk of player disharmony and friction with Michaels surfaced... It's true that nothing soothes as much as success... Jets' record of 10–5–1 last year took care of the bickering... "We became a team last year," added Michaels... Jets started off 0–3, then were perfect the rest of the way, excluding two losses to Seattle and a 28–28 overtime tie with Miami... It was the Jets' first playoff appearance in 12 years... Michaels was a great linebacker for the Cleveland Browns in the 1950s... He was drafted by Cleveland in 1951, out of Washington & Lee... Born Oct. 16, 1929, in Swoyersville, Pa.

GREATEST LINEBACKER

In 1960, the New York Titans drafted 52 players, only four of whom signed with the team. Only one was worth remembering: Larry Grantham.

A linebacker from Ole Miss, Grantham survived the tragicomedy of those early Titan teams and was still around when the Jets acquired Joe Namath and won Super Bowl III.

There was nothing comic about Grantham's performance, even from the beginning. He played in six AFL All-Star Games and was voted the Jets' Most Valuable Player in 1971, the only time a Jet linebacker has been so honored.

Grantham led the club in interceptions in 1967 (5) and ranks third on the Jets in career interceptions (24) behind Billy Baird (34) and Dainard Paulson (27).

Grantham was on the smallish size (6–1, 210), but made up for it on instincts and quickness. He was like Jim Otto, who came to the AFL in its first year as a raw talent, developed into an all-star and got better every year to keep up with the improving AFL.

The Jets' veteran linebacker stayed two years past the merger, retiring in 1972.

Awesome Joe Klecko leads the New York Sack Exchange.

INDIVIDUAL JET RECORDS

Rushing

Most Yards Game:	180	Matt Snell, vs Houston, 1964
Season:	1,005	John Riggins, 1975
Career:	5,135	Emerson Boozer, 1966–75

Passing

Most TD Passes Game:	6	Joe Namath, vs Baltimore, 1972
Season:	26	Al Dorow, 1960
	26	Joe Namath, 1967
Career:	170	Joe Namath, 1965–76

Receiving

Most TD Passes Game:	3	Art Powell, vs Denver, 1960
	3	Don Maynard, vs Denver, 1963
	3	Don Maynard, vs San Diego, 1967
	3	Don Maynard, vs Miami, 1968
	3	Rich Caster, vs Baltimore, 1972
Season:	14	Art Powell, 1960
	14	Don Maynard, 1965
Career:	88	Don Maynard, 1960–72

Scoring

Most Points Game:	19	Jim Turner, vs Buffalo, 1968
Season:	145	Jim Turner, 1968
Career:	697	Jim Turner, 1964–70
Most TDs Game:	3	Art Powell, vs Denver, 1960
	3	Don Maynard, vs Denver, 1963
	3	Emerson Boozer, vs Denver, 1967
	3	Emerson Boozer, vs Miami, 1967
	3	Don Maynard, vs San Diego, 1967
	3	Billy Joe, vs Boston, 1968
	3	Don Maynard, vs Miami, 1968
	3	Emerson Boozer, vs Buffalo, 1972
	3	Rich Caster, vs Baltimore, 1972
	3	Emerson Boozer, vs New England, 1972 (twice)
	3	John Riggins, vs San Diego, 1974
	3	Kevin Long, vs Buffalo, 1978
	3	Kevin Long, vs Detroit, 1979
Season:	14	Art Powell, 1960
	14	Don Maynard, 1965
	14	Emerson Boozer, 1972
Career:	88	Don Maynard, 1960–72

OAKLAND RAIDERS

TEAM DIRECTORY: Managing Gen. Partner: Al Davis; Gen. Partner: E. W. McGah; Exec. Asst.: Al LoCasale; Bus. Mgr.: Ken LaRue; Dir. Publications: Bill Glazier; Head Coach: Tom Flores. Home field: Oakland Coliseum (54,616). Colors: Silver and black.

SCOUTING REPORT

OFFENSE: The Raiders collapsed offensively last year, but it was due to injuries more than anything else. Quarterback Jim Plunkett tore ligaments in his right thumb in the season opener and never recovered, winding up on the bench. Wide receiver Bob Chandler ruptured his spleen in the same game and underwent surgery, missing two months. Fullback Mark van Eeghen's second straight year of injuries further affected the Raider offense.

It wasn't just injuries; age caught up with the Raiders as well. Curt Marsh replaced Gene Upshaw at guard, Steve Sylvester supplanted Dave Dalby at center and Derrick Ramsey took over for Raymond Chester at tight end.

Transition continues to be a factor: Oakland needs a fullback who can play every game if van Eeghen can't. That person might be Kenny King, switched over from halfback, who would then pair with ex-Brown Greg Pruitt or rookie Marcus Allen. If Plunkett can stay in one piece, he could challenge Marc Wilson at quarterback. This may be Plunkett's last hurrah as Wilson will in time be the Raiders' quarterback.

Tackle Art Shell's knee problems could make this his last hurrah, too. Who knows about Cliff Branch, who played in another world last year—one that was flat.

The Raiders are unsettled on offense, but never count them out.

DEFENSE: Difficult to figure out. Oakland had the best defense in football at the tail end of the '80 season, then collapsed last year.

Certainly, injuries had a lot to do with the fold. Nose tackle Reggie Kinlaw and inside linebacker Bob Nelson missed the entire season. Strong safety Mike Davis missed most of it. Getting these three back will be a big help.

However, outside linebacker Ted Hendricks and cornerback Lester Hayes—the AFC's two best defensive players in '80—weren't hurt. They just had sub-par seasons, making the Pro Bowl

Without Stickum, Lester Hayes had only three interceptions.

off their previous year's play. Defensive end John Matuszak didn't have the best of autumns, either.

Oakland, as a team, intercepted 13 passes, the worst mark in football. The Raiders are a funny club, though. Just when you think they are down, like two years ago, they come back and win the Super Bowl.

This team needs a pass-rushing defensive end (ex-Brown Lyle Alzado?) and new life at linebacker. Perhaps end Willie Jones will overcome his "personal problems," but Cedrick Hardman may retire.

KICKING GAME: Wanted: a return man, punts or kickoffs. Apply in Oakland. The Raiders have desperately needed a return man, one who is consistent, for years. They need a consistent kicker, too. Chris Bahr hasn't provided dependability in his two years at Oakland. Punter Ray Guy is still one of the best.

RAIDERS VETERAN ROSTER

HEAD COACH—Tom Flores. Assistant Coaches—Sam Boghosian, Willie Brown, Chet Franklin, Earl Leggett, Bob Mischak, Steve Ortmayer, Charles Sumner, Tom Walsh, Ray Willsey.

No.	Name	Pos.	Ht.	Wt.	NFL Exp.	College
77	Alzado, Lyle	DE	6-3	250	12	Yankton
10	Bahr, Chris	K	5-10	175	7	Penn State
	Bailey, Mark	RB	6-3	235	3	Cal State-Long Beach
56	Barnes, Jeff	LB	6-2	225	6	California
80	Barnwell, Malcolm	WR	5-11	185	2	Virginia Union
	Berns, Rick	RB	6-2	205	3	Nebraska
54	Bracelin, Greg	LB	6-1	215	3	California
81	Bradshaw, Morris	WR	6-1	195	9	Ohio State
21	Branch, Cliff	WR	5-11	170	11	Colorado
	Bright, Greg	S	6-0	205	3	Morehead State
73	Browning, Dave	DE	6-5	245	5	Washington
85	Chandler, Bob	WR	6-1	180	11	Southern California
88	Chester, Raymond	TE	6-4	235	13	Morgan State
46	Christensen, Todd	TE-RB	6-3	230	4	Brigham Young
50	Dalby, Dave	C	6-3	250	11	UCLA
79	Davis, Bruce	T	6-6	280	4	UCLA
36	Davis, Mike	S	6-3	200	5	Colorado
	Grossart, Kyle	QB	6-4	210	2	Oregon State
8	Guy, Ray	P	6-3	195	10	Southern Mississippi
86	Hardman, Cedrick	DE	6-4	245	13	North Texas State
27	Hawkins, Frank	RB	5-9	210	2	Nevada-Reno
37	Hayes, Lester	CB	6-2	200	6	Houston
83	Hendricks, Ted	LB	6-7	230	14	Miami
48	Hill, Kenny	S	6-0	195	2	Yale
42	Jackson, Monte	CB	5-11	195	8	San Diego State
31	Jensen, Derrick	RB	6-1	220	4	Texas
90	Jones, Willie	DE	6-4	250	4	Florida State
33	King, Kenny	RB	5-11	205	4	Oklahoma
62	Kinlaw, Reggie	DT	6-2	245	3	Oklahoma
70	Lawrence, Henry	T	6-4	270	9	Florida A&M
75	Long, Howie	DE	6-5	265	2	Villanova
60	Marsh, Curt	G	6-5	270	2	Washington
53	Martin, Rod	LB	6-2	210	6	Southern California
65	Marvin, Mickey	G	6-4	210	6	Tennessee
71	Mason, Lindsey	T	6-5	275	4	Kansas
72	Matuszak, John	DE	6-8	280	10	Tampa
57	McClanahan, Randy	LB	6-5	235	5	Southwestern Louisiana
23	McKinney, Odis	S	6-2	190	5	Colorado
	Miller, Mark	QB	6-2	185	3	Bowling Green
55	Millen, Matt	LB	6-2	255	2	Penn State
28	Montgomery, Cleotha	RB	5-8	185	2	Abilene Christian
51	Nelson, Bob	LB	6-4	235	6	Nebraska
	Odom, Cliff	LB	6-2	225	2	Texas
35	O'Steen, Dwayne	CB	6-1	195	5	San Jose State
44	Owens, Burgess	S	6-2	200	10	Miami
16	Plunkett, Jim	QB	6-3	220	12	Stanford
34	Pruitt, Greg	RB	5-10	190	10	Oklahoma
84	Ramsey, Derrick	TE	6-5	235	5	Kentucky
68	Robinson, Johnny	DT	6-2	260	2	Louisiana Tech
78	Shell, Art	T	6-5	290	15	Maryland State
66	Sylvester, Steve	C	6-4	260	8	Notre Dame
	Taylor, Billy	RB	6-0	215	5	Texas Tech
63	Upshaw, Gene	G	6-5	255	16	Texas A&I
30	van Eeghen, Mark	RB	6-2	220	9	Colgate
41	Watts, Ted	CB	6-0	190	2	Texas Tech
52	Westbrooks, Greg	LB	6-3	230	8	Colorado
22	Whittington, Arthur	RB	5-11	185	5	Southern Methodist
	Wilkinson, Jerry	DE	6-9	290	3	Oregon State
38	Willis, Chester	RB	5-11	195	2	Auburn
6	Wilson, Marc	QB	6-6	205	3	Brigham Young

TOP FIVE DRAFT CHOICES

Rd.	Name	Sel. No.	Pos.	Ht.	Wt.	College
1	Allen, Marcus	10	RB	6-2	202	Southern California
2	Squirek, Jack	35	LB	6-3	235	Illinois
2	Romano, Jim	37	C	6-3	241	Penn State
3	McElroy, Vann	64	DB	6-2	194	Baylor
4	Muransky, Ed	91	T	6-7	275	Michigan

THE ROOKIES: USC's Allen is a good athlete, though no O.J. Simpson. Allen's size and receiving ability should make him a factor as a rookie, though his fumbling in college also makes him a liability. Illinois linebacker Jack Squirek can play inside or outside, a possible starter in time. Penn State center Jim Romano could spell the end for Dalby.

OUTLOOK: Hard to tell. Raiders had their first losing season in 16 years, which drove Al Davis bananas. Too many muddled areas, too many unanswered questions to predict a playoff berth for Oakland. The best the Raiders should do is 8–8 and fourth place. Still, with Davis....

RAIDER PROFILES

MARC WILSON 25 6–6 205   Quarterback

Winner of football's Ray Bolger lookalike contest...Built like the Scarecrow with a long, gawky frame. But it all comes together with perfect coordination on a football field as Wilson has a perfect throwing motion. He only needs experience to be a top NFL quarterback for years...Pressed into a starting role his second year, Wilson completed 47.2 percent of his passes, 14 for touchdowns. He had 19 interceptions, but brought his team back several times from certain defeat...Born Feb. 15, 1957, in Bremerton, Wash....Broke 11 NCAA records in three varsity seasons at Brigham Young, which was 11–0 his senior year...All-American, No. 1 draft pick of Oakland in 1980...Deeply religious, family type.

JIM PLUNKETT 34 6–3 220   Quarterback

Cinderella story ended last year when the glass slipper no longer fit...True story, which Raiders never announced: Plunkett tore a ligament in his passing thumb in opener, couldn't grip the ball properly, later was benched...Raiders tumbled without him...Has chance to win his job back from Marc Wilson, if Plunkett's body (nine operations) holds together...One of the nicest people in the game, Plunkett went from rags to riches in 1980, leading the wild-card Raiders to Super Bowl championship... Born Dec. 5, 1947, in San Jose, Cal.... Heisman Trophy winner at Stanford, sparked school to 27–17 upset of Ohio State in Rose Bowl... First player taken in 1971 draft, traded from New England to San Francisco... Oakland got him on waivers.

KENNY KING 25 5–11 205   **Running Back**

Slippery runner—that applies to his feet and his hands... Fumbling is his only weakness. He picked up the habit at Oklahoma—the school for fumblers—and has had a hard time breaking it... If he can kick the habit, King can be one of the better backs in the game... Made the Pro Bowl his second year in the league, his first as a starter, after Oakland got him in a trade from Houston in 1980... Had a better year in '81 with 828 rushing yards (4.9), though he failed to score a touchdown... Born March 7, 1957, in Clarendon, Tex.... Fullback and blocking back for Billy Sims at Oklahoma, where King averaged 6.3 yards per carry over career... Third-round draft pick of Houston in 1979... Injury problems both years with Raiders.

CURT MARSH 23 6–5 265   **Offensive Guard**

The man who replaced Gene Upshaw... This will be Marsh's marker, and his measure, in years to come... Broke into Raiders' starting lineup as a rookie, moving Upshaw out of the left guard position he had owned since 1967... Marsh had his bad moments, but he had some good ones, too. Once he figures out all the defensive sets, the defenses are in trouble ... Mountain of a man, typical Raider lineman... Born Aug. 25, 1959, in Tacoma, Wash., moved to beautiful, downtown Snohomish as a youth... Standout tackle at the University of Washington after beginning college career on defense... Raiders' second of two first-round choices in 1981, the 23rd player taken... Wears No. 60, Otis Sistrunk's number, but has never been to Mars.

ART SHELL 35 6-5 290   Offensive Tackle

One of football's giants, both in size and stature... There aren't many better offensive tackles who have played over the NFL's 60-plus years... All-pro a number of times, played in eight Pro Bowls... Quiet, reflective type, Shell is quite a contrast to his friend and former running mate, the talkative Gene Upshaw... Father Time broke up the left side of the Raider line in 1981 by sending Upshaw (37) to the bench... Shell's trying to hold off young Lindsey Mason, who started several games in '81 after Shell received a knee injury... Shell will give it one last shot this fall, then retire with Upshaw. That's their plan anyway... Shell was born Nov. 26, 1946, in Charlestown, S.C.... No.3 pick in '68 from Maryland State.

LYLE ALZADO 33 6-3 250   Defensive End

Gerry Cooney of football... Fought Muhammad Ali in a publicized Denver exhibition and landed his share of punches, too... Considered turning to pro boxing, a la Too Tall Jones, but stayed with football... All-pro in Denver and one of the leaders of the Broncos' Orange Crush defense... Contract problem made him expendable and Broncos shipped him to Cleveland... Played three years with Browns before trade to Raiders on draft day... Born April 3, 1949, in Brooklyn... Rough-tough upbringing... But someone pointed a way out: Yankton, S.D.... Alzado became a superstar at little Yankton College... A fourth-round Broncos' pick in 1974... Still one of strongest players in league... Ask Ali.

JOHN MATUSZAK 31 6-8 280   Defensive End

Tooooooooooz... Peck's bad boy in shoulder pads... The last of the true football characters ... The Olivier of defensive ends... There aren't enough words or ways in which to describe John Matuszak, who has a great physique and an even greater appetite for life... Al Davis brought him to Oakland to stop the run, which Tooz has done in two Super Bowl victories...Last year wasn't one of Tooz' best, however, as the run often stopped him...Must fight to hold onto his starting job this fall...Born Oct. 25, 1950, in Oak Creek, Wis....Attended Missouri, punched out an ROTC cadet and transferred hurriedly to Tampa...First player taken in the 1973 draft, then bounced around...Made two movies: "North Dallas Forty" and "Caveman."

ROD MARTIN 28 6-2 210   Outside Linebacker

That's Rodney as in Dangerfield...Martin gets even less respect than the comedian...The best Raider defensive player throughout 1981, but received no recognition. The story of his life...Drafted in the 12th round by Oakland in '77, was cut by Raiders and 49ers before coming back to Oakland. Became a starter his second year and has won Raider Lineman-of-the-Year Award twice (sharing honor last year with Henry Lawrence)...Martin has league's strongest hands; it would be safer to shake hands with King Kong...Quick, powerful tackler despite smallish size...Born April 7, 1954, in Welch, W. Va....Two-year starter at USC...Intercepted three passes in one Super Bowl, which was a *career* record, yet "What's that guy's name again, Red Morgan?"

LESTER HAYES 26 6-2 200   Cornerback

Stuck without Stickum...Giant comedown from 18 interceptions (including playoffs) in 1980 to only three in '81...Hayes said the reason wasn't the NFL's outlawing of Stickum, but simply bad luck...Yet he had his hands on a number of passes he didn't hold onto...Could have been an off year as Hayes received the worst beating of his career the day Tampa's Kevin House turned him in circles...Hayes still made the Pro Bowl, so the year wasn't lost...Born Dec. 22, 1955, in Houston, Tex....Linebacker and strong safety at Texas A&M, drafted in the fifth round as a cornerback in '77...Became a starter late in his rookie year...Had a serious stutter problem, which he has all but corrected through special therapy.

GREG PRUITT 31 5-10 190   **Running Back**

Was once called "The Franchise" in Cleveland, but appears to be winding down career... That's what Browns thought, so they traded him to Oakland in April... He averaged 1,000 yard rushing from 1975–78, but constant pounding finally slowed him down to point where he'll now get 200–300 yards... Has really blossomed as a receiver, though. He caught 65 passes last season, ninth-best in the AFC, and his 9.8 yards-per-catch was the highest among running backs who finished in the top 20 in receptions... So he can still motor... Born Aug. 18, 1951, in Houston... Tough for his size, Pruitt was a high school tight end at 5–7½ and caught 80 passes his senior year.... Among the greatest backs ever to play at Oklahoma... Browns picked him No. 1 in 1976.

COACH TOM FLORES... Super Bowl to Super Hole. That's

what Flores fell into after injuries decimated the Raiders in 1981 and the team dropped to 7–9, its first losing season in 16 years... Flores said little during the demise, but then he said little when the Raiders won it all the year before... If John Wayne had been a football coach, he would have been Tom Flores, to whom 10 words is a speech... The Raiders' quiet man heard noises in the backroom, however, as owner Al Davis voiced his displeasure with Flores' coaching throughout the league. There is no tougher place to be a football coach than in Oakland... Flores' nickname, from his days as the Raider quarterback, is the "Iceman." He'll need ice in his veins to survive the upstairs pressure from Davis... Flores had never been a head coach until Davis tapped him in '79. After a 9–7 debut, the Raiders improved to 11–5 and a Super Bowl victory... Quite an accomplishment for the son of Mexican fruit pickers from the California valley town of Sanger (born March 21, 1937, in Fresno)... Flores quarterbacked at College of Pacific, then was the Raiders' first quarterback in 1960... Oakland's receivers' coach for seven years before his big chance.

GREATEST LINEBACKER

It is not a name Ted Hendricks particularly enjoys—the Mad Stork—but there is no better way to describe his playing style.

Long on height (6–7), range and talent, Hendricks has flapped about National Football League stadiums for 11 seasons, blocking kicks, sacking quarterbacks and generally raising havoc.

He has blocked 22 punts, field goals and extra points, high among active NFL players. He has four safeties, an NFL record. More often than not, Hendricks has led his team in sacks and pass deflections. He has 26 career interceptions.

Hendricks revolutionized linebacker play in the NFL. He was a three-time All-America defensive end at the University of Miami (Fla.), but was too lean to play the position for the Baltimore Colts, who drafted him second in 1969. The Colts made him football's tallest linebacker and quarterbacks have been under siege ever since against the blitzing Stork.

He was traded to Green Bay after a contract dispute in Baltimore, then signed as a free agent with Oakland in 1975 in exchange for two No. 1 draft picks. The Raiders have won two Super Bowls since this five-time all-pro arrived.

INDIVIDUAL RAIDER RECORDS

Rushing

Most Yards Game:	200	Clem Daniels, vs N.Y. Jets, 1963
Season:	1,273	Mark van Eeghan, 1977
Career:	5,907	Mark van Eeghan, 1974–81

Passing

Most TD Passes Game:	6	Tom Flores, vs Houston, 1963
	6	Daryle Lamonica, vs Buffalo, 1969
Season:	34	Daryle Lamonica, 1969
Career:	150	Ken Stabler, 1970–79

Receiving

Most TD Passes Game:	4	Art Powell, vs Houston, 1963
Season:	16	Art Powell, 1963
Career:	76	Fred Biletnikoff, 1965–78

Scoring

Most Points Game:	24	Art Powell, vs Houston, 1963
Season:	117	George Blanda, 1968
Career:	863	George Blanda, 1967–75
Most TDs Game:	4	Art Powell, vs Houston, 1963
Season:	16	Art Powell, 1963
	16	Pete Banaszak, 1975
Career:	77	Fred Biletnikoff, 1965–78

PITTSBURGH STEELERS

TEAM DIRECTORY: Chairman: Art Rooney; Pres.: Daniel Rooney; VP: John McGinley, VP: Art Rooney Jr.; Dir. Player Personnel: Dick Haley; Pub. Dir.: Joe Gordon; Head Coach: Chuck Noll. Home field: Three Rivers Stadium (54,000). Colors: Black and gold.

SCOUTING REPORT

OFFENSE: What the Steelers need more than anything else is a breakaway running back. If they get one and if their passing

Franco Harris is third on NFL all-time rushing list.

game stays in one piece, then you've got trouble right there in Three Rivers city.

Franco Harris will likely pass Jim Brown as the all-time leading rusher in two or three seasons. But Harris' days as a long-distance threat seem behind him. Maybe top pick Walter Abercrombie will be the speedy back who'll pair with Harris and eventually assume the bulk of the running from Franco the Fantastic.

Think what this would mean to the passing game, which has slipped in recent years because of injuries to Terry Bradshaw, Lynn Swann and John Stallworth. Throw in Jim Smith and the Steelers have the best quarterback-wide receiver situation in football. One more running back and....

Tight end Bennie Cunningham finally started to look like a football player in 1981. The Steelers' offensive line has added some new faces in the '80s, but the biceps remain the same and so does the quality of performance.

Pittsburgh only needs good health to have football's dominant offense again. The Steelers' MVP of late has been the team doctor.

DEFENSE: Where have all the great players gone? The defensive line once had names like Greene, Holmes, White and Greenwood. They put the steel in the Steel Curtain. Now there are names like Goodman, Beasley, Dunn and Banaszek. They finished ninth in AFC defense.

Unless Chuck Noll has some surprises planned, Pittsburgh doesn't look very strong on defense. Instead of great players, they now have merely good ones. L. C. Greenwood, once great, now is second team and playing out the string. Joe Greene is the latest Steeler great to call it quits. Those were the days, my friend....

The linebacking has fallen off, too. Jack Ham was once a 10, but now is a 6½. Jack Lambert remains the heart of the defense. Robin Cole is a good player, but he's no Andy Russell.

Pittsburgh finished 12th in the AFC against the pass despite a big year from Mel Blount. But even Blount is 34. Dwayne Woodruff will have a hard time holding off Anthony "Adverse" Washington, the Lambert of cornerbacks. Donnie Shell remains a top strong safety. J. T. Thomas battles Ron "Slo Mo" Johnson at strong safety.

Defensively, the Steelers are a poor imitation of their former selves.

KICKING GAME: Average. Punter Craig Colquitt (43.3) is among the best in the AFC. Kicker David Trout hammered through 12 of 17 field goals, but he was awful on PATs (38 of 46). Steelers need a new kicker. Return man Larry Anderson is adequate.

STEELERS VETERAN ROSTER

HEAD COACH—Chuck Noll. Assistant Coaches—George Perles, Rollie Dotsch, Tony Dungy, Dick Hoak, Jon Kolb, Tom Moore, Robert Widenhofer.

No.	Name	Pos.	Ht.	Wt.	NFL Exp.	College
30	Anderson, Larry	CB-KR	5-11	188	5	Louisiana Tech
76	Banaszak, John	DE-DT	6-3	250	8	Eastern Michigan
65	Beasley, Tom	DT	6-5	248	5	Virginia Tech
47	Blount, Mel	CB	6-3	205	13	Southern
12	Bradshaw, Terry	QB	6-3	215	13	Louisiana Tech
79	Brown, Larry	T	6-4	270	12	Kansas
56	Cole, Robin	LB	6-2	220	6	New Mexico
5	Colquitt, Craig	P	6-1	182	5	Tennessee
77	Courson, Steve	G	6-1	260	5	South Carolina
89	Cunningham, Bennie	TE	6-5	260	7	Clemson
45	Davis, Russell	RB	6-1	231	3	Michigan
67	Dunn, Gary	DT	6-3	260	6	Miami
95	Goodman, John	DE-DT	6-6	250	2	Oklahoma
68	Greenwood, L.C.	DE	6-6	250	14	Arkansas AM&N
84	Grossman, Randy	TE	6-1	225	12	Penn State
59	Ham, Jack	LB	6-1	225	4	Penn State
32	Harris, Franco	RB	6-2	225	11	Penn State
27	Hawthorne, Greg	RB	6-2	225	4	Baylor
62	Ilkin, Tunch	T	6-3	253	3	Indiana State
29	Johnson, Ron	CB-S	5-10	200	5	Eastern Michigan
90	Kohrs, Bob	DE	6-3	245	2	Arizona State
58	Lambert, Jack	LB	6-4	220	9	Kent State
50	Little, David	LB	6-1	220	2	Florida
16	Malone, Mark	QB	6-4	223	3	Arizona State
61	McGriff, Tyrone	G	6-0	267	3	Florida A&M
39	Moser, Rick	RB	6-0	210	5	Rhode Island
66	Petersen, Ted	T	6-5	244	6	Eastern Illinois
74	Pinney, Ray	T-C	6-4	256	6	Washington
44	Pollard, Frank	RB	5-10	210	3	Baylor
31	Shell, Donnie	S	5-11	190	9	South Carolina State
86	Smith, Jim	WR-KR	6-2	205	6	Michigan
82	Stallworth, John	WR	6-2	183	9	Alabama A&M
18	Stoudt, Cliff	QB	6-4	218	6	Youngstown State
88	Swann, Lynn	WR	6-0	180	9	Southern California
85	Sweeney, Calvin	WR	6-2	190	3	Southern California
24	Thomas, J.T.	S	6-2	196	9	Florida State
38	Thornton, Sidney	RB	5-11	230	6	Northwestern Louisiana
51	Toews, Loren	LB	6-3	220	10	California
1	Trout, David	K	5-6	165	2	Pittsburgh
54	Valentine, Zack	LB	6-2	220	4	East Carolina
42	Washington, Anthony	CB	6-1	204	2	Fresno State
52	Webster, Mike	C	6-1	255	9	Wisconsin
73	Wolfley, Craig	G	6-1	265	3	Syracuse
49	Woodruff, Dwayne	CB-S	5-11	198	4	Louisville

TOP FIVE DRAFT CHOICES

Rd.	Name	Sel. No.	Pos.	Ht.	Wt.	College
1	Abercrombie, Walter	12	RB	5-11	201	Baylor
2	Meyer, John	43	T	6-6	257	Arizona State
3	Merriweather, Mike	70	LB	6-2	215	Pacific
4	Woods, Rick	97	DB	6-0	196	Boise State
5	Dallafior, Ken	124	T	6-3	268	Minnesota

THE ROOKIES: Is Baylor's Abercrombie the answer at running back, or another Greg Hawthorne or Sidney Thornton? Pittsburgh has lost its draft-time magic. Tackle John Meyer of Arizona State is a late-bloomer who will develop his skills and biceps in Steeltown. Trading of Dirt Winston may open linebacking spot for Pacific's Mike Merriweather.

OUTLOOK: The Steelers are a victim of their own draft, the same draft which once propelled them to four Super Bowl victories. The best they can hope for, unless the town of Cincinnati drops into the Mississippi, is second place. Pittsburgh's frame of mind in training camp is a big key.

STEELER PROFILES

TERRY BRADSHAW 33 6-3 215   **Quarterback**

The duke of hazards...Wanted to be an actor in the good ol' boy mold, but his TV pilot with singer Mel Tillis failed, pushing Bradshaw back into football...He hasn't been the same mentally and physically the last two years, although his stats aren't bad...But how can a team look to a quarterback for leadership if he is thinking about other careers?...So the Dukes of Hazzard are safe, while Bradshaw deals now with other hazards—getting his body and mind in shape and lifting the Steelers back to playoff respectability...Born Sept. 2, 1948, in Shreveport, La....Still possesses the same cannon for an arm that he had at Louisiana Tech. First player taken in the 1970 draft...Great talent, nice person.

FRANCO HARRIS 32 6-2 225   **Running Back**

Old Man River as in the Allegheny, Monongahela and Ohio...The terror of Three Rivers, Harris has rushed for 10,339 yards in 10 NFL seasons, placing him third all-time and 898 yards behind second-place O.J. Simpson. Harris already is football's all-time leader in rushing attempts (2,462), which is testimony to his durability and a rebuttal to those who say that Harris runs out of bounds because he doesn't like punishment. He has scored 91 touchdowns; they weren't all end runs...Born March 7, 1950, at Fort Dix, N.J....Blocking back for Lydell Mitchell at Penn State, Harris became an instant sensation in

NFL...Rushed for seven 1,000-yard seasons...Won numerous awards for his humanitarian efforts...Keeps very low profile.

LYNN SWANN 30 6-0 180   Wide Receiver

The Baryshnikov of wide receivers...Graceful, agile and elusive, Swann's heart is a dancer. He appeared on a PBS special with Gene Kelly. Swann might be the first male Rockette...His acrobatic performance in Super Bowl X was the individual artistic highlight of all Super Bowls...Now 30, Swann can still be trusted. Hamstring pull hampered his play last year, though he caught five touchdown passes, making it 51 in eight pro seasons...He relies on precise patterns and extra-quick movements, so he devoted more time to conditioning than dancing this offseason...Born March 7, 1952, in Alcoa, Tenn....Great all-around athlete...USC All-American...Steelers' No. 1 pick in 1974.

JOHN STALLWORTH 30 6-2 183   Wide Receiver

The complete receiver...Runs all patterns well and runs cornerbacks into the ground when healthy...Foot surgery bothered him last fall, though he caught 63 passes (17.4) to lead the club and scored five touchdowns...Not nearly as flamboyant as Swann, but just as dangerous with his speed and versatility of routes...Many scouts would take Stallworth over Swann, though they would dearly love to have them both. Who wouldn't?...Stallworth was born July 15, 1952, in Tuscaloosa, Ala., but didn't play for the Bear. Went to Alabama A&M, where his jersey (22) was retired...Pittsburgh drafted him fourth in 1974, but he didn't come into his own until '77...Steelers may retire his jersey (82), too.

JIM SMITH 27 6-2 205   Wide Receiver

The best receiver not starting in football...Smith could start for 27 other NFL teams, but not Pittsburgh, with Swann and Stallworth. Smith plays when they are hurt, or in triple wide-receiver formations...The last two years he has caught 66 passes (19.4) for 16 touchdowns, and would have had more if he, himself, hadn't had injury problems...With more playing time, he could be one of the game's best pass-catchers. But where is he going to get the time? Not in Pittsburgh, unless Swann or Stallworth joins a gypsy caravan... Born July 20, 1955, in Blue Island, Mich.... Played at Ann Arbor and set several Michigan receiving records (23.1 yards per catch)... Third-round pick of Steelers in 1977.

JACK LAMBERT 30 6–4 220 **Middle Linebacker**

Grrrrrrrr... Down Jack, nice boy... Seven years in the NFL and as mean as ever... Maybe even better as a football player, if that's possible, intercepting six passes to lead all NFL linebackers. Now has 14 interceptions in last three seasons and 25 over seven... Built like an outside linebacker, Lambert excels in the middle because he has Dick Butkus' intensity... The blond Steeler already is one of the great middle linebackers in history. All-pro again last year and a Pro Bowl pick in each of his seven NFL seasons... Born July 8, 1952, in Mantua, Ohio... A hidden secret, except to the scouts, at Kent State... Second-round pick in Steelers' magnificent draft of '74, possible the best single draft ever by one team in any sport.

MEL BLOUNT 34 6–3 205 **Cornerback**

That's Blount, as in blunt, as in hunt... Malevolent Mel has been hunting wide receivers for 12 years and they still tread lightly when they come into his territory... A fierce hitter, Blount had a playback year in 1981, intercepting six passes—his highest in four years—including a 50-yard return for a touchdown off a Joe Montana throw... Blount was named all-pro, the first time that had happened in several years... Tied for club's all-time lead in interceptions with 52... Born April 10, 1948, in Vidalia, Ga.... Third-round pick out of Southern U. in 1970... Perfectly-conditioned athlete who still has a rookie's speed... Ran down Oakland's Kenny King from behind last year, saving a touchdown... Possible Hall of Famer.

MIKE WEBSTER 30 6–1 255   Center

The best there is...Not only as a center, but maybe at any position. Offensive linemen are terribly overlooked, but Webster may be further ahead at his position in terms of talent than any player at any position in football...Take that, John Hannah!...Seen Webster's arms? They look like thighs and pop out of that black Pittsburgh jersey, knocking middle guards and linebackers on their derrieres...Born March 18, 1952, in Tomahawk, Wis....A good college center at Wisconsin, Webster was drafted fifth by Pittsburgh in '74...He got on the weights and soon was a dues-paying member of the Steelers' bulging biceps brigade...Webster has been the NFL's best center for four years and an all-pro pick each of those years.

DONNIE SHELL 30 5–11 190   Strong Safety

His first name should be Missile...Missile Shell...He hits like one...Donnie doesn't know the meaning of the word half-speed...When it's time to go, he explodes...Hardest-hitting strong safety in the game the past four years, all of them Pro Bowl seasons...One of Pittsburgh's best big-play performers, intercepting 17 passes the last three years...Pittsburgh found Shell at South Carolina State after the NFL scouting services overlooked him. He signed with the Steelers as a free agent in '74...Born Aug. 26, 1952, in Whitmire. S.C....Became a pro starter in '77 and has pounded on tight ends ever since...Pittsburgh's MVP in '80.

CRAIG COLQUITT 28 6–1 182   Punter

How high the moon?...Colquitt seems determined to hit it as he keeps improving as a punter...Never been under 40-yard average in four seasons in Steeltown...Has gone from 40.0 to 40.2 to 40.7 to last year's sparkling 43.3 average...This was the highest by a Steeler in nine years, and where have you gone Bobby Walden?...Colquitt's 35.3 net mark was the third-highest in the conference . . . Only 40 percent of his punts were returned—the second lowest mark in the NFL—and his 25 punts inside the twenty ranked him third in the league . . . Born June 9, 1954, in Knoxville, Tenn. . . . Three-year punter at Tennessee, where he was a walk-on and averaged 42.5 for his career . . . Steelers' third pick in 1978.

COACH CHUCK NOLL . . . Used to vintage years, as in football, as in wine . . . Only head coach to have four Super Bowl rings, and in four tries, too . . . Appreciates winning football and California wines, and the latter has done better than the Steelers recently . . . Pittsburgh hasn't made the playoffs in two years and that's enough to pop Noll's cork . . . He grew up with excellence as an offensive guard under Paul Brown with the Cleveland Browns. He played seven years in Cleveland, then retired prematurely to get into coaching. After serving his apprenticeship with San Diego, Baltimore and the New York Jets, Noll got his chance with Pittsburgh in 1969 and immediately went 1–13. Three seasons later, the Steelers finished 11–3 and a dynasty was born . . . Noll produced nine straight winning seasons before the Steelers finished 8–8 last year . . . Though it's not like starting over, Noll will test his mettle again as a coach after a .500 season . . . He has the personality of an ice floe when his mind is on football, which is much of the time . . . A deep thinker who enjoys reading and classical music, he does have a dry wit . . . And he can say more in a short sentence than many coaches can say in a month . . . A Dayton grad who was born Jan. 5, 1932, in Cleveland.

GREATEST LINEBACKER

Jack Ham is not only the greatest linebacker in Pittsburgh's history, but one of the best football players of the '70s. He was a unanimous pick on the NFL Team of the Decade.

Ham is an intuitive outside linebacker who seems to know what the quarterback is thinking. He is intelligent and quick on his feet, which enables him to get into the runner before the latter can initiate full contact.

Tackling is only part of Ham's talent. His 31 interceptions lead active NFL linebackers. He has recovered 18 fumbles. And he has made many big plays for the Steelers, including two interceptions against Oakland in the 1975 AFC championship game that propelled Pittsburgh to its first Super Bowl.

"Jack Ham is the best linebacker in NFL history...as close to the perfect football player as is humanly possible," said a Steeler official who's obviously biased but isn't alone in his thinking.

Injuries have hampered Ham the last two years, so 1982 will either be the resurrection or the termination of this fine player's career.

INDIVIDUAL STEELER RECORDS

Rushing

Most Yards Game:	218	John Fuqua, vs Philadelphia, 1970
Season:	1,246	Franco Harris, 1975
Career:	10,339	Franco Harris, 1971–81

Passing

Most TD Passes Game:	5	Terry Bradshaw, vs Atlanta, 1981
Season:	28	Terry Bradshaw, 1978
Career:	193	Terry Bradshaw, 1970–81

Receiving

Most TD Passes Game:	4	Roy Jefferson, vs Atlanta, 1968
Season:	12	Buddy Dial, 1961
Career:	51	Lynn Swann, 1974–81

Scoring

Most Points Game:	24	Ray Mathews, vs Cleveland, 1954
	24	Roy Jefferson, vs Atlanta, 1968
Season:	123	Roy Gerela, 1973
Career:	770	Roy Gerela, 1971–78
Most TDs Game:	4	Ray Mathews, vs Cleveland, 1954
	4	Roy Jefferson, vs Atlanta, 1968
Season:	14	Franco Harris, 1976
Career:	91	Franco Harris, 1971–81

SAN DIEGO CHARGERS

TEAM DIRECTORY: Pres.: Eugene Klein; GM: John Sanders; Asst. to Pres.: Jack Teele; Asst. GM: Tank Younger; Dir. Pub. Rel.: Rick Smith; Head Coach: Don Coryell. Home field: San Diego Stadium (52,675). Colors: Blue, gold and white.

SCOUTING REPORT

OFFENSE: You want lots of points, plenty of yards? Hey, nobody does it better than San Diego. The Chargers averaged 29.8 points and 421.5 yards, tops in professional football. And there's no reason to believe they will be any less exciting this year.

Quarterback Dan Fouts has broken NFL passing records the last three seasons. Kellen Winslow, Wes Chandler and Charlie Joiner all surpassed 1,000 yards in receptions. Fouts, who can't run to save his life, was sacked only 19 times. So his offensive line is aging gracefully.

There is really nothing that could improve the offense, but coach Don Coryell insists on trying. He brought in Ricky Bell from Tampa Bay to fortify an already deep backfield.

Chuck Muncie had a superb season, but can't shake the stigma of fumbling in crucial situations. Rookie James Brooks gave Fouts still another passing target.

Three offensive linemen—Russ Washington, Ed White and Doug Wilkerson—are 35 years old and Washington is closing in on 36. This could be their last shot at a Super Bowl.

DEFENSE: What has 22 legs and continually runs in the wrong direction? That's right, San Diego's defense. The Chargers finished dead last in pass defense in the NFL, yielding 383 yards a game. San Diego surrendered 390 points—only Baltimore and St. Louis gave up more—and had a *winning* season. Those Chargers sure make life exciting, don't they?

There's nothing wrong with San Diego's ability to stop the run; they ranked second in the AFC in '81. With big ol' boys like Louie Kelcher, Gary Johnson and Leroy Jones, folks don't mess around much on the ground against the Chargers. The linebackers—Woodrow Lowe, Bob Horn and Linden King—are tough to run on, too.

But, pass the ball? Shoot, the Chargers are sitting ducks.

Mike Williams isn't a bad cornerback, but Willie Buchanon is over the hill and so is free safety Glen Edwards, brought out of retirement when injuries hit the secondary. Tim Fox, a talented safety acquired from the Patriots, should help.

Jack Pardee came in last year to coach the linebackers, saw that he didn't have much to work with and left after the season.

KICKING GAME: Great shape. Rolf Benirschke is a super place-kicker, Brooks a super return man and George Roberts a steady punter (41.0) who found new life in San Diego after getting his walking papers in Miami.

Kellen Winslow has caught 177 passes in just two seasons.

CHARGERS VETERAN ROSTER

HEAD COACH—Don Coryell. Assistant Coaches—Larrye Weaver, Dave Levy, Earnel Durden, Ernie Zampese, Tom Bass, Jerry Smith, Jim Wagstaff, Chuck Weber, Marv Braden, Birt Slater.

No.	Name	Pos.	Ht.	Wt.	NFL Exp.	College
37	Bauer, Hank	RB	5-11	204	6	California Lutheran
45	Beaudoin, Doug	S	6-0	190	7	Minnesota
42	Bell, Ricky	RB	6-2	220	5	Southern California
6	Benirschke, Rolf	K	6-1	175	6	California-Davis
50	Bradley, Carlos	LB	6-0	221	2	Wake Forest
21	Brooks, James	RB	5-9	180	2	Auburn
28	Buchanon, Willie	CB	6-1	185	11	San Diego State
25	Cappelletti, John	FB	6-1	224	8	Penn State
89	Chandler, Wes	WR	5-11	186	5	Florida
77	Claphan, Sam	T	6-6	267	2	Oklahoma
73	DeJurnett, Charles	DT	6-4	260	6	San Jose State
47	Duncan, Frank	S	6-1	188	4	San Francisco State
27	Edwards, Glen	S	6-0	183	12	Florida A&M
48	Ellis, Allan	CB	5-10	177	9	UCLA
81	Fitzkee, Scott	WR	6-0	187	4	Penn State
76	Ferguson, Keith	DE	6-5	240	2	Ohio State
14	Fouts, Dan	QB	6-3	210	10	Oregon
	Fox, Tim	S	6-0	190	7	Ohio State
43	Gregor, Bob	S	6-2	187	2	Washington State
12	Harris, James	QB	6-3	221	13	Grambling
39	Henderson, Wyatt	CB	5-10	180	2	Fresno State
82	Holohan, Pete	TE	6-4	226	2	Notre Dame
55	Horn, Bob	LB	6-4	230	7	Oregon State
79	Johnson, Gary	DT	6-3	252	8	Grambling
18	Joiner, Charlie	WR	5-11	183	14	Grambling
68	Jones, Leroy	DE	6-8	271	7	Norfolk State
74	Kelcher, Louie	DT	6-5	282	8	Southern Methodist
57	King, Linden	LB	6-4	237	5	Colorado State
54	Laslavic, Jim	LB	6-2	229	9	Penn State
	Lewis, David	LB	6-4	240	6	Southern California
64	Loewen, Chuck	G-T	6-3	259	3	South Dakota
51	Lowe, Woodrow	LB	6-0	227	7	Alabama
11	Luther, Ed	QB	6-2	211	3	San Jose State
62	Macek, Don	C	6-2	253	7	Boston College
46	Muncie, Chuck	RB	6-3	218	8	California
23	Phillips, Irvin	CB	6-1	192	2	Arkansas Tech
52	Preston, Ray	LB	6-0	218	7	Syracuse
4	Roberts, George	K	6-0	186	5	Virginia Tech
56	Rush, Bob	C-T	6-5	264	6	Memphis State
87	Scales, Dwight	WR	6-2	185	6	Grambling
	Selmon, Dewey	LB	6-1	240	6	Oklahoma
44	Shaw, Pete	S	5-10	183	6	Northwestern
66	Shields, Billy	T	6-8	275	8	Georgia Tech
59	Sievers, Eric	TE	6-4	234	2	Maryland
59	Thrift, Cliff	LB	6-2	232	4	East Central Oklahoma
70	Washington, Russ	T	6-7	288	15	Missouri
61	Webb, Jimmy	DT	6-5	252	8	Missouri State
67	White, Ed	G	6-2	271	14	California
63	Wilkerson, Doug	G	6-3	262	13	North Carolina Central
40	Williams, Clarence	FB	5-10	185	6	South Carolina
72	Williams, Jeff	G-T	6-4	260	5	Rhode Island
29	Williams, Mike	CB	5-10	176	8	Louisiana State
80	Winslow, Kellen	TE	6-6	240	3	Missouri
90	Woodcock, John	DE	6-3	255	6	Hawaii
99	Young, Wilbur	DT	6-6	290	12	William Penn, Iowa

TOP FIVE DRAFT CHOICES

Rd.	Name	Sel. No.	Pos.	Ht.	Wt.	College
7	Hall, Hollis	188	DB	5-9	173	Clemson
8	Buford, Maury	215	P	6-1	180	Texas Tech
9	Lyles, Warren	246	DT	6-3	253	Alabama
10	Young, Andre	273	DB	6-0	200	Louisiana Tech
11	Watson, Anthony	299	DB	6-0	205	New Mexico State

THE ROOKIES: If one Charger draft pick makes the squad, it will be Clemson defensive back Hollis Hall, and only because San Diego is weakest in the secondary. The Chargers, like the Redskins under George Allen, are trying to get rich quick through trades. Don Coryell didn't have a pick until the seventh round (Hall). Teams that trade instead of draft will die eventually.

OUTLOOK: Can the Tampa Bay Chargers save San Diego? Linebackers David Lewis and Dewey Selmon and new defensive coordinator Tom Bass are Tampa expatriates sent to California. But the Chargers need defensive backs, not linebackers. San Diego has enough offense to make the playoffs, but not enough defense to make the Super Bowl.

CHARGER PROFILES

DAN FOUTS 31 6–3 210   Quarterback

The 5,000-yard barrier . . . No quarterback has ever done it in one season, but Fouts came close with 4,802 last year . . . He could do it with a full training camp to work with Wes Chandler and if Charlie Joiner's legs hold up for one more season . . . Fouts has passed for more than 4,000 yards the last three seasons, setting an NFL record each year . . . He also established NFL records for most attempts (609) and completions (360) last year . . . Nevertheless, he completed 59.1 percent of his passes . . . Born June 10, 1951, in San Francisco . . . Broke numerous passing records at Oregon . . . Chargers' third-round pick in '73 . . . NFL career stagnated until Bill Walsh came to San Diego for '76 season . . . Fouts' strengths: great fire and determination.

CHUCK MUNCIE 29 6–3 218   Running Back

Extremely good back who can never do enough . . . Enjoyed his finest season last year with 1,144 yards rushing (4.6) and 19 touchdowns, but still couldn't satisfy his critics . . . Fumbled too much, they carped . . . They are right . . . Muncie doesn't know how to carry the ball correctly. He holds it against his chest instead of under his arm . . . Until he learns to protect the ball better, the fumbling will continue...It really is noticeable in pressure situations. Too bad. Muncie could really be something if he overcame fumbling stigma...Born March 17, 1953, in Uniontown, Pa....All-American and Heisman Trophy runnerup at California in '75...New Orleans' No. 1 pick in '76, but a myriad of problems there led to his San Diego trade.

JAMES BROOKS 23 5–9 180   Running Back

Football's Fuller Brush man...Need a big run, pass reception, punt return, kickoff return? Call on James Brooks...Amassed 2,093 all-purpose yards for Chargers his rookie year...Scored three touchdowns running, three receiving, and came close to breaking a number of returns all the way...San Diego drafted him in the first round and wound up with a four-dimensional talent...Played in the same Auburn backfield as Joe Cribbs and William Andrews...Brooks was born Dec. 28, 1958, in Warner Robins, Ga....Led the Warner Robbins High School Demons to a 31–2 three-year record, concluding with 13–0 his senior year as the Demons were declared co-national high school champs with Cincinnati's Moeller.

CHARLIE JOINER 34 5–11 183   Wide Receiver

Geritol Joiner...Charlie's getting old as wide receivers go, but either no one has told him or he doesn't care to listen...He'll turn 35 this autumn in what should be the winter of his career...However, the last three seasons, he has caught 70 or more passes for 1,000 or more yards...Don't put this old horse out to pasture just yet...Born Oct. 14, 1947, in Many, La. Only Many was too few and Joiner's family resettled in Lake Charles, La....James Harris' favorite receiver at Grambling...Houston selected Joiner in the fourth round of the 1969 draft as a defensive back...Won a job as a receiver, though, then traded to Cincinnati in '72...Came to Chargers in '76 for Coy Bacon...Joiner has 495 receptions, could wind up in the top three all-time.

KELLEN WINSLOW 24 6–6 240   Tight End

The very best and getting better...Better? A more appropriate word would be lethal...Winslow has caught 177 passes in two seasons, including 19 touchdowns...If he keeps this pace up for another five seasons, the NFL will have to retire him on the spot and immediately induct him into the Pro Football Hall of Fame...Winslow's 89 catches two years ago set an NFL record for tight ends; his 88 receptions last year were the most in the league by anyone...He is so talented, the Chargers put him in motion and set him out as wide receiver, too...Born Nov. 5, 1957, in St. Louis...Didn't play football until his senior year at East St. Louis (Ill.) High School...Chargers' No. 1 pick in '79 out of Missouri.

RICKY BELL 27 6–2 220   Running Back

The Bell system failed in Tampa and one long-distance call transferred it to San Diego...So John McKay loves only USC players, huh? Can't live without them, you say?...Well, he got rid of one of the more famous Trojans by sending Bell to the Chargers...Bell dropped off terribly the last two years from his 1,000-yard season in '79...He feels it was injuries. McKay obviously feels that Bell dogged it or, quite simply, lost it...San Diego is now a halfway house for NFL rejects...Bell might find happiness again in California...Born April 8, 1955, in Houston...Another of the great USC running backs, Bell was the No. 1 pick in the 1977 draft—ahead of Tony Dorsett.

WES CHANDLER 26 5–11 186   Wide Receiver

Another Saints' mistake...New Orleans has disposed of Ken Burrough, John Gillman, Chuck Muncie and now Chandler...What do the Saints have against talent anyway?...Chandler signed on with Air Coryell and joined the Chargers' 1,000-yard club (1,142 yards, including his New Orleans' stats). His 1981 totals: 69 catches, six touchdowns... That was enough to give him acceptance as the replacement for the popular John Jefferson, now relocated in Green Bay... Chandler may not be another Jefferson—who is?—but he's not a Jubilee Dunbar, either... Chandler is a tremendous athlete, one of the finest ever to play football for Florida... Born Aug. 22, 1956, in New Smyrna, Fla.

DOUG WILKERSON 35 6–3 262   Offensive Guard

Patience is golden... Or maybe it's Doug Wilkerson... Didn't get his first Pro Bowl invitation until two years ago, his 11th year in the NFL... To prove it was no fluke, he was invited back last year as a starter for the AFC... Toiled for many years without respect, except among his peers. NFL players knew Wilkerson was the real thing, a quality offensive guard... Houston gave up on him, though, back in 1970. The Oilers drafted him No. 1 out of North Carolina Central, then traded him his rookie year to San Diego... Wilkerson then survived (along with Russ Washington) terrible management, inept football teams and about everything that could go wrong with a franchise... Wilkerson was born March 27, 1947, in Fayetteville, N.C.

TIM FOX 28 6–0 190   Free Safety

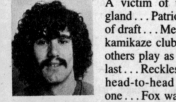

A victim of the housecleaning at New England... Patriots sent him to Chargers on day of draft... Member of the exclusive free-safety kamikaze club... Fox, Doug Plank and a few others play as if their next tackle will be their last... Reckless with their bodies, they'd go head-to-head with a rhino on third-and-one... Fox was one of the few bright spots on a weak New England defense last year... First-round pick out of Ohio State in 1976, he started from the first day of training camp... Born Nov. 1, 1953, in Canton, Ohio... Buckeyes were 40–5–1 during Fox's four years there... He once celebrated a touchdown in Columbus by doing a complete forward flip in the end zone... Pro Bowl pick in 1980... Enjoys anything reckless.

ROLF BENIRSCHKE 27 6–1 175   **Kicker**

Courageous kicker . . . Battled back from Crohn's disease, an intestinal ailment, two years ago to re-establish himself as the NFL's best place-kicker . . . Made 19 of 26 field goals last year to keep career accuracy percentage at 74.0, highest in NFL history . . . Had final operation this offseason to "clean out" any Crohn's aftereffects . . . Dropped 30-40 pounds in '79, prompting a sportswriter to say, "He looks like someone from Auschwitz.". . . Chargers picked Benirschke up on waivers from Oakland in '77 . . . He was Raiders' 12th-round draft pick that year . . . Born Feb. 7, 1955, in Boston . . . Made 23 of 49 kicks during University of California-Davis career . . . Degree in zoology . . . Works with San Diego Zoo in offseason.

COACH DON CORYELL . . . Close twice, but no cigar . . . Coryell

has gotten San Diego into the last two AFC championship games, with the Super Bowl in the balance, and each time the Chargers lost . . . Charger fans might say it was the weather—a rainy field against Oakland, miserable frost conditions against Cincinnati—that grounded Air Coryell. Others might point to the Chargers' defense, or the lack thereof . . . Coryell can teach offense—the Chargers put on a passing show second to none—and he knows how to win—Coryell has had only one losing season in 24 seasons of coaching. But he hasn't gotten enough defense in the pros to sustain him in five playoff appearances . . . San Diego averaged 421 yards in offense last year; the Chargers had to because they gave up 383 yards a game on defense . . . Coryell is a cheerleader on the field, keeping his players emotionally into the game and letting his assistants do most of the game coaching . . . He believes in preparation, then in stepping aside and delegating authority . . . A real Nervous Nellie, Coryell gets so preoccupied with football, he's lucky to find his car keys or the stadium during the season . . . He is 56, but in great shape for a man his age . . . He's a native of Seattle—born there Oct. 17, 1924—and was a defensive back at the University of Washington.

GREATEST LINEBACKER

Chuck Allen and Woodrow Lowe have something in common: they are blue-collar linebackers. You know the kind: they show up every game, bust their backsides to beat the other guys, never get any headlines, stay around a long time.

They played in different eras, Allen in the '60s and Lowe from the mid-'70s into the '80s. But they represent the best in San Diego Chargers' linebackers.

Allen came to the Chargers in 1961 from the University of Washington and was named All-AFL middle linebacker his rookie year. He played in two AFL All-Star Games and was a defensive captain five of his nine seasons in San Diego, retiring in 1969.

He burned Denver twice for touchdowns—a 59-yard interception return in 1961 and a 22-yard fumble return in 1963.

Lowe, an outside linebacker, scored twice on interceptions in 1979, including a 77-yard return against Pittsburgh. He has played in 92 consecutive games since joining the Chargers in '76.

"San Diego's getting Lowe in the fifth round is like getting a ten-dollar gold piece for 10 cents," said Lowe's college coach, Alabama's Bear Bryant, after the '76 draft.

INDIVIDUAL CHARGER RECORDS

Rushing

Most Yards Game:	206	Keith Lincoln, vs Boston, 1964
Season:	1,162	Don Woods, 1974
Career:	4,963	Paul Lowe, 1961–67

Passing

Most TD Passes Game:	6	Dan Fouts, vs Oakland, 1981
Season:	33	Dan Fouts, 1981
Career:	201	John Hadl, 1962–72

Receiving

Most TD Passes Game:	5	Kellen Winslow, vs Oakland, 1981
Season:	14	Lance Alworth, 1965
Career:	81	Lance Alworth, 1962–70

Scoring

Most Points Game:	30	Kellen Winslow, vs Oakland, 1981
Season:	118	Rolf Benirschke, 1980
Career:	500	Lance Alworth, 1962–70
Most TDs Game:	5	Kellen Winslow, vs Oakland, 1981
Season:	19	Chuck Muncie, 1981
Career:	83	Lance Alworth, 1962–70

SEATTLE SEAHAWKS

TEAM DIRECTORY: Managing Gen. Partner: Elmer Nordstrom; Dir. Oper.: Mike McCormack; GM: John Thompson; Dir. Player Personnel: Dick Mansperger; Dir. Pub. Rel.: Don Andersen; Dir. Publicity: Gary Wright; Head Coach: Jack Patera. Home field: Kingdome (64,757). Colors: Blue, green and silver.

SCOUTING REPORT

OFFENSE: The Seahawks have some strengths, but more obvious weaknesses. Jim Zorn is a fine pass-run quarterback and Steve Largent continually gets open on pass patterns, no matter what his speed is or what defenses do to try and stop him.

The Seahawks were proud of the draft-day maneuvering that made Tony Dorsett a Dallas Cowboy back in 1977. But Tom Lynch, whom the Seahawks drafted with a Dallas pick from the

Pro Bowl end Steve Largent had a club-record 75 catches.

Dorsett wheeling-dealing, now plays for the Buffalo Bills. So much for pride.

Seattle finished last in AFC rushing without Lynch. Sherman Smith's knee surgery finished him as a top-flight back. Theotis Brown was brought in and gave the Seahawks something to crow about. But how good is Brown if poor old St. Louis was willing to get rid of him?

The Seahawks still have backfield problems. They're not that well off at tight end, either. John Sawyer is average at best.

Seattle still has gaping holes in the line, at tight end and at running back. It just doesn't look like a winning act.

DEFENSE: What Seattle needs more than anything else on defense is a "set 11." Jack Patera has tinkered for several years trying to place the proper people in the right spots. At some point this has to stop. Sooner or later, the right combination must be found. Patera hasn't found it yet.

The Seahawks continue to pick up other team's rejects, a sign of confusion. Seattle brought in tackle Mike White from Cincinnati and shifted Manu Tuiasosopo to end. Manu T. had never played end before, making that move a major gamble. White and Robert Hardy must prove they can stop the run up the middle. Rookie DE Jeff Bryant may bolster AFC's 13th-best rushing defense.

Seattle showed improvement against the pass, ranking fifth. The front four, led by talented end Jacob Green, is best against the pass. Outside linebacker Michael Jackson is fast enough to blitz or cover the pass. But Patera is contemplating moving Jackson to the middle, a position the Seahawks can't solidify. Who would then replace Jackson on the outside? Maybe another reject.

The secondary *is* set. Keith Simpson and Dave Brown are capable corners. John Harris led the AFC in interceptions (10) and Kenny Easley, the other safety, is the best player the Seahawks have ever drafted. Where have you gone, Steve Niehaus?

KICKING GAME: More confusion. Why the Seahawks dumped punter Herman (Thunderfoot) Weaver remains a mystery. Jeff West averaged 39.1 last year. The Seahawks' longest return was 36 yards and the team has only one touchdown return in its history. Efren Herrera is a quality placekicker, which means he could be expendable.

THE ROOKIES: The Sleephawks drafted Clemson defensive lineman Bryant in the first round when they might have gotten him in the second. Strange. Texas linebacker Bruce Scholtz and Wabash tight end Pete Metzelaars could fit in right away. Seattle

SEAHAWKS VETERAN ROSTER

HEAD COACH—Jack Patera. Assistant Coaches—Jack Christiansen, Andy MacDonald, Frank Lauterbur, Howard Mudd, Jackie Simpson, Jerry Rhome, Rusty Tillman.

No.	Name	Pos.	Ht.	Wt.	NFL Exp.	College
12	Adkins, Sam	QB	6-2	214	6	Wichita State
2	Alvarez, Wilson	K	6-0	165	2	Southeast Louisiana
63	Anderson, Fred	DE	6-4	245	4	Prairie View
76	August, Steve	T	6-5	254	6	Tulsa
65	Bailey, Edwin	G	6-4	265	2	South Carolina State
58	Beeson, Terry	LB	6-3	235	6	Kansas
82	Bell, Mark	DE	6-4	240	3	Colorado State
68	Boyd, Dennis	T	6-6	255	5	Oregon State
36	Brinson, Larry	RB	6-0	214	5	Florida
22	Brown, Dave	CB	6-2	190	8	Michigan
30	Brown, Theotis	RB	6-3	225	4	UCLA
53	Butler, Keith	LB	6-4	225	5	Memphis State
33	Doornink, Dan	RB	6-3	210	5	Washington State
25	Dufek, Don	S	6-0	195	6	Michigan
66	Dugan, Bill	G	6-4	271	2	Penn State
45	Easley, Kenny	S	6-3	206	2	UCLA
64	Essink, Ron	T	6-6	254	3	Grand Valley State
50	Flones, Brian	LB	6-1	228	2	Washington State
56	Gaines, Greg	LB	6-3	220	2	Tennessee
79	Green, Jacob	DE	6-3	247	3	Texas A&M
75	Hardy, Robert	DT	6-2	250	4	Jackson State
44	Harris, John	S	6-2	200	5	Arizona State
1	Herrera, Efren	K	5-9	190	8	UCLA
46	Hughes, David	RB	6-0	220	2	Boise State
32	Ivory, Horace	RB	6-0	198	4	Oklahoma
55	Jackson, Michael	LB	6-1	220	4	Washington
43	Jodat, Jim	FB	5-11	213	6	Carthage
85	Johns, Paul	WR	5-11	170	2	Tulsa
27	Johnson, Greggory	CB	6-1	188	2	Oklahoma State
26	Justin, Kerry	CB	5-11	175	5	Oregon State
17	Krieg, Dave	QB	6-1	185	3	Milton
54	Kuehn, Art	C	6-3	255	7	UCLA
37	Lane, Eric	RB	6-0	195	2	Brigham Young
80	Largent, Steve	WR	5-11	184	7	Tulsa
84	McCullum, Sam	WR	6-2	190	9	Montana State
89	McGrath, Mark	WR	5-11	175	2	Montana State
21	Minor, Vic	S	6-0	198	3	Northeast Louisiana
78	Newton, Bob	G	6-5	260	12	Nebraska
52	Norman, Joe	LB	6-1	220	4	Indiana
83	Raible, Steve	WR	6-2	195	7	Georgia Tech
81	Sawyer, John	TE	6-2	230	7	Southern Mississippi
42	Simpson, Keith	CB	6-1	195	5	Memphis State
47	Smith, Sherman	RB	6-4	225	7	Miami, Ohio
69	Sutherland, Doug	DT	6-3	250	13	Wisconsin-Superior
59	Thomas, Rodell	LB	6-2	225	2	Alabama State
86	Tice, Mike	TE	6-7	250	2	Maryland
74	Tuiasosopo, Manu	DE	6-3	252	4	UCLA
60	Turner, Kevin	LB	6-2	225	3	Pacific
8	West, Jeff	P	6-2	220	7	Cincinnati
70	White, Mike	DT	6-5	266	4	Albany State
51	Yarno, John	C	6-5	251	6	Idaho
10	Zorn, Jim	QB	6-2	200	7	Cal Poly-Pomona

TOP FIVE DRAFT CHOICES

Rd.	Name	Sel. No.	Pos.	Ht.	Wt.	College
1	Bryant, Jeff	6	DE	6-5	260	Clemson
2	Scholtz, Bruce	33	LB	6-6	240	Texas
3	Metzelaars, Pete	75	TE	6-7	240	Wabash
6	Campbell, Jack	144	T	6-5	277	Utah
7	Williams, Eugene	174	LB	6-1	220	Tulsa

went after two basketball players, Sam Clancy of Pitt and Ken McAlister of USF, who last played football in high school. Clancy is projected as a defensive tackle and McAlister as a tight end or linebacker.

OUTLOOK: About as promising as the skies in cloudy Seattle. The Seahawks must have everything go right—no injuries, few turnovers, a number of over-their-head performances—to escape the AFC West cellar. It is a time for introspection in Seattle.

SEAHAWK PROFILES

JIM ZORN 29 6–2 200   Quarterback

Priming for the Super Bowl or Pablo Casals Award?...Zorn played the violin with the Seattle Symphony in a concert two years ago...Zorn's biggest goal is to take the Seahawks all the way. Since he's not yet 30, there's still time...Broke his ankle and missed the last three games in 1981...Played well up until that point, completing a personal-high 59.4 percent of his passes...Zorn's ability to scramble helped the Seahawks through their toddler years. Seattle finished 9–7 in 1978 and '79, remarkable for a third- and fourth-year franchise. Zorn's running helped...Born May 10, 1953, in Whittier, Cal....Played at Cal Poly-Pomona, then signed as free agent with Dallas...Been Seattle's only No. 1 quarterback.

STEVE LARGENT 27 5–11 184   Wide Receiver

"He's an amazing player," Jack Patera said of Steve Largent. "He makes the difficult catches look routine and the seemingly impossible receptions commonplace...I can't believe there is a better route-runner in football."...Largent caught a club-record 75 passes in 1981, surpassed the 1,000-yard receiving mark for the fourth straight year...He was named to the Pro Bowl for the third time in four seasons...He caught nine touchdown passes, giving him 46 in six years...He scored on a 10-yard run after lining up at tailback...Oh, yes, he was the team's MVP...Born Sept. 28, 1954, in Tulsa...Standout collegian at Tulsa...Traded from Houston to Seattle in '76.

THEOTIS BROWN 25 6–3 225   **Running Back**

Bigfoot, captured... By the Seahawks... Brown wears a 15EEE shoe, which earned him the nickname Bigfoot as a youngster... He represented big game to the Seahawks when they snatched him from St. Louis for a fourth-round pick midway through the 1981 season... Seattle finished 5–4 with Brown in the lineup... He rushed for 531 yards (3.8), caught 25 passes and scored six touchdowns... "He has size, adequate speed and, perhaps more important to us than other teams, outstanding ability to catch the ball," said Jack Patera... Brown was born April 20, 1957, in Oakland... Standout running back at UCLA... Drafted second by Cardinals in 1979, part of Ottis (Anderson) and Theotis backfield and radio team.

EFREN HERRERA 31 5–9 190   **Kicker**

Mr. Entertainment... All right, ladies and gentlemen, it's Monday Night Football, the Seahawks are playing and who knows what Mr. Herrera will do this time?... Will he kick the ball, will he catch it, will he go in motion, will he—you never know—throw it?... Maybe a more pertinent question would be: will he play?... Seattle likes backup Wilson Alvarez, who's 25... Herrera kicked a career-long 54-yarder, however... Born July 30, 1951, in Guadalajara, Mexico... Led the NCAA in kick-scoring his senior year at UCLA... Detroit drafted him seventh in 1974. He was waived and signed by Dallas that same year... Seattle got him in a trade in '78 and Howard Cosell has been unable to contain himself since... Herrera owns a Mexican restaurant in Dallas.

DAVID HUGHES 23 6–0 220   **Running Back**

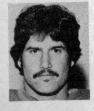

Possible sleeper... All-purpose back who doesn't have great speed or moves, but is tough, reliable and can catch the football... Seattle drafted him No. 2 out of Boise State in 1981 and he filled in for Dan Doornink at fullback... Hughes rushed for 135 yards and caught 35 passes for 263 yards and two touchdowns... Third-down type back who can make the necessary yard or catch the pass coming out of the back-field...Could play a lot more now that he has a feel for the pro game...Born June 1, 1959, in Honolulu...Helped lead Boise to the 1980 NCAA Division 1-AA championship with a 31–29 victory over Eastern Kentucky. Hughes scored on an 18-yard run in that game...Mostly lead blocker for Boise, however.

SAM McCULLUM 29 6-2 190   Wide Receiver

King of the leftovers...McCullum came to the Seahawks as table scraps in 1976, part of the Seahawks' veteran allocation. In other words, expansion draft...The undesirables...Steady Sam turned out to be a four-star, haute cuisine...He has caught 46 or more passes in each of the last three seasons...Best year was 1980, when he caught career-high 62 passes and was named the team's Most Valuable Player...Caught 13 touchdown passes the last three years...Born Nov. 30, 1952, in McComb, Miss....Left the warm South for the cold Big Sky country to grow up in Kalispell, Mont. and play for Montana State...Ninth-round pick of Minnesota in 1974, spent two years with the Vikings, scoring three times as a rookie on seven catches.

JOHN HARRIS 26 6-2 200   Safety

The name's Harris...John Harris...Intercepted 10 passes last year, tops in the AFC...Didn't make the Pro Bowl...The selectors acted as if it never happened...Harris must be wondering himself why Donnie Schell, Gary Barbaro and Bill Thompson were picked as AFC safeties for the Pro Bowl when they didn't have half his statistics...Harris has yet to learn that it takes the selectors one year to wake up. They'll probably recognize him this season...Twenty-two interceptions in four years with Seattle, which drafted him in the seventh round and got lucky...Born June 13, 1956, at Ft. Benning, Ga. ...Valedictorian of his high school class in Miami...Played college ball at Arizona State.

KENNY EASLEY 23 6–3 206   Safety

Easley the best? Easily . . . It will happen some-day, Kenny Easley becoming the best safety in football . . . Then it will be up to the NFL to figure out if he is a strong or free safety . . . Seattle doesn't use such designations: Easley and Harris are just left and right safeties . . . Whatever, Easley has as much talent as any safety who ever came into the league . . . He has the size, speed, enthusiasm, ability to react quickly and aggressiveness . . . Born Jan. 15, 1959, in Chesapeake, Va. . . . Three-year consensus All-American at UCLA . . . First Pacific-10 player named all-conference four years . . . Last year, Easley recovered four fumbles, finished second on the team in tackles (107) and intercepted three passes, returning one 82 yards for a touchdown.

JACOB GREEN 25 6–3 247   Defensive End

Who says it's not easy being Green? . . . Not Jacob, who set a Seattle club record last year with 12 sacks . . . This gives him 18 in two years with the Seahawks . . . "Jacob has the tools to excel at his position," said Jack Patera. "He has great quickness and anticipation and he improved tremendously against the run last year." . . . Green recovered a fumble and had 72 tackles the second time around . . . Born Jan. 21, 1957, in Pasadena, Tex. . . . His high school basketball team in Houston (Kashmere) won two consecutive state titles . . . Jacob was a defensive terror at Texas A&M, with 38 sacks, 12 forced fumbles and six recoveries . . . All-American pick . . . Drafted No. 1 by Seattle in 1980 . . . Started 13 games as a rookie.

MANU TUIASOSOPO 25 6–3 252   Defensive End

Manu T. . . . It's simpler to leave it at that . . . Manu T. was shifted from defensive tackle to end last year, finishing with 67 tackles and six sacks . . . His forte is strength and all-out intensity for four quarters . . . He is difficult to block because he is so active . . . Offensive tackles have named him to their All-Fatiguing team. He gives everyone a workout . . . Born Aug. 30,

1957, in Los Angeles, not American Samoa...But Manu T. is a cousin to every Samoan in the NFL, it seems...Second-team All-American at UCLA, he was drafted in the first round by Seattle in 1979...His full name is Manu'ula Asovalu Tuiasosopo....Manu'ula translated, means Happy Bird...Happy Bird, the happy sacker.

COACH JACK PATERA...Two losing seasons after two winning ones...In most organizations, that would be tantamount to See ya later, Charlie...But the Seahawks don't fly off the handle easily...They believe they have a good man in Patera, and that two straight losers are more a reflection of a still-young expansion team going through adolescent growing pains...Patera made the baby Seahawks a winner two years after their birth. This made a big impression on the Seattle management, one it's not apt to forget...The Seahawks are more of a family operation, anyway..."We're getting a little better each year," Patera said...Patera is a coaching stoic in the manner of Tom Landry and Bud Grant...It's no wonder: Patera played for Landry and coached under Grant...He played seven seasons in the NFL as a guard and linebacker...He coached the Fearsome Foursome in Los Angeles and the Purple Gang in Minnesota...The fledgling Seattle franchise liked this defensive line coach and named him as its first, and only, head coach in 1976...Seattle beat Pittsburgh, San Diego and the New York Jets (twice) over the last half of the 1981 season. Patera sees that as promise of things to come in '82...A University of Oregon grad, he was born Aug. 1, 1933, in Bismarck, N.D.

GREATEST LINEBACKER

The Seattle Seahawks haven't been around that long and neither has Michael Jackson, but they are growing up together on defense.

Jackson is the first quality linebacker the Seahawks have had in their six-year history, and he can only get better. He isn't very big (6–1, 220), along the order of another Jackson—Denver's Tom—but just as fast.

Michael Jackson was a quarterback, running back and safety at Pasco High School in Washington, but grew to linebacker proportions at the University of Washington.

He led the Huskies in tackles his junior and senior years, but his personal highlight was the game-saving interception against Michigan in the Rose Bowl.

The Seahawks drafted him in the third round in 1979 after other teams thought him too small to be taken any earlier. He broke in as a starting outside linebacker midway through his rookie year and has been getting better every fall.

His speed overcomes his lack of size and makes him a threat on pass coverage as well as the sweep. And the little man can hit too, as bruised rib cages around the NFL indicate.

INDIVIDUAL SEAHAWK RECORDS

Rushing

Most Yards Game:	152	Sherman Smith, vs Chicago, 1978
Season:	805	Sherman Smith, 1978
Career:	3,227	Sherman Smith, 1976–81

Passing

Most TD Passes Game:	4	Steve Myer, vs Tampa Bay, 1977
	4	Jim Zorn, vs Buffalo, 1977
	4	Jim Zorn, vs San Diego, 1977
Season:	20	Jim Zorn, 1979
Career:	93	Jim Zorn, 1976–81

Receiving

Most TD Passes Game:	2	Steve Largent (seven times, most recently vs Oakland, 1979)
	2	Sam McCullum, vs St. Louis, 1976
	2	Dan Doornink, vs Green Bay, 1981
Season:	10	Steve Largent, 1977
Career:	46	Steve Largent, 1976–81

Scoring

Most Points Game:	18	David Sims, vs New York Jets, 1978
	18	David Sims, vs Cleveland, 1978
	18	Sherman Smith, vs Cleveland, 1979
Season:	100	Efren Herrera, 1979
Career:	331	Efren Herrera, 1978–81
Most TDs Game:	3	David Sims, vs New York Jets, 1978
	3	David Sims, vs Cleveland, 1978
	3	Sherman Smith, vs Cleveland, 1979
Season:	15	David Sims, 1978
Career:	38	Sherman Smith, 1976–81

OFFICIAL 1981 NFL STATISTICS

(Compiled by Elias Sports Bureau)

RUSHING

TOP TEN RUSHERS

	Att	Yards	Avg	Long	TD
Rogers, George, N.O.	378	1674	4.4	t79	13
Dorsett, Tony, Dall.	342	1646	4.8	t75	4
Sims, Billy, Det.	296	1437	4.9	51	13
Montgomery, Wilbert, Phil.	286	1402	4.9	41	8
Anderson, Ottis, St.L.	328	1376	4.2	28	9
Campbell, Earl, Hou.	361	1376	3.8	43	10
Andrews, William, Atl.	289	1301	4.5	29	10
Payton, Walter, Chi.	339	1222	3.6	39	6
Muncie, Chuck, S.D.	251	1144	4.6	t73	19
Delaney, Joe, K.C.	234	1121	4.8	t82	3

AFC - INDIVIDUAL RUSHERS

	Att	Yards	Avg	Long	TD
Campbell, Earl, Hou.	361	1376	3.8	43	10
Muncie, Chuck, S.D.	251	1144	4.6	t73	19
Delaney, Joe, K.C.	234	1121	4.8	t82	3
Pruitt, Mike, Clev.	247	1103	4.5	21	7
Cribbs, Joe, Buff.	257	1097	4.3	35	3
Johnson, Pete, Cin.	274	1077	3.9	t39	12
Harris, Franco, Pitt.	242	987	4.1	50	8
Collins, Anthony, N.E.	204	873	4.3	29	7
King, Kenny, Oak.	170	828	4.9	60	0
Nathan, Tony, Mia.	147	782	5.3	46	5
Dickey, Curtis, Balt.	164	779	4.8	t67	7
Parros, Rick, Den.	176	749	4.3	25	2
Franklin, Andra, Mia.	201	711	3.5	29	7
Preston, Dave, Den.	183	640	3.5	23	3
McNeil, Freeman, N.Y.J.	137	623	4.5	43	2
Hadnot, James, K.C.	140	603	4.3	30	3
McMillen, Randy, Balt.	149	597	4.0	42	3
Brown, Theotis, St.L.-Sea.	156	583	3.7	43	8
Pollard, Frank, Pitt.	123	570	4.6	29	2

t = Touchdown
Leader based on most yards gained

	Att	Yards	Avg	Long	TD
Brooks, James, S.D.	109	525	4.8	t28	3
Jensen, Derrick, Oak.	117	456	3.9	33	4
Jackson, Billy, K.C.	111	398	3.6	31	10
Harper, Bruce, N.Y.J.	81	393	4.9	t29	4
Leaks, Roosevelt, Buff.	91	357	3.9	31	6
White, Charles, Clev.	97	342	3.5	26	1
Ferguson, Vagas, N.E.	78	340	4.4	t19	3
Augustyniak, Mike, N.Y.J. ..	85	339	4.0	12	1
Dierking, Scott, N.Y.J.	74	328	4.4	t15	1
Anderson, Ken, Cin.	46	320	7.0	25	1
Alexander, Charles, Cin. ...	98	292	3.0	16	2
Dixon, Zachary, Balt.	73	285	3.9	41	0
Woodley, David, Mia.	63	272	4.3	26	4
Davis, Russell, Pitt.	47	270	5.7	28	1
Long, Kevin, N.Y.J.	73	269	3.7	19	2
Cunningham, Sam, N.E.	86	269	3.1	12	4
Cappelletti, John, S.D.	68	254	3.7	30	4
Smith, Sherman, Sea.	83	253	3.0	21	3
Hooks, Roland, Buff.	51	250	4.9	19	3
Newton, Tom, N.Y.J.	73	244	3.3	13	1
Brown, Curtis, Buff.	62	226	3.6	13	0
Whittington, Arthur, Oak. ..	69	220	3.2	13	1
Calhoun, Don, N.E.	57	205	3.6	33	2
Thornton, Sidney, Pitt.	56	202	3.6	t17	4
Tatupo, Mosi, N.E.	38	201	5.3	43	2
McKnight, Ted, K.C.	54	195	3.6	26	5
Doornink, Dan, Sea.	65	194	3.0	11	1
Hawkins, Frank, Oak.	40	165	4.1	19	0
Miller, Cleo, Clev.	52	165	3.2	13	2
Griffin, Archie, Cin.	47	163	3.5	23	3
Bradshaw, Terry, Pitt.	38	162	4.3	16	2
Reed, Tony, Den.	68	156	2.3	10	0
Sipe, Brian, Clev.	38	153	4.0	22	1
van Eeghen, Mark, Oak.	39	150	3.8	11	2
Wilson, Marc, Oak.	30	147	4.9	18	2
Armstrong, Adger, Hou.	31	146	4.7	18	0
Hill, Eddie, Mia.	37	146	3.9	24	1
Zorn, Jim, Sea.	30	140	4.7	20	1
McCutcheon, Lawrence, Buff.	34	138	4.1	12	0
Hughes, David, Sea.	47	135	2.9	15	0
Todd, Richard, N.Y.J.	32	131	4.1	19	0
Pruitt, Greg, Clev.	31	124	4.0	15	0
Fuller, Steve, K.C.	19	118	6.2	27	0
Vigorito, Tommy, Mia.	35	116	3.3	t30	1
Canada, Larry, Den.	33	113	3.4	11	3
Taylor, Billy, N.Y.G.-N.Y.J.	38	111	2.9	14	2
Lytle, Rob, Den.	30	106	3.5	18	4

	Att	Yards	Avg	Long	TD
Jodat, Jim, Sea.	31	106	3.4	15	1
Bennett, Woody, Mia.	28	104	3.7	12	0
Cavanaugh, Matt, N.E.	17	92	5.4	11	3
Coleman, Ronnie, Hou.	21	91	4.3	30	1
Kenney, Bill, K.C.	24	89	3.7	21	1
Jones, Bert, Balt.	20	85	4.3	17	0
Marshall, Henry, K.C.	3	69	23.0	34	0
Malone, Mark, Pitt.	16	68	4.3	19	2
Hargrove, Jimmy, Cin.	16	66	4.1	27	1
Bledsoe, Curtis, K.C.	20	65	3.3	13	0
Hawthorne, Greg, Pitt.	25	58	2.3	16	2
Upchurch, Rick, Den.	5	56	11.2	37	0
Krieg, Dave, Sea.	11	56	5.1	29	1
Fouts, Dan, S.D.	22	56	2.5	13	0
Willis, Chester, Oak.	16	54	3.4	t15	1
Franklin, Cleveland, Balt. .	21	52	2.5	8	1
Grogan, Steve, N.E.	12	49	4.1	t24	2
Largent, Steve, Sea.	6	47	7.8	15	1
Schonert, Turk, Cin.	7	41	5.9	19	0
DeBerg, Steve, Den.	9	40	4.4	11	0
Ivory, Horace, Sea.	9	38	4.2	7	0
Plunkett, Jim, Oak.	12	38	3.2	t13	1
McCauley, Don, Balt.	10	37	3.7	8	0
Wilson, Tim, Hou.	13	35	2.7	7	0
Riddick, Robb, Buff.	3	29	9.7	12	0
Ferguson, Joe, Buff.	20	29	1.5	16	1
Adkins, Sam, Sea.	3	28	9.3	13	0
Williams, Clarence, S.D. ...	20	26	1.3	6	0
West, Jeff, Sea.	3	25	8.3	27	0
Hill, Calvin, Clev.	4	23	5.8	9	0
Lane, Eric, Sea.	8	22	2.8	5	0
Kreider, Steve, Cin.	1	21	21.0	21	0
Morgan, Stanley, N.E.	2	21	10.5	11	0
Howell, Steve, Mia.	5	21	4.2	9	0
Newsome, Ozzie, Clev.	2	20	10.0	14	0
Lewis, Kenny, N.Y.J.	6	18	3.0	7	0
Morton, Craig, Den.	8	18	2.3	5	0
Stallworth, John, Pitt.	1	17	17.0	17	0
Brammer, Mark, Buff.	2	17	8.5	11	0
Moore, Jeff, Sea.	1	15	15.0	15	0
Smith, Jim, Pitt.	1	15	15.0	15	0
Orosz, Tom, Mia.	1	13	13.0	13	0
Reaves, John, Hou.	6	13	2.2	13	0
Landry, Greg, Balt.	1	11	11.0	11	0
Wright, James, Den.	1	11	11.0	11	0
Verser, David, Cin.	2	11	5.5	9	0
Stoudt, Cliff, Pitt.	3	11	3.7	10	0

	Att	Yards	Avg	Long	TD
Bass, Don, Cin.	1	9	9.0	9	0
Colquitt, Craig, Pitt.	1	8	8.0	8	0
Bauer, Hank, S.D.	2	7	3.5	4	0
Watson, Steve, Den.	2	6	3.0	6	0
Moser, Rick, Pitt.	1	4	4.0	4	0
Garrett, Mike, Balt.	2	4	2.0	3	0
Miller, Terry, Sea.	2	4	2.0	2	0
Moore, Nat, Mia.	1	3	3.0	3	0
Pennywell, Carlos, N.E.	1	3	3.0	3	0
Roberts, George, S.D.	1	2	2.0	2	0
Nielsen, Gifford, Hou.	6	2	0.3	4	0
Butler, Jerry, Buff.	1	1	1.0	1	0
Johnson, Andy, N.E.	2	1	0.5	5	0
Anderson, Kim, Balt.	1	0	0.0	0	0
Jones, Johnny, N.Y.J.	2	0	0.0	5	0
McDonald, Paul, Clev.	2	0	0.0	2	0
Williams, Mike, K.C.	2	0	0.0	3	0
Ramsey, Chuck, N.Y.J.	3	0	0.0	0	0
Chandler, Wes, S.D.	5	-1	-0.2	9	0
Carson, Carlos, K.C.	1	-1	-1.0	-1	0
Feacher, Ricky, Clev.	1	-1	-1.0	-1	0
Robinson, Matt, Buff.	1	-2	-2.0	-2	0
Stabler, Ken, Hou.	10	-3	-0.3	4	0
Ryan, Pat, N.Y.J.	3	-5	-1.7	-1	0
Dixon, Al, K.C.	1	-5	-5.0	-5	0
Kush, Rod, Buff.	1	-6	-6.0	-6	0
Luther, Ed, S.D.	3	-8	-2.7	-1	0
Franklin, Byron, Buff.	1	-11	-11.0	-11	0
Jackson, Harold, N.E.	2	-14	-7.0	-5	0
Grupp, Bob, K.C.	1	-19	-19.0	-19	0
Strock, Don, Mia.	14	-26	-1.9	9	0
McInally, Pat, Cin.	1	-27	-27.0	-27	0

NFC - INDIVIDUAL RUSHERS

	Att	Yards	Avg	Long	TD
Rogers, George, N.O.	378	1674	4.4	t79	13
Dorsett, Tony, Dall.	342	1646	4.8	t75	4
Sims, Billy, Det.	296	1437	4.9	51	13
Montgomery, Wilbert, Phil. .	286	1402	4.9	41	8
Anderson, Ottis, St.L.	328	1376	4.2	28	9
Andrews, William, Atl.	289	1301	4.5	29	10
Payton, Walter, Chi.	339	1222	3.6	39	6
Tyler, Wendell, L.A.	260	1074	4.1	t69	12
Brown, Ted, Minn.	274	1063	3.9	34	6
Washington, Joe, Wash.	210	916	4.4	32	4

	Att	Yards	Avg	Long	TD
Ellis, Gerry, G.B.	196	860	4.4	29	4
Carpenter, Rob, Hou.-N.Y.G.	208	822	4.0	35	5
Riggins, John, Wash.	195	714	3.7	24	13
Eckwood, Jerry, T.B.	172	651	3.8	59	2
Springs, Ron, Dall.	172	625	3.6	16	10
Patton, Ricky, S.F.	152	543	3.6	28	4
Cain, Lynn, Atl.	156	542	3.5	35	4
Suhey, Matt, Chi.	150	521	3.5	26	3
Bussey, Dexter, Det.	105	446	4.2	23	0
Bryant, Cullen, L.A.	109	436	4.0	20	1
Guman, Mike, L.A.	115	433	3.8	18	4
Morris, Wayne, St.L.	109	417	3.8	14	5
Owens, James, T.B.	91	406	4.5	t35	3
Huckleby, Harlan, G.B.	139	381	2.7	22	5
Wilder, James, T.B.	107	370	3.5	t23	4
Kane, Rick, Det.	77	332	4.3	20	2
Cooper, Earl, S.F.	98	330	3.4	23	1
Oliver, Hubert, Phil.	75	329	4.4	39	1
Davis, Johnny, S.F.	94	297	3.2	14	7
Perry, Leon, N.Y.G.	72	257	3.6	23	0
Easley, Walt, S.F.	76	224	2.9	9	1
Evans, Vince, Chi.	43	218	5.1	25	3
Thompson, Vince, Det.	35	211	6.0	30	1
Williams, Doug, T.B.	48	209	4.4	29	4
Galbreath, Tony, Minn.	42	198	4.7	21	2
Bright, Leon, N.Y.G.	51	197	3.9	25	2
Holmes, Jack, N.O.	58	194	3.3	11	2
Hofer, Paul, S.F.	60	193	3.2	12	1
Jones, James, Dall.	34	183	5.4	t59	1
Tyler, Toussaint, N.O.	36	183	5.1	42	0
Jackson, Wilbur, Wash.	46	183	4.0	14	0
Middleton, Terdell, G.B. ...	53	181	3.4	34	0
Theismann, Joe, Wash.	36	177	4.9	24	2
Mitchell, Stump, St.L.	31	175	5.6	43	0
Hipple, Eric, Det.	41	168	4.1	18	7
Kotar, Doug, N.Y.G.	46	154	3.3	18	1
Harrington, Perry, Phil. ...	34	140	4.1	16	2
Wilson, Wayne, N.O.	44	137	3.1	13	1
Murray, Calvin, Phil.	23	134	5.8	20	0
Young, Rickey, Minn.	47	129	2.7	13	0
Jaworski, Ron, Phil.	22	128	5.8	26	0
Russell, Booker, Phil.	38	123	3.2	17	4
Thomas, Jewerl, L.A.	34	118	3.5	40	0
Campfield, Billy, Phil.	31	115	3.7	13	1
Ring, Bill, S.F.	22	106	4.8	16	0
Harper, Roland, Chi.	34	106	3.1	11	1
Haden, Pat, L.A.	18	104	5.8	16	0

	Att	Yards	Avg	Long	TD
Lomax, Neil, St.L.	19	104	5.5	t22	2
Giaquinto, Nick, Mia.-Wash.	20	104	5.2	20	0
White, Danny, Dall.	38	104	2.7	17	0
Giammona, Louie, Phil.	35	98	2.8	9	1
Montana, Joe, S.F.	25	95	3.8	t20	2
Bell, Ricky, T.B.	30	80	2.7	8	0
Jensen, Jim, G.B.	27	79	2.9	15	0
Thompson, Leonard, Det.	10	75	7.5	21	1
Forte, Ike, N.Y.G.	19	74	3.9	15	0
McClendon, Willie, Chi.	30	74	2.5	17	0
Ivery, Eddie Lee, G.B.	14	72	5.1	28	1
Jackson, Louis, N.Y.G.	27	68	2.5	9	1
Mayberry, James, Atl.	18	66	3.7	11	0
Green, Roy, St.L.	3	60	20.0	t44	1
Metcalf, Terry, Wash.	18	60	3.3	12	0
LeCount, Terry, Minn.	3	51	17.0	38	0
Whitehurst, David, G.B.	15	51	3.4	15	1
Nichols, Mark, Det.	3	50	16.7	30	0
Lawrence, Amos, S.F.	13	48	3.7	14	1
Solomon, Freddie, S.F.	9	43	4.8	16	0
Simms, Phil, N.Y.G.	19	42	2.2	24	0
Newsome, Timmy, Dall.	13	38	2.9	7	0
Rogers, Jimmy, N.O.	9	37	4.1	15	0
Cosbie, Doug, Dall.	4	33	8.3	15	0
Atkins, Steve, G.B.-Phil. ..	12	33	2.8	21	0
Newhouse, Robert, Dall.	14	33	2.4	6	0
Clark, Dwight, S.F.	3	32	10.7	18	0
Pearson, Drew, Dall.	3	31	10.3	25	0
Dennard, Preston, L.A.	6	29	4.8	21	0
Elliott, Lenvil, S.F.	7	29	4.1	9	0
Manning, Archie, N.O.	2	28	14.0	15	0
Groth, Jeff, N.O.	2	27	13.5	28	0
King, Horace, Det.	7	25	3.6	7	0
Scott, Freddie, Det.	7	25	3.6	10	0
Robinson, Bo, Atl.	9	24	2.7	5	0
Danielson, Gary, Det.	9	23	2.6	t11	2
Jefferson, John, G.B.	2	22	11.0	15	0
Redwine, Jarvis, Minn.	5	20	4.0	8	0
Brunner, Scott, N.Y.G.	14	20	1.4	23	0
Williams, Dave, Chi.	2	19	9.5	15	0
Claitt, Ricky, Wash.	3	19	6.3	11	0
Cromwell, Nolan, L.A.	1	17	17.0	17	0
Moroski, Mike, Atl.	3	17	5.7	14	0
Lewis, Leo, Minn.	1	16	16.0	16	0
Hill, Drew, L.A.	1	14	14.0	14	0
Dils, Steve, Minn.	4	14	3.5	7	0
Matthews, Bo, N.Y.G.	4	14	3.5	6	0

	Att	Yards	Avg	Long	TD
Kramer, Tommy, Minn.	10	13	1.3	8	0
DuPree, Billy Joe, Dall. ...	1	12	12.0	12	0
Margerum, Ken, Chi.	1	11	11.0	11	0
Love, Randy, St.L.	3	11	3.7	4	0
Wonsley, Otis, Wash.	3	11	3.7	7	0
Baschnagel, Brian, Chi.	1	10	10.0	10	0
Erxleben, Russell, N.O.	2	10	5.0	26	0
House, Kevin, T.B.	2	9	4.5	8	0
Kemp, Jeff, L.A.	2	9	4.5	7	0
Carano, Glenn, Dall.	8	9	1.1	11	0
Francis, Wallace, Atl.	1	8	8.0	t8	1
Stief, Dave, St.L.	1	8	8.0	8	0
Bell, Theo, T.B.	1	7	7.0	7	0
Harrell, Sam, Minn.	1	7	7.0	7	0
LeMaster, Frank, Phil.	1	7	7.0	7	0
Smith, Ron, Phil.	1	7	7.0	7	0
Stauch, Scott, N.O.	2	6	3.0	5	0
Strong, Ray, Atl.	3	6	2.0	3	0
Harrell, Willard, St.L.	5	6	1.2	4	1
Dickey, Lynn, G.B.	19	6	0.3	13	0
Bartkowski, Steve, Atl.	11	2	0.2	5	0
Benjamin, Guy, S.F.	1	1	1.0	1	0
Carmichael, Harold, Phil. ..	1	1	1.0	1	0
Wilson, Dave, N.O.	5	1	0.2	9	0
Pisarcik, Joe, Phil.	7	1	0.1	10	0
Blanchard, Tom, T.B.	1	0	0.0	0	0
Childs, Henry, L.A.	1	0	0.0	0	0
Connell, Mike, Wash.	1	0	0.0	0	0
Phipps, Mike, Chi.	1	0	0.0	0	0
Sciarra, John, Phil.	1	0	0.0	0	0
Siemon, Jeff, Minn.	1	0	0.0	0	0
Merkens, Guido, N.O.	2	-1	-0.5	2	0
Perkins, Johnny, N.Y.G.	2	-1	-0.5	10	0
White, Sammy, Minn.	2	-1	-0.5	1	0
Jones, June, Atl.	1	-1	-1.0	-1	0
Birdsong, Carl, St.L.	1	-2	-2.0	-2	0
Henry, Wally, Phil.	1	-2	-2.0	-2	0
Rutledge, Jeff, L.A.	5	-3	-0.6	4	0
Myers, Tommy, N.O.	2	-3	-1.5	6	0
Caster, Richard, N.O.	1	-3	-3.0	-3	0
Hill, Tony, Dall.	1	-3	-3.0	-3	0
Scott, Bobby, N.O.	3	-4	-1.3	-1	0
Monk, Art, Wash.	1	-5	-5.0	-5	0
Neal, Dan, Chi.	1	-6	-6.0	-6	0
Parsons, Bob, Chi.	1	-6	-6.0	-6	0
James, John, Atl.	1	-7	-7.0	-7	0
Swider, Larry, T.B.	1	-9	-9.0	-9	0

TOP TEN SCORERS – KICKERS

	XP	XPA	FG	FGA	PTS
Murray, Ed, Det.	46	46	25	35	121
Septien, Rafael, Dall.	40	40	27	35	121
Breech, Jim, Cin.	49	51	22	32	115
Lowery, Nick, K.C.	37	38	26	36	115
Luckhurst, Mike, Atl.	51	51	21	33	114
Leahy, Pat, N.Y.J.	38	39	25	36	113
Benirschke, Rolf, S.D.	55	61	19	26	112
von Schamann, Uwe, Mia.	37	38	24	31	109
Danelo, Joe, N.Y.G.	31	31	24	38	103
Franklin, Tony, Phil.	41	43	20	31	101
Stenerud, Jan, G.B.	35	36	22	24	101

TOP TEN SCORERS – NON-KICKERS

	TD	R	P	M	PTS
Muncie, Chuck, S.D.	19	19	0	0	114
Tyler, Wendell, L.A.	17	12	5	0	102
Johnson, Pete, Cin.	16	12	4	0	96
Sims, Billy, Det.	15	13	2	0	90
Jenkins, Alfred, Atl.	13	0	13	0	78
Riggins, John, Wash.	13	13	0	0	78
Rogers, George, N.O.	13	13	0	0	78
Watson, Steve, Den.	13	0	13	0	78
Andrews, William, Atl.	12	10	2	0	72
Springs, Ron, Dall.	12	10	2	0	72

TOP TEN PASS RECEIVERS

	No	Yards	Avg	Long	TD
Winslow, Kellen, S.D.	88	1075	12.2	t67	10
Clark, Dwight, S.F.	85	1105	13.0	t78	4
Brown, Ted, Minn.	83	694	8.4	63	2
Andrews, William, Atl.	81	735	9.1	t70	2
Senser, Joe, Minn.	79	1004	12.7	53	8
Largent, Steve, Sea.	75	1224	16.3	t57	9
Lofton, James, G.B.	71	1294	18.2	t75	8
Ross, Dan, Cin.	71	910	12.8	37	5
Jenkins, Alfred, Atl.	70	1358	19.4	67	13
Lewis, Frank, Buff.	70	1244	17.8	33	4
Joiner, Charlie, S.D.	70	1188	17.0	57	7
Washington, Joe, Wash.	70	558	8.0	32	3

PASSING

AFC INDIVIDUAL PASSING QUALIFIERS

	Att	Comp	Pct Comp	Yards	Avg Gain
Anderson, Ken, Cin. ..	479	300	62.6	3754	7.84
Morton, Craig, Den. ..	376	225	59.8	3195	8.50
Fouts, Dan, S.D.	609	360	59.1	4802	7.89
Bradshaw, Terry, Pitt.	370	201	54.3	2887	7.80
Zorn, Jim, Sea.	397	236	59.4	2788	7.02
Todd, Richard, N.Y.J.	497	279	56.1	3231	6.50
Jones, Bert, Balt. ...	426	244	57.3	3094	7.26
Ferguson, Joe, Buff.	498	252	50.6	3652	7.33
Woodley, David, Mia. .	366	191	52.2	2470	6.75
Stabler, Ken, Hou. ...	285	165	57.9	1988	6.98
Sipe, Brian, Clev. ...	567	313	55.2	3876	6.84
Kenney, Bill, K.C. ...	274	147	53.6	1983	7.24
Grogan, Steve, N.E. ..	216	117	54.2	1859	8.61
Cavanaugh, Matt, N.E.	219	115	52.5	1633	7.46
Wilson, Marc, Oak. ...	366	173	47.3	2311	6.31

NFC INDIVIDUAL PASSING QUALIFIERS

	Att	Comp	Pct Comp	Yards	Avg Gain
Montana, Joe, S.F. ...	488	311	63.7	3565	7.31
White, Danny, Dall. ..	391	223	57.0	3098	7.92
Bartkowski, Steve, Atl.	533	297	55.7	3829	7.18
Dickey, Lynn, G.B. ...	354	204	57.6	2593	7.32
Theismann, Joe, Wash.	496	293	59.1	3568	7.19
Williams, Doug, T.B. .	471	238	50.5	3563	7.56
Simms, Phil, N.Y.G. .	316	172	54.4	2031	6.43
Jaworski, Ron, Phil. .	461	250	54.2	3095	6.71
Hipple, Eric, Det. ...	279	140	50.2	2358	8.45
Kramer, Tommy, Minn. .	593	322	54.3	3912	6.60
Hart, Jim, St.L.	241	134	55.6	1694	7.03
Haden, Pat, L.A.	267	138	51.7	1815	6.80
Manning, Archie, N.O.	232	134	57.8	1447	6.24
Lomax, Neil, St.L. ...	236	119	50.4	1575	6.67
Evans, Vince, Chi. ...	436	195	44.7	2354	5.40

TOP TEN PUNTERS

	No	Yds	Long	Avg
McInally, Pat, Cin.	72	3272	62	45.4
Guy, Ray, Oak.	96	4195	69	43.7
Skladany, Tom, Det.	64	2784	74	43.5
Colquitt, Craig, Pitt. ...	84	3641	74	43.3
Jennings, Dave, N.Y.G. ...	97	4198	62	43.3
Swider, Larry, T.B.	58	2476	62	42.7
Cox, Steve, Clev.	68	2884	66	42.4
Corral, Frank, L.A.	89	3735	67	42.0
Birdsong, Carl, St.L.	69	2883	75	41.8
Camarillo, Rich, N.E.	47	1959	75	41.7

TD	Pct TD	Long	Int	Pct Int	Rating Points
29	6.1	t74	10	2.1	98.5
21	5.6	t95	14	3.7	90.6
33	5.4	t67	17	2.8	90.6
22	5.9	t90	14	3.8	83.7
13	3.3	t80	9	2.3	82.3
25	5.0	49	13	2.6	81.8
21	4.9	67	20	4.7	76.8
24	4.8	t67	20	4.0	74.1
12	3.3	t69	13	3.6	69.7
14	4.9	t71	18	6.3	69.5
17	3.0	62	25	4.4	68.3
9	3.3	t64	16	5.8	63.8
7	3.2	t76	16	7.4	63.0
5	2.3	65	13	5.9	60.0
14	3.8	t66	19	5.2	58.8

TD	Pct TD	Long	Int	Pct Int	Rating Points
19	3.9	t78	12	2.5	88.2
22	5.6	t73	13	3.3	87.5
30	5.6	t70	23	4.3	79.2
17	4.8	t75	15	4.2	79.1
19	3.8	t79	20	4.0	77.3
19	4.0	t84	14	3.0	76.5
11	3.5	80	9	2.8	74.2
23	5.0	t85	20	4.3	74.0
14	5.0	t94	15	5.4	73.3
26	4.4	63	24	4.0	72.8
11	4.6	t58	14	5.8	68.9
9	3.4	t67	13	4.9	64.4
5	2.2	55	11	4.7	64.0
4	1.7	75	10	4.2	60.1
11	2.5	t85	20	4.6	51.0

Total Punts	TB	Blk	Opp Ret	Ret Yds	In 20	Net Avg
73	11	1	42	416	17	36.1
96	15	0	45	514	23	35.2
64	5	0	39	299	21	37.3
84	16	0	34	358	25	35.3
97	12	0	61	561	19	35.0
60	4	2	39	409	13	33.1
70	12	2	30	253	11	34.2
89	3	0	52	481	19	35.9
69	8	0	37	276	18	35.5
47	9	0	20	209	12	33.4

TOP TEN INTERCEPTORS

	No	Yards	Avg	Long	TD
Walls, Everson, Dall.	11	133	12.1	33	0
Harris, John, Sea.	10	155	15.5	t42	2
Hicks, Dwight, S.F.	9	239	26.6	72	1
Brown, Cedric, T.B.	9	215	23.9	t81	2
Thurman, Dennis, Dall.	9	187	20.8	96	0
Allen, Jim, Det.	9	123	13.7	34	0
Ray, Darroll, N.Y.J.	7	227	32.4	t64	2
Pridemore, Tom, Atl.	7	221	31.6	t101	1
Lott, Ronnie, S.F.	7	117	16.7	t41	3
Greene, Ken, St.L.	7	111	15.9	47	0
Harris, Eric, K.C.	7	109	15.6	43	0
Downs, Michael, Dall.	7	81	11.6	25	0
Murphy, Mark, Wash.	7	68	9.7	29	0

TOP TEN KICKOFF RETURNERS

	No	Yards	Avg	Long	TD
Nelms, Mike, Wash.	37	1099	29.7	84	0
Roaches, Carl, Hou.	28	769	27.5	t96	1
Lawrence, Amos, S.F.	17	437	25.7	t92	1
Walker, Fulton, Mia.	38	932	24.5	t90	1
Tullis, Willie, Hou.	32	779	24.3	t95	1
Smith, Reggie, Atl.	47	1143	24.3	52	0
Verser, David, Cin.	29	691	23.8	78	0
Brooks, James, S.D.	40	949	23.7	47	0
Mitchell, Stump, St.L.	55	1292	23.5	67	0
Wilson, Wayne, N.O.	31	722	23.3	57	0

TOP TEN PUNT RETURNERS

	No	FC	Yards	Avg	Long	TD
Irvin, Leroy, L.A.	46	6	615	13.4	t84	3
Brooks, James, S.D.	22	6	290	13.2	42	0
Fisher, Jeff, Chi.	43	20	509	11.8	t88	1
Groth, Jeff, N.O.	37	6	436	11.8	36	0
Johns, Paul, Sea.	16	4	177	11.1	34	0
Nelms, Mike, Wash.	45	1	492	10.9	t75	2
Mitchell, Stump, St.L.	42	0	445	10.6	t50	1
Smith, J.T., K.C.	50	7	528	10.6	62	0
Vigorito, Tommy, Mia.	36	12	379	10.5	t87	1
Anderson, Larry, Pitt.	20	8	208	10.4	33	0

NFL STANDINGS
1921–1981

1921

	W	L	T	Pct.
Chicago Staleys	10	1	1	.909
Buffalo All-Americans	9	1	2	.900
Akron, Ohio, Pros	7	2	1	.778
Green Bay Packers	6	2	2	.750
Canton, Ohio, Bulldogs	4	3	3	.571
Dayton Triangles	4	3	1	.571
Rock Island Independents	5	4	1	.556
Chicago Cardinals	2	3	2	.400
Cleveland Indians	2	6	0	.250
Rochester Jeffersons	2	6	0	.250
Detroit Heralds	1	7	1	.125
Columbus Panhandles	0	6	0	.000
Cincinnati Celts	0	8	0	.000

1922

	W	L	T	Pct.
Canton, Ohio, Bulldogs	10	0	2	1.000
Chicago Bears	9	3	0	.750
Chicago Cardinals	8	3	0	.727
Toledo Maroons	5	2	2	.714
Rock Island Independents	4	2	1	.667
Dayton Triangles	4	3	1	.571
Green Bay Packers	4	3	3	.571
Racine, Wis., Legion	5	4	1	.556
Akron, Ohio, Pros	3	4	2	.429
Buffalo All-Americans	3	4	1	.429
Milwaukee Badgers	2	4	3	.333
Marion, O., Oorang Indians	2	6	0	.250
Minneapolis Marines	1	3	0	.250
Evansville Crimson Giants	0	2	0	.000
Louisville Brecks	0	3	0	.000
Rochester Jeffersons	0	3	1	.000
Hammond, Ind., Pros	0	4	1	.000
Columbus Panhandles	0	7	0	.000

1923

	W	L	T	Pct.
Canton, Ohio, Bulldogs	11	0	1	1.000
Chicago Bears	9	2	1	.818
Green Bay Packers	7	2	1	.778
Milwaukee Badgers	7	2	3	.778
Cleveland Indians	3	1	3	.750
Chicago Cardinals	8	4	0	.667
Duluth Kelleys	4	3	0	.571
Buffalo All-Americans	5	4	3	.556
Columbus Tigers	5	4	1	.556
Racine, Wis., Legion	4	4	2	.500
Toledo Maroons	2	3	2	.400
Rock Island Independents	2	3	3	.400

	W	L	T	Pct.
Minneapolis Marines	2	5	2	.286
St. Louis All-Stars	1	4	2	.200
Hammond, Ind., Pros	1	5	1	.167
Dayton Triangles	1	6	1	.143
Akron, Ohio, Indians	1	6	0	.143
Marion, O., Oorang Indians	1	10	0	.091
Rochester Jeffersons	0	2	0	.000
Louisville Brecks	0	3	0	.000

1924

	W	L	T	Pct.
Cleveland Bulldogs	7	1	1	.875
Chicago Bears	6	1	4	.857
Frankford Yellowjackets	11	2	1	.846
Duluth Kelleys	5	1	0	.833
Rock Island Independents	6	2	2	.750
Green Bay Packers	8	4	0	.667
Buffalo Bisons	6	4	0	.600
Racine, Wis., Legion	4	3	3	.571
Chicago Cardinals	5	4	1	.556
Columbus Tigers	4	4	0	.500
Hammond, Ind., Pros	2	2	1	.500
Milwaukee Badgers	5	8	0	.385
Dayton Triangles	2	7	0	.222
Kansas City Cowboys	2	7	0	.222
Akron, Ohio, Indians	1	6	0	.143
Kenosha, Wis., Maroons	0	5	1	.000
Minneapolis Marines	0	6	0	.000
Rochester Jeffersons	0	7	0	.000

1925

	W	L	T	Pct.
Chicago Cardinals	11	2	1	.846
Pottsville, Pa., Maroons	10	2	0	.833
Detroit Panthers	8	2	2	.800
New York Giants	8	4	0	.667
Akron, Ohio, Indians	4	2	2	.667
Frankford Yellowjackets	13	7	0	.650
Chicago Bears	9	5	3	.643
Rock Island Independents	5	3	3	.625
Green Bay Packers	8	5	0	.615
Providence Steamroller	6	5	1	.545
Canton, Ohio, Bulldogs	4	4	0	.500
Cleveland Bulldogs	5	8	1	.385
Kansas City Cowboys	2	5	1	.286
Hammond, Ind., Pros	1	3	0	.250
Buffalo Bisons	1	6	2	.143
Duluth Kelleys	0	3	0	.000
Rochester Jeffersons	0	6	1	.000
Milwaukee Badgers	0	6	0	.000
Dayton Triangles	0	7	1	.000
Columbus Tigers	0	9	0	.000

1926

	W	L	T	Pct.
Frankford Yellowjackets	14	1	1	.933
Chicago Bears	12	1	3	.923
Pottsville, Pa., Maroons	10	2	1	.833
Kansas City Cowboys	8	3	1	.727
Green Bay Packers	7	3	3	.700
Los Angeles Buccaneers	6	3	1	.667
New York Giants	8	4	1	.667
Duluth Eskimos	6	5	2	.545
Buffalo Rangers	4	4	2	.500
Chicago Cardinals	5	6	1	.455
Providence Steamroller	5	7	0	.417
Detroit Panthers	4	6	2	.400
Hartford Blues	3	7	0	.300
Brooklyn Lions	3	8	0	.273
Milwaukee Badgers	2	7	0	.222
Akron, Ohio, Indians	1	4	3	.200
Dayton Triangles	1	4	1	.200
Racine, Wis., Legion	1	4	0	.200
Columbus Tigers	1	6	0	.143
Canton, Ohio, Bulldogs	1	9	3	.100
Hammond, Ind., Pros	0	4	0	.000
Louisville Colonels	0	4	0	.000

1927

	W	L	T	Pct.
New York Giants	11	1	1	.917
Green Bay Packers	7	2	1	.778
Chicago Bears	9	3	2	.750
Cleveland Bulldogs	8	4	1	.667
Providence Steamroller	8	5	1	.615
New York Yankees	7	8	1	.467
Frankford Yellowjackets	6	9	3	.400
Pottsville, Pa., Maroons	5	8	0	.385
Chicago Cardinals	3	7	1	.300
Dayton Triangles	1	6	1	.143
Duluth Eskimos	1	8	0	.111
Buffalo Bisons	0	5	0	.000

1928

	W	L	T	Pct.
Providence Steamroller	8	1	2	.889
Frankford Yellowjackets	11	3	2	.786
Detroit Wolverines	7	2	1	.778
Green Bay Packers	6	4	3	.600
Chicago Bears	7	5	1	.583
New York Giants	4	7	2	.364
New York Yankees	4	8	1	.333
Pottsville, Pa., Maroons	2	8	0	.200
Chicago Cardinals	1	5	0	.167
Dayton Triangles	0	7	0	.000

1929

	W	L	T	Pct.
Green Bay Packers	12	0	1	1.000
New York Giants	13	1	1	.929
Frankford Yellowjackets	9	4	5	.692
Chicago Cardinals	6	6	1	.500
Boston Bulldogs	4	4	0	.500
Orange, N.J., Tornadoes	3	4	4	.429
Stapleton Stapes	3	4	3	.429
Providence Steamroller	4	6	2	.400
Chicago Bears	4	9	2	.308
Buffalo Bisons	1	7	1	.125
Minneapolis Red Jackets	1	9	0	.100
Dayton Triangles	0	6	0	.000

1930

	W	L	T	Pct.
Green Bay Packers	10	3	1	.769
New York Giants	13	4	0	.765
Chicago Bears	9	4	1	.692
Brooklyn Dodgers	7	4	1	.636
Providence Steamroller	6	4	1	.600
Stapleton Stapes	5	5	2	.500
Chicago Cardinals	5	6	2	.455
Portsmouth, O., Spartans	5	6	3	.455
Frankford Yellowjackets	4	14	1	.222
Minneapolis Red Jackets	1	7	1	.125
Newark Tornadoes	1	10	1	.091

1931

	W	L	T	Pct.
Green Bay Packers	12	2	0	.857
Portsmouth, O., Spartans	11	3	0	.786
Chicago Bears	8	5	0	.615
Chicago Cardinals	5	4	0	.556
New York Giants	7	6	1	.538
Providence Steamroller	4	4	3	.500
Stapleton Stapes	4	6	1	.400
Cleveland Indians	2	8	0	.200
Brooklyn Dodgers	2	12	0	.143
Frankford Yellowjackets	1	6	1	.143

1932

	W	L	T	Pct.
Chicago Bears	7	1	6	.875
Green Bay Packers	10	3	1	.769
Portsmouth, O., Spartans	6	2	4	.750
Boston Braves	4	4	2	.500
New York Giants	4	6	2	.400
Brooklyn Dodgers	3	9	0	.250
Chicago Cardinals	2	6	2	.250
Stapleton Stapes	2	7	3	.222

1933

EASTERN DIVISION

	W	L	T	Pct.	Pts.	OP
N.Y. Giants	11	3	0	.786	244	101
Brooklyn	5	4	1	.556	93	54
Boston	5	5	2	.500	103	97
Philadelphia	3	5	1	.375	77	158
Pittsburgh	3	6	2	.333	67	208

WESTERN DIVISION

	W	L	T	Pct.	Pts.	OP
Chi. Bears	10	2	1	.833	133	82
Portsmouth	6	5	0	.545	128	87
Green Bay	5	7	1	.417	170	107
Cincinnati	3	6	1	.333	38	110
Chi. Cardinals	1	9	1	.100	52	101

NFL Championship: Chicago Bears 23, N.Y. Giants 21

1934

EASTERN DIVISION	W	L	T	Pct.	Pts.	OP
N.Y. Giants	8	5	0	.615	147	107
Boston	6	6	0	.500	107	94
Brooklyn	4	7	0	.364	61	153
Philadelphia	4	7	0	.364	127	85
Pittsburgh	2	10	0	.167	51	206

WESTERN DIVISION	W	L	T	Pct.	Pts.	OP
Chi. Bears	13	0	0	1.000	286	86
Detroit	10	3	0	.769	238	59
Green Bay	7	6	0	.538	156	112
Chi. Cardinals	5	6	0	.455	80	84
St. Louis	1	2	0	.333	27	61
Cincinnati	0	8	0	.000	10	243

NFL Championship: N.Y. Giants 30, Chicago Bears 13

1935

EASTERN DIVISION	W	L	T	Pct.	Pts.	OP
N.Y. Giants	9	3	0	.750	180	96
Brooklyn	5	6	1	.455	90	141
Pittsburgh	4	8	0	.333	100	209
Boston	2	8	1	.200	65	123
Philadelphia	2	9	0	.182	60	179

WESTERN DIVISION	W	L	T	Pct.	Pts.	OP
Detroit	7	3	2	.700	191	111
Green Bay	8	4	0	.667	181	96
Chi. Bears	6	4	2	.600	192	106
Chi. Cardinals	6	4	2	.600	99	97

NFL Championship: Detroit 26, N.Y. Giants 7
One game between Boston and Philadelphia was canceled.

1936

EASTERN DIVISION	W	L	T	Pct.	Pts.	OP
Boston	7	5	0	.583	149	110
Pittsburgh	6	6	0	.500	98	187
N.Y. Giants	5	6	1	.455	115	163
Brooklyn	3	8	1	.273	92	161
Philadelphia	1	11	0	.083	51	206

WESTERN DIVISION	W	L	T	Pct.	Pts.	OP
Green Bay	10	1	1	.909	248	118
Chi. Bears	9	3	0	.750	222	94
Detroit	8	4	0	.667	235	102
Chi. Cardinals	3	8	1	.273	74	143

NFL Championship: Green Bay 21, Boston 6

1937

EASTERN DIVISION	W	L	T	Pct.	Pts.	OP
Washington	8	3	0	.727	195	120
N.Y. Giants	6	3	2	.667	128	109
Pittsburgh	4	7	0	.364	122	145
Brooklyn	3	7	1	.300	82	174
Philadelphia	2	8	1	.200	86	177

WESTERN DIVISION	W	L	T	Pct.	Pts.	OP
Chi. Bears	9	1	1	.900	201	100
Green Bay	7	4	0	.636	220	122
Detroit	7	4	0	.636	180	105
Chi. Cardinals	5	5	1	.500	135	165
Cleveland	1	10	0	.091	75	207

NFL Championship: Washington 28, Chicago Bears 21

1938

EASTERN DIVISION	W	L	T	Pct.	Pts.	OP
N.Y. Giants	8	2	1	.800	194	79
Washington	6	3	2	.667	148	154
Brooklyn	4	4	3	.500	131	161
Philadelphia	5	6	0	.455	154	164
Pittsburgh	2	9	0	.182	79	169

WESTERN DIVISION	W	L	T	Pct.	Pts.	OP
Green Bay	8	3	0	.727	223	118
Detroit	7	4	0	.636	119	108
Chi. Bears	6	5	0	.545	194	148
Cleveland	4	7	0	.364	131	215
Chi. Cardinals	2	9	0	.182	111	168

NFL Championship: N.Y. Giants 23, Green Bay 17

1939

EASTERN DIVISION	W	L	T	Pct.	Pts.	OP
N.Y. Giants	9	1	1	.900	168	85
Washington	8	2	1	.800	242	94
Brooklyn	4	6	1	.400	108	219
Philadelphia	1	9	1	.100	105	200
Pittsburgh	1	9	1	.100	114	216

WESTERN DIVISION	W	L	T	Pct.	Pts.	OP
Green Bay	9	2	0	.818	233	153
Chi. Bears	8	3	0	.727	298	157
Detroit	6	5	0	.545	145	150
Cleveland	5	5	1	.500	195	164
Chi. Cardinals	1	10	0	.091	84	254

NFL Championship: Green Bay 27, N.Y. Giants 0

1940

EASTERN DIVISION	W	L	T	Pct.	Pts.	OP	WESTERN DIVISION	W	L	T	Pct.	Pts.	OP
Washington	9	2	0	.818	245	142	Chi. Bears	8	3	0	.727	238	152
Brooklyn	8	3	0	.727	186	120	Green Bay	6	4	1	.600	238	155
N.Y. Giants	6	4	1	.600	131	133	Detroit	5	5	1	.500	138	153
Pittsburgh	2	7	2	.222	60	178	Cleveland	4	6	1	.400	171	191
Philadelphia	1	10	0	.091	111	211	Chi. Cardinals	2	7	2	.222	139	222

NFL Championship: Chicago Bears 73, Washington 0

1941

EASTERN DIVISION	W	L	T	Pct.	Pts.	OP	WESTERN DIVISION	W	L	T	Pct.	Pts.	OP
N.Y. Giants	8	3	0	.727	238	114	Chi. Bears	10	1	0	.909	396	147
Brooklyn	7	4	0	.636	158	127	Green Bay	10	1	0	.909	258	120
Washington	6	5	0	.545	176	174	Detroit	4	6	1	.400	121	195
Philadelphia	2	8	1	.200	119	218	Chi. Cardinals	3	7	1	.300	127	197
Pittsburgh	1	9	1	.100	103	276	Cleveland	2	9	0	.182	116	244

Western Division playoff: Chicago Bears 33, Green Bay 14
NFL Championship: Chicago Bears 37, N.Y. Giants 9

1942

EASTERN DIVISION	W	L	T	Pct.	Pts.	OP	WESTERN DIVISION	W	L	T	Pct.	Pts.	OP
Washington	10	1	0	.909	227	102	Chi. Bears	11	0	0	1.000	376	84
Pittsburgh	7	4	0	.636	167	119	Green Bay	8	2	1	.800	300	215
N.Y. Giants	5	5	1	.500	155	139	Cleveland	5	6	0	.455	150	207
Brooklyn	3	8	0	.273	100	168	Chi. Cardinals	3	8	0	.273	98	209
Philadelphia	2	9	0	.182	134	239	Detroit	0	11	0	.000	38	263

NFL Championship: Washington 14, Chicago Bears 6

1943

EASTERN DIVISION	W	L	T	Pct.	Pts.	OP	WESTERN DIVISION	W	L	T	Pct.	Pts.	OP
Washington	6	3	1	.667	229	137	Chi. Bears	8	1	1	.889	303	157
N.Y. Giants	6	3	1	.667	197	170	Green Bay	7	2	1	.778	264	172
Phil-Pitt	5	4	1	.556	225	230	Detroit	3	6	1	.333	178	218
Brooklyn	2	8	0	.200	65	234	Chi. Cardinals	0	10	0	.000	95	238

Eastern Division playoff: Washington 28, N.Y. Giants 0
NFL Championship: Chicago Bears 41, Washington 21

1944

EASTERN DIVISION	W	L	T	Pct.	Pts.	OP	WESTERN DIVISION	W	L	T	Pct.	Pts.	OP
N.Y. Giants	8	1	1	.889	206	75	Green Bay	8	2	0	.800	238	141
Philadelphia	7	1	2	.875	267	131	Chi. Bears	6	3	1	.667	258	172
Washington	6	3	1	.667	169	180	Detroit	6	3	1	.667	216	151
Boston	2	8	0	.200	82	233	Cleveland	4	6	0	.400	188	224
Brooklyn	0	10	0	.000	69	166	Card-Pitt	0	10	0	.000	108	328

NFL Championship: Green Bay 14, N.Y. Giants 7

1945

EASTERN DIVISION	W	L	T	Pct.	Pts.	OP	WESTERN DIVISION	W	L	T	Pct.	Pts.	OP
Washington	8	2	0	.800	209	121	Cleveland	9	1	0	.900	244	136
Philadelphia	7	3	0	.700	272	133	Detroit	7	3	0	.700	195	194
N.Y. Giants	3	6	1	.333	179	198	Green Bay	6	4	0	.600	258	173
Boston	3	6	1	.333	123	211	Chi. Bears	3	7	0	.300	192	235
Pittsburgh	2	8	0	.200	79	220	Chi. Cardinals	1	9	0	.100	98	228

NFL Championship: Cleveland 15, Washington 14

1946

EASTERN DIVISION

	W	L	T	Pct.	Pts.	OP
N.Y. Giants	7	3	1	.700	236	162
Philadelphia	6	5	0	.545	231	220
Washington	5	5	1	.500	171	191
Pittsburgh	5	5	1	.500	136	117
Boston	2	8	1	.200	189	273

WESTERN DIVISION

	W	L	T	Pct.	Pts.	OP
Chi. Bears	8	2	1	.800	289	193
Los Angeles	6	4	1	.600	277	257
Green Bay	6	5	0	.545	148	158
Chi. Cardinals	6	5	0	.545	260	198
Detroit	1	10	0	.091	142	310

NFL Championship: Chicago Bears 24, N.Y. Giants 14

1947

EASTERN DIVISION

	W	L	T	Pct.	Pts.	OP
Philadelphia	8	4	0	.667	308	242
Pittsburgh	8	4	0	.667	240	259
Boston	4	7	1	.364	168	256
Washington	4	8	0	.333	295	367
N.Y. Giants	2	8	2	.200	190	309

WESTERN DIVISION

	W	L	T	Pct.	Pts.	OP
Chi. Cardinals	9	3	0	.750	306	231
Chi. Bears	8	4	0	.667	363	241
Green Bay	6	5	1	.545	274	210
Los Angeles	6	6	0	.500	259	214
Detroit	3	9	0	.250	231	305

Eastern Division playoff: Philadelphia 21, Pittsburgh 0
NFL Championship: Chicago Cardinals 28, Philadelphia 21

1948

EASTERN DIVISION

	W	L	T	Pct.	Pts.	OP
Philadelphia	9	2	1	.818	376	156
Washington	7	5	0	.583	291	287
N.Y. Giants	4	8	0	.333	297	388
Pittsburgh	4	8	0	.333	200	243
Boston	3	9	0	.250	174	372

WESTERN DIVISION

	W	L	T	Pct.	Pts.	OP
Chi. Cardinals	11	1	0	.917	395	226
Chi. Bears	10	2	0	.833	375	151
Los Angeles	6	5	1	.545	327	269
Green Bay	3	9	0	.250	154	290
Detroit	2	10	0	.167	200	407

NFL Championship: Philadelphia 7, Chicago Cardinals 0

1949

EASTERN DIVISION

	W	L	T	Pct.	Pts.	OP
Philadelphia	11	1	0	.917	364	134
Pittsburgh	6	5	1	.545	224	214
N.Y. Giants	6	6	0	.500	287	298
Washington	4	7	1	.364	268	339
N.Y. Bulldogs	1	10	1	.091	153	368

WESTERN DIVISION

	W	L	T	Pct.	Pts.	OP
Los Angeles	8	2	2	.800	360	239
Chi. Bears	9	3	0	.750	332	218
Chi. Cardinals	6	5	1	.545	360	301
Detroit	4	8	0	.333	237	259
Green Bay	2	10	0	.167	114	329

NFL Championship: Philadelphia 14, Los Angeles 0

1950

AMERICAN CONFERENCE

	W	L	T	Pct.	Pts.	OP
Cleveland	10	2	0	.833	310	144
N.Y. Giants	10	2	0	.833	268	150
Philadelphia	6	6	0	.500	254	141
Pittsburgh	6	6	0	.500	180	195
Chi. Cardinals	5	7	0	.417	233	287
Washington	3	9	0	.250	232	326

NATIONAL CONFERENCE

	W	L	T	Pct.	Pts.	OP
Los Angeles	9	3	0	.750	466	309
Chi. Bears	9	3	0	.750	279	207
N.Y. Yanks	7	5	0	.583	366	367
Detroit	6	6	0	.500	321	285
Green Bay	3	9	0	.250	244	406
San Francisco	3	9	0	.250	213	300
Baltimore	1	11	0	.083	213	462

American Conference playoff: Cleveland 8, N.Y. Giants 3
National Conference playoff: Los Angeles 24, Chicago Bears 14
NFL Championship: Cleveland 30, Los Angeles 28

1951

AMERICAN CONFERENCE

	W	L	T	Pct.	Pts.	OP
Cleveland	11	1	0	.917	349	152
N.Y. Giants	9	2	1	.818	254	161
Washington	5	7	0	.417	183	296
Pittsburgh	4	7	1	.364	183	235
Philadelphia	4	8	0	.333	234	264
Chi. Cardinals	3	9	0	.250	210	287

NATIONAL CONFERENCE

	W	L	T	Pct.	Pts.	OP
Los Angeles	8	4	0	.667	392	261
Detroit	7	4	1	.636	336	259
San Francisco	7	4	1	.636	255	205
Chi. Bears	7	5	0	.583	286	282
Green Bay	3	9	0	.250	254	375
N.Y. Yanks	1	9	2	.100	241	382

NFL Championship: Los Angeles 24, Cleveland 17

1952

AMERICAN CONFERENCE

	W	L	T	Pct.	Pts.	OP
Cleveland	8	4	0	.667	310	213
N.Y. Giants	7	5	0	.583	234	231
Philadelphia	7	5	0	.583	252	271
Pittsburgh	5	7	0	.417	300	273
Chi. Cardinals	4	8	0	.333	172	221
Washington	4	8	0	.333	240	287

NATIONAL CONFERENCE

	W	L	T	Pct.	Pts.	OP
Detroit	9	3	0	.750	344	192
Los Angeles	9	3	0	.750	349	234
San Francisco	7	5	0	.583	285	221
Green Bay	6	6	0	.500	295	312
Chi. Bears	5	7	0	.417	245	326
Dallas	1	11	0	.083	182	427

National Conference playoff: Detroit 31, Los Angeles 21

NFL Championship: Detroit 17, Cleveland 7

1953

EASTERN CONFERENCE

	W	L	T	Pct.	Pts.	OP
Cleveland	11	1	0	.917	348	162
Philadelphia	7	4	1	.636	352	215
Washington	6	5	1	.545	208	215
Pittsburgh	6	6	0	.500	211	263
N.Y. Giants	3	9	0	.250	179	277
Chi. Cardinals	1	10	1	.091	190	337

WESTERN CONFERENCE

	W	L	T	Pct.	Pts.	OP
Detroit	10	2	0	.833	271	205
San Francisco	9	3	0	.750	372	237
Los Angeles	8	3	1	.727	366	236
Chi. Bears	3	8	1	.273	218	262
Baltimore	3	9	0	.250	182	350
Green Bay	2	9	1	.182	200	338

NFL Championship: Detroit 17, Cleveland 16

1954

EASTERN CONFERENCE

	W	L	T	Pct.	Pts.	OP
Cleveland	9	3	0	.750	336	162
Philadelphia	7	4	1	.636	284	230
N.Y. Giants	7	5	0	.583	293	184
Pittsburgh	5	7	0	.417	219	263
Washington	3	9	0	.250	207	432
Chi. Cardinals	2	10	0	.167	183	347

WESTERN CONFERENCE

	W	L	T	Pct.	Pts.	OP
Detroit	9	2	1	.818	337	189
Chi. Bears	8	4	0	.667	301	279
San Francisco	7	4	1	.636	313	251
Los Angeles	6	5	1	.545	314	285
Green Bay	4	8	0	.333	234	251
Baltimore	3	9	0	.250	131	279

NFL Championship: Cleveland 56, Detroit 10

1955

EASTERN CONFERENCE

	W	L	T	Pct.	Pts.	OP
Cleveland	9	2	1	.818	349	218
Washington	8	4	0	.667	246	222
N.Y. Giants	6	5	1	.545	267	223
Chi. Cardinals	4	7	1	.364	224	252
Philadelphia	4	7	1	.364	248	231
Pittsburgh	4	8	0	.333	195	285

WESTERN CONFERENCE

	W	L	T	Pct.	Pts.	OP
Los Angeles	8	3	1	.727	260	231
Chi. Bears	8	4	0	.667	294	251
Green Bay	6	6	0	.500	258	276
Baltimore	5	6	1	.455	214	239
San Francisco	4	8	0	.333	216	298
Detroit	3	9	0	.250	230	275

NFL Championship: Cleveland 38, Los Angeles 14

1956

EASTERN CONFERENCE

	W	L	T	Pct.	Pts.	OP
N.Y. Giants	8	3	1	.727	264	197
Chi. Cardinals	7	5	0	.583	240	182
Washington	6	6	0	.500	183	225
Cleveland	5	7	0	.417	167	177
Pittsburgh	5	7	0	.417	217	250
Philadelphia	3	8	1	.273	143	215

WESTERN CONFERENCE

	W	L	T	Pct.	Pts.	OP
Chi. Bears	9	2	1	.818	363	246
Detroit	9	3	0	.750	300	188
San Francisco	5	6	1	.455	233	284
Baltimore	5	7	0	.417	270	322
Green Bay	4	8	0	.333	264	342
Los Angeles	4	8	0	.333	291	307

NFL Championship: N.Y. Giants 47, Chicago Bears 7

1957

EASTERN CONFERENCE

	W	L	T	Pct.	Pts.	OP
Cleveland	9	2	1	.818	269	172
N.Y. Giants	7	5	0	.583	254	211
Pittsburgh	6	6	0	.500	161	178
Washington	5	6	1	.455	251	230
Philadelphia	4	8	0	.333	173	230
Chi. Cardinals	3	9	0	.250	200	299

WESTERN CONFERENCE

	W	L	T	Pct.	Pts.	OP
Detroit	8	4	0	.667	251	231
San Francisco	8	4	0	.667	260	264
Baltimore	7	5	0	.583	303	235
Los Angeles	6	6	0	.500	307	278
Chi. Bears	5	7	0	.417	203	211
Green Bay	3	9	0	.250	218	311

Western Conference playoff: Detroit 31, San Francisco 27
NFL Championship: Detroit 59, Cleveland 14

1958

EASTERN CONFERENCE

	W	L	T	Pct.	Pts.	OP
N.Y. Giants	9	3	0	.750	246	183
Cleveland	9	3	0	.750	302	217
Pittsburgh	7	4	1	.636	261	230
Washington	4	7	1	.364	214	268
Chi. Cardinals	2	9	1	.182	261	356
Philadelphia	2	9	1	.182	235	306

WESTERN CONFERENCE

	W	L	T	Pct.	Pts.	OP
Baltimore	9	3	0	.750	381	203
Chi. Bears	8	4	0	.667	298	230
Los Angeles	8	4	0	.667	344	278
San Francisco	6	6	0	.500	257	324
Detroit	4	7	1	.364	261	276
Green Bay	1	10	1	.091	193	382

Eastern Conference playoff: N.Y. Giants 10, Cleveland 0
NFL Championship: Baltimore 23, N.Y. Giants 17, sudden-death overtime

1959

EASTERN CONFERENCE

	W	L	T	Pct.	Pts.	OP
N.Y. Giants	10	2	0	.833	284	170
Cleveland	7	5	0	.583	270	214
Philadelphia	7	5	0	.583	268	278
Pittsburgh	6	5	1	.545	257	216
Washington	3	9	0	.250	185	350
Chi. Cardinals	2	10	0	.167	234	324

WESTERN CONFERENCE

	W	L	T	Pct.	Pts.	OP
Baltimore	9	3	0	.750	374	251
Chi. Bears	8	4	0	.667	252	196
Green Bay	7	5	0	.583	248	246
San Francisco	7	5	0	.583	255	237
Detroit	3	8	1	.273	203	275
Los Angeles	2	10	0	.167	242	315

NFL Championship: Baltimore 31, N.Y. Giants 16

1960 AFL

EASTERN DIVISION

	W	L	T	Pct.	Pts.	OP
Houston	10	4	0	.714	379	285
N.Y. Titans	7	7	0	.500	382	399
Buffalo	5	8	1	.385	296	303
Boston	5	9	0	.357	286	349

WESTERN DIVISION

	W	L	T	Pct.	Pts.	OP
L.A. Chargers	10	4	0	.714	373	336
Dall. Texans	8	6	0	.571	362	253
Oakland	6	8	0	.429	319	388
Denver	4	9	1	.308	309	393

AFL Championship: Houston 24, L.A. Chargers 16

1960 NFL

EASTERN CONFERENCE

	W	L	T	Pct.	Pts.	OP
Philadelphia	10	2	0	.833	321	246
Cleveland	8	3	1	.727	362	217
N.Y. Giants	6	4	2	.600	271	261
St. Louis	6	5	1	.545	288	230
Pittsburgh	5	6	1	.455	240	275
Washington	1	9	2	.100	178	309

WESTERN CONFERENCE

	W	L	T	Pct.	Pts.	OP
Green Bay	8	4	0	.667	332	209
Detroit	7	5	0	.583	239	212
San Francisco	7	5	0	.583	208	205
Baltimore	6	6	0	.500	288	234
Chicago	5	6	1	.455	194	299
L.A. Rams	4	7	1	.364	265	297
Dall. Cowboys	0	11	1	.000	177	369

NFL Championship: Philadelphia 17, Green Bay 13

1961 AFL

EASTERN DIVISION

	W	L	T	Pct.	Pts.	OP
Houston	10	3	1	.769	513	242
Boston	9	4	1	.692	413	313
N.Y. Titans	7	7	0	.500	301	390
Buffalo	6	8	0	.429	294	342

WESTERN DIVISION

	W	L	T	Pct.	Pts.	OP
San Diego	12	2	0	.857	396	219
Dall. Texans	6	8	0	.429	334	343
Denver	3	11	0	.214	251	432
Oakland	2	12	0	.143	237	458

AFL Championship: Houston 10, San Diego 3

1961 NFL

EASTERN CONFERENCE

	W	L	T	Pct.	Pts.	OP
N.Y. Giants	10	3	1	.769	368	220
Philadelphia	10	4	0	.714	361	297
Cleveland	8	5	1	.615	319	270
St. Louis	7	7	0	.500	279	267
Pittsburgh	6	8	0	.429	295	287
Dall. Cowboys	4	9	1	.308	236	380
Washington	1	12	1	.077	174	392

WESTERN CONFERENCE

	W	L	T	Pct.	Pts.	OP
Green Bay	11	3	0	.786	391	223
Detroit	8	5	1	.615	270	258
Baltimore	8	6	0	.571	302	307
Chicago	8	6	0	.571	326	302
San Francisco	7	6	1	.538	346	272
Los Angeles	4	10	0	.286	263	333
Minnesota	3	11	0	.214	285	407

NFL Championship: Green Bay 37, N.Y. Giants 0

1962 AFL

EASTERN DIVISION

	W	L	T	Pct.	Pts.	OP
Houston	11	3	0	.786	387	270
Boston	9	4	1	.692	346	295
Buffalo	7	6	1	.538	309	272
N.Y. Titans	5	9	0	.357	278	423

WESTERN DIVISION

	W	L	T	Pct.	Pts.	OP
Dall. Texans	11	3	0	.786	389	233
Denver	7	7	0	.500	353	334
San Diego	4	10	0	.286	314	392
Oakland	1	13	0	.071	213	370

AFL Championship: Dallas Texans 20, Houston 17, sudden-death overtime

1962 NFL

EASTERN CONFERENCE

	W	L	T	Pct.	Pts.	OP
N.Y. Giants	12	2	0	.857	398	283
Pittsburgh	9	5	0	.643	312	363
Cleveland	7	6	1	.538	291	257
Washington	5	7	2	.417	305	376
Dall. Cowboys	5	8	1	.385	398	402
St. Louis	4	9	1	.308	287	361
Philadelphia	3	10	1	.231	282	356

WESTERN CONFERENCE

	W	L	T	Pct.	Pts.	OP
Green Bay	13	1	0	.929	415	148
Detroit	11	3	0	.786	315	177
Chicago	9	5	0	.643	321	287
Baltimore	7	7	0	.500	293	288
San Francisco	6	8	0	.429	282	331
Minnesota	2	11	1	.154	254	410
Los Angeles	1	12	1	.077	220	334

NFL Championship: Green Bay 16, N.Y. Giants 7

1963 AFL

EASTERN DIVISION

	W	L	T	Pct.	Pts.	OP
Boston	7	6	1	.538	317	257
Buffalo	7	6	1	.538	304	291
Houston	6	8	0	.429	302	372
N.Y. Jets	5	8	1	.385	249	399

WESTERN DIVISION

	W	L	T	Pct.	Pts.	OP
San Diego	11	3	0	.786	399	255
Oakland	10	4	0	.714	363	282
Kansas City	5	7	2	.417	347	263
Denver	2	11	1	.154	301	473

Eastern Division playoff: Boston 26, Buffalo 8
AFL Championship: San Diego 51, Boston 10

1963 NFL

EASTERN CONFERENCE

	W	L	T	Pct.	Pts.	OP
N.Y. Giants	11	3	0	.786	448	280
Cleveland	10	4	0	.714	343	262
St. Louis	9	5	0	.643	341	283
Pittsburgh	7	4	3	.636	321	295
Dallas	4	10	0	.286	305	378
Washington	3	11	0	.214	279	398
Philadelphia	2	10	2	.167	242	381

WESTERN CONFERENCE

	W	L	T	Pct.	Pts.	OP
Chicago	11	1	2	.917	301	144
Green Bay	11	2	1	.846	369	206
Baltimore	8	6	0	.571	316	285
Detroit	5	8	1	.385	326	265
Minnesota	5	8	1	.385	309	390
Los Angeles	5	9	0	.357	210	350
San Francisco	2	12	0	.143	198	391

NFL Championship: Chicago 14, N.Y. Giants 10

1964 AFL

EASTERN DIVISION

	W	L	T	Pct.	Pts.	OP
Buffalo	12	2	0	.857	400	242
Boston	10	3	1	.769	365	297
N.Y. Jets	5	8	1	.385	278	315
Houston	4	10	0	.286	310	355

WESTERN DIVISION

	W	L	T	Pct.	Pts.	OP
San Diego	8	5	1	.615	341	300
Kansas City	7	7	0	.500	366	306
Oakland	5	7	2	.417	303	350
Denver	2	11	1	.154	240	438

AFL Championship: Buffalo 20, San Diego 7

1964 NFL

EASTERN CONFERENCE

	W	L	T	Pct.	Pts.	OP
Cleveland	10	3	1	.769	415	293
St. Louis	9	3	2	.750	357	331
Philadelphia	6	8	0	.429	312	313
Washington	6	8	0	.429	307	305
Dallas	5	8	1	.385	250	289
Pittsburgh	5	9	0	.357	253	315
N.Y. Giants	2	10	2	.167	241	399

WESTERN CONFERENCE

	W	L	T	Pct.	Pts.	OP
Baltimore	12	2	0	.857	428	225
Green Bay	8	5	1	.615	342	245
Minnesota	8	5	1	.615	355	296
Detroit	7	5	2	.583	280	260
Los Angeles	5	7	2	.417	283	339
Chicago	5	9	0	.357	260	379
San Francisco	4	10	0	.286	236	330

NFL Championship: Cleveland 27, Baltimore 0

1965 AFL

EASTERN DIVISION

	W	L	T	Pct.	Pts.	OP
Buffalo	10	3	1	.769	313	226
N.Y. Jets	5	8	1	.385	285	303
Boston	4	8	2	.333	244	302
Houston	4	10	0	.286	298	429

WESTERN DIVISION

	W	L	T	Pct.	Pts.	OP
San Diego	9	2	3	.818	340	227
Oakland	8	5	1	.615	298	239
Kansas City	7	5	2	.583	322	285
Denver	4	10	0	.286	303	392

AFL Championship: Buffalo 23, San Diego 0

1965 NFL

EASTERN CONFERENCE

	W	L	T	Pct.	Pts.	OP
Cleveland	11	3	0	.786	363	325
Dallas	7	7	0	.500	325	280
N.Y. Giants	7	7	0	.500	270	338
Washington	6	8	0	.429	257	301
Philadelphia	5	9	0	.357	363	359
St. Louis	5	9	0	.357	296	309
Pittsburgh	2	12	0	.143	202	397

WESTERN CONFERENCE

	W	L	T	Pct.	Pts.	OP
Green Bay	10	3	1	.769	316	224
Baltimore	10	3	1	.769	389	284
Chicago	9	5	0	.643	409	275
San Francisco	7	6	1	.538	421	402
Minnesota	7	7	0	.500	383	403
Detroit	6	7	1	.462	257	295
Los Angeles	4	10	0	.286	269	328

Western Conference playoff: Green Bay 13, Baltimore 10, sudden-death overtime

NFL Championship: Green Bay 23, Cleveland 12

1966 AFL

EASTERN DIVISION

	W	L	T	Pct.	Pts.	OP
Buffalo	9	4	1	.692	358	255
Boston	8	4	2	.667	315	283
N.Y. Jets	6	6	2	.500	322	312
Houston	3	11	0	.214	335	396
Miami	3	11	0	.214	213	362

WESTERN DIVISION

	W	L	T	Pct.	Pts.	OP
Kansas City	11	2	1	.846	448	276
Oakland	8	5	1	.615	315	288
San Diego	7	6	1	.538	335	284
Denver	4	10	0	.286	196	381

AFL Championship: Kansas City 31, Buffalo 7

1966 NFL

EASTERN CONFERENCE

	W	L	T	Pct.	Pts.	OP
Dallas	10	3	1	.769	445	239
Cleveland	9	5	0	.643	403	259
Philadelphia	9	5	0	.643	326	340
St. Louis	8	5	1	.615	264	265
Washington	7	7	0	.500	351	355
Pittsburgh	5	8	1	.385	316	347
Atlanta	3	11	0	.214	204	437
N.Y. Giants	1	12	1	.077	263	501

WESTERN CONFERENCE

	W	L	T	Pct.	Pts.	OP
Green Bay	12	2	0	.857	335	163
Baltimore	9	5	0	.643	314	226
Los Angeles	8	6	0	.571	289	212
San Francisco	6	6	2	.500	320	325
Chicago	5	7	2	.417	234	272
Detroit	4	9	1	.308	206	317
Minnesota	4	9	1	.308	292	304

NFL Championship: Green Bay 34, Dallas 27

Super Bowl I: Green Bay (NFL) 35, Kansas City (AFL) 10

1967 AFL

EASTERN DIVISION	W	L	T	Pct.	Pts.	OP
Houston	9	4	1	.692	258	199
N.Y. Jets	8	5	1	.615	371	329
Buffalo	4	10	0	.286	237	285
Miami	4	10	0	.286	219	407
Boston	3	10	1	.231	280	389

WESTERN DIVISION	W	L	T	Pct.	Pts.	OP
Oakland	13	1	0	.929	468	238
Kansas City	9	5	0	.643	408	254
San Diego	8	5	1	.615	360	352
Denver	3	11	0	.214	256	409

AFL Championship: Oakland 40, Houston 7

1967 NFL

EASTERN CONFERENCE

Capitol Division	W	L	T	Pct.	Pts.	OP
Dallas	9	5	0	.643	342	268
Philadelphia	6	7	1	.462	351	409
Washington	5	6	3	.455	347	353
New Orleans	3	11	0	.214	233	379

WESTERN CONFERENCE

Coastal Division	W	L	T	Pct.	Pts.	OP
Los Angeles	11	1	2	.917	398	196
Baltimore	11	1	2	.917	394	198
San Francisco	7	7	0	.500	273	337
Atlanta	1	12	1	.077	175	422

Century Division	W	L	T	Pct.	Pts.	OP
Cleveland	9	5	0	.643	334	297
N.Y. Giants	7	7	0	.500	369	379
St. Louis	6	7	1	.462	333	356
Pittsburgh	4	9	1	.308	281	320

Central Division	W	L	T	Pct.	Pts.	OP
Green Bay	9	4	1	.692	332	209
Chicago	7	6	1	.538	239	218
Detroit	5	7	2	.417	260	259
Minnesota	3	8	3	.273	233	294

Conference Championships: Dallas 52, Cleveland 14; Green Bay 28, Los Angeles 7
NFL Championship: Green Bay 21, Dallas 17
Super Bowl II: Green Bay (NFL) 33, Oakland (AFL) 14

1968 AFL

EASTERN DIVISION	W	L	T	Pct.	Pts.	OP
N.Y. Jets	11	3	0	.786	419	280
Houston	7	7	0	.500	303	248
Miami	5	8	1	.385	276	355
Boston	4	10	0	.286	229	406
Buffalo	1	12	1	.077	199	367

WESTERN DIVISION	W	L	T	Pct.	Pts.	OP
Oakland	12	2	0	.857	453	233
Kansas City	12	2	0	.857	371	170
San Diego	9	5	0	.643	382	310
Denver	5	9	0	.357	255	404
Cincinnati	3	11	0	.214	215	329

Western Division playoff: Oakland 41, Kansas City 6
AFL Championship: N.Y. Jets 27, Oakland 23

1968 NFL

EASTERN CONFERENCE

Capitol Division	W	L	T	Pct.	Pts.	OP
Dallas	12	2	0	.857	431	186
N.Y. Giants	7	7	0	.500	294	325
Washington	5	9	0	.357	249	358
Philadelphia	2	12	0	.143	202	351

WESTERN CONFERENCE

Coastal Division	W	L	T	Pct.	Pts.	OP
Baltimore	13	1	0	.929	402	144
Los Angeles	10	3	1	.769	312	200
San Francisco	7	6	1	.538	303	310
Atlanta	2	12	0	.143	170	389

Century Division	W	L	T	Pct.	Pts.	OP
Cleveland	10	4	0	.714	394	273
St. Louis	9	4	1	.692	325	289
New Orleans	4	9	1	.308	246	327
Pittsburgh	2	11	1	.154	244	397

Central Division	W	L	T	Pct.	Pts.	OP
Minnesota	8	6	0	.571	282	242
Chicago	7	7	0	.500	250	333
Green Bay	6	7	1	.462	281	227
Detroit	4	8	2	.333	207	241

Conference Championships: Cleveland 31, Dallas 20; Baltimore 24, Minnesota 14
NFL Championship: Baltimore 34, Cleveland 0
Super Bowl III: N.Y. Jets (AFL) 16, Baltimore (NFL) 7

1969 AFL

EASTERN DIVISION

	W	L	T	Pct.	Pts.	OP
N.Y. Jets	10	4	0	.714	353	269
Houston	6	6	2	.500	278	279
Boston	4	10	0	.286	266	316
Buffalo	4	10	0	.286	230	359
Miami	3	10	1	.231	233	332

WESTERN DIVISION

	W	L	T	Pct.	Pts.	OP
Oakland	12	1	1	.923	377	242
Kansas City	11	3	0	.786	359	177
San Diego	8	6	0	.571	288	276
Denver	5	8	1	.385	297	344
Cincinnati	4	9	1	.308	280	367

Divisional playoffs: Kansas City 13, N.Y. Jets 6; Oakland 56, Houston 7
AFL Championship: Kansas City 17, Oakland 7

1969 NFL

EASTERN CONFERENCE
Capitol Division

	W	L	T	Pct.	Pts.	OP
Dallas	11	2	1	.846	369	223
Washington	7	5	2	.583	307	319
New Orleans	5	9	0	.357	311	393
Philadelphia	4	9	1	.308	279	377

WESTERN CONFERENCE
Coastal Division

	W	L	T	Pct.	Pts.	OP
Los Angeles	11	3	0	.786	320	243
Baltimore	8	5	1	.615	279	268
Atlanta	6	8	0	.429	276	268
San Francisco	4	8	2	.333	277	319

Century Division

	W	L	T	Pct.	Pts.	OP
Cleveland	10	3	1	.769	351	300
N.Y. Giants	6	8	0	.429	264	298
St. Louis	4	9	1	.308	314	389
Pittsburgh	1	13	0	.071	218	404

Central Division

	W	L	T	Pct.	Pts.	OP
Minnesota	12	2	0	.857	379	133
Detroit	9	4	1	.692	259	188
Green Bay	8	6	0	.571	269	221
Chicago	1	13	0	.071	210	339

Conference Championships: Cleveland 38, Dallas 14; Minnesota 23, Los Angeles 20
NFL Championship: Minnesota 27, Cleveland 7
Super Bowl IV: Kansas City (AFL) 23, Minnesota (NFL) 7

1970

AMERICAN CONFERENCE
Eastern Division

	W	L	T	Pct.	Pts.	OP
Baltimore	11	2	1	.846	321	234
Miami*	10	4	0	.714	297	228
N.Y. Jets	4	10	0	.286	255	286
Buffalo	3	10	1	.231	204	337
Boston	2	12	0	.143	149	361

NATIONAL CONFERENCE
Eastern Division

	W	L	T	Pct.	Pts.	OP
Dallas	10	4	0	.714	299	221
N.Y. Giants	9	5	0	.643	301	270
St. Louis	8	5	1	.615	325	228
Washington	6	8	0	.429	297	314
Philadelphia	3	10	1	.231	241	332

Central Division

	W	L	T	Pct.	Pts.	OP
Cincinnati	8	6	0	.571	312	255
Cleveland	7	7	0	.500	286	265
Pittsburgh	5	9	0	.357	210	272
Houston	3	10	1	.231	217	352

Central Division

	W	L	T	Pct.	Pts.	OP
Minnesota	12	2	0	.857	335	143
Detroit*	10	4	0	.714	347	202
Chicago	6	8	0	.429	256	261
Green Bay	6	8	0	.429	196	293

Western Division

	W	L	T	Pct.	Pts.	OP
Oakland	8	4	2	.667	300	293
Kansas City	7	5	2	.583	272	244
San Diego	5	6	3	.455	282	278
Denver	5	8	1	.385	253	264

Western Division

	W	L	T	Pct.	Pts.	OP
San Francisco	10	3	1	.769	352	267
Los Angeles	9	4	1	.692	325	202
Atlanta	4	8	2	.333	206	261
New Orleans	2	11	1	.154	172	347

*Wild Card qualifier for playoffs
Divisional playoffs: Baltimore 17, Cincinnati 0; Oakland 21, Miami 14
AFC Championship: Baltimore 27, Oakland 17
Divisional playoffs: Dallas 5, Detroit 0; San Francisco 17, Minnesota 14
NFC Championship: Dallas 17, San Francisco 10
Super Bowl V: Baltimore (AFC) 16, Dallas (NFC) 13

1971

AMERICAN CONFERENCE

Eastern Division

	W	L	T	Pct.	Pts.	OP
Miami	10	3	1	.769	315	174
Baltimore*	10	4	0	.714	313	140
New England	6	8	0	.429	238	325
N.Y. Jets	6	8	0	.429	212	299
Buffalo	1	13	0	.071	184	394

Central Division

	W	L	T	Pct.	Pts.	OP
Cleveland	9	5	0	.643	285	273
Pittsburgh	6	8	0	.429	246	292
Houston	4	9	1	.308	251	330
Cincinnati	4	10	0	.286	284	265

Western Division

	W	L	T	Pct.	Pts.	OP
Kansas City	10	3	1	.769	302	208
Oakland	8	4	2	.667	344	278
San Diego	6	8	0	.429	311	341
Denver	4	9	1	.308	203	275

NATIONAL CONFERENCE

Eastern Division

	W	L	T	Pct.	Pts.	OP
Dallas	11	3	0	.786	406	222
Washington*	9	4	1	.692	276	190
Philadelphia	6	7	1	.462	221	302
St. Louis	4	9	1	.308	231	279
N.Y. Giants	4	10	0	.286	228	362

Central Division

	W	L	T	Pct.	Pts.	OP
Minnesota	11	3	0	.786	245	139
Detroit	7	6	1	.538	341	286
Chicago	6	8	0	.429	185	276
Green Bay	4	8	2	.333	274	298

Western Division

	W	L	T	Pct.	Pts.	OP
San Francisco	9	5	0	.643	300	216
Los Angeles	8	5	1	.615	313	260
Atlanta	7	6	1	.538	274	277
New Orleans	4	8	2	.333	266	347

*Wild Card qualifier for playoffs
Divisional playoffs: Miami 27, Kansas City 24, sudden-death overtime; Baltimore 20, Cleveland 3
AFC Championship: Miami 21, Baltimore 0
Divisional playoffs: Dallas 20, Minnesota 12; San Francisco 24, Washington 20
NFC Championship: Dallas 14, San Francisco 3
Super Bowl VI: Dallas (NFC) 24, Miami (AFC) 3

1972

AMERICAN CONFERENCE

Eastern Division

	W	L	T	Pct.	Pts.	OP
Miami	14	0	0	1.000	385	171
N.Y. Jets	7	7	0	.500	367	324
Baltimore	5	9	0	.357	235	252
Buffalo	4	9	1	.321	257	377
New England	3	11	0	.214	192	446

Central Division

	W	L	T	Pct.	Pts.	OP
Pittsburgh	11	3	0	.786	343	175
Cleveland*	10	4	0	.714	268	249
Cincinnati	8	6	0	.571	299	229
Houston	1	13	0	.071	164	380

Western Division

	W	L	T	Pct.	Pts.	OP
Oakland	10	3	1	.750	365	248
Kansas City	8	6	0	.571	287	254
Denver	5	9	0	.357	325	350
San Diego	4	9	1	.321	264	344

NATIONAL CONFERENCE

Eastern Division

	W	L	T	Pct.	Pts.	OP
Washington	11	3	0	.786	336	218
Dallas*	10	4	0	.714	319	240
N.Y. Giants	8	6	0	.571	331	247
St. Louis	4	9	1	.321	193	303
Philadelphia	2	11	1	.179	145	352

Central Division

	W	L	T	Pct.	Pts.	OP
Green Bay	10	4	0	.714	304	226
Detroit	8	5	1	.607	339	290
Minnesota	7	7	0	.500	301	252
Chicago	4	9	1	.321	225	275

Western Division

	W	L	T	Pct.	Pts.	OP
San Francisco	8	5	1	.607	353	249
Atlanta	7	7	0	.500	269	274
Los Angeles	6	7	1	.464	291	286
New Orleans	2	11	1	.179	215	361

*Wild Card qualifier for playoffs
Divisional playoffs: Pittsburgh 13, Oakland 7; Miami 20, Cleveland 14
AFC Championship: Miami 21, Pittsburgh 17
Divisional playoffs: Dallas 30, San Francisco 28; Washington 16, Green Bay 3
NFC Championship: Washington 26, Dallas 3
Super Bowl VII: Miami (AFC) 14, Washington (NFC) 7

1973

AMERICAN CONFERENCE

Eastern Division

	W	L	T	Pct.	Pts.	OP
Miami	12	2	0	.857	343	150
Buffalo	9	5	0	.643	259	230
New England	5	9	0	.357	258	300
Baltimore	4	10	0	.286	226	341
N.Y. Jets	4	10	0	.286	240	306

Central Division

	W	L	T	Pct.	Pts.	OP
Cincinnati	10	4	0	.714	286	231
Pittsburgh*	10	4	0	.714	347	210
Cleveland	7	5	2	.571	234	255
Houston	1	13	0	.071	199	447

Western Division

	W	L	T	Pct.	Pts.	OP
Oakland	9	4	1	.679	292	175
Denver	7	5	2	.571	354	296
Kansas City	7	5	2	.571	231	192
San Diego	2	11	1	.179	188	386

NATIONAL CONFERENCE

Eastern Division

	W	L	T	Pct.	Pts.	OP
Dallas	10	4	0	.714	382	203
Washington*	10	4	0	.714	325	198
Philadelphia	5	8	1	.393	310	393
St. Louis	4	9	1	.321	286	365
N.Y. Giants	2	11	1	.179	226	362

Central Division

	W	L	T	Pct.	Pts.	OP
Minnesota	12	2	0	.857	296	168
Detroit	6	7	1	.464	271	247
Green Bay	5	7	2	.429	202	259
Chicago	3	11	0	.214	195	334

Western Division

	W	L	T	Pct.	Pts.	OP
Los Angeles	12	2	0	.857	388	178
Atlanta	9	5	0	.643	318	224
New Orleans	5	9	0	.357	163	312
San Francisco	5	9	0	.357	262	319

*Wild Card qualifier for playoffs
Divisional playoffs: Oakland 33, Pittsburgh 14; Miami 34, Cincinnati 16
AFC Championship: Miami 27, Oakland 10
Divisional playoffs: Minnesota 27, Washington 20; Dallas 27, Los Angeles 16
NFC Championship: Minnesota 27, Dallas 10
Super Bowl VIII: Miami (AFC) 24, Minnesota (NFC) 7

1974

AMERICAN CONFERENCE

Eastern Division

	W	L	T	Pct.	Pts.	OP
Miami	11	3	0	.786	327	216
Buffalo*	9	5	0	.643	264	244
New England	7	7	0	.500	348	289
N.Y. Jets	7	7	0	.500	279	300
Baltimore	2	12	0	.143	190	329

Central Division

	W	L	T	Pct.	Pts.	OP
Pittsburgh	10	3	1	.750	305	189
Cincinnati	7	7	0	.500	283	259
Houston	7	7	0	.500	236	282
Cleveland	4	10	0	.286	251	344

Western Division

	W	L	T	Pct.	Pts.	OP
Oakland	12	2	0	.857	355	228
Denver	7	6	1	.536	302	294
Kansas City	5	9	0	.357	233	293
San Diego	5	9	0	.357	212	285

NATIONAL CONFERENCE

Eastern Division

	W	L	T	Pct.	Pts.	OP
St. Louis	10	4	0	.714	285	218
Washington*	10	4	0	.714	320	196
Dallas	8	6	0	.571	297	235
Philadelphia	7	7	0	.500	242	217
N.Y. Giants	2	12	0	.143	195	299

Central Division

	W	L	T	Pct.	Pts.	OP
Minnesota	10	4	0	.714	310	195
Detroit	7	7	0	.500	256	270
Green Bay	6	8	0	.429	210	206
Chicago	4	10	0	.286	152	279

Western Division

	W	L	T	Pct.	Pts.	OP
Los Angeles	10	4	0	.714	263	181
San Francisco	6	8	0	.429	226	236
New Orleans	5	9	0	.357	166	263
Atlanta	3	11	0	.214	111	271

*Wild Card qualifier for playoffs
Divisional playoffs: Oakland 28, Miami 26; Pittsburgh 32, Buffalo 14
AFC Championship: Pittsburgh 24, Oakland 13
Divisional playoffs: Minnesota 30, St. Louis 14; Los Angeles 19, Washington 10
NFC Championship: Minnesota 14, Los Angeles 10
Super Bowl IX: Pittsburgh (AFC) 16, Minnesota (NFC) 6

1975

AMERICAN CONFERENCE

Eastern Division

	W	L	T	Pct.	Pts.	OP
Baltimore	10	4	0	.714	395	269
Miami	10	4	0	.714	357	222
Buffalo	8	6	0	.571	420	355
New England	3	11	0	.214	258	358
N.Y. Jets	3	11	0	.214	258	433

Central Division

	W	L	T	Pct.	Pts.	OP
Pittsburgh	12	2	0	.857	373	162
Cincinnati*	11	3	0	.786	340	246
Houston	10	4	0	.714	293	226
Cleveland	3	11	0	.214	218	372

Western Division

	W	L	T	Pct.	Pts.	OP
Oakland	11	3	0	.786	375	255
Denver	6	8	0	.429	254	307
Kansas City	5	9	0	.357	282	341
San Diego	2	12	0	.143	189	345

NATIONAL CONFERENCE

Eastern Division

	W	L	T	Pct.	Pts.	OP
St. Louis	11	3	0	.786	356	276
Dallas*	10	4	0	.714	350	268
Washington	8	6	0	.571	325	276
N.Y. Giants	5	9	0	.357	216	306
Philadelphia	4	10	0	.286	225	302

Central Division

	W	L	T	Pct.	Pts.	OP
Minnesota	12	2	0	.857	377	180
Detroit	7	7	0	.500	245	262
Chicago	4	10	0	.286	191	379
Green Bay	4	10	0	.286	226	285

Western Division

	W	L	T	Pct.	Pts.	OP
Los Angeles	12	2	0	.857	312	135
San Francisco	5	9	0	.357	255	286
Atlanta	4	10	0	.286	240	289
New Orleans	2	12	0	.143	165	360

*Wild Card qualifier for playoffs
Divisional playoffs: Pittsburgh 28, Baltimore 10; Oakland 31, Cincinnati 28
AFC Championship: Pittsburgh 16, Oakland 10
Divisional playoffs: Los Angeles 35, St. Louis 23; Dallas 17, Minnesota 14
NFC Championship: Dallas 37, Los Angeles 7
Super Bowl X: Pittsburgh (AFC) 21, Dallas (NFC) 17

1976

AMERICAN CONFERENCE

Eastern Division

	W	L	T	Pct.	Pts.	OP
Baltimore	11	3	0	.786	417	246
New England*	11	3	0	.786	376	236
Miami	6	8	0	.429	263	264
N.Y. Jets	3	11	0	.214	169	383
Buffalo	2	12	0	.143	245	363

Central Division

	W	L	T	Pct.	Pts.	OP
Pittsburgh	10	4	0	.714	342	138
Cincinnati	10	4	0	.714	335	210
Cleveland	9	5	0	.643	267	287
Houston	5	9	0	.357	222	273

Western Division

	W	L	T	Pct.	Pts.	OP
Oakland	13	1	0	.929	350	237
Denver	9	5	0	.643	315	206
San Diego	6	8	0	.429	248	285
Kansas City	5	9	0	.357	290	376
Tampa Bay	0	14	0	.000	125	412

NATIONAL CONFERENCE

Eastern Division

	W	L	T	Pct.	Pts.	OP
Dallas	11	3	0	.786	296	194
Washington*	10	4	0	.714	291	217
St. Louis	10	4	0	.714	309	267
Philadelphia	4	10	0	.286	165	286
N.Y. Giants	3	11	0	.214	170	250

Central Division

	W	L	T	Pct.	Pts.	OP
Minnesota	11	2	1	.821	305	176
Chicago	7	7	0	.500	253	216
Detroit	6	8	0	.429	262	220
Green Bay	5	9	0	.357	218	299

Western Division

	W	L	T	Pct.	Pts.	OP
Los Angeles	10	3	1	.750	351	190
San Francisco	8	6	0	.571	270	190
Atlanta	4	10	0	.286	172	312
New Orleans	4	10	0	.286	253	346
Seattle	2	12	0	.143	229	429

*Wild Card qualifier for playoffs
Divisional playoffs: Oakland 24, New England 21; Pittsburgh 40, Baltimore 14
AFC Championship: Oakland 24, Pittsburgh 7
Divisional playoffs: Minnesota 35, Washington 20; Los Angeles 14, Dallas 12
NFC Championship: Minnesota 24, Los Angeles 13
Super Bowl XI: Oakland (AFC) 32, Minnesota (NFC) 14

1977

AMERICAN CONFERENCE

Eastern Division

	W	L	T	Pct.	Pts.	OP
Baltimore	10	4	0	.714	295	221
Miami	10	4	0	.714	313	197
New England	9	5	0	.643	278	217
N.Y. Jets	3	11	0	.214	191	300
Buffalo	3	11	0	.214	160	313

Central Division

	W	L	T	Pct.	Pts.	OP
Pittsburgh	9	5	0	.643	283	243
Houston	8	6	0	.571	299	230
Cincinnati	8	6	0	.571	238	235
Cleveland	6	8	0	.429	269	267

Western Division

	W	L	T	Pct.	Pts.	OP
Denver	12	2	0	.857	274	148
Oakland*	11	3	0	.786	351	230
San Diego	7	7	0	.500	222	205
Seattle	5	9	0	.357	282	373
Kansas City	2	12	0	.143	225	349

NATIONAL CONFERENCE

Eastern Division

	W	L	T	Pct.	Pts.	OP
Dallas	12	2	0	.857	345	212
Washington	9	5	0	.643	196	189
St. Louis	7	7	0	.500	272	287
Philadelphia	5	9	0	.357	220	207
N.Y. Giants	5	9	0	.357	181	265

Central Division

	W	L	T	Pct.	Pts.	OP
Minnesota	9	5	0	.643	231	227
Chicago*	9	5	0	.643	255	253
Detroit	6	8	0	.429	183	252
Green Bay	4	10	0	.286	134	219
Tampa Bay	2	12	0	.143	103	223

Western Division

	W	L	T	Pct.	Pts.	OP
Los Angeles	10	4	0	.714	302	146
Atlanta	7	7	0	.500	179	129
San Francisco	5	9	0	.357	220	260
New Orleans	3	11	0	.214	232	336

*Wild Card qualifier for playoffs
Divisional playoffs: Denver 34, Pittsburgh 21; Oakland 37, Baltimore 31, sudden-death overtime
AFC Championship: Denver 20, Oakland 17
Divisional playoffs: Dallas 37, Chicago 7; Minnesota 14, Los Angeles 7
NFC Championship: Dallas 23, Minnesota 6
Super Bowl XII: Dallas (NFC) 27, Denver (AFC) 10

1978

AMERICAN CONFERENCE

Eastern Division

	W	L	T	Pct.	Pts.	OP
New England	11	5	0	.688	358	286
Miami*	11	5	0	.688	372	254
N.Y. Jets	8	8	0	.500	359	364
Buffalo	5	11	0	.313	302	354
Baltimore	5	11	0	.313	239	421

Central Division

	W	L	T	Pct.	Pts.	OP
Pittsburgh	14	2	0	.875	356	195
Houston*	10	6	0	.625	283	298
Cleveland	8	8	0	.500	334	356
Cincinnati	4	12	0	.250	252	284

Western Division

	W	L	T	Pct.	Pts.	OP
Denver	10	6	0	.625	282	198
Oakland	9	7	0	.563	311	283
Seattle	9	7	0	.563	345	358
San Diego	9	7	0	.563	355	309
Kansas City	4	12	0	.250	243	327

NATIONAL CONFERENCE

Eastern Division

	W	L	T	Pct.	Pts.	OP
Dallas	12	4	0	.750	384	208
Philadelphia*	9	7	0	.563	270	250
Washington	8	8	0	.500	273	283
St. Louis	6	10	0	.375	248	296
N.Y. Giants	6	10	0	.375	264	298

Central Division

	W	L	T	Pct.	Pts.	OP
Minnesota	8	7	1	.531	294	306
Green Bay	8	7	1	.531	249	269
Detroit	7	9	0	.438	290	300
Chicago	7	9	0	.438	253	274
Tampa Bay	5	11	0	.313	241	259

Western Division

	W	L	T	Pct.	Pts.	OP
Los Angeles	12	4	0	.750	316	245
Atlanta*	9	7	0	.563	240	290
New Orleans	7	9	0	.438	281	298
San Francisco	2	14	0	.125	219	350

*Wild Card qualifier for playoffs
First-round playoff: Houston 17, Miami 9
Divisional playoffs: Houston 31, New England 14; Pittsburgh 33, Denver 10
AFC Championship: Pittsburgh 34, Houston 5
First-round playoff: Atlanta 14, Philadelphia 13
Divisional playoffs: Dallas 27, Atlanta 20; Los Angeles 34, Minnesota 10
NFC Championship: Dallas 28, Los Angeles 0
Super Bowl XIII: Pittsburgh (AFC) 35, Dallas (NFC) 31

1979

AMERICAN CONFERENCE

Eastern Division

	W	L	T	Pct.	Pts.	OP
Miami	10	6	0	.625	341	257
New England	9	7	0	.563	411	326
N.Y. Jets	8	8	0	.500	337	383
Buffalo	7	9	0	.438	268	279
Baltimore	5	11	0	.313	271	351

Central Division

	W	L	T	Pct.	Pts.	OP
Pittsburgh	12	4	0	.750	416	262
Houston*	11	5	0	.688	362	331
Cleveland	9	7	0	.563	359	352
Cincinnati	4	12	0	.250	337	421

Western Division

	W	L	T	Pct.	Pts.	OP
San Diego	12	4	0	.750	411	246
Denver*	10	6	0	.625	289	262
Seattle	9	7	0	.563	378	372
Oakland	9	7	0	.563	365	337
Kansas City	7	9	0	.438	238	262

NATIONAL CONFERENCE

Eastern Division

	W	L	T	Pct.	Pts.	OP
Dallas	11	5	0	.688	371	313
Philadelphia*	11	5	0	.688	339	282
Washington	10	6	0	.625	348	295
N.Y. Giants	6	10	0	.375	237	323
St. Louis	5	11	0	.313	307	358

Central Division

	W	L	T	Pct.	Pts.	OP
Tampa Bay	10	6	0	.625	273	237
Chicago*	10	6	0	.625	306	249
Minnesota	7	9	0	.438	259	337
Green Bay	5	11	0	.313	246	316
Detroit	2	14	0	.125	219	365

Western Division

	W	L	T	Pct.	Pts.	OP
Los Angeles	9	7	0	.563	323	309
New Orleans	8	8	0	.500	370	360
Atlanta	6	10	0	.375	300	388
San Francisco	2	14	0	.125	308	416

*Wild Card qualifier for playoffs
First-round playoff: Houston 13, Denver 7
Divisional playoffs: Houston 17, San Diego 14; Pittsburgh 34, Miami 14
AFC Championship: Pittsburgh 27, Houston 13
First-round playoff: Philadelphia 27, Chicago 17
Divisional playoffs: Tampa Bay 24, Philadelphia 17; Los Angeles 21, Dallas 19
NFC Championship: Los Angeles 9, Tampa Bay 0
Super Bowl XIV: Pittsburgh (AFC) 31, Los Angeles (NFC) 19

1980

AMERICAN CONFERENCE

Eastern Division

	W	L	T	Pct.	Pts.	OP
Buffalo	11	5	0	.688	320	260
New England	10	6	0	.625	441	325
Miami	8	8	0	.500	266	305
Baltimore	7	9	0	.438	355	387
N.Y. Jets	4	12	0	.250	302	395

Central Division

	W	L	T	Pct.	Pts.	OP
Cleveland	11	5	0	.688	357	310
Houston*	11	5	0	.688	295	251
Pittsburgh	9	7	0	.563	352	313
Cincinnati	6	10	0	.375	244	312

Western Division

	W	L	T	Pct.	Pts.	OP
San Diego	11	5	0	.688	418	327
Oakland*	11	5	0	.688	364	306
Kansas City	8	8	0	.500	319	336
Denver	8	8	0	.500	310	323
Seattle	4	12	0	.250	291	408

NATIONAL CONFERENCE

Eastern Division

	W	L	T	Pct.	Pts.	OP
Philadelphia	12	4	0	.750	384	222
Dallas*	12	4	0	.750	454	311
Washington	6	10	0	.375	261	293
St. Louis	5	11	0	.313	299	350
N.Y. Giants	4	12	0	.250	249	425

Central Division

	W	L	T	Pct.	Pts.	OP
Minnesota	9	7	0	.563	317	308
Detroit	9	7	0	.563	334	272
Chicago	7	9	0	.437	304	264
Tampa Bay	5	10	1	.343	271	341
Green Bay	5	10	1	.343	231	371

Western Division

	W	L	T	Pct.	Pts.	OP
Atlanta	12	4	0	.750	405	272
Los Angeles*	11	5	0	.688	424	289
San Francisco	6	10	0	.375	320	415
New Orleans	1	15	0	.063	291	487

*Wild Card qualifier for playoffs
First-round playoff: Oakland 27, Houston 7
Divisional playoffs: San Diego 20, Buffalo 14; Oakland 14, Cleveland 12
AFC Championship: Oakland 34, San Diego 27
First-round playoff: Dallas 34, Los Angeles 13
Divisional playoffs: Philadelphia 31, Minnesota 16; Dallas 30, Atlanta 27
NFC Championship: Philadelphia 20, Dallas 7
Super Bowl XV: Oakland (AFC) 27, Philadelphia (NFC) 10

1981

AMERICAN CONFERENCE
Eastern Division

	W	L	T	Pct.	Pts.	OP
Miami	11	4	1	.719	345	275
N.Y. Jets*	10	5	1	.656	355	287
Buffalo*	10	6	0	.625	311	276
Baltimore	2	14	0	.125	259	533
New England	2	14	0	.125	322	370

Central Division

	W	L	T	Pct.	Pts.	OP
Cincinnati	12	4	0	.750	421	304
Pittsburgh	8	8	0	.500	356	297
Houston	7	9	0	.438	281	355
Cleveland	5	11	0	.313	276	375

Western Division

	W	L	T	Pct.	Pts.	OP
San Diego	10	6	0	.625	478	390
Denver	10	6	0	.625	321	289
Kansas City	9	7	0	.563	343	290
Oakland	7	9	0	.438	273	343
Seattle	6	10	0	.375	322	388

NATIONAL CONFERENCE
Eastern Division

	W	L	T	Pct.	Pts.	OP
Dallas	12	4	0	.750	367	277
Philadelphia*	10	6	0	.625	368	221
N.Y. Giants*	9	7	0	.563	295	257
Washington	8	8	0	.500	347	349
St. Louis	7	9	0	.438	315	408

Central Division

	W	L	T	Pct.	Pts.	OP
Tampa Bay	9	7	0	.563	315	268
Detroit	8	8	0	.500	397	322
Green Bay	8	8	0	.500	324	361
Minnesota	7	9	0	.438	325	369
Chicago	6	10	0	.375	253	324

Western Division

	W	L	T	Pct.	Pts.	OP
San Francisco	13	3	0	.813	357	250
Atlanta	7	9	0	.438	426	355
Los Angeles	6	10	0	.375	303	351
New Orleans	4	12	0	.250	207	378

*Wild card qualifier for playoffs

First-round playoff: Buffalo 31, N.Y. Jets 27
Divisional playoffs: San Diego 41, Miami 38 (OT); Cincinnati 28, Buffalo 21
AFC Championship: Cincinnati 27, San Diego 7
First-round playoff: N.Y. Giants 27, Philadelphia 21
Divisional playoffs: Dallas 38, Tampa Bay 0; San Francisco 38, N.Y. Giants 24
NFC Championship: San Francisco 28, Dallas 27
Super Bowl XVI: San Francisco (NFC) 26, Cincinnati (AFC) 21

1982 NFL DRAFT

Player	Order No.	Pos.	College	Club	Round
Abercrombie, Walter	12	RB	Baylor	Pittsburgh	1
Abraham, Robert	77	LB	North Carolina State	Houston	3
Allen, Gary	148	RB	Hawaii	Houston	6
Allen, Marcus	10	RB	Southern California	Oakland	1
Andersen, Morten	86	K	Michigan State	New Orleans	4
Anderson, Gary	171	K	Syracuse	Buffalo	7
Anderson, Stuart	104	LB	Virginia	Kansas City	4
Armstrong, Harvey	190	DT	Southern Methodist	Philadelphia	7
Atha, Bob	317	K	Ohio State	St. Louis	12
Atkins, Kelvin	212	LB	Illinois	Tampa Bay	8
Austin, Craig	258	LB	South Dakota	Seattle	10
Babb, Mike	115	C	Texas	Cleveland	5
Bailey, Stacey	63	WR	San Jose State	Atlanta	3
Baker, Milton	227	TE	West Texas State	Cleveland	9
Baldinger, Rich	270	T	Wake Forest	New York Giants	10
Baldwin, Keith	31	DE	Texas A&M	Cleveland	2
Banks, Chip	3	LB	Southern California	Cleveland	1
Barbian, Tim	279	DT	Western Illinois	San Francisco	10
Barnes, Roosevelt	266	LB	Purdue	Detroit	10
Barrett, Dave	103	RB	Houston	Tampa Bay	4
Barnett, Doug	118	DE	Azusa Pacific	Los Angeles	5
Bates, Phil	175	RB	Nebraska	Detroit	7
Beach, Pat	140	TE	Washington State	Baltimore	6
Bechtold, Bill	67	C	Oklahoma	Los Angeles	3
Becker, Kurt	146	G	Michigan	Chicago	6
Bedford, Vance	119	DB	Texas	St. Louis	5
Bell, Jerry	74	TE	Arizona State	Tampa Bay	3
Bennett, James	250	WR	N.W. Louisiana	Cincinnati	9
Berryhill, Tony	225	C	Clemson	Baltimore	9
Bingham, Craig	167	LB	Syracuse	Pittsburgh	7
Boatner, Mack	248	RB	S.E. Louisiana	Miami	9
Boliaux, Guy	283	LB	Wisconsin	Chicago	11
Boures, Emil	182	C	Pittsburgh	Pittsburgh	7
Bowser, Charles	108	LB	Duke	Miami	4
Boyd, Thomas	210	LB	Alabama	Green Bay	8
Bradley, Matt	234	DB	Penn State	Houston	9
Brodsky, Larry	268	WR	Miami	Kansas City	10
Brown, Reggie	95	RB	Oregon	Atlanta	4
Brown, Robert	98	LB	Virginia Tech	Green Bay	4
Bryant, Jeff	6	DE	Clemson	Seattle	1
Bryant, Steve	94	WR	Purdue	Houston	4
Buford, Maury	215	P	Texas Tech	San Diego	8
Burroughs, Jim	57	DB	Michigan State	Baltimore	3
Burtness, Rich	332	G	Montana	Dallas	12
Byford, Lyndle	241	T	Oklahoma	Kansas City	9

Player	Order No.	Pos.	College	Club	Round
ampbell, Jack	144	T	Utah	Seattle	6
ampbell, Jim	287	TE	Kentucky	Houston	11
annon, John	83	DE	William & Mary	Tampa Bay	3
arlstrom, Tom	330	G	Nebraska	New York Jets	12
arpenter, Brian	101	DB	Michigan	Dallas	4
arter, Bob	297	WR	Arizona	Kansas City	11
hivers, De Wayne	160	TE	South Carolina	Buffalo	6
lancy, Sam	284	DE	Pittsburgh	Seattle	11
lark, Brian	253	K	Florida	New England	10
lark, Brian	327	G	Clemson	Denver	12
lark, Bryan	251	QB	Michigan State	San Francisco	9
lark, Steve	239	DE	Utah	Miami	9
offey, Ken	226	DB	S.W. Texas State	Washington	9
offman, Ricky	285	WR	UCLA	Los Angeles	11
oley, Raymond	312	DT	Alabama A&M	Los Angeles	12
ollins, Glen	26	DE	Mississippi State	Cincinnati	1
ollins, Ken	197	LB	Washington State	New England	8
ooks, Johnie	2	LB	Mississippi State	Baltimore	1
oombs, Tom	191	TE	Idaho	New York Jets	7
ooper, Chester	201	WR	Minnesota	Seattle	8
owan, Larry	192	RB	Jackson State	Miami	7
rable, Bob	23	LB	Notre Dame	New York Jets	1
raft, Donnie	314	RB	Louisville	Houston	12
rouch, Terry	113	G	Oklahoma	Baltimore	5
rum, Gary	303	T	Wyoming	Miami	11
rump, George	85	DE	East Carolina	New England	4
rutchfield, Dwayne	79	RB	Iowa State	New York Jets	3
ailey, Darnell	232	LB	Maryland	St. Louis	9
allafior, Ken	124	T	Minnesota	Pittsburgh	5
'Amico, Rich	263	LB	Penn State	Oakland	10
aniels, Calvin	46	LB	North Carolina	Kansas City	2
aniels, Terry	265	DB	Tennessee	Washington	10
aum, Charles	165	DT	Cal Poly-SLO	Dallas	6
avis, Jeff	128	LB	Clemson	Tampa Bay	5
avis, Russell	305	RB	Idaho	Cincinnati	11
ean, Vernon	49	DB	San Diego State	Washington	2
e Bruijn, Case	214	P-K	Idaho State	Kansas City	8
eery, Tom	252	DB	Widener	Baltimore	10
De Vaughan, Dennis	132	DB	Bishop	Philadelphia	5
iana, Richard	136	RB	Yale	Miami	5
oerger, Jerry	200	LB	Wisconsin	Chicago	8
oig, Steve	69	LB	New Hampshire	Detroit	3
uckett, Ken	68	WR	Wake Forest	New Orleans	3
uper, Mark	52	WR	N.W. Louisiana	Miami	2
berhardt, Ricky	203	DB	Morris Brown	Atlanta	8
ckerson, Todd	277	T	North Carolina State	Dallas	10
delman, Brad	30	C	Missouri	New Orleans	2
dwards, Dennis	245	DT	Southern California	Buffalo	9
dwards, Stan	72	RB	Michigan	Houston	3
liopulos, Jim	81	LB	Wyoming	Dallas	3
lliott, Tony	114	DE	North Texas State	New Orleans	5
pps, Phillip	321	WR	Texas Christian	Green Bay	12
ahnhorst, Jim	92	LB	Minnesota	Minnesota	4
arrell, Sean	17	G	Penn State	Tampa Bay	1
eraday, Dan	333	QB	Toronto	Cincinnati	12
errari, Ron	195	LB	Illinois	San Francisco	7
errell, Earl	125	RB	East Tennessee	St. Louis	5
isher, Robin	271	LB	Florida	Miami	10
loyd, George	107	DB	Eastern Kentucky	New York Jets	4

Player	Order No.	Pos.	College	Club	Round
Floyd, Ricky	255	RB	Southern Mississippi	Cleveland	
Foster, Roy	24	G	Southern California	Miami	
Fritzsche, Jim	217	T	Purdue	Philadelphia	
Galloway, David	38	DT	Florida	St. Louis	
Garcia, Eddie	264	K	Southern Methodist	Green Bay	
Gary, Joe	249	DT	UCLA	Dallas	
Gaylord, Jeff	88	LB	Missouri	Los Angeles	
Gentry, Dennis	89	RB	Baylor	Chicago	
Gibson, Gary	306	LB	Arizona	San Francisco	
Goff, Jeff	322	LB	Arkansas	Washington	
Goodlow, Eugene	66	WR	Kansas State	New Orleans	
Goodson, John	209	P	Texas	Pittsburgh	
Graham, William	127	DB	Texas	Detroit	
Grieve, Curtis	159	WR	Yale	Philadelphia	
Griggs, Anthony	105	LB	Ohio State	Philadelphia	
Guilbeau, Rusty	73	DT	McNeese State	St. Louis	
Haley, Darryl	55	G	Utah	New England	
Hall, Hollis	188	DB	Clemson	San Diego	
Hallstrom, Ron	22	G	Iowa	Green Bay	
Hammond, Ken	143	G	Vanderbilt	Dallas	
Hancock, Anthony	11	WR	Tennessee	Kansas City	
Harmon, Kirk	206	LB	Pacific	Minnesota	
Hartnett, Perry	116	G	Southern Methodist	Chicago	
Hatchett, Mike	230	DB	Texas	Chicago	
Haynes, Louis	100	LB	North Texas State	Kansas City	
Heflin, Van	204	TE	Vanderbilt	Cleveland	
Hemphill, Darryl	275	DB	West Texas State	New York Jets	
Hester, Ron	164	LB	Florida State	Miami	
Higgins, John	240	DB	Nevada-Las Vegas	New York Giants	
Hill, Rod	25	DB	Kentucky State	Dallas	
Hirn, Mike	236	TE	Central Michigan	Pittsburgh	
Hogue, Larry	278	DB	Utah State	Cincinnati	
Holly, Bob	291	QB	Princeton	Washington	
Holman, Rodney	82	TE	Tulane	Cincinnati	
Horan, Mike	235	P	Cal State-Long Beach	Atlanta	
Howard, Bryan	233	DB	Tennessee State	Minnesota	
Hubble, Robert	213	TE	Rice	New York Giants	
Hughes, Al	320	DE	Western Michigan	Pittsburgh	
Hunter, Monty	109	DB	Salem, W. Va.	Dallas	
Ingram, Brian	111	LB	Tennessee	New England	
Ingram, Ron	301	WR	Oklahoma	Philadelphia	
Jackson, Bill	211	DB	North Carolina	Cleveland	
Jackson, Ed	123	LB	Louisiana Tech	Oakland	
Jackson, Jeff	177	DE	Toledo	Oakland	
James, Vic	272	DB	Colorado	Buffalo	
Jeffers, Lemont	153	LB	Tennessee	Washington	
Jefferson, David	228	LB	Miami	Seattle	
Jenkins, Fletcher	169	DT	Washington	Baltimore	
Jerue, Mark	135	LB	Washington	New York Jets	
Johnson, Dan	170	TE	Iowa State	Miami	
Jones, A.J.	202	RB	Texas	Los Angeles	
Jones, Cedric	56	WR	Duke	New England	
Jones, Wayne	276	T	Utah	Miami	1
Jordan, Steve	179	TE	Brown	Minnesota	
Kab, Vyto	78	TE	Penn State	Philadelphia	
Kafentzis, Mark	199	DB	Hawaii	Cleveland	
Kalil, Frank	298	G	Arizona	Buffalo	

Player	Order No.	Pos.	College	Club	Round
Keller, Jeff	288	WR	Washington	Atlanta	11
Kelley, Mike	149	QB	Georgia Tech	Atlanta	6
Kersten, Wally	117	T	Minnesota	Los Angeles	5
King, Arthur	166	DT	Grambling	Cincinnati	6
Klever, Rocky	247	RB	Montana	New York Jets	9
Kofler, Matt	48	QB	San Diego State	Buffalo	2
Krimm, John	76	DB	Notre Dame	New Orleans	3
Lane, Bob	242	QB	N.E. Louisiana	Tampa Bay	9
Lankford, Paul	80	DB	Penn State	Miami	3
Laster, Don	309	T	Tennessee State	Washington	12
Lee, Edward	292	WR	South Carolina State	Detroit	11
Levenick, Dave	315	LB	Wisconsin	Atlanta	12
Lewis, Marvin	142	RB	Tulane	New Orleans	6
Lewis, Rodney	58	DB	Nebraska	New Orleans	3
Liebenstein, Todd	99	DE	Nevada-Las Vegas	Washington	4
Lindstrom, Chris	205	DT	Boston University	St. Louis	8
Locklin, Kerry	145	TE	New Mexico State	Los Angeles	6
Loia, Tony	196	G	Arizona State	Baltimore	8
Lucear, Gerald	260	WR	Temple	Minnesota	10
Luck, Oliver	44	QB	West Virginia	Houston	2
Lyles, Warren	246	DT	Alabama	San Diego	9
Macaulay, John	294	C	Stanford	Green Bay	11
Machurek, Mike	154	QB	Idaho State	Detroit	6
Mansfield, Von	122	DB	Wisconsin	Atlanta	5
Marion, Fred	112	DB	Miami	New England	5
Marve, Eugene	59	LB	Saginaw Valley	Buffalo	3
Mc Daniel, Orlando	50	WR	Louisiana State	Denver	2
Mc Elroy, Reggie	51	T	West Texas State	New York Jets	2
Mc Elroy, Vann	64	DB	Baylor	Oakland	3
Mc Gill, Eddie	259	TE	Western Carolina	St. Louis	10
Mc Lemore, Dana	269	KR	Hawaii	San Francisco	10
Mc Mahon, Jim	5	QB	Brigham Young	Chicago	1
Mc Norton, Bruce	96	DB	Georgetown, Ky.	Detroit	4
Mc Pherson, Miles	256	DB	New Haven College	Los Angeles	10
Meacham, Lamont	280	DB	Western Kentucky	Baltimore	11
Meade, Mike	126	RB	Penn State	Green Bay	5
Merriweather, Mike	70	LB	Pacific	Pittsburgh	3
Metzelaars, Pete	75	TE	Wabash	Seattle	3
Meyer, John	43	T	Arizona State	Pittsburgh	2
Michuta, Steve	282	QB	Grand Valley State	Cleveland	11
Miller, Dan	281	K	Miami	Washington	11
Miller, Mike	324	DB	S.W. Texas State	Kansas City	12
Milner, Hobson	318	RB	Cincinnati	Minnesota	12
Morris, Joe	45	RB	Syracuse	New York Giants	2
Morris, Tom	185	DB	Michigan State	Tampa Bay	7
Morton, Michael	325	KR	Nevada-Las Vegas	Tampa Bay	12
Moss, Martin	208	DE	UCLA	Detroit	8
Munchak, Mike	8	G	Penn State	Houston	1
Muransky, Ed	91	T	Michigan	Oakland	4
Murdock, Kelvin	224	WR	Troy State	New England	9
Naylor, Frank	311	C	Rutgers	Seattle	12
Needham, Ben	194	LB	Michigan	Cincinnati	7
Nelson, Bob	120	DT	Miami	Miami	5
Nelson, Darrin	7	RB	Stanford	Minnesota	1
Nelson, Edmund	172	DT	Auburn	Pittsburgh	7
Nicholson, Darrell	156	LB	North Carolina	New York Giants	6
Nicolas, Scott	310	LB	Miami	Cleveland	6
Pagel, Mike	84	QB	Arizona State	Baltimore	4
Parlavecchio, Chet	152	LB	Penn State	Green Bay	6

Player	Order No.	Pos.	College	Club	Round
Parmelee, Perry	302	WR	Santa Clara	New York Jets	11
Paris, Bubba	29	T	Michigan	San Francisco	2
Peoples, George	216	RB	Auburn	Dallas	8
Perko, Mike	155	DT	Utah	Pittsburgh	6
Perrin, Benny	65	DB	Alabama	St. Louis	3
Phea, Lonell	163	WR	Houston	New York Jets	6
Plater, Dan	106	WR	Brigham Young	Denver	4
Porter, Ricky	319	RB	Slippery Rock, Pa.	Detroit	12
Powell, Carl	61	WR	Jackson State	Washington	3
Pozderac, Phil	137	T	Notre Dame	Dallas	5
Purifoy, Bill	193	DE	Tulsa	Dallas	7
Quick, Mike	20	WR	North Carolina State	Philadelphia	1
Randle, Tate	220	DB	Texas Tech	Miami	8
Raymond, Gerry	102	G	Boston College	New York Giants	4
Redden, Barry	14	RB	Richmond	Los Angeles	1
Reese, Booker	32	DE	Bethune-Cookman	Tampa Bay	2
Reeves, Ron	261	QB	Texas Tech	Houston	10
Reilly, Mike	207	DE	Oklahoma	Los Angeles	8
Riggins, Charles	237	DE	Bethune-Cookman	Green Bay	9
Riggs, Gerald	9	RB	Arizona State	Atlanta	1
Robbins, Tootie	90	T	East Carolina	St. Louis	4
Roberts, Jeff	168	LB	Tulane	New England	7
Rodrique, Mike	331	WR	Miami	Miami	12
Rogers, Del	71	RB	Utah	Green Bay	3
Rogers, Doug	36	DE	Stanford	Atlanta	2
Rohrer, Jeff	53	LB	Yale	Dallas	2
Romano, Jim	37	C	Penn State	Oakland	2
Roquemore, Durwood	157	DB	Texas A&I	Kansas City	6
Rouse, Curtis	286	G	Tennessee-Chattanooga	Minnesota	11
Ruben, Alvin	189	DE	Houston	Denver	7
Rubick, Rob	326	TE	Grand Valley State	Detroit	12
Sampleton, Lawrence	47	TE	Texas	Philadelphia	2
Sandon, Steve	296	QB	Northern Iowa	New England	11
Schachtner, John	180	LB	Northern Arizona	Washington	7
Schlichter, Art	4	QB	Ohio State	Baltimore	1
Scholtz, Bruce	33	LB	Texas	Seattle	2
Scott, Lindsay	13	WR	Georgia	New Orleans	1
Seale, Mark	323	DT	Richmond	New York Giants	12
Sebro, Bob	178	C	Colorado	St. Louis	7
Shaffer, Craig	150	LB	Indiana State	St. Louis	6
Sharpe, Luis	16	T	UCLA	St. Louis	1
Shearin, Joe	181	G	Texas	Los Angeles	7
Simmons, Victor	187	WR	Oregon State	Detroit	7
Sims, Ken	1	DT	Texas	New England	1
Slaughter, Chuck	198	T	South Carolina	New Orleans	8
Smith, Greg	184	DT	Kansas	Kansas City	7
Smith, Harold	254	DE	Kentucky State	Washington	10
Smith, Randy	316	WR	East Texas State	Oakland	12
Smith, Ricky	141	DB	Alabama State	New England	6
Sorboor, Mikal Abdul	293	G	Morgan State	Pittsburgh	11
Sorenson, Paul	138	DB	Washington State	Cincinnati	5
Speight, Bob	229	T	Boston University	Los Angeles	9
Squirek, Jack	35	LB	Illinois	Oakland	2
Stark, Rohn	34	P	Florida State	Baltimore	2
Storr, Gregg	147	LB	Boston College	Minnesota	6
Stowers, Curtis	262	LB	Mississippi State	Atlanta	10
Suber, Tony	329	DT	Gardner-Webb	Buffalo	12
Sullivan, Dwight	221	RB	North Carolina State	Dallas	8
Sunseri, Sal	267	LB	Pittsburgh	Pittsburgh	10

Player	Order No.	Pos.	College	Club	Round
Tabron, Dennis	134	DB	Duke	Chicago	5
Tate, Rodney	110	RB	Texas	Cincinnati	4
Tausch, Terry	39	T	Texas	Minnesota	2
Taylor, Greg	308	WR	Virginia	New England	12
Taylor, Malcolm	121	DE	Tennessee State	Houston	5
Taylor, Rob	328	T	Northwestern	Philadelphia	12
Texada, Lawrence	219	RB	Henderson, Ark.	New York Jets	8
Thompson, Delbert	130	RB	Texas-El Paso	Kansas City	5
Thompson, George	295	WR	Albany State, Ga.	Dallas	11
Tippett, Andre	41	LB	Iowa	New England	2
Toloumu, David	176	RB	Hawaii	Atlanta	7
Tousignant, Luc	218	QB	Fairmont State	Buffalo	8
Trautman, Randy	238	DT	Boise State	Washington	9
Turner, Joe	257	DB	Southern California	Chicago	10
Turner, Willie	289	WR	Louisiana State	Oakland	11
Tutson, Tom	161	DB	South Carolina State	Miami	6
Tuttle, Perry	19	WR	Clemson	Buffalo	1
Tyler, Andre	158	WR	Stanford	Tampa Bay	6
Uecker, Keith	243	T	Auburn	Denver	9
Umphrey, Rich	129	C	Colorado	New York Giants	5
Waechter, Henry	173	DT	Nebraska	Chicago	7
Wagoner, Danny	231	DB	Kansas	Detroit	9
Walker, Dwight	87	WR	Nicholls State	Cleveland	4
Warthen, Ralph	223	DT	Gardner-Webb	Washington	8
Washington, Tim	334	DB	Fresno State	San Francisco	12
Watkins, Bobby	42	DB	S.W. Texas State	Detroit	2
Watson, Anthony	299	DB	New Mexico State	San Diego	11
Weathers, Robert	40	RB	Arizona State	New England	2
Weaver, Emanuel	54	DT	South Carolina	Cincinnati	2
Weishuhn, Clayton	60	LB	Angelo State	New England	3
Whiting, Mike	304	RB	Florida State	Dallas	11
Whitley, Joey	183	DB	Texas-El Paso	Green Bay	7
Whitwell, Mike	162	WR	Texas A&M	Cleveland	6
Willhite, Gerald	21	RB	San Jose State	Denver	1
Williams, Eugene	174	LB	Tulsa	Seattle	7
Williams, James	290	DE	North Carolina A&T	St. Louis	11
Williams, Jimmy	15	LB	Nebraska	Detroit	1
Williams, Lester	27	DT	Miami	New England	1
Williams, Michael	133	TE	Alabama A&M	Washington	5
Williams, Newton	139	RB	Arizona State	San Francisco	5
Williams, Van	93	RB	Carson-Newman	Buffalo	4
Williams, Vince	151	RB	Oregon	San Francisco	6
Winder, Sammy	131	RB	Southern Mississippi	Denver	5
Wiska, Jeff	186	G	Michigan State	New York Giants	7
Wisniewski, Leo	28	DT	Penn State	Baltimore	2
Woodruff, Tony	244	WR	Fresno State	Philadelphia	9
Woods, Rick	97	DB	Boise State	Pittsburgh	4
Woodward, Ken	274	LB	Tuskegee State	Denver	10
Woolfolk, Butch	18	RB	Michigan	New York Giants	1
Wright, Johnnie	307	RB	South Carolina	Baltimore	12
Wrightman, Tim	62	TE	UCLA	Chicago	3
Yatsko, Stuart	300	G	Oregon	Denver	11
Yli-Renko, Kari	222	T	Cincinnati	Cincinnati	8
Young, Andre	273	DB	Louisiana Tech	San Diego	10
Young, Ricky	313	LB	Oklahoma State	Chicago	12

1982
NFL SCHEDULE

*NIGHT GAME

SUNDAY, SEPT. 12
Atlanta at New York Giants
Chicago at Detroit
Cleveland at Seattle
Houston at Cincinnati
Kansas City at Buffalo
Los Angeles vs. Green Bay
  at Milwaukee
Miami at New York Jets
New England at Baltimore
Oakland at San Francisco
St. Louis at New Orleans
San Diego at Denver
Tampa Bay at Minnesota
Washington at Philadelphia

MONDAY, SEPT. 13
*Pittsburgh at Dallas

THURSDAY, SEPT. 16
Minnesota at Buffalo

SUNDAY, SEPT. 19
Baltimore at Miami
Cincinnati at Pittsburgh
Dallas at St. Louis
Detroit at Los Angeles
New Orleans at Chicago
New York Jets at New England
Oakland at Atlanta
Philadelphia at Cleveland
San Diego at Kansas City
San Francisco at Denver
Seattle at Houston
Washington at Tampa Bay

MONDAY, SEPT. 20
*Green Bay at New York Giants

THURSDAY, SEPT. 23
*Atlanta at Kansas City

SUNDAY, SEPT. 26
Buffalo at Houston
Chicago at San Francisco
Dallas at Minnesota
Denver at New Orleans
Los Angeles at Philadelphia
Miami at Green Bay
New York Giants at Pittsburgh
New York Jets at Baltimore
Oakland at San Diego
St. Louis at Washington
Seattle at New England
Tampa Bay at Detroit

MONDAY, SEPT. 27
*Cincinnati at Cleveland

SUNDAY, OCT. 3
Baltimore at Detroit
Cleveland at Washington
Houston at New York Jets
Kansas City at Seattle
Los Angeles at St. Louis
Miami at Cincinnati
Minnesota at Chicago
New England at Buffalo
New Orleans at Oakland
New York Giants at Dallas
Philadelphia vs. Green Bay
  at Milwaukee
Pittsburgh at Denver
San Diego at Atlanta

MONDAY, OCT. 4
*San Francisco at Tampa Bay

SUNDAY, OCT. 10
Atlanta at Los Angeles
Buffalo at Baltimore
Cincinnati at New England
Cleveland at Oakland
Denver at New York Jets
Detroit at Miami
Green Bay at Chicago
Houston at Kansas City
Minnesota at Tampa Bay
St. Louis at New York Giants
San Francisco at New Orleans
Seattle at San Diego
Washington at Dallas

MONDAY, OCT. 11
*Philadelphia at Pittsburgh

SUNDAY, OCT. 17
Atlanta at Detroit
Baltimore at Cleveland
Chicago at St. Louis
Cincinnati at New York Giants
Dallas at Philadelphia
Denver at Houston
Kansas City at San Diego
Los Angeles at San Francisco
New England at Miami
New Orleans at Minnesota
Oakland at Seattle
Pittsburgh at Washington
Tampa Bay at Green Bay

MONDAY, OCT. 18
*Buffalo at New York Jets

SUNDAY, OCT. 24
Cleveland at Pittsburgh
*Dallas at Cincinnati
Detroit at Buffalo
Green Bay at Minnesota
Miami at Baltimore
New Orleans at Los Angeles
New York Jets at Kansas City
Oakland at Denver
St. Louis at New England
San Diego at Seattle
San Francisco at Atlanta
Tampa Bay at Chicago
Washington at Houston

MONDAY, OCT. 25
*New York Giants at Philadelphia

SUNDAY, OCT. 31
Atlanta at New Orleans
Buffalo at Denver
Chicago at Green Bay
Dallas at New York Giants
Houston at Cleveland
Los Angeles at San Diego
Miami at Oakland
New England at New York Jets
Philadelphia at St. Louis
Pittsburgh at Cincinnati
San Francisco at Washington
Seattle at Kansas City
Tampa Bay at Baltimore

MONDAY, NOV. 1
*Detroit at Minnesota

SUNDAY, NOV. 7
Atlanta at Chicago
Baltimore at New England
Denver at Seattle
Detroit at Philadelphia
Green Bay at Tampa Bay

Houston at Pittsburgh
Kansas City at Oakland
Los Angeles at New Orleans
Minnesota at San Francisco
New York Giants at Cleveland
New York Jets at Buffalo
St. Louis at Dallas

MONDAY, NOV. 8
*San Diego at Miami

SUNDAY, NOV. 14
Buffalo at New England
Chicago at Tampa Bay
Cincinnati at Houston
Cleveland at Miami
Dallas at San Francisco
Denver at Kansas City
Green Bay at Detroit
Minnesota at Washington
New Orleans at San Diego
New York Giants at Los Angeles
New York Jets at Pittsburgh
Oakland at Baltimore
Seattle at St. Louis

MONDAY, Nov. 15
*Philadelphia at Atlanta

SUNDAY, NOV. 21
Baltimore at New York Jets
Cincinnati at Philadelphia
Detroit at Chicago
Kansas City at New Orleans
Los Angeles at Atlanta
Miami at Buffalo
Minnesota vs. Green Bay
    at Milwaukee
New England at Cleveland
Pittsburgh at Houston
San Francisco at St. Louis
Seattle at Denver
Tampa Bay at Dallas
Washington at New York Giants

MONDAY, NOV. 22
*San Diego at Oakland

THURSDAY, NOV. 25
Cleveland at Dallas
New York Giants at Detroit

SUNDAY, NOV. 28
Baltimore at Buffalo
Chicago at Minnesota
Denver at San Diego
Green Bay at New York Jets
Houston at New England
Kansas City at Los Angeles

New Orleans at San Francisco
Oakland at Cincinnati
Philadelphia at Washington
Pittsburgh at Seattle
St. Louis at Atlanta

MONDAY, NOV. 29
*Miami at Tampa Bay

THURSDAY, DEC. 2
*San Francisco at Los Angeles

SUNDAY, DEC. 5
Atlanta at Denver
Buffalo vs. Green Bay
    at Milwaukee
Cincinnati at Baltimore
Dallas at Washington
Houston at New York Giants
Kansas City at Pittsburgh
Minnesota at Miami
New England at Chicago
St. Louis at Philadelphia
San Diego at Cleveland
Seattle at Oakland
Tampa Bay at New Orleans

MONDAY, DEC. 6
*New York Jets at Detroit

SATURDAY, DEC. 11
Philadelphia at New York Giants
San Diego at San Francisco

SUNDAY, DEC. 12
Baltimore at Minnesota
Chicago at Seattle
Cleveland at Cincinnati
Denver at Los Angeles
Detroit at Green Bay
Miami at New England
New Orleans at Atlanta
Oakland at Kansas City
Pittsburgh at Buffalo
Tampa Bay at New York Jets
Washington at St. Louis

MONDAY, DEC. 13
*Dallas at Houston

SATURDAY, DEC. 18
Los Angeles at Oakland
New York Jets at Miami

SUNDAY, DEC. 19
*Atlanta at San Francisco
Buffalo at Tampa Bay
Green Bay at Baltimore

Houston at Philadelphia
Kansas City at Denver
Minnesota at Detroit
New England at Seattle
New Orleans at Dallas
New York Giants at Washington
Pittsburgh at Cleveland
St. Louis at Chicago

MONDAY, DEC. 20
*Cincinnati at San Diego

SUNDAY, DEC. 26
Baltimore at San Diego
Chicago at Los Angeles
Cleveland at Houston
Denver at Oakland
Detroit at Tampa Bay
Green Bay at Atlanta
New England at Pittsburgh
New York Giants at St. Louis
New York Jets at Minnesota
Philadelphia at Dallas
San Francisco at Kansas City
Seattle at Cincinnati
Washington at New Orleans

MONDAY, DEC. 27
*Buffalo at Miami

Nationally Televised Games

(CBS and NBC also will televise a national doubleheader game each Sunday during the regular season. All games carried on CBS Radio Network.)

REGULAR SEASON

Monday, Sept. 13–Pittsburgh at Dallas (night, ABC)
Thursday, Sept. 16–Minnesota at Buffalo (night, ABC)
Monday, Sept. 20–Green Bay at New York Giants (night, ABC)
Thursday, Sept. 23–Atlanta at Kansas City (night, ABC)
Monday, Sept. 27–Cincinnati at Cleveland (night, ABC)
Monday, Oct. 4–San Francisco at Tampa Bay (night, ABC)
Monday, Oct. 11–Philadelphia at Pittsburgh (night, ABC)
Monday, Oct. 18–Buffalo at New York Jets (night, ABC)
Sunday, Oct. 24–Dallas at Cincinnati (night, ABC)
Monday, Oct. 25–New York Giants at Philadelphia (night, ABC)
Monday, Nov. 1–Detroit at Minnesota (night, ABC)
Monday, Nov. 8–San Diego at Miami (night, ABC)
Monday, Nov. 15–Philadelphia at Atlanta (night, ABC)
Monday, Nov. 22–San Diego at Oakland (night, ABC)
Thursday, Nov. 25–(Thanksgiving) Cleveland at Dallas (day, NBC)
Thursday, Nov. 25–(Thanksgiving) New York Giants at Detroit (day, CBS)
Monday, Nov. 29–Miami at Tampa Bay (night, ABC)
Thursday, Dec. 2– San Francisco at Los Angeles (night, ABC)
Monday, Dec. 6–New York Jets at Detroit (night, ABC)
Saturday, Dec. 11–Philadelphia at New York Giants (day, CBS)
Saturday, Dec. 11– San Diego at San Francisco (day, NBC)
Monday, Dec. 13–Dallas at Houston (night, ABC)
Saturday, Dec. 18–Los Angeles at Oakland (day, CBS)
Saturday, Dec. 18–New York Jets at Miami (day, NBC)
Sunday, Dec. 19–Atlanta at San Francisco (night, ABC)
Monday, Dec. 20–Cincinnati at San Diego (night, ABC)
Monday, Dec. 27–Buffalo at Miami (night, ABC)

POSTSEASON

Sunday, Jan. 2–NFL First Round Playoffs (CBS and NBC)
Saturday, Jan. 8–AFC and NFC Divisional Playoffs (NBC and CBS)
Sunday, Jan. 9–AFC and NFC Divisional Playoffs (NBC and CBS)
Sunday, Jan. 16–AFC Championship Game (NBC)
Sunday, Jan. 16–NFC Championship Game (CBS)
Sunday, Jan. 30–Super Bowl XVII at Rose Bowl, Pasadena, Cal. (NBC)
Sunday, Feb. 6–AFC-NFC Pro Bowl at Honolulu, Hawaii (ABC)

MONDAY NIGHT GAMES AT A GLANCE (ABC)

Sept. 13–Pittsburgh at Dallas
Sept. 20–Green Bay at New York Giants
Sept. 27–Cincinnati at Cleveland
Oct. 4–San Francisco at Tampa Bay
Oct. 11–Philadelphia at Pittsburgh
Oct. 18–Buffalo at New York Jets
Oct. 25–New York Giants at Philadelphia
Nov. 1–Detroit at Minnesota

Nov. 8–San Diego at Miami
Nov. 15–Philadelphia at Atlanta
Nov. 22–San Diego at Oakland
Nov. 29–Miami at Tampa Bay
Dec. 6–New York Jets at Detroit
Dec. 13–Dallas at Houston
Dec. 20–Cincinnati at San Diego
Dec. 27–Buffalo at Miami

SUNDAY-THURSDAY NIGHT GAMES AT A GLANCE (ABC)

Thursday, Sept. 16–Minnesota at Buff.
Thursday, Sept. 23–Atlanta at KC
Sunday, Oct. 24–Dallas at Cincinnati

Thursday, Dec. 2–San Fran. at LA
Sunday, Dec. 19–Atlanta at San Fran.